DATE DUE

OCT 0 5 1995	
NOV - 3 1999	

BRODART   Cat. No. 23-221

Aesthetic Frontiers

AESTHETIC
FRONTIERS

The Machiavellian Tradition

and the Southern Imagination

RICHARD NELSON

University Press of Mississippi • Jackson and London

Copyright © 1990 by the University Press of Mississippi
All rights reserved
Manufactured in the United States of America

93 92 91 90   4 3 2 1

The paper in this book meets the guidelines for permanence
and durability of the Committee on Production Guidelines
for Book Longevity of the Council on Library Resources. ⊗

Library of Congress Cataloging-in-Publication Data

Nelson, Richard, 1948–
　　Aesthetic frontiers : the Machiavellian tradition and the
　Southern imagination / Richard Nelson.
　　　p.　cm.
　　Includes bibliographical references.
　　ISBN 0-87805-439-1 (alk. paper)
　　1. American literature—Southern States—History and
　criticism—Theory, etc.　2. Politics and literature—
　Southern States—History.　3. Machiavelli, Niccolò,
　1469-1527—Influence.　4. Southern States—Intellectual
　life.　5. Southern States—Historiography.　I. Title.
　PS261.N4　1990
　810.9′975—dc20　　　　　　　　　　　　　　90-32055
　　　　　　　　　　　　　　　　　　　　　　　　　CIP

British Library Cataloguing-in-Publication data available

For two generations:

Solveig, Kirsten, Karl, Kristian, and Britta;

and their Grandparents

CONTENTS

PREFACE

Since the end of World War II, American historians have been forced to make a fundamental reorientation in their understanding of the movement of space and time. The end of American exceptionality, the contradictions in the American story of liberty, and the failure of older heroic narratives to square with the consequences of twentieth-century economic and social realities have brought about a crisis of cultural awareness. That crisis, in turn, demands new interpretations for the configurations of space and time out of which, finally, we all must construct our understanding of the purpose and meaning of our own lives.

The legacy of the counter-Progressive, or Consensus, historians of the 1950s in explaining the movement of Anglo-American space and time into unexpected and even contradictory conclusions to Progressive hopes was a new appreciation of the role of irony in shaping human affairs. Under the tutelage of Modernist aesthetics, historians of Anglo-America learned to use irony as a sophisticated instrument for interpreting the twists and turns of historical transformations, while preserving faith in progress as a living process of human growth, separate from the sometimes quite opposite experience of individual lives. Once more, the irony that seemed to reveal fundamental patterns of historical change in Perry Miller's New England or C. Vann Woodward's new South, in Lionel Trilling's literary imagination or Reinhold Niebuhr's political religion, was a special form of irony, which served to justify a particular view of the world within the context of economic and political liberalism.

In recent years, many scholars have come to believe that liberalism replaced earlier Anglo-American political and economic ideals that had been fashioned in the Renaissance, most particularly by Niccolò Machiavelli. I believe, however, that Lockean values are continuous with older Machiavellian values, which share similar assumptions about political virtue and corruption and remain controlling values in the present. From this perspective, the appeal of irony in post–World War II Anglo-American political thought, historiography, and literary theory may reflect its usefulness less as a description of reality than as an unconscious and paradoxical strategy for preserving the authority of doubtful political and economic forms. That is to say that irony, in post–World War II America, has become a powerful aesthetic formula, which expresses the conundrums and contradictions within a particular variation on Machiavellian political culture even as it preserves the legitimacy of the contradictory values it helps expose. That the process is most visible at the level of historiography and literary theory does not mean it is unique to those areas. Rather, it is because history in America has long been practiced within the conventions for offering public interpretations of order in changing time and space, either as a ritualized form of complaint—a jeremiad—or as a frontier, offering hope and opportunity, while literature has come to serve the private and personal side of these same needs.

This book is not meant to be a comprehensive description of Machiavellian political culture in America since 1890, but it is an interpretation of the transformation of space and time in Anglo-American culture between 1890 and the present in the context of its dominant Machiavellian values in crisis. For reasons that I will make clear in the Introduction, I have found the central conflict in the crisis of Machiavellian values to be inherent in the divisions of America's most visible internal family quarrels: Declaration *versus* Constitution, sectionalism, conflicts over race, and conflicts within gender. Indeed, all of these intersecting and continuing political conflicts have been fought and refought through American history within the aesthetic divisions of Romanticism and Realism. As variations on a common pattern, I suggest that such aesthetic divisions are really complementary in character, despite the widening formal separation between the worlds of politics and aesthetics since the 1890s, a process that was completed during the Cold War. My interpretation of Anglo-American cultural change, therefore, is offered as an exploration of an aesthetic frontier and an effort to map the course of the transformation of twentieth-century American space and time. However, I have consciously resisted the temptation to appeal to irony as if it were some objective political force or natural law of cultural movement, existing outside the particular culture that spawned it.

I wish to express my gratitude to the many friends, colleagues, and teachers who have shaped my own historical and moral perspective which made this study possible. These include Robert Foster and Carl Skrade, two fine undergraduate teachers and friends who, along with the late Wilhelm Pauck, helped me understand the contours of American

Protestantism. Bernard Mehl helped me see the implications of the New Criticism. Steve Peterson offered many helpful ideas on the relation of the heroic narrative to Machiavellianism. Erik Peterson helped me in innumerable ways, and I learned a great deal from discussions with him, Gail Olson, and Nancy Enstad. Kim and John Olson, Brian LeCloux, J. Gordon Nelson, and John Bailey all offered much-needed help and gave me the benefit of their insights. Richard Abel, director of the University Press of Mississippi, has been patient and more understanding and supportive than any writer should even hope, and his advice has been invaluable in making possible whatever merits this work may have. Richard suggested directions for linking Machiavelli and Shakespeare in Southern writers which I found very helpful, though any defects in my treatment of that theme are my fault, not his.

The staff at the University Press of Mississippi has been most capable and considerate throughout this project, and it has been a pleasure to work with them. In addition, I particularly wish to acknowledge the high standard of Dr. Lys Shore's copyediting of the manuscript. Her ability to choose the better word and to catch mistakes improved the book immensely. I owe her many thanks for saving me from the cause of many embarrassments.

I wish to express my appreciation, as well, to the staff of the Southern Collection of the University of North Carolina Library, Chapel Hill, for their special help in making the papers of Tom Watson available when they were in the midst of recataloguing and microfilming them. I also wish to thank the staff of the Manuscript Department of Duke University's William R. Perkins Library for material on Thomas Dixon and the staff of the Archives of the University of Wisconsin-Madison for opening the collection of Frederick Jackson Turner's papers to me. I wish to thank the University of Wisconsin's Institute for Race and Ethnicity, which generously provided a travel grant for me to visit these collections. I also wish to thank Alan P. Twyman, who through the Rohauer Collection, generously made it possible for me to read Thomas Dixon's autobiography, *Southern Horizons*.

Perhaps my greatest debts incurred in the completion of this study are to my immediate and extended family. My wife, Jane Solveig Nelson was, my most important collaborator and critic. I consider this book to be as much a result of her time, energy and interest as my own. Together, we especially wish to thank our parents, Robert and Solveig Bailey for their unreserved and selfless support. They have been more important in this process than they can imagine, or than we can express in words. We wish to thank our parents, William R. and Jane Nelson who have encouraged us through their concern and faith in the value of this project. We wish to thank our children who have been subjected to the crisis of time and space that goes along with a parent's preoccupation with completing a book. Finally, we wish to thank David W. Noble for reading and discussing this manuscript. Jane and I both wish to acknowledge David's patience and generosity in sharing his prodigious historical knowledge and wisdom. Most of all, we wish to thank him as a teacher and scholar for personally offering an alternative to a Machiavellian view of life.

Machias, Maine

December 1989

Aesthetic Frontiers

INTRODUCTION

Of Spider's Webs and Frontiers: Literary Theory, Historiography, and the Anglo-American Frontier

In the mid-1970s, J. G. A. Pocock created a stir among American historians by arguing that Anglo-American political culture derived from the ideas of Niccolò Machiavelli.[1] Many scholars now accept Pocock's thesis that the Founding Fathers espoused an agrarian variation on Machiavelli's view that power and value had become separated in his contemporary world and that some way must be found to balance them if liberty were to flourish and political chaos to be constrained. This variation was, of course, republicanism. Scholars have now begun to argue that its codification of the inherent political conflict between the ambition for dominance and the desire for liberty was fundamental to the tragically violent divisions between Northerners and Southerners which culminated in the Civil War.

Recently, David W. Noble has extended this line of research to show that the Progressive historians Frederick Jackson Turner and Charles Beard wrote within the same republican paradigm, which the English theorist James Harrington developed in the 1600s.[2] Harrington theorized that it was possible to use freehold property as a counterweight to economic and political centralization, preserving liberty against tyranny and political virtue against corruption in an expanding empire. Neither Turner nor Beard, however, was successful in reformulating a Harringtonian solution to the disintegration of republican political and economic values in America once the agrarian frontier closed at the end of the nineteenth century. The major role of the counter-Progressive or Consensus school of American historians, which developed during the Cold

War, Noble argues, was to adjust to new arrangements of cultural and political power, bringing an end to republicanism by mediating from within the academy the public's acceptance of a centralized capitalist economy.

This book is indebted to both Pocock's and Noble's work and begins with the fatal crisis for republican political culture, which both historians place in the 1890s. This was the historical moment when Harrington's hopeful balance of time and space, linking both commercial and freehold property into a dynamic yet stable commonwealth, collapsed as a consequence of its own internal contradictions. For according to Harringtonian principles, a republican polity could not long survive without a frontier of free space to support an economics of independent production. However, because republicanism was but one variation within a far larger and much more comprehensive Machiavellian tradition in the West, its death in the years between 1890 and 1945 did not mean that the patterns upon which it had been based had come to an end. Quite to the contrary, new patterns of Machiavellian values were generated as part of the same process that swept aside the old discredited republican forms. New styles of balancing contradictory requirements for dynamic economic expansion and stable civic institutions replaced republican methods and mores, which were incapable of balancing power and value under the new conditions of accelerating change.

This book is an exploration of that process. Thematically, it lies at the crossroads where historiography, literary criticism, and political ideology meet. That conceptualized intersection of cultural space and creative change represents a twentieth-century Anglo-American frontier line. That frontier line is not between artificial civilization and nature, as it was for Frederick Jackson Turner, when he codified the meaning of the frontier experience for Americans at the turn of the century. Rather, it is an equally imaginary line, which divides the mundane realm of politics from the creative realm of aesthetics. This new frontier of the imagination slowly came to replace Turner's agrarian frontier. Perhaps because cultural forms are less likely simply to disappear than to become transformed by the conditions of social change, the frontier persisted as a redemptive conception for balancing freedom and order, even after it came to an end in its agrarian form. In its transformation into a dividing line between politics and aesthetics, the frontier occupied a strategically necessary ground for Americans between 1890 and 1945: it permitted a successful transition from the death of republicanism as a mode of heroic politics to a new world with no heroes but merely celebrities. This new world substituted an economics of self-absorbed consumerism for one based upon production. Deeply rooted in Anglo-American history, it was only established on a national scale with the advent of the Cold War.

The story of how this new frontier of the imagination came to be established in the twentieth century is also a story of cultural tensions and inversions of power and value, which intersected along regional, racial, gender, and aesthetic lines of conflict. These conflicts involved not just politicians and advertisers, corporate executives and educators, but also the guardians of Anglo-American redemptive culture: Protestant theologians, American historians, composers of music and poetry. The role of these cultural guardians, who traffic in ideas, meanings, and value, frames the interrelated elements of this study in transforming political decay into aesthetic vitality.

The framework within which this transformation occurred may be viewed as a spider's web, stretched between two poles of cultural conflict. The web forms what I suggest is a single aesthetic and political reformulation of a national Machiavellian culture. One of the poles may be identified with the Southern Literary Renaissance and the so-called "Harlem Renaissance" with which it was intimately tied, if geographically separated. The other pole is New England's redemptive culture, which had dominated the whole nation since the Civil War but was perceived as sliding into failure even before the moment of its identification with military victory and moral rectitude.

If my image may be stretched a bit further, think of the spider's web as representing the crisis of space between those poles. Then consider the central place of the spider's web metaphor in the fiction of Robert Penn Warren, and his preoccupation with frontiers. In this way, we may recognize that the confined space of the jeremiad belongs to the same frame of reference as the open frontier. If we follow the significance of the web of responsibilities and communal or even covenantal interconnections, which Warren has integrated with his many symbols of renewal through an inverted experience of liberation in the West, we may see the central theme that integrates these two poles of cultural renewal: the family romance, which was as strongly tied to New England as to the South. The family romance nicely summarizes the necessity of a balance between the destiny of the household and the heroic quest away from it, which must be successfully completed to bring about renewal.

This same Southern family romance, however, symbolized the familial tragedy of the Civil War and the possibility of a permanent cultural failure in history. The Civil War sat massively and bloodily in brooding silence for both Southerners and Northerners, and it was in terms of the war that the southern family romance was refashioned from its antebellum forms, which had been constructed of still earlier variations on this same republican theme. Therefore, by recognizing the availability and appropriate structure of the southern family romance narrative, we may bring together the elements that permitted the emergence of a new Machiavellian balance in Anglo-American political culture. Here we may isolate the implications of those two contradictory but mutually dependent cultural symbols of detachment and intimacy—dynamic progress and stagnation, chaos and stability—inherent within the languages of the jeremiad and the frontier.

Fundamentally, the crisis of republicanism between 1890 and 1945 was a crisis of a whole genre of politics, initiated by the political and economic failure of the agrarian frontier. As a result, republicanism suddenly appeared to its disillusioned critics as transparently romantic in style. Once characterized as romantic, it lost its cultural force along with its claim to realism. Republicanism then literally disappeared into the liberal political, economic, and social framework that replaced it.[3] Only in the mid-1960s, when liberalism found itself embroiled in a crisis of "realism" over the relation of power and value in Vietnam and over civil rights at home, was republicanism recovered as a historiographical lever for demythologizing another failed form of American exceptionalism—the ironically redemptive nationalism as formulated by Reinhold Niebuhr.

I argue that this pattern of political and cultural transformation must be viewed as Machiavellian in character, for Machiavelli was at once an artist and a political theorist preoccupied with the dilemmas of legitimacy and change behind heroic forms of political action. He was a conscious stylist of a particular mode of heroic literature, through which he aesthetically mediated a profound sense of loss of a classical standard. At the same time, he offered a practical, "realistic" alternative, which conservatively defended an essentially romantic heroic ideal in a negative way—that is, by revealing its absence. The Machiavellian aesthetic, then, is a hidden aesthetic standard of politics based on the inversion of the heroic ideal as a formula for conservatively preserving a political authority that has lost its legitimacy. To call this aesthetic Machiavellian is not to make a historical claim for Machiavelli as a romantic antihero of Western culture but simply to recognize that it has become associated with his name through time and familiarity. As such, American culture may be said to have been steeped in Machiavellian controversies since it was the product of Renaissance Europeans.

We may point to Shakespeare in America as a useful example of Machiavellianism functioning on both a political and an aesthetic level. Shakespeare was the common cultural property of rich and poor, literate and unlettered alike, among Americans of the eighteenth and nineteenth centuries. His plays were filled with allusions to a Machiavellian ethos: sophisticated confrontations with the dilemmas of heroism, power and value, innovation and tradition, piety and murder. Before the imposition of a distinction between "highbrow" and "lowbrow" culture towards the end of the nineteenth century—the same period in which centralized political and economic power was supplanting decentralized democratic republicanism—Shakespeare's ideas were common currency, like baseball or football today.[4] Shakespeare offers one of many instances of Machiavelli's pervasive presence in American cultural life. However, the example of Shakespeare emphasizes the continuity of aesthetic and political values and explains why Shakespeare found his greatest American popularity, and has held it the longest, in the South. The South was the original center of republican ideology during the Revolution and the area of the country which retained its republican character the longest. It should not be surprising, therefore, to find Southern audiences responding warmly to familiar dilemmas they shared with the Elizabethan audiences of Shakespearean plays. Nor should it be surprising that the American South, as the most militant center of republicanism in the antebellum period, remained the militant center of the effort to revive it in the period after 1890.

Until the 1890s, while republicanism remained a viable political and economic philosophy, a self-styled hero of Jeffersonian democracy such as the Populist and historian Tom Watson was able to balance aesthetics and politics within a single personality. By the end of the 1890s, Watson had begun to divide himself into a literary and political man. Watson's inability to use his identification with the Romantic poet Byron outside of a tragic sense of self-defeat provides one example of a failing Machiavellian synthesis in the years before World War I. At the same time, Watson's younger contemporary Thomas Dixon, historical novelist and filmmaker, became disillusioned with both politics and democracy while Watson was trying to fashion a role for himself as a champion of both. By the turn of the century and with his infamous novels of Reconstruction,

The Leopard's Spots and *The Clansman,* Dixon had begun to distance himself aesthetically from republicanism in ways that anticipated the New Critics.[5] However, he was hampered by his loyalty to the lost heroic ideal he associated with the Old South. He found himself trapped within the terms of a pastoral elegy, in which mourning a lost heroic ideal led to a personal identification with failure and mortality. This was not far different from Watson's Byronic self-identification as a tragic hero. Both men ended their lives sadly out of style aesthetically and as bitterly defeated political leaders who felt betrayed and misunderstood by the public and their critics.

Yet in the 1930s and 1940s, C. Vann Woodward was able to transform Watson, a discredited leader of a discredited agrarian movement, into a positive new symbol of Southern identity. He did so in his dissertation, which was published in 1938 as *Tom Watson: Agrarian Rebel* to high public and professional acclaim.[6] At about the same time, W. J. Cash, virtually imitating Dixon's theories in his acclaimed book of 1941, *The Mind of the South,* gained a reputation as a prophet of liberal enlightenment.[7] Woodward and Cash both wrote within the Machiavellian convention of inverting heroic forms, and both attacked romanticism while appealing to a higher realism that was actually a submerged form of heroic romanticism. Both too were influenced by the Southern Renaissance, especially the New Agrarian Critics of Nashville and the Regionalist sociologists of Chapel Hill.

The Southern Renaissance, and particularly the New Criticism of Allen Tate and Robert Penn Warren, can guide us into a comprehension of Woodward's and Cash's ability to use the failure of the southern family romance to generate new frontiers of political and aesthetic hope. Tate and Warren consciously worked with Machiavellian themes on the frontier between politics and aesthetics and between historiography and literary criticism. Thus, they are ideally suited to reveal the transformation of a failed Machiavellian culture into a successful alternative. They provide a mirror, to use one of their favorate metaphors, reflecting not only the Southern crisis in the twentieth century, but its reverse image in the complementary crisis within New England.

The New Criticism, which the New Agrarians embraced only after losing their bid to revitalize agrarianism, presents a key to understanding the transformation of twentieth-century Machiavellian culture because it was essentially a process of aesthetic distancing from a dead heroic tradition of republicanism. The New Criticism attempted to escape the implications of a failed political identity in order to locate another frontier space of freedom, beyond the tragedy of lost possibility. This transformation of an Old World of shriveled political hope into a New World of unlimited aesthetic potential was finally mediated through what Kenneth Bruffee has identified as the Romantic elegy.[8]

The elegy is a ritualistic literary formula associated with death and loss, especially in the context of heroic defeat. While the pastoral elegy has long been a standard formula for poetic identification with a friend's or hero's death, the Romantic elegy is apparently of more recent origin. Bruffee dates its presence as an identifiable formula from about 1890, the period when Harrington's balance between space and time was shattered by the vastly increased scale of loss and change, not only in America but throughout the Atlantic political culture. Like the pastoral elegy, the narrator of a Romantic elegy begins with a deeply felt identification with the dead hero. The pastoral elegist avoids sentimentality or nostalgia by turning the death of the hero into an autobiographical consciousness of the poet's own mortality. The Romantic elegist presents a different formula for release. The poet begins by identifying with the dead hero but then, over the course of the tale, succeeds in freeing himself and the reader. The elegist accomplishes this release "through an aesthetic act and imaginative 'research' into the past, a *recherche du temps perdu,* to discover the roots of the fundamental structure of meaning that each of us has grown up with." [9] The central virtue of this aesthetic act, continues Bruffee, is to preserve a dead tradition or convention in amber, at once to preserve it and to dismiss it as irretrievably lost. In this sense, the Romantic elegy is an inversion of the quest romance in which the lost hero—or tradition—stands as a barrier to the elegist's own freedom. In the effort to discover the hero's true significance or the real meaning of a lost tradition, the elegist fixes him in the past and emerges from the hero's shadow into his own powerful and central place in the universe.[10]

The Romantic elegy as a literary form is closely related to the Machiavellian dilemma of legitimacy and the problem of balancing innovation and tradition in order to defend patriarchal power conservatively. It presents a formula for turning a minor actor in a great external historical tragedy (for example, the critic or the reader) into a legitimate heir who may aesthetically replace the defeated external hero or tradition. Since the Romantic elegy is both a eulogy and a quest, the dead tradition may be external or may also, and simultaneously, be another, failed heroic self-identification. Death through skillful aesthetic politics may then be transformed into a personal resurrection. The conflagration that Machiavelli predicted when all virtue is used up may be turned into the rebirth of virtue, which he prophesied would rise from the ashes.

The New Agrarian critics thus provide us with a literary program for observing the aesthetic escape from Southern history and the laying to rest of republicanism. They also established the terms on which republicanism was recovered by a New England historian, Bernard Bailyn, in the 1960s. Significantly, the historiographical recovery of republicanism coincided with the height of the New Agrarian critics' influence of Anglo-American national culture. But just as important for the politics of aesthetics, it was also the point at which their influence was becoming conscious. A rising tide of dissent against the New Critics among literary historians, who believed the group dominated literary criticism, seemed to parallel dissent against economic and political liberalism and Consensus historiography. Simultaneously, each of these interrelated cultural conventions, which had appeared natural and timeless since the 1940s, lost its status as assumed truth. Social, economic, political, artistic, and even scientific criticism burgeoned from every possible perspective and persuasion. Solid cultural patterns fragmented and began to appear as particular, self-interested positions. Against this background of new perspectives on established forms, Bernard Bailyn happened to look at some pamphlets from the Revolutionary period. He did so not to challenge liberal interpretations of the Revolution, but merely to organize the pamphlets for publication, a mundane editorial chore. Bailyn thought he recognized a distinct pattern within this well-worn and familiar material. When he followed that pattern to its conclusions, he recovered a republican political ideology that had suffered years of historiographical neglect.[11]

The word *recovery* is important here because republicanism was not lost to American historians when documents were locked away and forgotten in some dusty archive only to reappear suddenly and transform the historical record. Rather, republican values had been rendered invisible through the familiarity of clichéd language. As Bailyn noted in his path-breaking study of republican ideology in 1967, *The Ideological Origins of the American Revolution*, these ideas had become so ordinary for American historians that scholars could no longer see the pattern within them.[12] Republican ideology had, in effect, dissolved into a taken-for-granted state of invisibility. But, as the Danish philosopher Sören Kierkegaard noted over one hundred fifty years ago, trivialization is a political use of aesthetic form, not an accident of changing style.[13]

Besides recognizing a lost pattern in the pamphlets and political discourses of the Revolutionary era, Bailyn described three significant characteristics of republican ideology that these sources revealed. First, rather than being purely American, republicanism was rooted in eighteenth-century British common law and in the European Enlightenment. This meant that the American Revolutionary ideals were rooted in older British formulas that were aimed at the defense of political virtue and leveled warnings against the dangers of economic and political corruption. The American political culture drew upon the same conventions that had supported the relation between power and liberty among the English dissenters of the country party in opposition to the court and its mercantile interests. Those similar and long-standing political tensions not only framed Bailyn's explanation of the origin of the American Revolution but also served as the starting point for his description of the process of transformation that shaped the revolutionary movement in unexpected ways. A political movement for the defense of English rights became a social movement. Bailyn explained. "Defiance to constituted authority leaped like a spark from one flammable area to another, growing in heat as it went." [14]

Bailyn's investigation into the origins of the American Revolution led directly to a recognition that it had ended in a crisis of authority. The analogy of a child's disobedience toward its parent appeared as apt to Bailyn as it had to the post-Revolutionary War writers he read. The literature suggested an Anglo-American family quarrel that had turned into an open rebellion, and not a simple conflict of economic interests.

The ideological origins of the new republican scholarship lay in the breakdown of the persuasiveness of arguments that maintained America was an unqualifiedly liberal political culture—a perspective that had been characteristic of post–World War II counter-Progressivism. As such, the new republican scholarship emerged from conditions similar to those that had prevailed within American historiography during the years of Bailyn's undergraduate and graduate study. Those were the years when Progressivism was giving way to counter-Progressive interpretations of American history, and republicanism was disappearing from American political language. Indeed, Bailyn's argument was quite out of fashion in the 1960s. His contention that the Revolution rested in a family conflict over ideas signaled a modified return to Carl Becker's ironic interpretation of the Revolution. For Becker viewed the Revolution through the eyes of Jeremiah Wynkoop, a fictional colonist of conservative disposition who discovered himself to be engaged in an unrecognized collision course with the authority of the Empire. [15]

Becker's frankly literary use of irony, and his open skepticism, however, had little appeal for Bailyn or for the whole generation of historians who came of professional age after World War II. They preferred the irony of political realism practiced by Reinhold Niebuhr. Specifically, Niebuhr modified the jeremiad from a defense of American exceptionalism to a challenge for a now *un*exceptional nation to fulfill a special mission of retaining freedom in a divided world. For Niebuhr, the world was divided not only between capitalist democracy and communist totalitarianism, but also between values and science, art and politics, and private and public life. Bailyn therefore offered a conclusion to *The Ideological Origins of the American Revolution* that was far closer to the perspective of the Niebuhr of *The Children of Light and the Children of Darkness* (1944) or *The Irony of American History* (1952) than to Becker's *How New Will the Better World Be?* (1944).[16] Bailyn described the new and transformed world created out of revolutionary disobedience as one of realistic limits but also of shining promise. For it was only in America "where there was this defiance, this refusal to truckle, this distrust of all authority, political or social, that institutions would express human aspirations, not crush them."[17]

Despite his retreat from a history of a unique America, separate from European influences in its origins, Bailyn, like Niebuhr, still assumed a kind of unique transformation of American history mediated by the ironic consequences that followed from its birth. This perspective meant that Bailyn, again like Niebuhr, both challenged the mythic picture of America as being born innocent and fully formed at its birth and assumed a focal point of crisis to account for the unique events that brought it into the world. Consequently, the second of the surprising characteristics that struck Bailyn did not strike him at once. He became aware of it, he wrote, only after a reconsideration of the material that made up his original collection of the *Pamphlets of the American Revolution* (1965).

This second characteristic was the unexpectedly early presence of republican rhetoric within American political discourse. Bailyn found that republican sentiments were already well established by the 1730s. Indeed, he thought he could see them "in partial form" as far back as the beginning of the seventeenth century. Bailyn was surprised to find that there was "no sharp break between the placid pre-Revolutionary era and the turmoil of the 1760s and 1770s." Why should this have been the case? Why did the mixture of politics and ideology remain potent for so long, lying beneath the "surface tranquility" for so many years before being "detonated"? Bailyn did not really answer these questions. But in asking them, he underscored the contradiction between the central place he had accorded the American Revolution in his narrative and the wider context of space and time in which this event was now seen to be imbedded.[18]

The third characteristic Bailyn noted—and the one that has remained unconsidered in subsequent studies of republicanism—is the degree to which republicanism should be defined as a literary movement as well as a political one. Bailyn himself recognized that the written word was central to the dissemination of republican ideology.[19] The pamphlets that contained this material, he acknowledged, were indeed a form of literature. Once more, Bailyn drew comparisons from at least one pre-Revolutionary pamphlet to *Tristram Shandy* and pointed out the frequent use in other pamphlets of satire, allegory, and aphorisms; "apostrophes, hyperboles and clever personifications"; dramatic dialogues; and any number of "artful literary constructions." Bailyn further recognized that these literary efforts were highly self-conscious imitations of the English model, which had raised the pamphlet to the level of an art form in the eighteenth century. In England, the great pamphleteers were also the great artists, such as Swift or Defoe. Bailyn, however, discounted the importance of the pamphlets of the American Revolution as literature because he was critical of the aesthetic merit of such pamphlets in comparison to their English models. They were crude and lacking in such literary values as characterization and verisimilitude. As literature they were "peculiarly incongruous to the deeper impulses of the time" in which they were written. But the problem was "not simply the presence or absence of literary imagination or technical skill," he argued in dismissing this aspect of the pamphlets' form from consideration, "but its employment." His criticism of that employment was based upon the failure of these early American literary efforts to achieve the intensity and polish of the English canon. "Beneath the technical deficiencies of the belletristic pieces lies an absence of motivating power," he wrote, "of that 'peculiar emotional intensity' that so distinguishes the political writing of Jonathan Swift." Similarly, the poetry—or versification, since it seemed too wooden and painfully constructed for Bailyn to call it poetry—exhibited the same technical weaknesses as the prose. Sense and sound were alternatively sacrificed to each other, he wrote. As poetry, these works lacked control and order and a coherence of idea and form.

Bailyn judged the romantic world of early American literature too far removed from the cool rationalism that nourished the American writers who produced such calm and reasonable pamphlets. Yet, paradoxically, this expository and explanatory writing, which was so "didactic, systematic and direct rather than imaginative and metaphoric," fired the passions of the Enlightenment-bred American Revolution. "In this rationality, this everyday, businesslike sanity so distant from the imaginative mists where artistic creations struggle into birth," he said of the pamphlets, "they were products of their situation and of the demands it made in politics."

The consequences of Bailyn's application of such literary criticism to the historical record of republican rhetoric in America was to define the Revolution and its ideology as an Enlightenment movement rather than as a Romantic one. In making that claim, however, he had actually provided an ahistorical justification for separating aesthetic elements of Anglo-American culture from political and economic ones. This separation in the American context served to explain the success of the Revolution and to justify it as a reasoned and liberating event. Despite the spirit of intoxication, the emotions of conspiratorial fear, the physical violence, the American Revolution could be characterized as a Neoclassical moment of realist calm. It was a rational alternative to the romantic excesses of the Europeans. American writers, he said, communicated understanding, they did not seek to annihilate their opponents as did the romantic English pamphleteers, or as would the French and, still later, the Russian revolutionists. Americans sought to persuade, they did not appeal to the unbridled imagination.

The effect of Bailyn's analysis of the literature of the Revolution was to define aesthetic expression and political rhetoric as discontinuous from each other. The coolness of political rhetoric, with the violent passions it ignited, was not seen as complementary to the pallid, lifeless, and transparent qualities characteristic of the poems written to inspire vigorous rebellion by the reader. Instead, these similarly inverted tensions between forms of passion and decorum within Revolutionary discourse were statically opposed to each other. Once more, though he was writing a political history of social transformation through revolution, Bailyn had adopted a formal criticism of Revolutionary literature that defended a traditional canon and subjected all writing to a timeless set of universal principles. In doing so, he specifically followed the New Criticism and applied it to the historical record and to historical method as well.

Bailyn's ahistorical application of New Criticism to historiography may seem surprising in the abstract. But besides revealing how thin the line is between literary theory and historiography in actual practice, it also shows the powerful influence of the New Criticism in shaping academic life between 1940 and 1960. No highly educated young person in those years—especially if he or she attended such Anglophile eastern colleges or universities as Williams and Harvard, Bailyn's almae matres—could have avoided drinking in the assumptions and standards inherent in the New Criticism. Yet despite the formative influence of New Critical methodology and standards on the emerging republican scholarship in the 1960s, the self-conscious recognition of its dominance among literary historians was already building a movement of rebellion against it. In the 1960s literary theorists like Harold Bloom were turning to a new appreciation of Romanticism. By the late 1970s and early 1980s, a new turn to historicity challenged the New Critical standards in the academy. From a number of directions came vocal claims that the New Criticism was dead.

The apparent passing of the New Criticism as the dominant formula for mediating the past of the written word and the present of the reader of those words has generated controversy and also created a great deal of confusion about what the passing may mean. The once-unassailed legitimacy of the New Critical effort to separate art from ideology and universal aesthetic laws from the particulars of history crumbled in the 1970s, but no clear replacement of the New Criticism has arisen. There was not a new New Criticism, only a failure of legitimacy of the old New Criticism. As Frank Lentricchia recently put it, the New Criticism may be dead in the official sense—that is, as a nineteenth-century description of literary space as a timeless universal—but "it is dead in the way that an imposing and repressive father figure is dead."[20]

For despite the innovative challenge to old authority among a new generation of New Critics and their collective sense that a privileged universe of aesthetic discourse no longer seems tenable, Lentricchia, like other observers of recent literary theorists, notes a similar and continuing effort to escape the implications of time within the mainstream of Anglo-American literary criticism. For Northrop Frye, Lentricchia points out, the aesthetic became a democratic vista, available anywhere the individual experiences the spiritual freedom of a creative moment.[21] In Frank Kermode, Lentricchia finds the centralizing power of myth placed in opposition to fictions as an aesthetic avenue to a free and independent self.[22] In more recent literary criticism Lentricchia sees a complementary effort by structuralists and poststructuralists to restore a pure literary space of freedom through opposing means. In one instance, the mastery of self-elucidating grammars of "reading" and "writing" creates a sort of frontier of freedom between the two structures. In a second, the indeterminacy of shattered conventions opens new spaces of positive freedom through their absence.[23] At the heart of the American jeremiad, origins and ends—like the alpha and omega of Christian symbolism or the negative inversions of Machiavellian—both point to a common redemptive frontier in Anglo-American literary thought. Whether considering the old New Critics or the structuralists or poststructuralists, according to Lentricchia, "the formalistic critic, is concerned to demonstrate the history-transcending qualities of the text, and whether he wields the textual cleaver of difference or that of irony, he portrays the writer as a kind of Houdini, a great escape artist whose deepest theme is freedom, whose great and repetitious feat is the defeat of history's manacles."[24]

This is a fairly well-defined fault line along which twentieth-century Anglo-American literary criticism runs, despite the wide variation within its particular forms. Each variation of formalist criticism offers an idealized conception of history "as the teleological unfolding of a promised end, whether in a secular or a theological sense; history as continuity or mere repetition, according to certain notions of 'tradition'; history as discontinuity—a series of 'ruptures' which mark 'periods' of semantic saturation and plenitude: these are the ruling conventional senses of a convention that leans on a temporally and culturally uncontaminated ideal meaning situated at some primal origin or at the end of things, or within temporality as its secret principle of coherence." Such a history, Lentricchia notes, provides security against fragmentation and contradiction. "A 'history,' in short, which would deny 'histories.'"[25]

This recurring crisis in Anglo-American aesthetic space closely parallels the historiographical interpretation of the crisis in Anglo-American political and economic space, as we have seen in Bernard Bailyn and as codified by Frederick Jackson Turner in the 1890s. Curiously, J. G. A. Pocock, like Bailyn, applied this formula of interpretation as well. For after demonstrating that the Machiavellian political conventions had been creatively regenerated from Savonarola's Florence in 1490 down to the Populist revolt in the 1880s, Pocock concluded his narrative as if Machiavellian conventions were incapable of surviving the same pattern of crisis in political exceptionalism that had originally created them.[26] In the first part of *The Machiavellian Moment,* Pocock had acknowledged that Machiavelli's political theory was developed in direct response to the failure of Savonarola's blend of aesthetic myth and practical politics, unsuccessfully aimed at preserving Florentine exceptionalism. Yet, in the second half of the book, he defined the subsequent defeat of political exceptionalism in England and the United States as though Savonarola's defeat and death had not anticipated them and as if Machiavelli had not fashioned his own response to transcend its consequences aesthetically and politically.

Pocock wrote of the Machiavellian tradition as if it were a political sensibility separated from a tragic reality, which became less and less real as it approached the twentieth century. In so doing, he was following the same cultural conventions as the New Agrarian Critics and the post–New Critics described by Lentricchia, except that he substituted the political world for an aesthetic one. This was in essence the same post–New Critical pattern that was being recognized as an internal contradiction within the symbol-myth school of American studies at just about the time when *The Machiavellian Moment* was published (the mid-1970s). At that time, a number of historicist-oriented critics were pointing to a submerged Romanticism in symbol-myth studies, such as Henry Nash Smith's *Virgin Land* and Leo Marx's *The Machine in the Garden* (which paradoxically defined itself as a new realism).[27] Still more recently, the literary historians Russell Reising and Robert Weismann have closed this circle by explicitly relating the conventions of the symbol-myth school to those of the New Criticism, as well as the post–New Criticism.[28] Reising, like Lentricchia, has found a common thread in their common and paradoxical efforts to escape history through history. But that same phrase, as the historian David W. Noble noted a quarter-century ago, has long applied to historians as well.[29]

For example, Pocock, like Henry Nash Smith, to whose scholarship he was indebted, assumed that myth and symbolism flourished and then died with free space and a fee-simple agrarian economy in the 1890s.[30] However, as early as 1953, Barry Marks had challenged that assumption by pointing out that Smith's *Virgin Land* created the impression that myth gave way to empirical fact as it approached an ideal and empirically objective present.[31] One implication of Smith's division of time and space was that the agrarian past was viewed as feminine. For Smith both the land and the ideal of its virginity had been compromised by history. Therefore, twentieth-century realism had rendered this feminine past as merely foolish, like the dime novel heroines who evolved or devolved into the Beadle western stories, slowly losing their own distinctive gender differences as the nineteenth century came to a close. The present, on the other hand, was defined as stolid, impenetrable, and, more than a little sadly, as neuter.[32] Within the divided time and space of Smith's myth-symbolism, there was a Romantic past in which fact and value, and aesthetics and politics, were integrated on one side of the twentieth century. On the other side of that time line lay a realistic though sterile present, in which politics and aesthetics are distinctly separated as facts and myths.

Pocock, writing more than a quarter-century after Smith's *Virgin Land,* did not mourn a lost myth of virgin promise. Identifying himself as an Antipodean, orphaned by time and distance from a shattered masculine British Empire of commercial power, which collapsed only in the twentieth century, Pocock looked to the other side of Turner's—and Smith's—equation. Pocock wrote of political ideology and not art, until he came to describe the death of the last republican culture on earth.[33]

In contrast to his use of Smith's perspective in concluding the death of Anglo-American republicanism, Pocock's earlier arguments did not even consider Machiavelli's complementary aesthetic role as a poet and dramatist to be relevant to a description of republican rhetoric or its deeper cultural significance. In evoking his "ghostly father figure" of doubtful legitimacy—that is, in tracing Anglo-American republicanism to Machiavelli—Pocock assumed that objective economic conditions alone had slain agrarian republicanism in the United States and that aesthetic fashion was irrelevant to explaining the nature of its demise. Therefore, Pocock did not consider the possibility that Machiavellian political values had simply been transformed with the death of republican virtue in a continuing process of adaptation, rather than having come to an end. Consequently, Pocock could only describe the recurring republican patterns of rhetoric in American political language—even as late as the 1970s—as a vestige that should have disappeared but, unaccountably, had not.[34]

When viewed aesthetically as well as politically, however, the closing of the frontier may be seen as a symbol "waiting to happen." It provided a formula for expressing dismay over the sociology of urbanization, the economics of industrial capitalism, and a host of other dilemmas that involved finding ground for stability while consuming time and space far more intensely than had been possible in the agrarian past. The growth of mass organizations of economic and social power exacerbated already-existing cultural tensions of time and space. Such changes might be compared to the advent of the hypodermic syringe as a mass-produced item, which was coupled with the development of new and powerful chemical opiates, such as heroin, at the turn of the century. Together, they permitted the *scale* of drug addiction to grow exponentially by radically increasing the speed and quantity with which opiates were introduced into the consumer's bloodstream. The closing of the frontier was an expression of a lost aesthetic balance as well as a lost political and economic balance within Anglo-American institutions and mores. But it was a balance lost within the context of the existing Machiavellian patterns of aesthetics and politics. The defeat of agrarian republican aesthetic and political formulas for balancing power and value, universals and particulars, and, above all, innovation and the order of law and tradition did not lead to the death of the Machiavellian political culture, as Pocock, following Smith, suggested it should. Instead, it led to new variations within Machiavellian conventions, answering the need for credible new Machiavellian formulas within a consumer economy as far removed from a producer's economy as Machiavelli's Florence was from Dante's. A postrepublican society required new aesthetics as well as new politics, just as did the postmedieval society of the Renaissance.

Historians such as Turner and then Charles Beard had captured the public ear in their time, as they led the Progressive effort to escape history through history, to find a new ground for another pure reality that time could not corrupt. But while Turner could still admit a common perspective for the Romantic artist and the objective historian, Beard forcefully rejected Romanticism as a vestige of a failed agrarian national identity. So too did Henry Nash Smith, who presented a complementary argument to Beard's for the division between realistic economics and aesthetic space. But Smith's perspective was an inversion of the New Agrarian Critics' point of view.[35] Smith's disdain for the Romantic tradition in popular Anglo-American literature—which he equated with the republican economic values of Turner—merged history and literature as aesthetic symbols of free space. But this was a dessicated and infertile space of the American past, which, he argued, both outmoded Romantic forms shared. In the 1930s, as an editor of the *Southwest Review*, Smith had placed the New Agrarian Critics in that same Romantic tradition.[36] Yet in *Virgin Land* Smith separated the realistic economic policies of the New Deal from this negatively integrated Romantic past. In contrast, he placed twentieth-century ideology completely outside of aesthetics—a stance he shared with his contemporary critics Leo Marx and F. O. Matthiessen, as Russell Reising has noted.[37] Though each of these critics in his own way experienced serious tension with the New Agrarian Critics, all shared a deeper hostility towards Romanticism as a code word for sentimentality and unrealizable visions of social harmony.

Machiavellian realism, itself a submerged form of Romanticism, has transcended the particular differences even among antagonistic critical perspectives on American history and literature. Together, historians and literary theorists, bound by their common desire to escape history, have preserved the same division of art and ideology that the New Agrarian Critics first championed in the 1930s and 1940s. That powerful cultural convention has proven extraordinarily adaptive and shows no sign of disappearing. Instead it seems to fuel a proliferation of variations, not only in historiography and literary theory, but also in popular political rhetoric. Yet, there is nothing predetermined or inevitable about the exceptionally strong hold that Machiavellian values continue to exert upon American moral and political choices. Other values are available, as they were in fifteenth-century Florence or sixteenth-century Europe, and could be substituted for them; indeed, sometimes they are substituted for them. Nor is Machiavellianism monolithic or so rigid in its forms that it blinds us to those other constructions of reality.

One useful place to begin the exploration of this Machiavellian spider's web of assumptions, ideals, and practices that shape American political and aesthetic life is to locate its national context. Such a context permits us to view republicanism as one expression of a continuing form of cultural tragedy, which at once anticipated the Civil War, was defeated by its implications, and remains locked within our present experience. I suggest that this context may be established by considering the writings and the changing literary and historiographical reputation of America's first popular writer to confront the heroic tensions within republican aesthetics and politics: Mason Locke Weems.

Parson Weems, George Washington's contemporary and his most popular biographer, sought to balance the contradictory tensions of Jeffersonian democracy and Federalist paternalism, capitalistic ambition and republican citizenship. At the same time he successfully straddled a growing antagonism between North and South following the Revolution. As the first American of letters to write in an identifiably Romantic mode, he combined politics and aesthetics in a republican jeremiad, warning against the destructive implications at the heart of the heroic innovation that had formed the nation. Weems was, in short, an American Machiavelli, who creatively and seamlessly joined aesthetics and politics to make a civic community, which he saw unraveling even before the death of the American founder-father, George Washington.

Weems was preoccupied with the tensions within the Machiavellian poles of innovation and tradition. His pamphlets and biographies of the heroes of the Revolution were jeremiads aimed at countering a growing threat to a *civitas* which he recognized as having been established by fraternal murder and parricidal rebellion. But, perhaps more important, the Anglican clergyman's fall from critical grace in the 1890s tells us a great deal about the intertextuality of literary criticism, historiography, and political ideology. For Weems was dismissed as a pious romantic, irrelevant to understanding objective historical fact, just as republicanism was dying with the agrarian frontier. And Weems was not rehabilitated, either as an artist or as an observer-historian of the Revolutionary era, until after the recovery of republican historiography in the 1960s.

At the turn of the century, when Weems's popularity with the public was attributed to his shallowness and greed for book sales, Romantic literature was at the same time negatively contrasted with Realism, and the Romantic historians suffered denigration by the scientific historians trained in the new university seminar system. Just as the corporations were destroying an agrarian producer's dream, Lockean materialism, which had been pilloried by Bancroft in the 1830s, became respectable.[38] Lockean economic and political conventions became acceptable as a guide to reality for historians as different in sensibility as New England's Henry Cabot Lodge and Henry Adams. Both men's lives were wracked by the growing gap that they, like their contemporaries Frederick Jackson Turner, Tom Watson, and Thomas Dixon, perceived between aesthetic and political truths. All of them viewed themselves as creative artists and realistic men of the world. Each struggled to come to terms with this division through the study of history. None of them believed they had succeeded.

CHAPTER ONE

Machiavelli in America: Parson Weems, Romanticism, and the Anglo-American Crisis of Legitimacy

For Henry Cabot Lodge, the conservative New England historian and politician, heroism was a highly problematic proposition at the close of the nineteenth century. The descendant of a Boston Brahmin family, Lodge held in disdain Populists trying to restore agrarian virtue to the South and Midwest along with the northeastern corporate business leaders who were advancing a new consumer's democracy against them. Lodge expressed the growing isolation of the post-Mugwump type, desperately in search of a revitalizing heroism in nationalism. Though he disdained Southerners as sentimental romantics, his great heroes, Lincoln and Washington, were both Southerners.[1]

Lodge extolled these two Southerners for having forged national policies through the power of their personalities and for having escaped the mindless romanticism of the South from which they sprang. These Southerners were able to rise to the greatness that national crises required of them because, like Lodge himself, they were realists and not romantics. Lincoln did not try to preserve a defeated republican past of agrarian virtue, nor did Washington seek to preserve the false values of luxurious self-indulgence that were characteristic of the spendthrift planter class. Instead, Lincoln and Washington—one from the rough frontier and the other from planter aristocracy—stood as shining beacons of nationalist patriotism, which Lodge believed the leaders of the United States needed to emulate in his day. Unlike their fellow Southerners, they were realists. And unlike the commercial men of dynamic leadership found in Lodge's own urban Northeast, they were more concerned for the country's needs than for narrow personal interests or private financial gain.

Therefore, when Lodge wrote a highly laudatory biography of Washington in 1898, he was as intensely engaged in exposing Jeffersonian republicanism as a failed Romantic myth as he was in rejecting the new crass commercialism, which he believed might ultimately triumph through the negative consequences of another form of Romanticism—popular sentimentality.[2] For Lodge, pious and patently false anecdotes about great leaders such as Washington could only help destroy the basis for a realistic and modern heroic alternative to the fading greatness of the Anglo-American past and the growing corruption of a purely commercial future. His hope lay in using history as a partisan weapon against terminally weakened myth and in fashioning a realistic heroic formula within a middle way of corporate nationalism. History could accomplish this reorientation of popular democracy because it could put that democracy back in touch with a universal classical tradition, based on a timeless standard of aesthetic taste with "the immortal vitality which appeals alike to the rich and poor, to the ignorant and to the learned."[3]

In trying to find a way to a realistic heroic standard for the present, beyond myth, Lodge challenged dual Romantic myths of the past in which he and his classical ideal of a truly timeless and universal Washington were imprisoned. In one myth, that of the cultivated elite's veneration of greatness, the heroes of the past had been separated from the present by the desire to worship them. As a result, Washington the man had been lost to the image of the great founder-father figure, "a man of lofty intellect, vast moral force, supremely successful and fortunate, and wholly apart from and above his fellow-men."[4] This was the myth of Romantic historians such as Bancroft, and belonged to the unreality of the earlier nineteenth century. It was now being challenged by the realism of the new scientific history taught to men like Lodge himself, who earned doctoral degrees in university seminars. Entrusting the study of past heroes to inspired amateurs, who were men of letters rather than true historians, Lodge suggested, resulted in an icon or statue but not the whole truth. "In the progress of time," he complained, "Washington has become in the popular imagination largely mythical: for mythical ideas grow up in this nineteenth century, not withstanding its boasted intelligence, much as they did in the infancy of the race."[5]

The second of the Romantic myths was the opposite of the first, according to Lodge's dichotomy of the unreal past. It was the humorist's burlesque, which made a mockery of Washington by turning him into "the blameless and priggish boy, and the equally faultless and uninteresting man"[6] whom the newspapers parody every February 22. This myth had created a national reaction of laughter at the mention of Washington's name because it was based on outmoded moralisms of a bygone era.

Though Lodge saw himself in combat with both myths in his effort to discover the true Washington—and, incidentally, to justify his addition to the surfeit of existing biographies—the second myth seemed to him more destructive. For while the first myth was rooted "in the genuine love and veneration springing from the inborn gratitude of man to the founders and chiefs of his race," the second was not even derived from the real Washington. It was a reaction against a Romantic fiction, invented by Parson Mason Locke Weems, which put Washington in "a ridiculous light to an age which has outgrown the educational foibles of seventy-five years ago."[7] Yet, though discredited and made into self-parodying jokes, Weems's fictions had become ingrained in the fabric of the nation. They had been carried west by the democratic tide and taught to generations of children in their schoolbooks. Eventually, Weems's fictions had infected everyone. At last, "even the most stately and solemn of the Washington biographers adopted the unsupported tales of the itinerant parson and book-peddler."[8] But how had this strange transformation occurred, in which popular piety passed into Romantic myth and then into the derision characteristic of the modern masses in a commercial society?

According to Lodge, the answer was not that Weems was a cold-blooded liar, but rather that he was a man without historical sense, training, or morals. Anxious for adventure, notoriety, and financial gain, he stumbled onto George Washington by accident and instinctively recognized a source of book sales. Weems knew how to appeal to the vulgar taste for heroes. As such, he was "an approved myth maker" who needed to be disposed of before Lodge could fulfill his own mission to "get at the real Washington" and restore an aesthetically and politically virtuous heroic ideal. Lodge succeeded in both aims. He began by denying Weems's moral and historical sense and criticizing his talent as a writer. "Judged solely as literature the book is beneath contempt," he wrote of Weems's *Life of Washington.*[9] "The style is turgid, overloaded, and at times silly." He continued, "The statements are loose, the mode of narration confused and incoherent, and the moralizing is flat and common-place to the last degree." Perversely, however, these very defects commended the book to the pioneers and backwoodsmen to whom it was directed (to Lodge, these frontiersmen were discredited mythic figures of the Romantic past). In their naive ignorance, they confused Weems's "heavy and tawdry style" and his moralism and patriotism with aesthetic and historical truth.[10]

Having disposed of Weems, Lodge then proceeded with his own task to restore the true Washington as a classical heroic figure. His Washington was "a fighting man, hot blooded and fierce in action, and utterly indifferent to the danger which excited and delighted him." He was also a man of prudence and learning, one with whom to stir and educate the public. Lodge's model was self-consciously drawn from a portrait by Savage on the dining room wall in Memorial Hall at Cambridge, Mass. (Harvard). Unlike Stuart's "serene and beautiful" portrait—which Lodge did not add was painted in a plain, anti-heroic republican style—Lodge's ideal image, remembered from student days, "was cold and dry, hard enough to serve for a signboard of an inn, and able, one would think, to withstand all kinds of weathers." This Washington had a rugged strength in his face which made Lodge pause before it. The jaw was massive, "telling of an iron grip and a relentless will."[11]

Clearly, in Lodge's view, such a Washington would never have done anything so patently absurd as to lecture his playmates against the wickedness of fighting or to allow himself to be knocked down in front of his soldiers and then ask for forgiveness from his assailant. Yet these were precisely the stories that Parson Weems asked his unsophisticated readers to believe. Lodge said that even to attempt to offer a serious historical criticism of such "wretched fables" would be to "break a butterfly." Instead, Lodge's Washington was a stoic and dignified hero for an age that needed but no longer believed in heroes:

The day when the commander held his place merely by virtue of personal prowess lay far back in the centuries, and no one knew it better than Washington. But the old fighting spirit awoke within him when the clash of arms sounded in his ears, and though we may know the general in the tent and in the council, we can only know the man when he breaks out from all rules and customs, and shows the rage of battle, and the indomitable eagerness for the fray, which lie at the bottom of the tenacity and courage that carried the war for independence to a triumphant close.[12]

John S. Bassett, the southern historian and liberal editor of *The South Atlantic Quarterly*, echoed Lodge's sentiments during the twilight years of

Progressivism. In his contribution to the *Cambridge History of American Literature* (1917), he accorded Weems a paragraph. Bassett admitted that Weems's life of Washington was "the most successful historical book of the day," but as "a romance, interlarded with pious stories," the book appealed only to the uneducated and unsophisticated reader. "Except as a curiosity, it is beneath contempt or criticism."[13]

Marcus Cunliffe notes several similar examples of criticism by Bassett's and Lodge's contemporaries, such as Albert J. Beveridge and William Roscoe Thayer. In the 1920s, Rupert Hughes was still echoing Lodge's charge that Weems simply made up false stories of Washington's youth; he referred to Weems's stories of young Washington as the "slush of plagiarism and piety."[14]

Yet in the 1980s, historians and students of American literature, such as Dwight Anderson, Jay Fliegelman, and Garry Wills, came to view Weems in a very different light.[15] Anderson considers Weems's biography of Washington "a surprisingly dependable guide to the Revolution and the Constitution." For Wills, "Weems's books live—especially his *Washington.*" Those who mock Weems, Wills argues, have mistaken both his genre and his intent. Agreeing with Bassett and Lodge that Weems was the most popular of Washington's early biographers, Wills also claims that Weems "had more, and more truthful, things to tell those readers." Wills, Fliegelman, and especially Dwight Anderson not only find Weems to be a trustworthy guide for understanding Washington and his legacy for pre–Civil War America but also view him as a key architect of a particular heroic narrative within antebellum American political culture. They portray Weems as the opposite of the pious dispenser of improbable anecdotes, so disdainfully dismissed by Lodge and his Progressive-era contemporaries. They see Weems as centrally engaged in containing a bitter legacy of a violent family quarrel—the Revolution—which was already building up once again between Northerners and Southerners in the new nation. Anderson views Weems as consciously fashioning a heroic image of Washington and then intentionally undermining it to warn his contemporaries against tyranny and corruption in the nation's political birthright. Fliegelman sees a similar antipaternalism, a deeply Protestant attack upon false earthly fathers who would assume Heaven's prerogative. In his view, Weems sought to restore harmony between natural and spiritual fatherhood by undermining all false earthly claims of authority. Wills sees Weems as a tireless fashioner of a new heroic icon, not in the shape of Moses, as one would expect from Christian piety, but in a sccular form, as Cincinnatus. Wills's Weems was deliberately using books, tracts, sermons, and speeches to create a common hero who was his own anti-hero, the military leader as farmer who returns to his fields after victory and not to a throne. This Weems was obsessed with public duty, civic virtue, religious tolerance, antislavery, and the containment of political passions.

This problematic twist in the interpretation of Parson Weems who once seemed so patently—and piously—simple has by the 1980s become conventional among historians of the early republic. That preoccupation with the implications of Weems's dualisms between true and false heroes, and private and public virtue, and with his warnings that self-indulgent vices would lead to despair, parricide, and fratricide, reflects the renewed interest of historians in republican political ideology and popular Romantic literature. Weems's language no longer seems peripheral as it did to the earlier historians of a neoclassically reserved Revolution. Rather, Weems appears to recent historians, who view the Revolution through the republican paradigms of Bernard Bailyn and J. G. A. Pocock, as someone who was personally engaged in confrontation with the same crisis of authority that produced the Revolution.

Mason Locke Weems was born in Maryland in 1759. The youngest in a family of nineteen, he did not become a young volunteer in Washington's army but instead remained in England and studied during the Revolution, though he returned to Maryland briefly to attend his father's funeral in 1779. He first studied medicine, may have had some experience at sea, and finally elected to seek ordination in the Church of England. After his return to America about 1784, he served as rector of two parishes in Maryland. About 1791 or 1792, while still serving as rector of St. Margaret's parish in Westminster, Maryland, Weems first began to promote himself as a seller of books and pamphlets. Apparently, Weems did not begin his career of selling books for purely financial reasons, since he was still the incumbent of St. Margaret's at the time and did not marry until 1795. A possible explanation for Weems's entering into bookselling may have been his desire to influence public morals around his preoccupation with republican themes of patriarchal legitimacy and family virtue. These were the twin grounds for confronting the dangers to the nation, which underlay everything Weems later wrote, including his life of Washington and his pamphlets against bachelorhood, adultery, gambling, and drinking.[16]

One of the first publications Weems promoted was a pamphlet titled

Onania "or the heinous sin of self-pollution, and all its frightful consequences in both sexes, considered."[17] The pamphlet seems to have confined its discussion to the moral rather than the physiological aspects of
the practice of masturbation. However, it apparently created a minor
scandal, and Weems became the subject of ridicule. Quite possibly the
affair led to the loss of his position and his inability or unwillingness to
find another. From about 1793 on, Weems led an itinerant life. He was
constantly on the road, visiting out-of-the-way taverns and villages from
New York to Georgia. Weems was better able to take the popular pulse
than any other individual in America, as he catered to the needs and
wants of his customers and listened to their homespun tales. He was in a
position to hear conversations in taverns and churches, to feel the growing antagonism of the sections toward each other, and to witness the daily
tragedies of small-town quarrels and private vices. By the end of the decade and the century, he was bringing out his own books and pamphlets,
not just promoting those of others. In 1799 he issued *The Philanthropist;
Or A Good Twenty-Five Cents Worth of Political Love Powder, for the Fair
Daughters and Patriotic Sons of Virginia.*[18] He dedicated the work to "that
great Lover and Love of his Country, George Washington, Esquire," and
pushed an endorsement from Washington himself. The pamphlet was a
plea for love between the "sister states" of the union so that "quarrels
vile / 'Twixt A's and D's / may cease."[19] Conscious of the implications
of the French Revolution for America, Weems confirmed the truth of the
natural equality of man but prayed for the nation's deliverance from "the
mobs of the sans-Culottes." The antidote to civic chaos, Weems said, is
Christian love. The avenue for the dispensation of that healing balm and
the deliverance from self-destruction lay in marriage. For that holy state
alone "preserves Youth from Black eyes and Broken Heads." The unat-
tached young man soon falls in with others who are as strongly self-
willed and passionate as himself. Contradictions lead to contentions, and
tragedy must inevitably follow. Males are hard and unloving, Weems explained, "and fond of quarrelling and throat cutting." Lovely women
have the power to soothe and soften, and "verily the young man who
walks without one of these charming guards, *walks in jeopardy every
hour.*"[20] Weems's life of Washington followed this same theme but with a
far more difficult contradiction to be contained than could be ameliorated through the softening influence of gender on the violent male passions that threatened civic peace. The central problem of Washington as
a heroically violent rebel and as loving father to his political family was

that these mutually contradictory qualities had to be balanced in the same man. Weems's dedication to Washington in *The Philanthropist* acknowledged this purpose in writing a children's biography of America's father, a man who had learned to control his violent passions and who had established a national family that was now in danger of dissolution. Washington's personal triumph over the dangers of heroism had to be transferred to later generations so that the inherent sinfulness of men would not end in fratricide in America's streets.

Weems introduced his biography of Washington with praise from Napoleon, the very real alternative to Washington's sterling example. "*Ah, gentleman!*" Napoleon says to a visiting American delegation, ". . . *Posterity shall talk of him with reverence as the founder of a great empire, when my name shall be lost in the vortex of Revolutions.*"[21] Weems went on to describe a number of British and American false heroes, particularly Benedict Arnold. Arnold's presence within Weems's narrative emphasized the problematic nature of Weems's heroic Washington, even for Weems. In part, this was because Arnold fought valiantly with Washington against the British in the Revolutionary War, yet his heroism in that noble cause failed to prevent him from becoming a traitor. Perhaps even more important than the implication of Arnold's fall, however, was the fate of the virtuous young man who bound Arnold and Washington together in the public imagination: Major John Andre, the dashing young spy who was captured while on a mission from Arnold and executed by Washington's order.[22] Washington, over the objections of his own staff, had Andre hanged, denying his request to avoid that ignoble end with a bullet. As James Fenimore Cooper's 1821 novel, *The Spy*, confirmed, Washington was angrily denounced as a tyrant by many in sympathy with Andre, whose personal grace and courage reflected badly on Washington's humanity.[23] Weems drove this same message home by inserting a story into his narrative recounting Andre's personal act of mercy towards a young and impetuous rebel who was taken prisoner by the British.

According to the story, Andre was unlike the harsh soldiers who were preparing to incarcerate this frightened boy in a dank prison cell behind the enemy's line. "He appeared to me like a *brother; they like brutes*," the young man remembered. Then, approaching the crying lad tenderly, the dashing officer set him free. Later, Major Andre himself was captured. While others were thinking of self-preservation, Weems said, he was "thinking of nothing but *duty* and *generosity*." Andre's virtue led him to be more concerned with Arnold's safety than his own fate.

Though the false self-glorification of Arnold was evoked as a contrast to the private virtues of Andre's mercy and forgiveness, the implied criticism for Andre's death on the gallows certainly included Washington as well.[24]

If even Washington's public persona could fail him, permitting him to participate, ironically, with the traitor Arnold in a moral failure that resulted in the unsavory sacrifice of a virtuous young man, no public virtù, or heroic action, could be trusted. Private virtues alone must be the only reliable sources for true acts of heroism. For only in the private virtues of industry, civility, and obedience did Washington overcome the temptations of pride, and this saved him and the union from the disastrous self-destruction that became Arnold's fate. But Weems's dilemma was that because private heroism defeats self-aggrandizement through humility and harmony with nature and with others, it is directly in contradiction with the requirements of the public acts of heroism through which the Republic was born. For Weems, public expressions of heroism, as a form of virtù, were deeply suspect as a measure of character because they represented the self-willed usurpation of God's prerogatives by father-founders, which leads to fratricide in the next generation. Therefore, the war hero of public acclaim had to be described as having been a child of peace. Young George never engaged in fighting, unlike his companions. If he could not bring peace to their "savage passions," he would go to the schoolmaster and inform him of their intention to fight. Though his young companions were angry with George for this, he countered that an act shameful "even in *slaves* and *dogs*" ought to be scandalous for boys in school.[25] Yet, as Weems's readers knew, the mature Washington would lead one side of the fratricidal warfare between Britannia's children on American soil; Weems had Britannia, hearing the groans of her children, thrice begin to "*curse* the destroyers of her race; but thrice she remembered that *they too were her sons.*"[26]

Britannia's response, like any other mother's, was to rend the air with her cries of anguish. Parents should see their children returning home with smiles and joy, instead of "creeping in like blackguards," with their heads "*bound up, black eyes and bloody clothes!*" said Weems. But, he asked, what is the misguided children's answer when asked what all this violence is for? "Why that we *may get praise!!*" is the tragic answer.[27] Though Weems never questioned the right of Americans to kill to preserve their birthright as free Englishmen or the fact that the failure of the king to exercise his patriarchal responsibility was the cause of the war, he insisted it was a self-destructive family quarrel for all involved. This led Weems to emphasize Washington as "the *dutiful son*—affectionate brother—the cheerful school-boy—the diligent surveyor—the laborious farmer—the widow's husband—the orphan's father—the poor man's friend," and not as "Washington the HERO, and the Demigod . . . Washington the *sun beam* in council, or the *storm* in war."[28] Weems's Washington, then, had to be portrayed in dutiful relation to his own father, who in turn taught him that God was the only true father, so that George could escape the fate of a Benedict Arnold. For this reason, too, young George had to prefer his father's company to that of his playmates at school, though he loved them like brothers. It was his own inconsolable sorrow at his beloved father's death that made Washington "worthiest to be the founder of a JUST and EQUAL GOVERNMENT, lasting as thy own deathless name."[29] The memory of that father's guidance in pointing to God as his son's true father, sustained the bereaved George as it must sustain the next generation of young Georges for whom Weems was writing. Washington's dutifulness to his father's authority had to be translated to his acceptance of the authority of the schoolmaster, as new generations of Georges must translate their adoration of their political father to the legitimate government, after his death.

If, however, the rebel Washington had to acquit himself in the field, "where LIBERTY, heaven born goddess, was to be bought for blood," Weems needed to show that Washington had not been corrupted privately by the public stain of his own heroism. The effort to do so was the source of tales of Washington asking the pardon of a Mr. Payne, who knocked him down in front of his troops, and the prayer scene witnessed by a pious farmer named Potts at Valley Forge. For in meeting General Washington again after the war, Mr. Payne could be a credible witness to the fact that "his long familiarity with war had not robbed him of a single spark of the goodness and nobleness of his heart." Potts, the Quaker farmer who came upon "the commander and chief of the American Armies on his Knees in prayer," upon a dark, cold Pennsylvania night, was no partisan of either warring faction. Therefore, what more credible witness could be conceived to recognize what he or any other Christian apologist would never have expected to see? For, as he confessed later that night to his wife, "Thee knows that I always thought the sword and the gospel utterly inconsistent; and that no man could be a soldier and a christian at the same time. But George Washington had this day convinced me of my mistake."[30]

Were such tales manufactured by Weems out of a belief that Americans must have a mythic father-founder to contain the violence in their own origins? There is evidence for this in Weems's willingness to borrow and/or rearrange events to support his message. One example is his attribution of the contemporary cabbage-seed story of a Scottish poet-philosopher named James Beattie to Washington's father; the obvious point of the story was the necessity of earthly fathers teaching their children to abjure tyrannical designs through self-abnegation of their own authority.[31]

There is evidence as well in Weems's seeking out an endorsement of his *Life of Washington* from Thomas Jefferson, claiming that he had not, like some of his eulogists, "set him up as a Common Hero for military ambition to idolize and imitate—Nor an Aristocrat, like *others*, to mislead and enslave the nation, but a pure Republican whom all our youth should know, that they may love and imitate his Virtues, and thereby immortalize 'the *last Republic now on earth*'."[32]

Or did Weems, in his travels, simply collect the fragments of the people's own will to believe in a father-founder, whom they themselves made Washington symbolize? On this score, there is much evidence for Weems's veracity about worshipful public attitudes towards Washington, according to Marcus Cunliffe. Catherine Albanese offers many examples of the widespread veneration of Washington as father-founder as early as 1775.[33] When Washington assumed command of the army, for example, she quotes one chaplain as saying that he appeared "born to command" and clearly "reserved for some great destiny." An American correspondent noted that not a single king in Europe could look like more than "a valet de chambre" by his side. Harvard and Yale awarded him honorary doctorates, he was eulogized from the stage, and by the early 1790s his name was conventionally spelled in large or small capitals. According to Isaac Weld, by February 22, 1796, "not one town of any importance was there in the whole union where some meeting did not take place in honor of this day." Yet, it was also true, that, even then, Washington was not universally acclaimed, leading John Adams to comment on "the general sentiment in America that Washington must retire" out of fear of his ambitions and the factionalism he might inspire.[34]

Did Washington, as his critics feared, view himself as a father-founder and persuade his "children," of his special God-given status as rebel and as the new nation's legitimate leader? It was, after all, Washington himself—not Weems's Washington—who confessed in 1775, when called to exercise his talent for waging war, "*My diffidence in my own abilities, was superceded by a confidence in the rectitude of our cause and the patronage of Heaven.*"[35] Or as Weems quotes him upon his acceptance of the presidency:

When I contemplate the interposition of Providence, as it was visibly manifested in guiding us through the revolution, in preparing us for the reception of a general government, and in conciliating the good will of the people of America towards one another after its adoption; I feel myself oppressed and almost overwhelmed with a sense of the divine munificence. I feel that nothing is due to my personal agency in all those complicated and wonderful events, except what can simply be attributed to the exertions of an honest zeal for the good of my country.[36]

And, more problematically, it was Washington himself, and not Weems, who warned against tyranny and fratricide in his farewell address. In that solemn address, Washington warned his "children" that he would soon enter the "mansions of rest" and that no changes in government must occur through usurpation: "For though this, in one instance, may be the instrument of good, it is the customary weapon by which free governments are destroyed." The double bind of innovative violence and piety toward tradition at the heart of the Revolution was therefore tragically and palpably present for Washington, his public, and his biographer, at this, the focal moment of uncertain time in which he departed from public life. "The precedent," Washington continued, in a phrase pregnant with interpretive possibilities, "must always greatly overbalance in *permanent* evil any partial or transient benefit which the use can at *anytime* yield."[37]

Were the dark anxieties about tyranny and fratricidal war in the nation's future, then, Weems's distinctive contribution to the eighteenth-century fin de siècle American political culture in which the Neoclassical Enlightenment gave way to Romanticism? Is the reading of such anxiety and self-contradiction into the heroic age of the Revolutionary generation a mistake of style, the misprison of reading Romantic struggles between solipsism and communal responsibility into a classical Enlightenment formalism? Or, alternatively, was it only Washington out of the confident generation of the "heroic age" of revolution who experienced this sense of dread, because he alone bore the full burden of national fatherhood? Did the lesser Founding Fathers sense their own self-contradiction and fear that one day other heroic father-founders would mirror their actions? Did Washington serve as a shield against the intrusion of such fears and yet embody that very nightmare at the same time?

These interrelated questions of interpretation concerning Weems, patriarchal authority, and aesthetic standards of judgment confirm the problematic nature of the Anglo-American heroic narrative. Weems's true motives and his influence on American political culture remain as murky as Washington's—or Lincoln's, for whom both problematic images of the father-founder merged. For the Washington Lincoln knew as his political father was largely the one supplied by Parson Weems, making Weems, in a sense, the father of Lincoln's father. To ask which is the true Washington, now that both Weems and Washington must be read through Lincoln's Lyceum speech of 1838, is simply to compound the levels of interpretive confusion already considered.[38] For in that speech, the twenty-eight-year-old legislator from Illinois entered the same problematic heroic narrative structure as Weems by warning against the very tyranny over the national family to which he aspired. In referring to Weems's biography, Lincoln seemingly merged politics with aesthetics to make it possible for an unknown neophyte with aspirations for achieving greatness to conceive himself as a self-sacrificing savior of the Revolutionary promise of fraternity in union.

Thus, though the questions concerning the actual heroic ideals of Weems or Washington or Lincoln remain locked in an interminable objective confusion, the pattern of that confusion stands out starkly. In each case, the tensions between the poles of piety and murder, virtue and virtù, and innovation and tradition, run as a scarlet thread through the discourses of these historical figures and their interpreters, from Lodge to the present. Within the pattern of these tensions it becomes possible to recognize a continuing series of crises in balancing power and value within Anglo-American republican political culture. Defined purely as political discourse, however, this problematic heroic narrative, as Bernard Bailyn's recovery of republican ideology made explicit, was not confined within the tensions of the supposed post-heroic age. Rather, Bailyn's analysis of republican rhetoric identified republicanism as a conservative challenge to patriarchal authority, extending the same context of familial tensions, which exploded in Revolution in 1775, back to the turn of the seventeenth century. Since then, Bailyn's Anglocentric perspective on the republican language of patriarchal crisis has given way to a still larger Atlantic political context of space and time. J. G. A. Pocock, who has defined himself as neither a European nor an American but an "Antipodean," personally confronting a decentralized Anglo culture shaped by oceanic distance and the contingency of history, has placed the crisis of political legitimacy at the very doorstep of Niccolò Machiavelli.[39] In doing so, he has provocatively located the Anglo-American crisis, confronted by doubtful patriarchs such as Weems, Washington, and Lincoln, at the Florentine address of the most doubtful father-founder available in Western political history.

This new context for understanding the roots of the conflicts within Anglo-American republican values in an Atlantic-wide Machiavellian political culture reveals the need for a new aesthetic context for considering the relation of republicanism to Romanticism and Neoclassicism. While the political boundaries of republican culture have been largely erased, making it possible to see the Machiavellian roots of Anglo-American political culture, the aesthetic conventions of Neoclassicism and Romanticism have been much slower to dissolve. Yet recent literary and art historians, such as Marilyn Butler, Robert Rosenblum, and Hugh Honour, have challenged these divisions in ways that may offer a broader insight into the continuing aesthetic and political implications of Machiavellian patterns within contemporary American society.[40] Such a merging of political and aesthetic form into an identification of republican political culture as a form of Romanticism, however, must cut to the heart of the assumptions of both the New Criticism and counter-Progressive historiography. Both assume a stable Neoclassical ground for political and aesthetic consensus, either in the Revolution in the first case or in the aesthetic realm in the second. Denying such a ground must shatter the avenues of escape from history into aesthetics and from Romanticism into realism, which have been the twin legacies of counter-Progressivism and the New Criticism.

But when Machiavellian aesthetics and politics are seen together, as complementary patterns of the same problematic heroic narrative structure, the pattern of transformation becomes visible as well. At this juncture of aesthetics and history, Machiavellian political culture may be separated into a deep structure of political discourse and its *stylistic* deconstruction as an Agrarian tradition of virtue in the 1890s. Despite the deconstruction of republicanism as a recognizable nineteenth-century form of Agrarianism in the United States, a parallel form of this same Machiavellian convention persists in the aesthetic category of 'Neoclassicism' as a stable and timeless aesthetic formula, contrasted with a distinct turn-of-the-century movement called 'Romanticism'.

Classicism, for political historians as well as historians of aesthetics, has long been defined as a timeless and universal style. It appears cool, detached, and rational as opposed to the extravagant opulence of the earlier Rococo or the intense emotionalism of later Romanticism. Neoclassicism, in politics as in aesthetics, has become defined retrospectively as an oasis of repose between turbulent eras of self-indulgence and decline into overwrought emotionalism. Ironically, the literary historian Marilyn Butler argues that that image was likely derived directly from a Romantic prejudice against a preceding style and was absorbed afterwards by anti-Romantics. The category itself, therefore, came into general use only in the late nineteenth century, and it became an analytical abstraction for comparison with other periods in literary history only in the twentieth century.[41] Recent critics of the visual arts, such as Hugh Honour and Robert Rosenblum, have demonstrated that, far from being a cool, detached aesthetics, Neoclassicism represented a turn to revolutionary purity against a corrupted style of ornamentation. They suggest a profoundly deconstructive moralism in the work of Neoclassicist artists from the mid-eighteenth century on, which complements the revolutionary rhetoric Bernard Bailyn found in Anglo-American political expression at the same time. One example of the effect of this moralism on subject and style in the visual arts was that deathbed scenes of heroes or simply of fathers became highly popular, expressing a purifying catharsis of Rococo hedonism in the arts. Similarly, the preoccupation with ruins, particularly Greco-Roman ruins, pointed simultaneously to a nostalgia for a lost past and towards a prospective future of reconstructed glories. The ruin could be at once a random and irrational expression of time's destructive course in human affairs and history, and a geometric return to first principles, which anticipated twentieth-century Futurism.[42]

By the early 1780s, artists like John Flaxman and Henry Fuseli found in Dante's poetry, in particular, a model for their aesthetic ideal of purified form.[43] Dante's poetic heroism offered both a new political vision and an inspiration for a deeply ethical aesthetic response against ornamentation and color and towards clean lines and simple harmony with nature. However, these artists so solidly rooted in Neoclassical style shared this enthusiasm for Dante as a source for inspiration with the younger and primitively Romantic artist and poet, William Blake. Yet Blake, as Marilyn Butler notes, is one of those often credited with initiating Romanticism with his *Songs of Innocence* (1789), along with Wordsworth and Coleridge in 1798.[44] Revivals of interest in Dante by visual and literary artists around 1848, in the 1880s and 1890s, and then in the 1920s, in both Europe and the United States, carried the same rebellious connotations as had the earlier Neoclassical and Romantic revivals.

This Neoclassical revival, at least in England, began with Fuseli (1741–1825), who had worked on illustrations to the *Divine Comedy* in 1777 in Italy. Upon his return to England in 1780, he joined with Blake (1757–1827) and Flaxman (1755–1826) in pursuing his interest in Dante's aesthetic and political idealism. Blake, however, waited nearly thirty years before executing his own drawings. Blake had come to find Dante's Hell disconcerting, perhaps because of the similarity of Dante's images to industrial furnaces, which may have seemed all too real by 1824. Fuseli and Flaxman, working earlier, found Dante to be a voice of pure liberation.[45] Dante's meaning was necessarily subject to historical context, but he nevertheless remained a favored source of inspiration for such Romantics as Keats and Leigh Hunt. The focus provided for Fuseli and Flaxman by Dante's *Divine Comedy* was as iconoclastic in its own way as it was for Blake. They belonged to the same period, beginning about the middle of the eighteenth century, which saw the triumph of Classicism in the arts and literature and also coincided with a new popularity of Gothic and primitive styles. Perhaps, suggests Marilyn Butler, the affinity between the apparently contradictory styles of Neoclassical rationality and Primitivist experience rested in a common "revulsion against sophisticated urban life in favor of a dream of the pastoral."[46] At the very least, it suggests a deeply problematic relation between an ideal of timeless stability and a violent aesthetic assault on decadent forms, which somehow promised to restore social and aesthetic vitality to art as well as within social relations.

All this suggests that the problematic relation of artist to authority and the explosive separation of the individual's heroic sense of a self alienated from a corrupt society, usually associated with "Romanticism" around the turn of the nineteenth century, were present far earlier in the eighteenth century than has commonly been assumed. In Neoclassicism itself, the cool detachment of style contrasted with an intense undercurrent of emotionalism. Innovation served traditionalism or, alternately, the equation was reversed. Once more, these conservative or radical implications were often expressed in the same work of art. This raises the questions of just what 'Romanticism' means as the contrasting period to Neoclassicism and when it actually began. As Marilyn Butler has observed, the standard foundational assumptions about Romanticism rest on shaky and often untenable historical grounds, such as postulating an aesthetic change among artists in general from defining art in static mimetic terms of objective rationality to defining it as a subjective and emotionally intense expression of subjectivity.[47] Paradoxically, since aesthetics and politics have been formally separated with the New Criticism and counter-Progressivism, yet simultaneously linked in the belief that aesthetic work may transcend its time and therefore offer a redemptive alternative to historical determinism, Romanticism claims a dual origin. Scholars sometimes attempt to date its appearance by referring to a particular political event, such as the French Revolution, or to an aesthetic moment, such as the writings of Friedrich Schlegel in Germany and Wordsworth in England. This provides "a watershed between the old and the new, at a date conveniently close to 1800 and to the turn of the century." However, Butler asks how is it "that Blake, who was designing and writing great works in the 1780s, contrived to be so early?"

How is it that on the whole English and French painting is thought of as affected by Romanticism so much later than English poetry? In France the Romantic movement is represented taking hold of painters only after the end of the Napoleonic Wars, for example with Gericault's "Raft of the Medusa" (1819). In England the "revolution" seems to take place even later, with the work in the 1820s of the apocalyptic John Martin and the impressionistic J. M. W. Turner.[48]

That tableau seems even more irrational, Butler points out, when we recognize that Wordsworth is seen as a transitional figure, and not yet a full-blown Romantic. A completely subconscious aesthetic does not appear in England, for example, until J. S. Mill, Thomas Carlyle, and John Keble, in the 1830s.[49] Beyond that, this subjective doctrine of art inhabiting a mysterious realm of creativity rather than consisting in mimesis of the natural world gained general acceptance only in the generation after the English Romantics. More confusing still is that while the advent of Romanticism is often associated with the turn of the nineteenth century in England, France, and the United States, it is often traced to the same Dante who is equally associated with the Renaissance revival of Classicism in fourteenth-century Italy.[50]

With such fluctuation in date and style across national boundaries and across the borders of the arts themselves, it seems plain that no single Romantic movement existed. Rather, "Romanticisms" of various form have been present within a complex relation to more static ideals of aesthetic order, at least since the Renaissance.[51]

The dominant aesthetic patterns for balancing particular emotion and universal form, for mounting a conservative revolt for purity of line against the opulence of color, and for an effort to return to the harmony in nature over the artificiality of civilization all rested on a conception of the artist as a problematic hero capable of redeeming society aesthetically.[52]

Robert Rosenblum has placed this self-conscious reaction among eighteenth-century artists against the sensual and materialistic qualities of Rococo. He has traced its evolution from the simple and abstract chasteness of early Neoclassicism to the spartan rejection of the "sentimentality" of the family in favor of the clean disinterestedness of allegiance to the state before the era of revolutions in artists such as West, David, and Fuseli.[53] Marilyn Butler suggests that the stress associated with new commercial processes for the public consumption of art, in an era of uneasiness about expanding capitalism, should not be overlooked. During this period the artist became self-identified as a kind of producer, increasingly alienated from his or her society.[54] Such quarrels with the implications of a public world around the dilemmas of paternal legitimacy, brotherhood, citizenship, purity, and independence point to many of the same economic and political anxieties that were simultaneously experienced by other kinds of producers over dangers to republican virtue.[55]

This similarity of aesthetic and political conventions provides a surprisingly cohesive framework for the integration of formally different perspectives around the dilemmas codified by Machiavelli. For example, whatever religious and political ideals Dante may have expressed as a defender of a chastened Christian polity, his heroic narrative did not seek to subvert the authority of pope, king, Florentine institutions, or public standards of virtue. Quite to the contrary, his redemptive mission was to restore a basically sound tradition in which individuals had failed in their God-given responsibilities of authority and thus had corrupted the community as a whole. It is another Dante from the medieval heroic poet of purified mission, a more problematic Dante shaped into Machiavellian categories of subversion, who informed the rebellious conservatism of Fuseli, Flaxman, and Blake; Rossetti, Shelley, and Byron; or Eliot, Pound, Robert Penn Warren, and Allen Tate in the twentieth century.[56] And it was this same problematic heroism, which Machiavelli codified politically, that informed the Romantic writing and iconoclastic conservatisms of Anglo-Americans as different in sensibility as Parson Weems and Henry Cabot Lodge.

Ironically, however, the key to the success of this creative hope through cultural deconstruction has been to escape such conjunctions of styles by artists, historians, and political leaders distancing themselves from cultural styles that have become outworn or have grown too transparent in their political implications. Such stylistic innovation in the name of a conservative defense of tradition is, by its very nature, a form of the Machiavellian problem of patriarchal legitimacy—an aesthetic confrontation with the poles of piety and murder which Machiavelli sought to balance in order to preserve endangered republican political values.

In the case of Parson Weems, we have already seen a man who, like Machiavelli, was preoccupied with the problem of patriarchal legitimacy, specifically addressed to the problems associated with innovation and piety. Weems celebrated virtù as a dynamic ambition, whether in selling books, extolling leaders in war, such as Washington and Francis Marion, or urging procreation as the way to defeat British expansionism.[57] But, as we have also seen, he considered virtù a threat to the stable feminine virtues, which alone could preserve liberty. Like Machiavelli, Weems inverted the heroic, using negative forms of personal behavior such as drinking and adultery to reveal positive public ideals of citizenship.[58] Weems, too, placed natality, with its dual Christian and Classical associations of heroic sacrifice, at the center of his concern for extending the life of the *civitas*. Nor was Weems above using contrivances and dishonesty in the service of higher civic ideals. Indeed, Weems somehow gained a reputation for excessive piety; at the same time he gained a complementary reputation for having no scruples over selling the sacred. Scholars remain divided, not only among but within themselves, over the question of Weems's character. Was Weems a charlatan seeking cash, a patriot trying to save the union, or an underground priest hoping to save souls? Neither Lodge nor more recent commentators on Weems have been entirely sure, but all have agreed on some combination of these characterizations.[59] One example frequently cited is a comment Weems wrote to his publisher Mathew Carey: "You have a great deal of money lying in the bones of old George, if you will but exert yourself to extract it."[60] Was Weems appealing to Carey's greed or to his own? Or did he see greed, patriotism, and true religion all happily in harmony according to his own purposes? In another example, Weems sold Paine's atheistic *Age of Reason*, and when chastised for it, immediately produced Watson's *Apology for the Bible*, declaring that if he carried the poison, he also was prepared to sell the antidote.[61] Weems, like Machiavelli, played the fox to classical heroes, the better to use the lions for his own purposes in an attempt to redeem a degenerate age, to advance his own interests, or both.

Machiavellianism, then, is not simply a cynical use of power, as its popular connotation suggests. Instead, it represents a particular pattern of ambiguity between power and value, which are balanced in the interests of prolonging the life of a republic. Above all, *it is based on a conservative defense of patriarchal values of doubtful legitimacy.*[62]

In the case of Machiavelli himself, as for Weems, this created, politically, a distinctly divided attitude toward authority. The writings of both were devoted to a consideration of the political consequences of the *problematic* nature of the father-founder. For Machiavelli, piety towards the father-founder, whether of the Classical past or of the present, seemed essential. He always considered parricide abhorrent because it destroyed the foundation for, and possibility of, political legitimacy. Yet Machiavelli also thought that political renewal was possible only through the establishment of new authorities in a degenerate age.[63] Innovation, he explained, comes only when the son, capable of generating manhood in others, replaces the ineffectual father. But since manhood is a condition of freedom, the father-founder's virtù is in conflict with the virtue he seeks to restore. As a result of this contradiction, fraternity may turn into fratricide and the pious effort to restore ancient principles may turn into parricide. The ideal of citizenship and the dynamic ambition of the would-be father-founder are, therefore, as much in opposition as are tyranny and republican government. Apparently, for Machiavelli, in a time of degenerate men only the heroic restoration of political virtue by a new father-founder can resuscitate a languishing republic. The real problem for Machiavelli—who was so deeply conscious of the dilemmas of time for human meaning, yet who stylistically created only static characterizations—was that no one's life is long enough to establish new traditions in a population.[64] The would-be father-founder is a kind of cruel joke on himself and those he would save, but a joke that Machiavelli took with the utmost seriousness. The hero of virtue must use contrivance to establish natural affections; he must frighten and inspire at the same time. The successful father-founder, in Machiavelli's description, must be an innovator of tradition, one whose life is balanced perfectly between piety and murder. In comedies such as *Mandràgola* and *Clizia,* therefore, he portrayed the family as a romance gone absurd. Fathers are shown as fools in their desire to retain their patriarchal authority as generators of children. The legitimate love of the young can only be saved, along with the foolish father, by vice. Since nobility is absent, jealousy and spite must save the situation.[65]

What does all this mean? Was Machiavelli mocking himself and his generation for degenerating from the heroic standards of the true father-founders of the Classical past? Was he praising himself for recognizing the inadequacy of every father-founder, since each was trapped in an absurd contradiction of means and ends? When the right things are done in the wrong way and the wrong things are being done in the right way, does the fox alone know how to save the situation? Or is the fox a sorry substitute for an ideal reformer who will someday balance the contradictions and restore authority to tradition?[66]

Perhaps one reason for the inability of commentators on Machiavelli's texts to decide on his true motives is that a politics of *ressentiment*, by definition, is Janus-faced. It envies the power of father-founders and levels each of them so that it seems their preeminence is arbitrary. The powerful fathers are, at once, mythic in proportion, fulfilling human destiny, and they are accidents of fate whose roles might as easily have been filled by another, especially oneself. But whatever Machiavelli may have ultimately thought of the relation between his comedies and his treatises and histories, he plainly hoped to aid in the restoration of an eternal ideal of heroic action in an age of degenerated custom. In service to that end, both his apparently serious works, such as *The Art of War*, and his comedies were Romantic in their ironic equivocation between the real and the ideal. He debunked both the real and the ideal, but never at the same time, and therefore preserved each against the other. All his writing was essentially an inversion of the heroic ideal—a literary innovation through which he contrived to portray the real world as it is. As he forthrightly admitted in his plays, he sought in this way to render the private public and so to deceptively deliver the truth:

> How gentle is deception
> when carried to fruition as intended,
> For it defies perception
> and soothes the blissful dupes we have befriended
> Oh draught by heaven blended,
> You show the quickest way to true contentment.[67]

Because Machiavelli pointed to a timeless standard negatively, he made the presence of that absence compellingly real to his audiences. His stylistic innovation of defining negative space to reveal a positive ideal was an entirely new form of artistic as well as political discourse. The paradigmatic style of this artistic expression and its capturing of the character of the Renaissance crisis of cultural and political authority have defined a central place for Machiavelli in subsequent Atlantic political and cultural history.[68] But the very wedding of his style with his political message means that we cannot know either Machiavelli's motives or his message with certainty. We cannot know whether Machiavelli himself thought his relation to tradition was pious or murderous, because it may very well have been both.[69] Similarly, we cannot know whether Machiavelli is really our own political father or one who cleverly held a mirror to reveal a culture's already existing sense of its illegitimacy. We know only that the contingencies of history, possibly with his connivance and possibly without it, have revealed his deception. By the twentieth century, Americans have come to recognize a living kinship between Machiavelli's idea of republicanism and our own contradictory ideals of political virtue.

For this reason, when J. G. A. Pocock credited Machiavelli with fathering Atlantic republican political thought, he argued for the fact of Machiavelli's success in establishing his own stylistic innovation among his posterity at the same time.[70] For Machiavelli's paradigmatic confrontation with the problematic nature of the father-founder presaged Pocock's own tracing of the roots of republicanism to Niccolò Machiavelli himself. Through revealing the Machiavellian origins of a historically compulsive form of political virtue, Pocock attempted to expose the borrowed ideology behind the mythically enshrined political exceptionalism of the American Revolution. This permitted Pocock to engage personally in a paradoxically conservative rebellion against liberal America's compulsively moralistic demands, as well as to provide an explanation for the historical impotence of Marxism in transforming these claims into a revolutionary mode of class conflict as its Agrarian political and economic promise disappeared with the frontier by 1890. Americans, he claimed, remain suspended in a contradictory quarrel with themselves for failing to sustain the eighteenth-century ideal of *homo politicus*, a people of timeless Classical virtue, in a centralizing economic world. Echoing Hannah Arendt's analysis, Pocock explained that the alternative of a Marxian ideal of *homo faber*, which might have cut the gordian knot, left most Americans unmoved because it abandoned the primacy of personality in defining its solution. This locked American political culture into a double bind. Self-contradiction was inherent in the tragic legacy that republicanism had inherited, through Machiavelli, from a lost Classical past.[71]

This lost Classical past was no longer directly available to modern men and women because the fall of Greece and Rome had delivered them into the hands of time. Having become history, the Classical past had been transformed into memory. As Hannah Arendt explained, the Classical political universe had begun to come undone the moment private meaning eclipsed the public realm within the Christian polity of the Middle Ages. Yet, deeply buried within the rhetorical formulae of political discourse, she reminded her readers in *The Human Condition,* the fundamental link to the Classical political culture remained, and that link was natality.[72]

According to Arendt, natality as the origin of all human presence, and thus action, in the world is the central category of political thought. However, natality is also the central category for the Christian understanding of Providence, the incarnation. Natality, therefore, intersects the religious and political traditions of Western culture and, therefore, focuses the moment of balance between time and eternity and between the particular and the universal. It rests in the center of both republican ideology and Christian eschatology. Just as each new generation must replace the old generation to achieve the universality of the *polis* in time, the incarnation of God in time promises a universal salvation through the baby at Mary's breast. Both images of natality are based on innocence, a state of new beginnings. Classically, that meant the transformation of flesh and blood into divinity.[73] For, as Hannah Arendt noted, a new beginning inherently assumes action. And the ability to realize the self through action, generating action in others, is the province of the gods. In participating in the *polis,* the citizen transcends flesh and blood to participate in a timeless universal body, whose eyes may behold and remember the individual who founds the city or nation, or who heroically sacrifices himself for its sake. This is why the father-founder must be drawn innocent from nature and quickly pass through his humanity to live eternally in legend. He must potently generate new sons through their memory of his life-giving deeds. Yet the hero's life-giving actions must be established through the spilling of blood. Consequently, if Classical ideals of innocence led to the power of the demigod-founder or -citizen, Christian, innocence looked to the transcendence of flesh and blood through the spiritual renunciation of power. In Christianity, innocence belonged to the only perfectly obedient son of the only perfect Father.[74]

This dual but contradictory legacy for understanding the mystery of natality was entwined in the Renaissance reappropriation of Classical history from within the context of medieval Christian culture. The conflicting understandings of public and private, and universal and particular, that these two traditions entailed found expression in the jeremiad, a blend of political and religious rhetoric that was at once liturgical in form and progressive in movement.[75] The jeremiad merged cyclical and linear understandings of time because it combined two very different versions of Holy Rome: church and empire. The myths of restoration and mission inherent in the jeremiad, even in its earliest expressions at the end of the Middle Ages, codified time as a cycle of promise, declension, and return that could guarantee a redemptive conclusion to human history, despite the persistent failures of mortal men and women.

The Divine Comedy was among the most compelling and beautiful expressions of this dual jeremiad.[76] It was probably composed about 1313, after the death of Henry VII, contender for the crown of Charlemagne. Though written in bitter exile and with dashed hopes for a restoration of mythic Holy Rome, Dante's great allegory retained faith in the jeremiad's message. Despite his personal disappointments and suffering, he remained faithful to the pure ideal of the fallen church and its eventual regeneration through a still unrestored empire. Even for the gentle Dante, poet of love, the divinely inspired power of empire appeared as the avenue for the rebirth of the church's tarnished innocence.

Most commentators on *The Divine Comedy* consider that work to be at once a religious and political allegory.[77] Having read Aristotle, Dante viewed politics as a legitimate avenue to the good life which needed to be balanced against the higher, truly universal, model of religious salvation, gained only through the heavenly city. But the church, having become tainted by papal power politics and greed for secular luxuries, was guilty of destroying this balance. St. Peter castigated Dante's contemporary church for failing to fulfill its mission against sin, while impeding the secular authorities from fulfilling their God-given responsibility of governance. Without proper governance, innocence turned into corruption. Fathers failed to direct the moral growth of their children, leaders of the city failed to fulfil their responsibilities of office, and the pope, as spiritual father, failed his flock. The failure to exercise true guidance led unavoidably to a repetition of Adam's fall. In Dante's imagination, Florence served as his model for Hell. The world was turned upside down, and the offices of salvation were reversed. It was now the universal empire of secular Rome that must arise to save Christian Rome from its degeneration into a "stinking sewer" of iniquity. Purification and restoration, so it appeared to the visionary poet, could now occur only negatively, by the legitimate power of the secular state depriving the church of its illegitimate worldly power.[78]

Despite this crisis of authority, leading to a paradoxical reversal of roles, the traditional divisions between Classical and Christian innocence retained their legitimacy. Though he bore witness to a crisis in time, Dante kept his cosmos firmly in the hand of Providence. For the classically learned poet, the same Providence that had ordained Scipio to save pagan Rome for divine purposes of world salvation would soon act to secure the state's triumph and with it the salvation of the church. St. Peter's authority remained intact, despite the apostasy of those who inherited his keys to authority. Dante's positive vision of restoring tradition through God's providential agency led him to hold up saints Bernard and Benedict, Francis, Peter, Damian, and Bonaventure as reformers.[79] In comparison, Machiavelli's famous remark to Guicciardini about imagining a suitable preacher for Florence while sitting on the privy reveals an inversion of perspective from that of Dante. Dante hoped for a preacher who would guide the lost out of confusion and into Paradise. Machiavelli advocated instead "one who would teach them the way to go to the house of the Devil . . . because I believe that the true way of going to Paradise would be to learn the road to Hell in order to avoid it."[80]

Dante's heroic vision was expressed in his personal transformation from sinful man into demigod. As Christian artist, he succeeded Statius and Virgil, not through parricide, but by fulfilling their roles as artist-precursors, through his own humble obedience to God's message of love's salvation. Machiavelli, in contrast, is unable to fulfil the Classic ideals because he lives in a diminished time and acts as a diminished man. He is the manipulative fox, the underling who alone lives autonomously and, therefore, alone can achieve successful innovation in such times. But if he must play the fox to uphold heroic memory when the traditions of the forefathers have become remote, he is for the same reason a lesser man than the forefathers because he cannot directly create manliness in others.[81] It is true that Machiavelli, like Dante, reveres the ancients. But Machiavelli joins with the ancients only in his imagination after "exchanging" the soiled clothes of daily life for the ideal garments of imaginary discourse. As an innovator Machiavelli envies and levels his hosts as he dons regal and courtly robes like their own. He feeds "on the food that is only mine." Dante, on the contrary, had felt called to a mis-

sion and gained the ability to present truthful guidance through a pu
rified poetic style, purged of selfish preoccupations.[82] The source of this
purged sense of self, leading to an Isaiah-like vocation, included both feminine symbols of grace—Beatrice and Mary—and father-founders—
Virgil, Peter, and Bernard. For Machiavelli, *both* feminine and patriarchal symbols were now problematical. Fortune had to be wooed and
beaten; the prince at once destroys and confirms the manhood of his fellow citizens.[83]

Dante had identified himself as a new kind of hero: the poet, who
brings the eternal ideal of love into the world as the translator of heavenly speech into the discourse of men.[84] In doing so, he honored and
sought to fulfill the same institutions the father-founders had long ago
established but which had since fallen victim to corruption through
fraudulent servants. Machiavelli, too, viewed himself as a new kind of
poet-hero, one who imitated and quoted Dante, while reversing his message. Machiavelli would establish *The Divine Comedy* through corrosive
humor. Fraud would unmask fraud.

Dante's medieval distrust of commercial values and faith in communal
ones had made fraud a central conception in his criticism of his age. In
identifying this vice so fundamentally with his mission of renewal in *The
Divine Comedy*, Dante clearly drew on a tension that he shared with his
fellow Florentines. For, despite the growth of trading vocations at the
end of the Middle Ages, religious strictures against exploitation and luxurious living continued to influence social values. Fraud, perhaps more
than any other vice, embodied the dangers of individual ambition, or
virtù, for the harmony and mutuality of community, or virtue. As a
member of a merchant-banking family who had been unfairly exiled
for misusing public funds, Dante must have felt the double pain of guilt
for participating in a social sin and of suffering unjustly for acts he did
not commit.[85]

The jeremiad, however, was designed to mediate this tension, because
it expressed a promise of social renewal through the individual consciousness of sin. For this reason, *The Divine Comedy* was at once a
confession of personal unworthiness and a social broadside aimed at exposing Florentine profligacy. As Dante personally gained a new spiritualized poetic vision beyond lyrical celebration of the flesh, a renewed
Florence could discover new spiritual meanings to the commercial values
in which it was mired. Dante's use of art in the service of the divine word
meant that the language of spiritual usury, multiplying God's grace,

could evoke images of redemption instead of corporal corruption. Dante's heroic language of art could still participate in a unified political and religious ideal, despite injustice and corruption in the world.[86]

At the end of the fifteenth century, Dante's poetic vision of a restored spiritual and temporal order, held together by the loving hand of Providence, mediating time and eternity, collided with the historical events that destroyed a similar dream of another Florentine believer and patriot, Fra Girolamo Savonarola. Though the friar dreamed of a restoration of republican Rome, and not of empire, he, like Dante, accepted a heroic role in fulfilling the promise of the jeremiad.[87]

Savonarola, unlike the artist Dante, was both a political and religious leader, who embodied the dual myths of eternal Rome. His prophetic condemnation of Florence before the invasion of the French king in 1494 rested on his status as a father, criticizing his wayward children for their sins of economic corruption. However, he was thrust into political leadership in the city when fulfillment of his warning of God's coming chastisement of Florence by the hand of Charlemagne's heir seemed imminent. By averting the destruction of the city through the power of his spiritual jeremiad, Savonarola was placed in the position of becoming a new father-founder to a miraculously restored Florence. Suddenly, Florentine political events had revealed a hidden denouement to the progress of the jeremiad, making the aesthetic vision actually present in the world of time. But it also, equally and unavoidably, meant that the jeremiad's promise was now exposed to the possibility of being proved a false hope of salvation. Savonarola preached the jeremiad of repentance, but historical events of civic need required that he also preach that repentance would bring economic as well as spiritual wealth. For only by this wedding of sacred and profane history could Florence be saved from being swallowed up by its more powerful papal and national rivals.

Yet Savonarola's redemption was fraught with contradictions. Religiously, he found himself in a power struggle between friar and pope, placing himself at odds with his own spiritual father and the ecclesiastical symbol of the eternal church. Ultimately, that patriarchal authority gave a particular friar his prophetic legitimacy as a leader of the children of God. Politically, the friar's message, proclaiming a "new Jerusalem," was accomplished by rejecting the claims of loyalty to Rome—but at the sacrifice of the political exceptionalism, which alone could guarantee the defense of vulnerable Florence from the particulars of history. These contradictions were not lessened when a realistic appraisal of papal power persuaded Florentine citizens to turn over their new father-founder of a new eternal republic for an ignominious death by torture. Nor were they reduced when, after torture, the heroic defender of "God's city" confessed he had been a false prophet all along.

Machiavelli, who was conscious of Dante's vision and Savonarola's agony, is said to have been present in the crowd and to have witnessed the death of Savonarola. In *The Prince*, Machiavelli placed the martyred friar in the company of Moses, Cyrus, Theseus, and Romulus—great innovators who made themselves into father-founders without benefiting from inherited tradition for legitimacy.[88] Each was an innovator whose authority was artificial, gained only through imposition and not established over time. Usurpers, as Machiavelli cynically—or not so cynically—warned, must not rely on fickle and easily manipulated public acclaim. Innocent trust in the people is as foolish as trust in the false innocence of the would-be father-founder himself—a truth that Savonarola failed to appreciate.

History had deprived Machiavelli of a progressive theory of redemption which could link either the Christian or Classical past to the present. He was faced with the fundamental contradiction of the *polis*, the simple realization that the promise of natality is simultaneously the assurance of eventual death. He recognized that the eternal values of civic virtue in which he continued to believe passionately could not be maintained indefinitely in time.[89] The loss of mythic innocence meant the loss of faith in the Classical myth that the father-founder could be ahistorical, and therefore an innocent and immortal foundling, and that henceforth the innocence of Christ must remain in eternity. The incarnation of Providence would not transform the city of man into the city of God because, in this world, slippery Fortuna, and not Beatrice or Mary, guided the seeker of wisdom. Under such conditions, Machiavelli counseled autonomy as the preferable strategy of survival.[90]

History had destroyed the legitimacy of traditional patriarchy, and with it feminine virtue, as Machiavelli humorously informed his audiences in his plays. But he also reminded them that the *polis* remained rooted in the midst of life in its absurd center—the household. Machiavelli had recognized that the ordinary father of the ordinary household is subject to time and decay. Therefore, he could not be identified with the mythic founder of the *polis*, unless the latter was admitted to be mortal, therefore limited, and therefore fraudulent. Yet the possibility of political virtue required a father-founder who could establish a new tradition

modeled on ancient forms. The effort to balance this contradictory situation between reverence on one side and mayhem on the other, as we have
seen, became a central theme of his writing and of his legacy. The
Machiavellian formula for codifying the contradictory cultural dilemmas
for mediating time and eternity, universals and particulars, into a balanced tension was inherently unstable. It was less a "tradition" than a
nagging tension in which dissolution seemed always on the political horizon. Republicanism was an ideology suspended between a lost center
and an incipient chaos, its moorings ever eroding through the tragic consequences of time.[91]

Machiavelli witnessed a Copernican Revolution in the political universe, in which the providential center no longer held against the practical consequences of power and accident, and in which usurpers rushed
into the vacuum to assume new earthbound centers of doubtful legitimacy. The result was a removal of God, the Father, to the periphery of
human affairs and a corresponding ambiguity in the relation of all fathers
to their children. The space of the New World, however, provided a new
possibility to extend the sphere of Providence through the beneficence of
nature, just because it was on the periphery. The United States, like the
Massachusetts colony of Puritan faith before it, and Scotland and Ireland
before that, was protected from the centers of power and ambitious patriarchs who would try in their own persons to replace God. "Far from
the furious passions and politics of Europe," wrote Parson Weems, "you
are placed here by yourselves, the sole proprietors of a vast region, embracing all the soils and climates of the earth, and abounding with all
the conveniences of life."[92] The tragic end of Savonarola's exceptional
Florence, surrounded by the contradictions of power and value, did not
need to be the end of all political hope, though the hostile intentions of
"our brethren, the nations of Europe," left Weems anxious over the future.[93] The jeremiad could remain a promise so long as space, insulating
Americans from such evil, could ensure political virtue until the end of
time, when "the last refining flames shall then kindle on this *tear bathed,
blood-stained globe,* while from its ashes a new earth shall spring, far
happier than the first."[94]

The resurrection would come when all political virtue was exhausted,
consumed in a fire which would inaugurate a new, eternal, and glorious
republic of brotherhood, ruled by the true "Great Founder of your
holy republic."[95] But, said Weems, such a world-sustaining promise
of brotherhood depended on North and South putting away their di-

visiveness to escape impending civil war. For "when brethren turn their swords into each other's bowels, war degenerates into murder and battles into butchery." The tragedy of such a free government, "madly divided and destroying itself," must lead to a "proud tyrant, who, looking on our country but as his estate, and ourselves as his cattle, shall waste our wealth on the pomps of his court or the salaries of his officers; destroy our sons in ambitious wars, and beggar us with exactions, as long as his ministers can invent, or we, by hard labour can raise money to pay them."[96]

In calling on the memory and example of Washington to avert this impending tragic end to the American republic, the last such republic on earth, Weems was already conscious of being a voice crying in the wilderness against the division of North and South. The Civil War ended the promise of fraternity that Weems had posited against the growing threat of political and economic tyranny. Sacred space alone, whether as bloody battleground or as virgin land, remained as a symbol of freedom and renewal within post–Civil War Anglo-American republican culture.

But time, as the enemy of memory and the force transforming frontiers into the settled conditions of towns, was also the source of tradition and law, the restraining bond of commercial predators as well as of natural ones. Time could also be the ground of a new frontier of expanding promise, within the language of the jeremiad, as destiny. The time of the clock, the railroad schedule, and the stock exchange was one such possible identification of cyclical time with the frontier. However, there was also the possibility of time lived, the experience of personal uniqueness which could be gratified through consumption of life—or its artificial substitutes—in ever-new variations.

Before either or both of these contradictory redemptive formulas could be embraced, whether on a public or personal level, the corpse of republicanism had to be removed and buried. Only then would a new cycle of Machiavellian realism begin its long or short slide—depending on the vagaries of fortune—back into Romanticism.

CHAPTER TWO

Frederick Jackson Turner to the New Agrarian Critics: Space, Time, and the Aesthetic Frontier

When the young historian Frederick Jackson Turner declared the end of the agrarian frontier at the Columbian Exposition of 1893, he stood upon a symbolic site of the new international frontier of consumerism to do so. The very existence of the World's Fair in Chicago, a midwestern city of one million inhabitants that had doubled its size during the previous decade, graphically illustrated the defeat of agrarian space and local time through the harnessing of universal laws of mechanical power and through the imposition of the standards of universal time. In Chicago, farming as a way of life met and merged with the organized force of industrialism. The city's growth paralleled the absorption of the agrarian landscape of American exceptionalism into a worldwide commodity market from which it has never escaped.[1] However, beyond this tragic denouement to the particular agrarian identity of nineteenth-century America, a world-wide acceleration was occurring in the transforming experiences of time and space. That transformation, as Stephen Kern has shown, fueled a "crisis of abundance" that intensified until it exploded into world war.[2]

A dualistic contradiction lay at the heart of that "crisis of abundance," which paradoxically brought Turner and many Anglo-Americans of his generation to despair long before World War I shattered faith in a Progressive ideal of a national industrial frontier or the post-Progressive faith, for a much smaller minority, in the international frontier of the Russian Revolution. That despair, which pervaded the turn-of-the-century Anglo-American consciousness despite the official optimism of the time, suggests a far more desperate meaning to faith in progress than was publicly admitted by its proponents or has usually been attributed by historians.[3]

Industrial and technological progress through commercial expansion held great promise for a republican political culture in an age of abundance—but, paradoxically, both abundance and expansion demonstrably created scarcity in the natural world. Despite the heroic cultural implications of technological wonders and expanding commercial horizons, they threatened to dwarf the individual personalities of those who lived within them. Inevitably, economic motives were sundered from ideals of political virtue; therefore, this new abundance was ironically and necessarily self-defeating through the very terms of its marvelous successes. For Frederick Jackson Turner, as an heir to republican ideology, the ambitions that fueled expansion seemed as necessary to the winning and defense of civic virtues as they were destructive to the stability necessary for their survival. Turner and those who, like him, understood political virtue from the then dominant perspective of republicanism found themselves confronting a moment of deep doubt over the future of Anglo-American political culture.[4] Turner's paper of 1893, "The Significance of the Frontier in American History," sounded an alarm that America stood at what J. G. A. Pocock would later characterize as a "Machiavellian moment": the crisis-experience of mortality in republican cultures in which the admission of participation in the irrational particulars of birth and death fundamentally challenges the legitimacy of any republic.[5]

Machiavelli had recognized that the effort to establish universal and timeless political virtue in the context of history could only be temporarily successful because time, and therefore mortality, makes all human experience inherently unstable. The universal good of the *polis*, political stability capable of enduring from generation to generation, could be achieved only so long as the legitimacy of the republic could be maintained through piety rooted in tradition. But as tradition lost its vitality through the contingencies of time, the republic could be restored only through heroic action. Such innovation, however, called into question the legitimacy of the republic even as it saved it. The violence of innovation contradicted the continuity required to prolong the life of the republic, even as it provided the only avenue for restoring it within the contingent events of history. Therefore, from Machiavelli's pessimistic view of political virtue, no republic could retain its life indefinitely. Only by balancing the contradictory poles of ambition and duty, piety and murder, tradition and innovation could political virtue momentarily create a rational space of calm in a sea of irrational particulars, all too frequently churned to a froth in the flux of time.[6]

Following these Machiavellian political conventions as modified by the seventeenth-century English Agrarian theorist, James Harrington, Frederick Jackson Turner also assumed that political virtue could be only temporarily achieved. However, for him, as for Harrington, corruption and revitalization were part of a process and not a static moral condition, as for Machiavelli.[7] Harrington's Agrarian variation on Machiavelli emphasized the role of space in opposition to time. Corruption was tied less to the loss of specific virtues than to the loss of a relation to property as a necessary economic base for the practice of those virtues. So long as England, as both an island and an agrarian territory, could balance a commonwealth of independent yeomen at home while simultaneously sending forth dynamic conquerors abroad, political virtue could be preserved. According to Harrington, the process of corruption could be contained within a cyclical pattern in which the dynamic conquering of space inevitably led to corruption through the growth of centralizing power, but in which new frontiers would revive the cycle, temporarily making new moments of balance possible. The movement from virtue to corruption, cyclically returning, could be sustained by the timeless linear expansion into new space.[8]

The American Revolution had been premised, however, on a recognition of the limits of space. Presumably, at least for the revolutionists, the limits of space in the island commonwealth accounted for the triumph of Court corruption over the balancing virtue of Country opposition. Capitalism, the driving force of that expansion, was seen as the engine that hastened the demise of freehold space, leaving the corrupting effects of time unchecked. But if the Revolution pointed to a Machiavellian pessimism about the ability of any republic to maintain an indefinite balance between the cycles of corruption and advancing space, it also seemed to confirm the suspicion that the linear movement of history was progressing from England to the western periphery of the empire, and thus, to America as a new Rome.[9]

In the Jacksonian era, this ambiguity between the pessimistic and optimistic consequences of time's relation to space was expressed in terms of democracy and manifest destiny, which together balanced the dynamic movement of space with the centralizing consequences of time. A return to primitivism offered a return to the cycle of virtue, but it did not arrest the linear movement of time, which was seen as simultaneously necessary and self-defeating. Given the underlying pessimism of the American Revolution—evident not only in the uneasy balance of piety and innovation in the public pronouncements of the Founding Fathers but also in the Romantic pessimism of America's earliest popular republican author, Mason Locke Weems—it should not be surprising to find similar but graver doubts about Jackson's ambition and to see a popular Romantic republican literature begin to grow up around those doubts.[10] The Jacksonian era was a time of widening class division, industrialism, and urbanization. There was already confusion about whether the frontiersman embodied primitive energy or entrepreneurial power, and whether Jackson represented a return to the virtues of the Founding Fathers or to the despotism from which they revolted.

So long as open space remained, the frontier, as an abstraction resting between civilization and savagery, remained an ambiguous realm of possibility between the cycle of virtue and corruption and some indeterminate culmination of linear time in an apocalyptic future. Yet, especially with the Civil War, the speed with which time was overcoming space through its transformation into standardized forms of power steadily undermined the possibility of balancing corruption with timeless space. In slightly different terminology, the heroic qualities, which still seemed the only values that could lift ordinary experience into redemptive action, ironically appeared to be creating a society in which heroes had no space to exist.

There were, to be sure, other frontiers of heroic possibility besides agrarian republican ones available to Americans in the closing decade of the nineteenth century. Such new frontier conditions were generated precisely by the remarkable triumph of time over space in the period between the Civil War and 1890. Grandiose public dreams were spawned and private energies focused towards using time itself to conquer space. By November 1883, for example, the railroads had imposed standardized time on American communities. With the Prime Meridian Conference of the following year, the exact length of the day, the division of the world into twenty-four time zones, and even the precise beginning of the universal day were established. Jules Verne's fantasy of freedom on air, to circle the globe in eighty days, was published as a novel in 1873. But the feat was actually accomplished by Nellie Bly in 1890. Through a close scrutiny of steamship and railroad schedules and the new technologies of worldwide communications, it was possible for the American journalist to race against time to conquer space and defeat her fictional British rival by eight days. Just two years later, George Train reduced the travel time to only sixty days.[11] Joseph Pulitzer's *World* began publication in 1883, and based its success on popular craving for the excitement of reading about events as they happened, each and every day. Leisure time became a commodity to be sought and purchased, as play became a business that catered to popular fantasies. Football placed time in the center of the sports arena, as hierarchically ordered teams were cheered on by their fans in their drive to conquer space. Funerals became exorcisms of death, as undertakers began to call themselves "funeral directors" and promised to stop decay through embalming and hermetically sealed coffins. For the survivors, seances promised to permit a "breakthrough to the other side." Canned foods and refrigeration released individuals from nature's boundaries and the routine of daily shopping. Most important, these sundry processes physically suspended time's decay. And the invention of time-saving devices became a national mania.

Between the Civil War and 1890, Darwin's theory of evolution introduced the possibility for considering time itself as a frontier. Darwin's evolutionary theory turned time into a process of progressive transformation; the new sciences of history, geology, sociology, biology, and economics promised to identify and shape its linear direction. At the same time philosophers began to explore the inner experience of time, and novelists, following the psychologist William James's lead, began to write "stream of consciousness" prose. Psychologists began to explore the developmental stages of inner frontiers of behavior. G. Stanley Hall, for example, discovered—or invented—adolescence as another sort of frontier experience, one that each child must traverse as part of the biological necessity of moving from the primitive ego to the complexity of social cooperation. Young people could explore this new realm through guidebooks such as the Horatio Alger stories, western dime novels, and science fiction: all variations on the development of independent self-reliant character by overcoming, through fantasy, life's hardships.[12]

But none of these time-bound frontiers resolved the Machiavellian contradiction of locating timeless universal meaning within the context of changing, controlled, and limited personal and public space. Indeed, the victory of time over space seemed to increase anxiety about the future. This anxiety was expressed in the passionately fought controversy over the time-frame of creation and the process by which the biblical canon entered history—a controversy that split Anglo-American Protestants into fundamentalists and liberals in the 1890s. It surfaced as an epidemic of neurasthenia and a sense of ennui among the upper-middle class, and as a growing fear of centralized economic and political forms of oppression in all classes and in all sections of the country. At least on a personal scale, the new frontiers of time had not overcome the barrier of death, a subject that permeated the popular consciousness of the time.

Machiavellian categories for understanding political experience were part of the Atlantic heritage, along with the suspicions, doubts, and contradictions that followed from them. Therefore, neither those categories nor the attitudes that accompanied them evaporated from the American urban political landscape because of the burgeoning population of Irish, Italian, and German immigrants. Nor did the European immigrants require acculturation into those basic values through Anglo-American institutions. Nevertheless, as of 1890, an Anglo-American identity remained the cultural core of the nation, and its Harringtonian variation on Machiavelli's republicanism was still the dominant form of American political culture.

It was for this reason that Frederick Jackson Turner's short paper so powerfully shocked the new professional class of historians who were the keepers of the Anglo-American national culture and its promise for the future. As historians, they were charged with explaining the exceptional nature of American space through time. Turner's paper shattered the possibility of an exceptional national history and thus confirmed the death of the republican political tradition and the Anglo-Protestant Agrarian values upon which it was based.[13]

In Chicago in 1893 Turner delivered a pastoral elegy for the passing Agrarian order. Its purpose was to eulogize the dead heroic promise of exceptional space and to fashion a new vision by looking forward to a frontier of time: the next period of American history. But in laying to rest the failed history of space, Turner found himself unable to complete the transformation into a new form of heroic prediction. Instead, Turner's historical perspective revealed his own inability to escape the pessimistic implications of the failing balance he had recognized between power and personality as a cyclical process of creating and conquering frontiers.

As Turner described this process, there was in reality a long history of frontiers, often antagonistic to one another. One frontier succeeded another in a relentless movement from virtue to corruption. "Moving westward the frontier became more and more American"; the advance of the frontier meant "a steady movement away from the influence of Europe," he wrote. Yet Turner believed this progress simultaneously meant an ever-accelerating movement toward the complete triumph of Old World conditions and the death of an exceptional America. Once more, this was not only an apocalyptic catastrophe that loomed for the immediate future but also an old story that had already been repeated in the failure of each successive frontier.[14] Turner's paradoxical description of historical progress as a violent movement toward Armageddon was similarly inherent in his description of American development as a constant "return to primitive conditions on a continually advancing frontier line."

Though that conception of change was incorporated into evolutionist thought about time, it was rooted in far older conceptions of the Classical heroic father-founder raised in nature. This heroic image had become sterile for Turner by 1893, when he reformulated it into a concept of advancement through disintegration. This heroic vision was confirmed in its own ironic self-destruction (present in the first paragraph of Turner's famous paper) with the bland official announcement that the frontier line would no longer have a place in the American census report.

Turner insisted that each vanquished frontier had left its imprint, for both good and evil, in subsequent frontiers. Thus, though the trader's frontier was antagonistic to the farmer's frontier, the cumulative growth from both led to ever-greater social complexity and new forms of economic centralization. The Indian trail gave way to the trader's trace, which in turn was widened into a road, roads became turnpikes, and turnpikes became railroads. The eastern frontier shaped the West, which eclipsed it and then came to rule it in the democratic revolution of Jackson. "This new democracy, that captured the country and destroyed the ideals of statesmanship came from no theorist's dreams of the German forest," Turner wrote in 1896. "It came, stark and strong and full of life, from the American forest."[15] In the relentless and accelerating phases of change that followed, the centralized commercial cotton planter displaced the diversified small farmer in his forest log cabin; and in the Northwest, the centralized power of the railroad destroyed the sectional balance nature had provided in the flow of rivers into the heart of the South. Then, it was Lincoln, the "very flower of frontier training and ideals," who brought a premature end to the sectional character of America, turning it into a centralized nation of federal power. Though Turner may have understated the considerable influence of German geopolitical thinkers like Friedrich Ratzel on his own frontier thesis, it was also true that the increasing intensity, scope, and speed of change since the Civil War was "no theorist's dream" but was visible all around.[16]

Turner was born in the first year of the first great modern war and nurtured and educated by the generation who were direct participants in that cataclysm. When he declared the end of the frontier in 1893, the world had already entered the period leading up to "the great civil war among the Western nations" of 1914–18. His was an age of shifting and porous frontiers. And, as we have seen, it was an age when the Jeffersonian values of an agrarian-based political economy of republican virtue were on the wane. In his novel of 1890, *A Hazard of New Fortunes*, the novelist William Dean Howells, who shared Turner's republican values and anguish over their defeat, described this emerging new world.[17] He described the ugly Indiana boom town of Moffitt, a town bathed in the eerie flames belching from its gas wells, a town which, during the day, you could smell before you could see. Moffitt's new-found prosperity was constructed on manufacturing and the unlimited bonanza promised—no longer by land—by natural gas. The transformation from agrarian simplicity to commercial exploitation had been both abrupt and devastating. As one of his entrepreneurial characters observed, everything seemed to be moving, and farms that had only recently been filled with stumps now looked as smooth as a checkerboard and as old as England.

Natural gas had always been there; farmers plowed around the old burn-off pipes and horses ignored it. But when Standard Oil offered high prices, the boom was on and the town was transformed. The old settler families, especially the most frugal, were turned into capitalists, one of whom, a stolid farmer called old Dryfoos, went to Europe and bought the family's way into nobility by the end of the novel. In apocalyptic imagery, Howells explained that, fueled by a kind of frenzy of greed, even nature itself was distorted, creating an artificial Eden: "They say that when they let one of their big wells burn away all winter before they had learned how to control it, that well kept up a little summer all around it; the grass stayed green, and the flowers bloomed all through the winter."[18]

In the novel, the frugal farmer from Moffitt, Dryfoos, editor Basil March and his wife from Boston, and even a southern "colonel" who espoused a return to slavery as an alternative to crass commercialism were irresistibly drawn to the commercial center of New York, despite its incompatibility with their personalities and ideals. Howells described

New York City, the burgeoning center of mass culture, as a kind of twilight world. At Forty-Second Street, his protagonists, the Marches, contemplated the Central Depot at which the track "found and lost itself a thousand times in the flare and tremor of the innumerable lights; the moony sheen of the electrics mixing with the reddish points and blots of gas far and near: the architectural shapes of houses and churches and towers, rescued by the obscurity from all that was ignoble in them; and the coming and going of trains marking the stations with vivider or fainter plumes of flame-shot steam." Mrs. March had once protested that nothing under the sun would induce her to travel on one of the elevateds, but now she loved nothing more than night transit when one could establish "fleeting intimacy" with people in second- and third-floor interiors while the usual street life continued underneath. It was, Mr. March agreed, better than the theater. Meanwhile, the great trains lay "dim under the rain of gas lights that starred without dispersing the vast darkness of the place." They evoked reveries of "what forces, what fates, slept in those bulks which would soon be hurtling themselves north and east and west through the night!" But for the moment they rested, tractably and willessly—"organized lifelessness full of strange semblances of life." In this, they were much like the upper-story flats of city life, reached by elevators and cluttered with all kinds of bric-a-brac and which were neither public nor private but a sort of twilight between them.[19]

As the sleeping trains reminded the Marches of the fabled monsters of Arab story, ready for the magician's touch, they agreed that the boasted charms of home were nothing compared to the Arabian Nights magic of their hotel apartment, always there, ready for everyone and anyone—a generic adventure that seemed to speak to each person alone because it spoke to no person in particular.

But even Howells's contemporary novel hardly captured the enormous scale of change that made up this simultaneously expanding and shrinking world. The frontier of urban growth, continuing both day and night as described by Howells, was changing from a world lighted by gas to an even more abstract and insensible force, electricity. The electric light brought daylight into the city's night, thus opening a new kind of frontier of time, even as it ended the old barriers of darkness. Trolleys shrank the distances to work and created suburban frontiers of city life while permitting new divisions in living areas, which constricted dwelling location according to class or ethnic boundaries.

The telephone, which provided long-distance service from Chicago to New York beginning in 1891, not only defied distance, but made it possible, as Stephen Kern observes, to be, at least in some sense, in two places at once. Yet by disembodying the voice from the person, the telephone abstracted and distanced human contact even as it made it more immediate. The invention of the cinema between 1893 and 1896 similarly telescoped the past and the present into a single repeatable experience. The x-ray penetrated solid objects, to reverse perceptions about what was indeed solid and what was void. Perceptions proliferated, and homogeneous space was broken into innumerable fragments and then put together in constantly changing combinations.[20]

Space took on a special significance throughout the Atlantic culture as the century came to a close. In music, sculpture, and painting, as well as in sociology, physics, mathematics, and the novel, space took on a positive significance and was no longer just an assumed interval between entities in a predictable world. In this sense, Turner's historiographical revolution was situated within a wider context than the particular American space whose disappearance had so forcibly invaded his imagination along with those of his readers.

In part, then, Turner's perspective must be seen as one outcome of the interrelation of a series of inventions, artistic and scientific movements and discoveries, and physical changes in the economy and landscape. These changes on both sides of the Atlantic—and increasingly of the Pacific, too—shattered the world of routine perceptions that people in all walks of life had taken for granted. Together, the interrelated consequences of these changing speeds and distances shrank the world and subjected it to the rigid controls of time clocks, work schedules, and hierarchical corporate bureaucratic and militaristic organizations. Simultaneously, these same new conditions provided the possibilities of escape from growing urban-industrial squalor through suburban living for the middle class or a steerage ticket to Eboli for an Italian emigrant factory worker at the end of the season. The dualism of public and private experience was pushed to the breaking point by separating work from family and the economic from the moral life. The new consumer abundance provided myriad therapeutic avenues for constructing elaborately separate public and private realms through mass advertisements, public amusements, and personal consumer goods.

But the emphasis on novelty as the source of this obsession with time may well be misleading, whether that novelty is defined as some inevitable process of modernization or as a form of culture shock triggered by the proliferation of ways of perceiving speed and distance. Despite the scale of change experienced by Turner's contemporaries, the essential dilemmas of power and stability and of the relation of universals and particulars in an expanding capitalist society remained similar to those which had plagued Atlantic societies since the Renaissance. Indeed, the similarity of these crises was dictated by the common world-view and values out of which they were created again and again in almost monotonous repetition. Only the scale of the crises continued to escalate. And it was the crises' scale rather than their novelty which finally proved insurmountable within the Machiavellian conventions that had spawned them. This was clearly the case in the crisis of free space that Turner identified in 1893. For that crisis was essentially the same one that New Englanders confronted on a regional level in the 1780s, only raised to a national scale. The Machiavellian conventions that assured the death of American political exceptionalism in the 1890s had already anticipated the form of its demise at the moment of the nation's birth.[21]

New England was founded upon patriarchal principles, and the form those male-dominated values took reflected the central religious ideal of a corporate mission. But as George Mosse noted more than thirty years ago, English Calvinists owed far more to Machiavelli than they were willing to admit to themselves.[22] From the beginning of New England's history, the Calvinists' own sense of community legitimacy rested upon the authority of the farmer-father in the private sphere and the minister-father in the public sphere. By the mid-eighteenth century, however, a crisis was brewing around the shrinking availability of the free land upon which the economic and political structure of these colonies depended. The success of the colonies had led to both increased birth rates and further migration from England, which in turn hastened the closing of the regional frontier.

As patriarchal political communities, the legitimacy of the Puritan-dominated society rested on both virtù, or manly ambition, and virtue, or selfless giving for the greater good of others. The power and personal integrity of the fathers, therefore, depended on their ability to pass on the autonomy necessary to establish their male heirs as independent patriarchs. In that way, they proved their legitimacy and potency as fathers and selflessly carried on the continuity of the religious and civic community from generation to generation. The corporate civic and spiritual identity of the original Puritan mission had made the family the corncrstonc of thc community, so the successful completion of family responsibility was vital in sustaining the legitimacy of the public families, or congregations. These public families in turn were both autocratically ruled over and selflessly served by the ministers.

One consequence of this spiritual agrarianism was that each child, like each believer, expected to share in the blessings mediated by patriarchal authority. Therefore, throughout New England, partible inheritance was the rule. So long as there were free lands that fathers could pass on to their children, this system functioned smoothly and helped perpetuate the dual authority of the farmers and the ministers. It assured obedience from dependent children, kept the new families in close proximity to the parents after they gained their autonomy, and forged a self-perpetuating structure for assuring strong political alliances to protect group interests against those of other families.

For the ministers, on the other hand, the process was more complicated; as a group, they traded financial and physical dependency for spiritual autonomy. The clergy's prestige was gained in inversion to its direct access to secular forms of power. Practically, this meant that the system of partible inheritance worked against the ministers' ability to consolidate private networks of family power. Having only a single pulpit to pass on, even a very influential clergyman could pass on his authority to only one of his male children. The continued high status of his family, therefore, depended upon trading on his prestige to marry his children into the families of powerful landowners, magistrates, or merchants. This guaranteed the close integration of the clergy with the most influential members of their congregations and with the magistrates of the colony. But it also placed clergymen's prestige with the status quo, which until the mid-eighteenth century was solidly more agrarian than commercial.

Once the large landholdings of the farmer-fathers had dwindled through generations of inheritance and the common lands of the villages had been lost, the economic and political foundation of the whole standing order began to collapse. The farmer-father might be forced to limit the size of his family. The children he did have might be forced to put off starting their own families. When the children did attempt to establish autonomous lives, they might be given too little land to establish their birthrights of independence, or they might be forced to apprentice themselves to other patriarchal figures, diluting the authority of their fathers in another way.

As power and influence within a particular family eroded, the family's standing in the community and influence over public affairs deteriorated. Ministers became more dependent on those who could financially support them and thus lost the authority that once had accompanied their rule. They became hostage to the congregations they served and especially to the increasingly wealthy merchants on whose resources they found themselves ever more dependent. At last, the agrarian economy and the spiritual mission of these transplanted Englishmen became the double victims of the original impetus out of which the colonies had been chartered in the first place: the needs of British commercial expansion, which they thought they had left behind generations before in heroic flight from a corrupt parent country.

Ironically, the merchants emerged as the leaders of New England precisely because they were excluded from the highest positions in the old standing order. Their patriarchal authority was not based upon the partible inheritance of land. The dispersal of individual fortunes under that system had worked against the prestige of merchant-fathers by diluting wealth throughout their families. But when the frontier closed, and with it the opportunities that had given the old order its prestige, the merchants were in the best position to take advantage of the new commercial opportunities for manufacturing and trade that the resulting urbanization extended. Under the new economic conditions fostered by British commercial policy, colonial merchants had both greater opportunity and less risk to their investments. Because wealth was inherently more flexible than land, the merchants had more options to pursue. Above all, they were able to adapt the corporate ethic of their New England heritage to take advantage of such opportunities. They could establish partnerships, pool resources, and spread losses. By availing themselves of many cooperative schemes, including the creation of corporations, the merchants prospered and grew powerful while the old standing order was absorbed into their orbit of control.

By the 1780s, the merchants were capable of providing the patriarchal goods of advancement to autonomy for their children. They were able to supply positions in their firms for many more family members and employees than could any local merchant or landowner of the regionalist past. It was the merchants who could provide financial support for orphans and insane asylums; they, not the farmers, built roads and improved the common property of the towns. They paid for emergency repairs to churches and supported the formerly church-dominated universities, turning them into national institutions for training the young into new roles as employees for the continued expansion of corporate businesses.

Despite the phenomenal growth in the fortunes of the merchant class in New England in the fifty years before the Revolution, it remained only a minority segment among the different sociologies of the middle Atlantic and southern sections of the country. The southern-dominated nation that formed itself out of a desire to escape the corruption perceived in the British commercial empire did so at the precise moment when New England was experiencing an opposite conclusion regionally. But while New England's agrarian patriarchs were being replaced by commercial ones, the national economy and sentiment were overwhelmingly committed to an agrarian future.

Despite the vicissitudes of historical change, Anglo-American political culture remained locked within the Machiavellian patterns that had produced it, struggling to balance the consequences of virtù on one side and virtue on the other. This recurring formula for balancing patriarchal responsibility and power offered a heroic redemption from time's dual corruptions of dependency, resulting from too little patriarchal power, and oppression, resulting from too much. But the heroic nature of the republican ideal of redemption, classically rooted in the demigod founder but codified by Machiavelli within the romantic dilemmas it spawned, could offer no timeless position from which to defend the legitimacy of the father as hero. Trapped within time—which turns vital father-heroes into doddering fools, discredited providers, or tyrants who refuse autonomy to the next generation—the Machiavellian heroic ideal had to be as ambiguous in practice as it was contradictory in form.[23]

The resolution for holding together such a self-defeating balance of contradictions reflected Machiavelli's own dual identity as a stylist-poet and theorist-politician; it was necessarily as much aesthetic as political. Within the context of Anglo-American economic and social change, the poles of power and stability, passion and duty, innovation and tradition, or even more fundamentally, parricide and fraternal self-sacrifice, functioned like variations on an aesthetic genre. Change did occur in the world and had to be incorporated into a continuing order. Old styles, like old fathers, lost their potency. New names replaced old ones. But the aesthetic conventions of heroic politics were capable of almost infinite reformulation and reapplication because the Machiavellian hero was by definition neither wholly successful nor completely failed but deeply problematical.[24] As New Englanders discovered in one way and Southerners learned in another, the obsession with virtue could be as aesthetic a form of moralism as it could be politically and economically astute. Its tragic form provided the flexibility that only ambiguity can give.

Consequently, during the 1780s New Englanders did not surrender their agrarian values en masse and join the Federalist party, which became the party of the merchant class. Nor did all Federalists support Hamiltonian principles (another Machiavellian variation on power and virtue, offering a heroic alternative to the yeoman). Nor did most New Englanders, in embracing trade and manufacturing, necessarily reject the need for some balance with agrarianism to preserve virtue. The range of differences among Federalists and anti-Federalists and the variations within the economies of each section were too ambiguous for such a surgically clean division.[25] What did occur, however, was a crisis of legitimacy among the Founding Fathers and among Anglo-Americans generally concerning the implications for the future held by the innovative violence from which the new nation had been born.

In this sense, the Declaration of 1776 assumed the Constitution of 1789. The former document attacked the paternity of the king in the name of liberty. It was a defense of innovation. For this reason, the necessity of the second document (if not its actual form) was ordained by the other pole of Machiavellian common sense: law and tradition as a check on fratricide. The intense disagreement that attended the drafting and ratification of the Constitution reflected the depth of the tension between innovation and law within republican values. The Declaration and the Constitution, therefore, did not represent the transformation from promise to betrayal, as Beardians argued, in decrying what they saw as the movement from disinterested democracy to elitist privilege. Rather, the Constitution followed the Declaration because the tragic betrayal was inseparable from the promise itself. That is to say that the relations between Lincoln and Washington on one side and the Declaration and the Constitution on the other were expressions of a continuing tension of innovation and law, not breaks with the past. This dichotomy suggests as well an insight into Charles Beard's personal odyssey from savage critic to defender of the Constitution by the late 1930s.[26] Consequently, there was never a stable heroic age of republican virtue at any time between the Revolution and the Civil War—or after.

If the tensions between liberty and fratricide became manifest in the American Revolution, it was because they were already inherent in the Declaration. As an act of innovative violence that brought forth political freedom and fratricide, the Revolution only served to raise the level of urgency concerning those republican tensions, not to resolve them. When the struggle seemed joyfully and successfully to have been concluded, the self-defeating contradiction in the revolutionaries' obsession to preserve the traditions of English liberty through innovative violence began to emerge, driving the North and South into an increasingly suspicious opposition to each other. The Machiavellian contradictions between virtù and virtue, commercial expansion and free space, would be stirred into the pressure cooker of sectional and inter-sectional rivalries, racism, and competing claims of political legitimacy.

Following Jefferson's agrarian revolution of 1800, the Federalist party was driven from national power and remained a sectional party until its demise. But privately, through educational institutions and through developing networks of influence built upon a New England base, the corporations continued to grow and to expand, often claiming high moral purpose in justification for challenges to hostile legislation. By the 1890s, having harnessed the industrial power of steam and the organizational power of the clock, corporations were poised to repeat nationally and then internationally the Hamiltonian transformation of New England.

Between the Jacksonian period and the end of the national frontier, a new patriarchal order had grown into local positions of prominence. Reflecting the diluted consequences of the New England way, the new patriarchy was not so solidly agrarian as its progenitors but represented the diversified economy that was changing the political and cultural structure of the nation. These new middle-class community leaders were on the periphery of the corporations and were usually well insulated from direct control by them. The new middle-class leaders were often professionals who had been college educated, small businessmen, manufacturers, and along with them members of the old landed gentry. These men were found all over the East and Midwest, but they were frequently from New England families or had been educated there. They were active in local patriotic and civic organizations, and—as befitted successful Anglo-American Protestant father-figures representing the oldest and most established families—they were preoccupied with virtue. Somewhat doubtful about the corporations for which they sometimes worked, particularly as lawyers, and independent of strong party loyalty, the Mugwumps, as they were called, assumed a decentralized ideal of America. In a still largely rural society characterized by strong attachment to place, they held sway as leaders of their local communities, where they were strongly imbedded in local economies.

By the dawn of the Progressive era, however, this new middle class had become an old middle class. The children found that the rapidly urbanizing America of the post–Civil War years had left their literal and figurative fathers out of date and trapped in ineffectual provincialism. The corporations that had continued to expand their influence since the 1780s once again offered an opportunity not merely for an improved status, but also for tangible power and access to a fertile future.[27]

In embracing the virtù of national corporate capitalism as the only reality for the future, there was a far stronger sense of crisis than of euphoric promise, even among the minority of the new middle class who worked to consolidate the corporate victory through government regulation, social engineering, and aesthetic forms of propaganda. We have already seen this profound doubt about the consequences of the triumph of a corporate capitalist order in the widespread anxiety by Turner's day about the role of time as a harnessed formula for centralizing power in the absence of free space. In terms that are highly suggestive of the Machiavellian form of the Progressive generation's revolt, historian Robert Crunden has characterized the mood of reform as one of "innovative nostalgia."[28]

That phrase suggests not only the Machiavellian conundrum Progressives faced in attempting to balance the necessities of innovation with the requirements of tradition—or in other words, virtù with virtue. It also reveals a subtle shift towards distancing themselves from the genteel republicanism of their fathers and turning their ethical qualms into a form of aestheticism, shorn of political reality. That shift amounted to a repudiation of Agrarian politics, particularly in the form of the Agrarian radicalism, which grew to its highest pitch in the Populist movement.[29] Signaled by Turner's funeral oration for the national agrarian frontier, Progressive historiography defined agrarian values as reactionary and out of step with the evolutionary movement of history towards industrial progress. According to Charles and Mary Beard's eulogy, "there were to be no more Boones, Houstons, and Fremonts; the long wagon trains of homeseekers had gone down over the western horizon for the last time."[30] The passing of the frontier, they informed their readers in 1930—the same year as Twelve Southerners published their agrarian manifesto, *I'll Take My Stand*[31]—meant that "the army of untrained and wasteful farmers who had prospered by raising huge crops on virgin soil, in spite of their methods, could never again take refuge from themselves by leaving the exhausted lands of their first settlements for new sections in the West." Finally, the Beards concluded, inefficient and backward farmers would have to face up to scientific farming and marketing.[32] That assessment stood far from the perspective offered by the New Agrarians, such as the poets John Crowe Ransom, Allen Tate, Donald Davidson, and Robert Penn Warren. They and the other contributors to *I'll Take My Stand* decried the juggernaut of industrialism rolling down from the North and "the melancholy fact that the South itself has wavered a little and shown signs of wanting to join up behind the common or American industrial ideal."[33] In the opinion of the Twelve Southerners, to the contrary of the Beards, "the capitalization of the applied sciences has now become extravagant and uncritical; it has enslaved our human energies to a degree now clearly felt to be burdensome."

The New Agrarians were critical of the very idea of progress, arguing that the corporate development that promised to "liberate" local economies and social structures from their regional limitations was simply a form of organized expropriation. They followed the Harringtonian convention that political virtue was possible only when producers were in control of their own means of production. They expressed a Jeffersonian dismay over the implications of democracy under the conditions of industrialism. For, as Donald Davidson put it, only when democracy becomes politically and socially impotent or exists in an extreme form, as in the Soviet Union, does it become really dangerous.[34] Industrial democracy was clearly such a dangerous entity for all the contributors, not just Davidson. But Davidson also sounded a common theme among his fellow poets when he extended the Harringtonian warning about political virtue to aesthetics. He argued in his contribution, "A Mirror for Artists," that industrialism had sundered the artist from an economic base that could support political or aesthetic virtue.[35] The artist, as an expression of his objective circumstances, can find personal wholeness only in communion with society, Davidson wrote. But, he said, such a wholeness in an industrialized and scientific society as the United States was becoming could only be a "monstrous and misshapen nightmare which we pray we may not survive to witness."

On one point, the industrial republicanism of the Beards and the Agrarian republicanism of the Twelve Southerners found agreement. This was their common and intense rejection of romanticism and celebration of realism. The Beards attributed this romanticism to the agrarian frontier: "And with the passing of romance," they wrote of the coming of industrialism, "slowly dawned an age of realism."[36] For Davidson, as for his friends, the Romantic movement expressed the alienation and self-absorbed fragmentation that revealed its origins in the Industrial Revolution. Romanticism, he warned, is the "antitoxin that industrialism produces."[37] The escape from such a self-destructive reflection of contemporary society, he declared, is in joining the common struggle by becoming a citizen. "Whether he chooses, as citizen-person, to be a farmer or to run for Congress is a matter of individual choice; but in that general direction his duty lies." Davidson's celebration of the citizen-farmer was clearly meant as a bow to the Jeffersonian yeoman-hero, capable of redeeming the democratic ideal as the violence of the new industrial pioneers could not. But its context was the Machiavellian moment in Davidson's problematic view of the heroic. Thus, in his poem "The Tall Men," published in 1927, he had celebrated the heroic virtù of the forefathers, whose "words were bullets."[38] But his autobiographical narrator was merely a fox, who substitutes a typewriter for the forefather's rifle, and asks if "words pass for bullets, dabbed in a scribble of ink?" Like Machiavelli, Davidson would use his art to ask if there is any way to transform corrupt and degenerate Southerners into citizens. Could art restore men who had been reduced to foxes into men of virtù?[39]

Similarly, John Crowe Ransom's arcane but seminal book of 1930, *God Without Thunder,* complained of the loss of a God of heroic proportions to a god of utility and logic.[40] Revealingly, Ransom's original title was to be *Giants for Gods,* reflecting his own identification as an artist with the Classical demigod, standing between nature and God, as the mythical problematical hero. "All the saviors in the myths are Giants," said Ransom, "*and the problem is in what sense they can save, and for what purpose they are to be worshipped.*" The problem of religion, he explained to Allen Tate, is the problem of space and time, in relation to contingency, indeterminateness, and chaos on one side and necessity, determinateness, and cosmos, as order, on the other. The god of a genuine religion will appear evil to the soft humanist, while on the other side the god of soft humanism will appear to the stern religionist as an impotent giant.[41]

In his problematical response to contingency and necessity, neither wholly naturalist nor moralist, Ransom was repeating the Machiavellian convention of requiring a heroic response to a condition of divided sensibilities that had become part of the Western condition with the Renaissance. For this reason he followed the Machiavellian path of unorthodoxly defending orthodoxy and of lamenting the cultural consequences of Christianity, a religion based on sloth rather than vigor.[42] *God*

Without Thunder was a challenge to a defeated Anglo-Protestantism to regain a sense of autonomy by recovering the natural energy, or virtù, which was being tamed by science and progress, yet which remained alive and locked within the aesthetic potential at the heart of all ritual, whether of art, myth, or religion.[43]

The second major theoretician of the New Agrarian critics, Allen Tate, was also preoccupied with the problem of heroic legitimacy, but his concern was for the legitimacy of the southern heroic past itself. Tate found himself living in a degenerate age within memory of heroic history but barred by time from participating in it. Time's disintegration appeared to him the fate of all myths because all are born into history. But history, for Tate, was the medium of experience through which a society recognizes its responsibility to a specific set of values. Like Ransom, he called for a revitalization of religion and history as mythic conventions for reestablishing an organic and redemptive link between the present and the past and between sensation and abstraction. But Tate's persistent struggle was how that could be accomplished in a culture so self-divided as the West had become since the Reformation. This was a division he felt personally in his desire for the mythic universality of Catholic wholeness and his attachment to a particular, local identity, grounded in history, as an Anglo-Protestant Southerner. In his poem "Ode to the Confederate Dead" (1927), Tate expressed the anguish of his personally divided condition, in which he saw the larger cultural contradiction of being at once romantic and traditionalist. Though the romantically solipsistic narrator may long for the intensity of experience through the evocation of memory, he says, "These 'buried Caesars' will not bloom in the hyacinth but will only make saltier the sea."[44]

The same theme informs his biography *Stonewall Jackson: The Good Soldier,* published in 1928. Tate's mythically innocent southern landscape is filled with mechanical devices of death. His innocent hero, undivided in mind and loyal and responsible to a fault, is a father to the lad raised on Parson Weems's Washington in preparation for a heroic destiny. However, this heroic figure, who in his simple religious faith and direct intuition of military tactics might have been the source of a different southern, and hence national, history, is uncomprehendingly and senselessly cut down by his own soldiers' artillery fire.[45] In both works, the artistic act alone confers life on dead memory, and so the artist alone is the hero-father who is capable of passing on life to others in a shattered age. Death provides Tate's own aesthetic legitimacy as a creative hero, even as he mourns the defeated past that calls his own life's meaning into question.

During the 1920s, Charles Beard and the leading New Agrarians had steeped themselves in Machiavelli's works.[46] They drew different lessons from those studies about progress and the ways to pursue virtue. Yet in the early 1930s, as leading theorists of opposing variations on republicanism, both extolled similar values of civic activism. Both recognized a dilemma of innovation and tradition at the heart of contemporary political life, though their solutions were mutually exclusive. Most important, both the New Agrarian poets and the Progressive historian Beard continued to use the Romantic conventions associated with republicanism while submerging any awareness that they were doing so.

In Beard's case, the winning of industrial democracy from capitalist exploitation was viewed as great national destiny. Beard looked to Franklin Roosevelt as a heroic figure who would lead Americans out of the shadow of capitalism and from the impending doom of a foreign war among corrupted powers. The New Agrarians defended a pure South of the imagination with as much quarrelsome posturing as any alienated artists could muster, despite their vituperative attack on the southern family romance genre upon which it was based. They embraced Dante, just as had Blake and Flaxman, Eliot and Pound, for escaping the limits of the logical world through a universal vision; like the earlier writers, the New Agrarian poets were rebellious, conservative iconoclasts against a sterile and oppressive industrial order.[47]

However, from the vantage point of the early 1930s it would have been very difficult to predict that the eminent and popular historical evolutionist Charles Beard was about to fall from public grace and that the "provincial and reactionary" defenders of the South of the Scopes trial would become the most influential and prestigious literary critics in the nation, courted by major national universities and publishing houses. Yet that was precisely the case by the mid-1940s, when the New Agrarians had been transformed into the New Critics and Beard's realism had been eclipsed by the ideas of an ex-Marxist theologian named Reinhold Niebuhr.[48] That transition came at the point at which corporate capitalism fully completed its rise to dominance, as prophesied by Frederick Jackson Turner in 1893. Reinhold Niebuhr's funeral oration for an exceptional America completed the burial of republican political culture, anticipated in Frederick Jackson Turner's eulogy for an exceptional American space. While Turner could still believe that the innovative violence of the western frontier could find its resolution in the growth of civilization from the East, he could no longer hide the Machiavellian contradiction that held such a promise together. In the new realism of nuclear deterrence and the requirements of a national security state, there could be no heroic final resolution of harmony. Only irony seemed capable of balancing such irreducible contradictions to create a way out through the very absurdity of there being no way out.[49] Niebuhr's irony was not only, as he claimed and used it in his writings, a formal law of oppositions capable of holding together two contradictory poles of human experience at the same time. Rather, irony was an aesthetic formula that Niebuhr borrowed from Romanticism. It was, therefore, both a literary device and a political instrument. Irony, as Niebuhr defined it, was a variation on Machiavellian ambiguity; *ambiguity* was another word with strong resonances of mystical truth for Niebuhr and his generation.[50]

Niebuhr deeply resisted any recognition of the aesthetic side of life, or of its central role in his own ironic analysis. Instead, for Niebuhr and apparently for his readers, irony, despite its literary associations, masqueraded as mere trope and so never directly contradicted his claim of providing laws of political transformation. The amateur actor and political theorist liked to use such theatrical phrases as "the drama of human existence" or "the vastness of the historical drama," and to elicit ironic comparisons with Cervantes and Tolstoy. He defended his use of irony as a plausible interpretive structure without recognizing that his political analysis had subtly taken on the character of a literary exegesis. In this way, Niebuhr translated Machiavellian political conventions into a new context for a triumphant corporate capitalism, even as he helped bring the Anglo-American republican political tradition to a close. The separation of aesthetic life from politics played a key role in his ability successfully to provide an avenue of escape for a political culture facing the stark vision of its own demonic contradictions.[51]

But Reinhold Niebuhr was not alone in ushering in a new Machiavellian synthesis in the 1940s and in burying the rotting corpse of republicanism. The New Agrarian critics were simultaneously fulfilling the same role as Niebuhr by turning to a complementary rejection of politics in the name of an aesthetic mission to separate art from ideology—and from a failed history. This process of separating art from history was in essence a process of aesthetic distancing from the dead heroic tradition of republican virtue. It was an effort to escape the implications of a failed political identity in order to locate another frontier space of freedom beyond the tragedy of lost possibility, which followed from that death. This transformation from an Old World of shriveled political hope to a New World of unlimited aesthetic potential was mediated through an application of the Romantic elegy to Machiavellian politics.[52]

For the New Critics, that moment of death and resurrection accompanied the triumph of corporate capitalism. By the mid-1930s, the New Critics were confirmed in the abandonment of their self-identification as Agrarians. Politically and economically, the New Deal and the scientific-realist regionalism of the southern New Sociologists, such as Howard Odum and Rupert Vance, fatally wounded any lingering hopes for a national or regional impact from a decentralized activist group of intellectuals, led by a few poets.[53] After the mid-1930s, the logic and organized commitment of such alternative movements quickly overtook the New Agrarians' own ambivalent republican solutions. The New Agrarians perceptively recognized that the monism of science and the claims of evolution as a creative theory of nature rendered their own artistic theory of universal standards a static formalism when viewed from outside the human condition. And it was precisely the imaginative removal from a standard of human scale that characterized those who believed in a scientific industrial future and, conversely, those (often from their own ranks) whom the New Agrarians criticized as nostalgic defenders of a dead traditionalism. In abandoning their defeated republican tradition, the New Critics' formal separation of power from aesthetics dramatically reversed their place in the national culture. As Alexander Karanikas wrote in 1966, the New Critics "and their methods of evaluation became the most exciting subject of comment on the literary scene." Their textbooks became standards; they published widely, taught, lectured, judged writing contests, reviewed books, and "reaped all the rewards reserved for the highest authorities in literature." More importantly, Karanikas noted, they profoundly influenced the standards for judging literature, by denigrating the popular and democratic authors of the past as well as the present.[54]

However, in recognizing the pervasiveness of the New Critics in the mid-1960s, Karanikas also signaled the beginning of their displacement as arbitrators of aesthetic power within the academy. For once self-consciously defined, rather than taken for granted, any dominant Machiavellian style must necessarily lose its legitimacy to newer, more subversive styles in the politics of culture.[55]

One implication of this Machiavellian style of Romantic elegiac dis-

placement, constantly renewed through the demand for aesthetic novelty, is that it calls into doubt the New Critics' claim of having recovered
universal meaning of texts by discovering a New World of aesthetic potential waiting beyond political disappointment. Instead, the hegemony
of the New Critics between 1940 and 1960 rested upon their service,
through ambiguity, in helping to restore a shattered aesthetic and political balance, making possible a new Machiavellian synthesis of power and
value. The southern New Critics, very much as the "New Standing
Order" of New England in the 1780s and 1790s, translated the political
failure of a regional patriarchy into an apology for a more abstract patriarchy of institutional centralization. The New Critics achieved this
precisely as the New Standing Order did, by attaching their Romantic
elegy to the greater power of corporate institutions. In that sense, the
professionalization of criticism in the universities in the 1930s and 1940s
paralleled the professionalization of virtue in the Federalist-dominated
universities in Jefferson's era. Both the Federalists and the New Critics
found themselves orthodoxly defending unorthodox religion as a means
of establishing order for an antidemocratic cultural aristocracy. Though
the New Critics, again like the New Standing Order, denied they had
politically schemed to gain control of cultural institutions of power, they
certainly did so, even after giving up Agrarian-style political action.
For example, in the 1950s Allen Tate participated in the "Congress for
Cultural Freedom" funded by the Central Intelligence Agency, though
Martin Buber rejected his invitation because he viewed it as a forum for
Cold War propaganda.[56] In a different context, Richard M. Weaver, who
studied with Cleanth Brooks and Robert Penn Warren in the 1940s,
though nursing his own conservative political agenda, remembered them
as political activists. The New Critics wished to establish a "radiating
center" of impulse—a "new Rome," Weaver called it—to spread their
influence.[57] Style-setting journals such as the *Kenyon Review*, edited by
Ransom, and the *Southern Review*, edited by Warren and Brooks, were
made more exclusive by rejecting some contributions of the famous,
while promoting young writers' careers.[58] For the power the New Critics
embraced was the power of the Romantic elegist, not the power of a
Huey Long. Yet in Warren and Brooks's case, the *Southern Review* and
Louisiana State University owed a great deal to Long's problematical heroic ambitions, constructed on an ambiguous alliance between disinterested altruism and political ruthlessness.[59] Long not only saved the
university during the Depression years but actually built it into a major

institution with the funds needed to launch and sustain a small magazine such as the *Southern Review*. Warren suffered no editorial interference by Long. But he nevertheless was disturbed by the situation and was prepared to resign if such interference came. Warren acknowledged and explored this web of shared implication in corruption in *Night Rider* and *All the King's Men*—both novels that confront the problem of guilt and innocence within the context of a morally compromised and politically defeated Agrarian idealism.[60] That association between aesthetic innocence and political corruption similarly attracted Warren's friend and Agrarian sympathizer, the historian C. Vann Woodward. As Richard H. King has said, Woodward's 1938 biography of the Georgia Populist Tom Watson and Warren's 1938 play *The Proud Flesh*, or as it became in 1946, the novel *All the King's Men*, are the same kind of book.[61]

The hallmark of the New Critical synthesis was its acceptance of a dualism in the human condition that required a *mimetic* division within the writer, as citizen and as artist. This dualism, which the theorists and followers of the New Criticism considered in various ways, could be mediated but never escaped. This meant that the artist-writer not only embodies a dualism between the universals of art and the particulars of political experience but also is trapped within an ironic condition. The artist-writer must strive to resolve the division between the public and private realms of experience without being able to transcend his or her own space and time. Only by confronting and balancing the resulting contradictions for the self and society, according to this formulation, can a moral order be established. The avenue for mediating the oppositions inherent in the purity of art and the impurity of experience, within a literary context, is criticism. As a form of written communication with a public, criticism intersects vision and ideology, creation and application, self and society. The critic as defined by the New Criticism is therefore a kind of demigod who mediates between God and Nature, reason and emotion, and art and science. He or she does so in the immediacy of his or her apprehension of reality, not in the artificial constructions of the historical method or the rigid categories of political ideology.

Correspondingly, the New Critics felt that they had a special mission beyond politics, economics, or even the older boundaries of literary criticism. They believed the vital distinction between the ideal and real had almost wholly left the practical world of science, industrialism, and capitalism, and the false communities and languages of communism and fascism.[62]

As poets, the New Agrarian critics sought a vision, as Robert Penn Warren explained in 1942, that was capable of surviving the contradictions of reality. They wished to preserve the purity of the poetic imagination without indulging in Romanticism, through opposing the purity of poetics to the imperfect and earth-bound language-form of prose. The poet, Warren wrote, desires the beautiful, an ineffable singleness of vision. But prose requires the acknowledgment of ugliness—ugly words, ugly thoughts, colloquialisms, and other jagged incongruities to a pure vision. The ironic terms of life, said Warren, may not be escaped, so the poem must be in eternal contradiction with its own mission. It must seek out the imperfection and include it within itself if the poet is to remain faithful to complexity.

This inability to transcend the ironic, and the necessity of living within poles of contradiction, may similarly be seen in John Crowe Ransom's counterpoint to Warren, in which he described a poem as being like a democratic state and prose, like a totalitarian one. The poem must have a logical structure but it also must preserve the free play of local textures. Prose, like all forms of scientific language, ruthlessly aims for a singleness of purpose, sacrificing everything to the dominant theme. The critic-poet must attack the "tidy universe" of scientific thinking to restore the democratic freedom of the poetic life of community. According to Ransom, the poet-critic must be Aristotelian and realistic against the scientist who is Platonic and idealist.

Both Warren and Ransom eventually modified their positions in order to accommodate a positive resolution to the problem of irony. But even within this formulation their position was problematic, especially since the New Agrarian critics disagreed among themselves over just which side of the opposition needed emphasis. Yet despite these differences, they remained united in their purpose of providing and defending a theoretical formula for judging literature's impact on life. They were also agreed that a ground for a social reformation, through literature, must be discovered and applied from outside either a historical or sociological context in terms of an independent, universal standard of aesthetics.[63]

The original self-identification of the leading theorists of the New Agrarian critics—led by Ransom, Tate, and for a time, Davidson, and by the considerably younger Warren and Cleanth Brooks—in the 1920s had been as Fugitives. This name was a double entendre, coined to express their alienation from both the false sentimentality of southern self-identification and the cold logic of scientific industrial progress, which they associated with the North.[64] But the tension in their stance between nostalgia and innovation was delicately equivocated by their poetry, which was at once fantastic and mystical in subject and spare and understated in style. As the 1930s approached, however, they found themselves unable to contain these tensions either within their own poetic creations or within an intimate circle of like-minded friends. With the publication of *I'll Take My Stand*, they had shifted their emphasis from poetry to prose, from the individual artist to a community of prophets, and from an escape from southern localism to its defense. They did so in an attempt to respond to the practical conditions of dynamic virtù swallowing up the virtues of community in corporate-industrial America, as well as from a desire to apply aesthetic creativity, politically and economically, to build another South capable of transcending its provincialism. They had come to view the former and dominant struggle in terms of defending a feminine, colonized South from a threatening and voracious, masculine North, much as they had defended poetic language from the rigid objective language of scientific discourse. But that battle against virtù was intimately tied to their preoccupation with virtue as Southerners. A traditional society, Allen Tate wrote, is a society capable of handing down something living, even if it were just invented. To this end, they had actively organized themselves into political action groups, and they wrote manifestos for Agrarian economic reform like *Who Owns America?* (1936).[65]

This sequel to *I'll Take My Stand* included more non-Southerners and was clearly more active in intent than the previous volume, since it was distributed to President Roosevelt and other prominent New Dealers. The poetically abstract and equivocal values of the Fugitives had given way to the concrete economic and political values of the New Agrarians. In the midst of the Great Depression the poets had become committed to making their vision physically real; therefore, the aesthetic frontier they had championed as alienated southern intellectuals suddenly had a specific agenda against which its ideals could be judged. Their platform, as builders of a national coalition of Agrarian and Distributist groups, was vintage Agrarian Populism; it condemned plutocracy and communism, praised the decentralization of agriculture, called for the defense of the family farm, and decried the rise of corporate capitalism. "In politics we are losing our freedom," it read. "In economics we are losing our independence. In life we are losing our proper sense of values."[66]

Until the mid-1930s, the New Agrarians continued to believe that a new balance could be achieved through the aesthetics of regionalism and the politics of sectionalism. That stance appeared to have added legitimacy because, as they noted, it echoed Frederick Jackson Turner's postfrontier thesis of a continuing balance against economic and national centralization.[67] But for Turner sectionalism was less a positive program to restore republican virtue than a practical defense to enforce harmony in its absence. For Turner, the organic unity of the nation had been defeated with the frontier, and sectionalism was an attempt to make a virtue out of a necessity of division. The hope that centralizing power could be balanced through sectional reconciliation was a hope against the possibility that violent competition in America might follow the historical pattern of the nations of Europe.[68] The New Agrarians, as Southerners, however, were already convinced that no balance was possible with a voracious industrial North. Sectionalism, for them, meant legitimacy for the South, but it provided no means for merging that legitimacy in practical terms with their aesthetic ideal of regionalism. How were they to construct a Machiavellian balance of aesthetic regionalism and political sectionalism in which the contradiction within their own values would not shatter their synthesis? How was a decentralized economy to survive, even if it could be constructed, now that industrial capitalism had been restored through government power? As poet-critics the New Agrarians could stand between science and romanticism. But, in practical political and economic terms, they could offer no clear alternative to either the New Deal or fascism. They wished to restore an agrarian ideal of rural self-sufficiency while also defending urban civilization against ignorance and unending labor. As political activists they were, therefore, trapped within the Machiavellian dilemmas of power and value. As cosmopolitan writers with classical educations and southern identities, they were unprepared to admit their own participation in the Machiavellian conventions of the republican political tradition. They preferred to believe that, as artists, they had discovered a New World that released them from the limitations of a tyrannical and provincial Old World of particulars.

Interestingly, the New Agrarian critical turn to a rigid dichotomy between art and politics found an immediate echo among the northern literary and social critics who have since become identified as the "New York intellectuals."[69] In the late 1930s, these intellectuals were just turning in disillusionment from the failure of an exceptional international frontier in Soviet communism. In the face of history, the promise of a universal economy of virtue had given way to a somber reality of self-interested national policies and to the tyranny of centralized power, graphically and unavoidably displayed in such political atrocities as the Moscow trials of 1936–38. Leon Trotsky, the dissident Russian revolutionist, intellectual, and opponent of Stalin, briefly appeared to many in the disaffected Left to offer a resolution to the feeling of betrayal and hopelessness created by Stalin's ruthless grasp of power. As a legitimate leader of the revolution, Trotsky seemed to offer a last possibility for restoring faith in the promise of an international and truly universal communism by challenging the sectarian, self-interested nationalism of Stalinism. He was a legitimate political son of Lenin and bona fide hero of the October Revolution, so his assurances that art and ideology could remain separate yet were ultimately harmonious provided new hope for redemption of a lost cause among these urban Northerners, much as the New Agrarianism had embodied hope for a renewed nation through a restored South.

The literary critic Edmund Wilson, the editors of the *Partisan Review*, Philip Rahv and William Phillips, and critics such as Lionel Trilling, among many others, found in Trotsky a way to retain their leftist hopes for a New World while opposing Stalinism. But in their turn to Modernism from proletarian literature, they were already moving away from a faith in a socialist alternative. Wilson sought to restore Trotsky to his legitimate heroic place in the revolution, but he could not wholly endorse either the revolution or Trotsky. Rahv and Phillips published Trotsky in the newly organized *Partisan Review*, created when the division between politics, the province of the *New Masses*, and culture had become intolerable. In reorganizing the *Partisan Review* in 1937, they had expressed their desire to bring politics and aesthetics together in a new synthesis. But neither Rahv nor Phillips was persuaded by Trotsky to become a committed follower. Even before his assassination in 1940, Trotsky had lost his bid to refashion a persuasive balance between aesthetics and political ideology among his most sympathetic audience.[70]

The process of burying failed heroic dreams of political and economic virtue was similar for the New York intellectuals and the Southerners. Though the context in the two sections was different, the result was very much the same. The Northeasterners, like their southern contemporaries, and the Missouri-born Niebuhr, rejected romanticism for realism and intensely defended the division between art and ideology. In doing so, these anticapitalist Northerners and Southerners together helped pave the way for an unchallenged acceptance of a rigidly capitalist new social order.

During this Cold War period of equation of capitalism with democracy and of American internationalist policies for spreading freedom and geopolitical control, republicanism disappeared from the lexicon of historians and political scientists in the North and South. A celebration of the values of consumerism in a precarious world of nuclear deterrence smothered any direct admission that the nation had quite reversed itself from its historical roots in agrarianism, political isolationism, and an economics of production. Liberalism was accepted as the only political ideology Americans had ever known.

As a viable political program, republicanism was dead. It was laid in a common grave with socialism. As an aesthetic pattern, however, it continued to live on in political rhetoric, cinematic clichés, and public rituals. It can still be seen in pervasive and persistent attachment to an aesthetics of power and of violence in relation to gender and race. Through these forms, republicanism was, in Kenneth Bruffee's phrase, preserved in amber as a traditional or conventional structure of meaning. Republicanism became merely an aesthetic sensibility. It lived on only in the Machiavellian political synthesis that replaced it. But through that continuity of form, republicanism could still haunt the dreams and fuel the nightmares of later generations of Americans.

CHAPTER THREE

The Pastoral Elegy
of Tom Watson, Agrarian Hero

Frederick Jackson Turner, unlike the younger New Agrarian critics, was never able to transcend the destruction of the agrarian republican political culture. He recognized that the triumph of virtù, centralized power and personal ambition, over virtue, decentralized political community and self-sacrificing citizenship, must result with the end of free space. Though he intellectually admitted the inevitability of the closing of the agrarian frontier and, therefore, the mortality of political virtue for any republic born in time, Turner could not emotionally confront so stark and despairing of a historical conclusion. Therefore, as Gene Wise and David Noble have both noted, Turner, who died in 1930, was never able to offer a coherent argument for a democratic future for America.[1] His response, as Noble has shown, was unconsciously to separate culture from politics and then to appeal to each side against the other in an attempt to sustain a hopeful future. When he looked to the East, according to the conventions of republicanism, he saw political and economic catastrophe, but he also saw civilization, aesthetics, and the progress of enlightenment through education—the qualities of virtue. When he looked to the West, he saw rude savagery but also youthfulness and political independence—the attributes of virtù. Unable to admit to the internal contradiction of this republican heritage and unable—or unwilling—to surrender its divided legacy, Turner's creativity, at least as measured by the books he could not complete, seemed to abandon him. His scholarship became trapped within the conundrums of a lost Machiavellian synthesis of virtù and virtue in active contradiction with each other.

Ironically, Turner would later claim that his "frontier thesis" developed out of resentment against the eastern academic establishment for its antiwestern attitude.[2] Yet, he gained both his Ph.D. and his professional stature from that eastern academic establishment for his pastoral elegy for the closing of the frontier. He accepted an invitation to join the Harvard faculty in 1910 but seemed unsure whether the move reflected his vanity and ambition to be recognized or his disillusionment with the University of Wisconsin and a selfless desire to sacrifice himself to shake the institution and public out of their provincialism. Ambition and modesty both personally and symbolically, in his divided attitude towards the East and West, warred in Frederick Jackson Turner's breast. For whatever reasons, at Johns Hopkins, Wisconsin, or Harvard, he alternately voiced frustration at midwestern provincialism and eastern elitism. Turner found himself blocked from exploring further creative interpretations of the role of the frontier in American history but escaped into the woods outside Madison or in Maine at every opportunity. When he left Madison for Cambridge, Massachusetts, he consoled himself that he was leaving many explorers in the field to study the West. Turner confined his own writings to the problems associated with preserving a fading past. He expressed dismay over the crowds of Eastern European immigrants he encountered in Boston, viewing them as threats to America's democratic future. As a theorist of Anglo-American democracy, Turner was not prepared to endorse the wisdom of the fifteenth amendment. For Turner, people of color were inferior culturally and physically and needed to be restrained from full access to American life. At the same time that he extolled Jacksonian democracy, he defined the Populists as economic primitives doomed to extinction in the light of the growing complexity of rational economics, evolving out of the Northeast.[3]

The Populists, however, presented a particularly tortuous dilemma for Turner because like him they derived their political values from Jeffersonianism. Like Turner, they remembered a different, agrarian America of Anglo-Saxon Protestantism and wished to defend the American future from the new urban masses pouring into the cities from Eastern Europe. However, just as Turner feared the disruption of the balance between capital and free land that hordes of alien immigrants might bring, he was dismayed by militant Populist protests against the new corporate order. The Populists seemed to Turner to express the primitive violence of the West in their naively irresponsible resistance to change—even though that change, in Turner's own view, augured the end of Jacksonian democracy. He was therefore ambivalent: at once sympathetic to the Populists' desire to preserve agrarian virtue in the West, yet compelled to reject their insurgent political activism because he no longer believed in the vitality of the agrarian frontier. Not until Populism was safely dead did Turner modify his assessment of its legitimacy, but by then his hope for a balance between virtù and virtue had shifted from the lost frontier and even the Middle West as a section to a beleaguered and fragmented middle class embodying the fading memory of an earlier vitality.[4]

As a republican in the tradition of Jefferson and Jackson, Turner accepted the necessity of virtù, or innovative violence, in order to advance the cause of virtue, peace and social harmony. But for Turner the celebration of violence as a life-affirming force for regeneration on the agrarian frontier lay in the past. He therefore strongly defended American militarism as a necessary act of expansive virtù for extending national economic frontiers abroad. But on the domestic front he emphasized the need for peaceful balancing of interests among sections, which could serve "as breakwaters" against overwhelming surges of national emotions.

He could do so because he equated the nationalizing expansion of the Union, led by Abraham Lincoln's personal march away from the western frontier of his youth, with the triumph of rational corporate economics, while conversely he equated Populism with the decentralized, irrational agricultural economy of the South. Like other frontier experiences, the Civil War offered Turner a paradigm of revitalized political progress through destruction. But it was a paradigm that required him to make an unacknowledged separation of aesthetic, or cultural, hope on one side, and hard economic and political reality on the other, just as it required a division of time into a romantic past and a realist present.[5]

So long as there was a frontier line between East and West, the two mutually exclusive conditions of virtù and virtue had creatively intermingled. Together, they promoted a salutary balance, preserving civilization against savagery, and political and economic independence against organized exploitation. But, Turner wrote in 1896, "a people composed of heterogeneous materials, with diverse and conflicting ideals and social interests, having passed from the task of filling up the vacant spaces of the continent, is now thrown back upon itself, and is seeking an equilibrium." As a result, he pessimistically concluded, "the forces of reorganization are turbulent and the nation seems like a witches' kettle."[6] In place of the frontier, "the Center of the Republic," as he called the Middle West—an entity created by the transformation of the West into a settled section—was left to balance European nation-like interests competing within American geographical space. This remnant of defeated frontier vitality alone challenged an imposed national unity of political and economic centralization, even as it participated in fragmenting higher national interests. With something less than persuasive evidence to back up his statements, this academic empiricist who later emigrated to the Northeast expressed hope for the nation in the legacy of a burgeoning Chicago. Speaking in the momentous political year of 1896, he said that Chicago's "complex and representative industrial organization and business ties, its determination to hold fast to what is original and good in its Western experience, and its readiness to learn and receive the results of the experience of other sections and nations, make it an open minded and safe arbiter of the American destiny."[7] In similar terms, on the eve of World War I, Turner declared in a commencement address that "legislation is taking the place of the free lands as the means of preserving the ideal of democracy," even as it endangered "the other pioneer ideal of creative and competitive individualism."[8] He expressed hope that Americans would not capitulate to "some Old World discipline of socialism or plutocracy, or despotic rule, whether by class or by dictator." Americans, he anxiously prophesied, would avoid these alternatives because "our ancient hopes, our courageous faith, our underlying good humor and love of fair play will triumph in the end." Give and take would prevail under disinterested leadership serving the best American ideals. "Nowhere is this leadership more likely to arise than among the men trained in the Universities, aware of the promise of the past and the possibilities of the future," concluded Turner.[9] Perhaps at that moment he was thinking of his former friend and instructor, President Wilson, a historian who had once echoed Turner's call to include the West in American national history by calling for the same sensitivity to the role of the South.[10] It was not a faith that even Turner's most loyal students, Carl Becker and Merle Curti, could find to be persuasive.[11]

Frederick Jackson Turner's tragic self-division as a historian of Anglo-American republican political culture marked a Machiavellian moment of crisis within the profession when he could no longer balance the contradictory implications of virtù and virtue, dynamic expansion as innovative violence and culture as lawful respect for authority, in republican terms. Unable to embrace the new order of corporate innovation and political deference to elites, Turner continued to defend a fatally problematic agrarian tradition by shutting his eyes to the contradiction at the heart of his narrative. His training in the new scientific history only partially mediated his personal separation from the Anglo-Protestant tradition of Harringtonian republicanism of his midwestern youth. Only later with Charles Beard—helped by John Dewey and a whole generation of social scientists who transformed nostalgia for their agrarian pasts into a dynamic urban future through evolutionary theory—would agrarianism be confidently replaced with industrialism. This resolution was anticipated for historiography by form criticism, a German method for tracing the transformation of memory through time, which made possible the integration of eternal religious truths with the dynamic flux of culture.[12]

Looking back from 1938, in an essay honoring the impact of Turner's frontier thesis, Charles Beard wrote that the 1890s were volatile years throughout the American political and economic system.[13] The agitation for urban reform was intensifying, and "the most powerful socialistic movement that has shaken American politics"—the Populist movement—"was in full swing at the very moment when Turner read his essay at Chicago in 1893." As the obscure young professor read his academic paper before a lukewarm gathering of bored antiquarians, making little or no immediate impact, one of those Populist insurgents, lately of the U.S. Congress, was sweeping crowds of thousands into passionate ecstasy. While Turner was eulogizing the agrarian values of America, Tom Watson was in the forefront of a gathering crusade to restore agrarianism's tarnished promise. As Turner prophesied the triumph of European conditions over the agrarian space of an exceptional America, Tom Watson warned that the traditions of the fathers were being forgotten by their degenerate sons. "No longer do we seek to depart as far as possible from European models," the agitator told his audiences. "No longer do we proudly adhere to republican simplicity and to the high dignity of natural manners, governed by common sense."[14]

Tom Watson chose to be an orator and journalist, to promote an active transformation of a defeated, agrarian South to the national leadership of its birthright as the land of Jefferson. He was a historian who was motivated by the belief that the South and the common people deserved to be included in "mankind's reading of mankind's achievement." He believed that if the South were to make history it must take the interpretation of its past out of the hands of the northeastern academic professionals who wrote history in the service of corporate power.[15]

Watson, the southern historian, like Turner, the midwestern historian, believed that the promise of American history was embodied in the balance of independence and cooperation, which Thomas Jefferson had located in the yeoman farmer and which Andrew Jackson had preserved through his own force of will when he heroically restored a failing American democracy. Both Watson and Turner had grown up under the republican political values of Jefferson and Jackson and both knew that in the present, as in the sacred past, virtù, manly force, was necessary to preserve political virtue. But both historians also knew, according to the same complementary balance codified by Machiavelli, that violent force, like other forms of virtù, threatened the continued existence of virtue itself. Consequently, excessive or centralized violence or the ambition that spawned it could undermine the civic harmony it was needed to save.

Watson and Turner attempted to maintain a balance between these problematic poles. Each tried to find, through historical study, the right combination of progress and stability necessary to stave off the inevitable fall of all high-wire acts. However, Watson in 1890, unlike Turner, still retained his political faith that the republican virtue of Jefferson and Jackson was viable and that a political movement, Populism, could spread out of the South to help save national virtue from its enemies. Turner, to the contrary, had abandoned faith in the practical economic foundation for agrarian politics with the closing of the frontier. He therefore celebrated a purifying and regenerating quality of heroic violence in the past but could not, like Watson in the years before the national election of 1896, believe in a Jeffersonian solution to modern social conditions. This meant that to decide which *forms* of violence were appropriate for preserving what remained of political liberty in a time of crisis, Watson and Turner appealed to the same republican ideal of balance, while drawing opposing conclusions.

From within the effort to balance virtù and virtue, Watson and Turner could equally subscribe to the republican-inspired faith that civic values must be guarded by the common virtue of an armed citizenry. Each accepted the Jeffersonian convention that an active and committed public participating in the violent redress of conditions of inequality constitutes a broad defense against corruption. Watson and Turner would both have agreed with Andrew Jackson and Machiavelli that the people have a spirit that professional armies cannot equal. Yet because he assumed that the republican virtue of America had come to a tragic end by 1890, Turner accepted the necessity of national centralization directed by elites, and of a foreign policy based upon seeking out international frontiers and requiring a professionalized military. Turner therefore affirmed the regenerative force of war in preserving the virtue of America, from the

Civil War to intervention in Mexico. He made an early and vociferous demand that the United States enter World War I. At that time, too old to enlist, Turner volunteered his services to a new propaganda department sponsored by the government, the National Board for Historical Services.[16]

Watson, in contrast, because he believed that republican virtue was still viable, feared the growing militarism of the national government as a threat to civic virtue.[17] Though he celebrated the virtù of personal violence and in later years fanned the flames of racial violence, Watson found himself in opposition to every American military conflict from the Civil War to World War I. Indeed, far from romanticizing the Civil War as a glorious lost cause, Watson characterized it as having initiated a disastrous centralization of the nation. Not only did the military and corporations gain a dynamic centralizing power in the North, he said, but the centralization of the Confederate military helped pave the way for postwar corruption in the South. Similarly, after the Spanish-American War, Watson wrote that "the blare of the bugle drowned the voice of the reformer." It was this crisis of virtù and virtue that sent him, like Machiavelli and the Roman historians, to a study of the decline of republican virtue. "Loathing the war and foreseeing many of the evil consequences that it brought upon us," he wrote, "I quit the active agitation of Populism and shut myself up in my library to write books."[18]

The developing contradiction between power and value in Turner between 1890 and World War I has not haunted the historical imagination to the same degree as has the complementary but far more intense contradiction of Tom Watson in the same period. Perhaps Turner's academic style and the context of his career as a professor, in contrast to Watson's provocative language and aggressively public life, have tended to render his pronouncements on race ("hyphenated Americans") or war more abstract and therefore less troubling than Watson's. For whatever reason—perhaps the need for exorcism—however, the contradictions within Watson's character and in his career as a reformer have remained the source of a continuing historiographical controversy since C. Vann Woodward published his biography of the Georgia Populist in 1938.[19] Indeed, Woodward purposely set out to expose the existence of such contradictions when he chose to develop his biography around the theme of the tragic transformation of an agrarian South into the New South and of an idealistic champion of the people before 1896 into a bitter and disillusioned fomenter of hate afterward. That transformation was strikingly illustrated by focusing abstract economic and political conditions onto a personal plane by writing a biography rather than a more general study. The personal change in Watson was also illustrated visually, through a series of photographs in the center section of the book (later reduced to twin frontispieces in subsequent editions). They showed a marked change in a mere six years: a slight, youthful-looking man of forty-eight with an intense but sensitive face gained a grim middle-aged countenance with sagging chin and swollen eyes. The first of the portraits was labeled: "At forty-eight: Historian and Presidential Candidate." The second: "At fifty-four: Anti-Catholic Crusader and State Boss." Woodward explained that the futility of Watson's early Populist battles had "made his life a personal tragedy," and that this was also the source of "the tragedy of a class and more especially a section."[20] Woodward did not, however, explain just why this frustration should have led to the sudden violent turn of Watson's racial rhetoric following the election of 1896, or why one so bellicose should have opposed U.S. military engagements. Nor, lacking the language of republicanism, was Woodward able to explain Watson's continuing ambivalence toward socialism or his odd—for an egalitarian Populist—but persistent defense of his lifelong hero, Napoleon.

For good or ill, however, Woodward's biography linked Watson's name to the Populist legacy, both by evoking the spirit of economic frustration and political unrest among the newly disfranchised farmers and by drawing attention to the destructive consequences of racism in American political culture. Woodward dualistically described a Watson whose brash and eloquent rhetoric forcefully challenged the exploitive structure of an emerging corporate economic and political system between 1880 and World War I, and a Watson whose anti-Semitic, antiblack, and anti-Catholic celebration of violence invited comparison to the Nazi *herrenvolk* Reich and its call for one people, one leader, one blood. In 1944, the sociologist Daniel Bell pointed out the cultural contradictions of Tom Watson's life as presented by Woodward and, with the horrors of Nazi atrocities freshly in mind, drew a direct comparison between Watson and Hitler.[21] Bell was conducting social research at Columbia University under the émigré sociologists of the Frankfurt school for a study of anti-Semitism in America. To him, Watson symbolized the risk that a fascist movement in the United States might grow out of the backward-looking, uneducated Populist *ressentiment* against progress. Bell's association of political violence with Populism and Tom Watson, an association that he compared forty years later to the dangers of Ronald Reagan's "new Populism," was echoed by Richard Hofstadter in his 1955 study, *The Age of Reform*.[22] Both men discerned an object lesson about the higher wisdom of the Founding Fathers in the shadow side of Watson's radical Populism. Both invested their dark fears of democracy into the particulars of Watson's evolution from a reformer to a demagogue at the turn of the century.

In 1976, however, an alternative view of Populism emerged with Lawrence Goodwyn's *The Democratic Promise: The Populist Moment in America*.[23] Goodwyn acknowledged his deep indebtedness to Woodward's scholarship. His version of Populism drew tangentially on Watson's early career, before his—and Populism's—national defeat, as Hofstadter's and Bell's interpretation had rested on the other Watson. This was the Populism of democratic social spaces, the last great third-party movement of democratic anticapitalism in the United States. In Goodwyn's account, American political virtue was defeated with Populism, rather than saved from it, in the national election of 1896. With the triumph of the business interests that controlled both national parties, Goodwyn explained, the reforms of the Progressive era ironically served to extinguish the light of democratic independence.

Populism, through self-defeating political compromises, was tragically co-opted by the economically centralizing elites who controlled corporate economic growth in America. "The people" became an empty phrase as the public acquiesced to its inability substantively to affect its own government. In accepting the inevitability of economic hierarchy, the social vision of equal citizenship at the heart of Populism's Jeffersonian agrarian message was surrendered. The result of this defeatism was that a popular resignation to hierarchies in personal relations inevitably filtered down from the hierarchies of the economic conventions of capitalism and socialism. Perversely, though based on antidemocratic economic theories that were themselves unworkable in their existing forms, the corporate capitalist forces and their socialist critics managed to define Populism as an irrational economic theory, staking the field of combat between themselves. Without an effective third-party alternative, capitalism and socialism were locked into a self-perpetuating choice of hierarchical models—a situation that assured the absolute triumph of corporate capitalism in Progressive-era American political culture.[24]

Clearly one of the legacies of Woodward's dualistic portrait of Watson was that it portrayed him one-dimensionally, as a man defined by politics. Critics and admirers of Woodward's biography might emphasize an earlier or later Tom Watson, or they might dismiss him as an undivided opportunist, but all would see him primarily as a political activist who turned to writing in disillusionment or while rebuilding his political fortunes after 1896. Yet, the Watson of 1880 or 1890 knew no such division between aesthetics and politics.

The combination of self-effacing idealism and self-interested ambition, which remained characteristic of Watson his whole life, was already evident in the first speech Watson composed, an address on Robert E. Lee's character delivered in 1871.[25] The fifteen-year-old orator evoked the expected pastoral sense of the loss of Lee, who had died some months before. "In ages to come, the patriot-scholar will turn from the decaying shrines of Roman and Grecian heroism," and turn to even more noble devotions at the "grass covered sepulcher of Lee," he intoned. Then, in the margin he scribbled, "I chose this subject because I knew it would engage the sympathies of the audience." Young Watson may have chosen a formulaic "lost cause" theme, but as an ambitious orator-to-be he confidently turned it to his own ends. At that time, he was reading and re-reading Byron and the other Romantic poets. He steeped himself in the conventions of Romantic literature and, like Byron before him, created himself as a poet-champion of political liberty out of identification with his themes. In this sense, there were never two Watsons—one, the idealistic young reformer before the ruinous election of 1896, and the other, the embittered demagogue of later years, as his biographer, C. Vann Woodward, portrayed him. The selfless reformer, the gloomy egotist, the man of deep feeling, the child of nature, and the satanic villain—all were aspects of one Byronic persona through which he defined himself in the world. True to that persona, Watson cultivated a self-identification as an aristocrat of suffering, born under a shadow of destiny that condemned him to a lonely heroic quest. His student notebooks and journals, to which he returned again and again in his later years, were filled with pastoral poetry and composition themes on the ruins of time, worthy ambition, the vanity of striving, and the power of literature—especially poetry—to transform lives.[26]

Thus, as he left Mercer University, this ardent if self-admittedly mediocre eighteen-year-old poet mused in his journal for November 7, 1874: "It was sad, very sad to think that I could never come back home again as a boy, that hereafter youth with its thoughtless pleasures would be but a recollection and a dream." The following year he composed an address on "The Fate of Reformers," in which he informed his audience that "every important discovery, every valuable and great invention, every political improvement has been almost a curse to its originator." The reformer confronts a herculean task because ordinary people have a fear of change. "They cling with filial devotion to the customs of their fathers, and the reformer who introduces a political, philosophical or religious change is met with bitter persecution." Watson assured his listeners that by the reformer he did not mean the man activated by selfish ambition, or the enthusiast who is led astray by the wild utopian dreams of an overheated imagination. "I mean," he said, "the spirit, pure and heaven[born?], which soars above the things of corruption and revels in the pure ether of truth and holiness." Such a reformer does not fear to leave the beaten path where principle is at stake, and "smiles in contempt at the bitter pangs of persecution." While the imposter may gain temporary fame, receive the plaudits of the rabble, and momentarily rise on the bloody wave of power, his ill-gotten garlands wither before the sun of the true reformer. For the mission of true reformers is an exalted one, "and as a race of men they have ever promulgated their opinions at the sacrifice of their earthly prospects and of their lives." Nevertheless, beginning like a small stream, the reformer's sacrifice slowly turns his movement into a torrent. Swept along "by the drama of history" he feels the "glorious thrill of ambition," and though he struggles in pain and without recognition, he finally knows success in his striving to benefit mankind.[27]

By 1880, a twenty-four-year-old Watson had tasted both the exhilaration of the reformer's mission and some of the suffering that his Romantic literary model of heroism had prepared him to face unflinchingly. After intense study and exploitation of his rhetorical talents as a successful lawyer, Watson made his first foray into politics as one of the young insurgents within the Democratic party. He made a name for himself by challenging the New Departure party machine, but soundly lost in supporting one Thomas M. Norwood, the independent candidate of weak reform. But his quixotic duel with the successful machine actually increased his confidence, for he had stood solidly behind moral principle, even at the price of personal advancement in terms that, he gambled, would assure his eventual vindication as a heroic leader of ordinary voters.

He did not hesitate to re-enter the political fray. After a shooting scrape with a competing lawyer and political rival named W. D. Tutt, the volatile Watson was elected a state representative in 1882 and was deeply engaged in insurgent Agrarian politics by the late 1880s. In August 1889, while in the full swing of a campaign that would take him to Congress in 1890, Watson announced that a new era was dawning in Georgia politics and the old order was passing away: "The masses are beginning to arouse themselves, reading for themselves, thinking for themselves. The great currents of thought quicken new impulses. At the bar of public opinion the people are pressing their demands and insisting they be heard." [28]

Watson began writing sketches of great Greek and Roman heroes in the *People's Party Paper,* which he edited in the early 1890s. The theme for the sketches, as for the paper, was the triumph of heroic virtue through adversity. Tom Watson knew that his political service as a Jeffersonian was the duty of a man of literary sensibility. He knew, too, from reading Gibbon, Macaulay, and Carlyle, that history was a literary art that should inspire as well as inform the public for whom it was written. Such sketches were placed side by side with similar messages drawn from contemporary events. For example, in an early number of the *Paper,* Watson described a lecture on the massacre of Armenian Christians by the Turks. As usual, Watson was equally interested in the speaker's dramatic ability—his effect upon the crowd—as in his message. Then a voice in the crowd asked, "Where is God?" As the speaker "sank into discreet silence," Watson's voice took up the challenge: "Left to *this* publican, the answer would be, he lives in the high aims and noble hearts, in all lives given to duty, in all work done for human rights and human happiness." God lives, he said, in the "upward tendency . . . that strikes the shackels from off the slave, which quenches the fire of persecution, which destroys the domination of priest and king, which lights the lamp of knowledge in the hut, as in the temple and palace," and "gives to each man the weapon of peace with which to fight for wife and child and fireside." God lives in the power of public opinion, Watson continued, which when aroused restrains tyranny, "as even now the angry remonstrance of Europe and America has checked the Turk in Armenia." God is present in Armenia or the Hocking Valley or in the nation's slums, in "the voice of human woe that awakens human help, for the cry of human anguish never yet was lost to the ear of the world." Watson promised his readers that there was a leaven at work in suffering "that shall permeate the whole loaf—the striving for Law which shall bring order out of chaos, and devotion to duty among the good of both Church and State that shall splendidly maintain against all assaults." That is where God is, he concluded, "*Where are You?*" [29]

Watson's rising career seemed to confirm his heroic destiny despite the shadow of poverty and a diminished family under which he had been born. Then, in the midst of this early success, Watson's three-year-old daughter Louise died suddenly. Watson wrote out his grief in the pages of his ever-present journal, sandwiched between newspaper clippings of his speeches. The journal entries, however, have the solipsistic air of an author's desire to capture an experience of loneliness and suffering for himself, as if it provided him with a heightened self-awareness, as it would for a Byronic hero. Watson affected the style of a pastoral elegy as he chose to linger over the hours just after her death.[30] He wrote of her touch, still warm upon the leaves and twigs she had gathered to decorate her hat, and of her footprints being the freshest to be seen by those who went to gather flowers for her funeral. The obsessive theme of this and subsequent entries was fading memory, along with his own heroic resolve to resist its decay. He rehearsed again and again the emptiness of his life without her presence, leaving space in his journal to muse on this subject ritually on each Christmas Eve.

He railed against the emptiness of ambition, asking, "What praise could ever be so sweet as one echo of her laughter? What monument ever could make me forget the little slab that covers her?" Riches, he said, would only "be embittered by the thought she will share them with us no more." Courage and duty must be met, but he asked, "Can duty keep still the dull throb of the old wound? Can courage always keep tears from the eyes?" Christmas henceforth will be "night of all nights the coldest," he wrote on Christmas Eve, 1889. In words that anticipated his intense turn to writing after 1896, Watson wrote, "Lock thy self, Oh student amid the books and let memory search with sighs, thro the ashes of the dead years to find if by chance an ember of the old glad life is there— Bend your ear to catch the tone of her voice growing fainter every day." Perhaps, he wrote in reaffirmation of ambition, courage, duty, and riches, through regeneration of her memory, light may come out of the gloom, "and purposes, purified—leading to achievements without stain may become the monument best holding her [remembrance?]." "Tell me what it all means: tell me whence you are whence you come and where you are bound: Tell me what life means and where ends the horror of pain and decay and death," he wrote on Christmas Eve, 1890. It was, he wrote, a night "for recollections, and regrets, and suffering."

As a politician, Watson was at this time experiencing what thirty years later he remembered as the most exhilarating period of his life.[31] Writing simultaneously as a bereaved father composing pastoral elegies to his deceased daughter on Christmas Eve (Watson returned to these same pages to write of his son's death in 1918), he appears as almost a self-parody of the Romantic identity. Every line expressed his destiny as a hero of sensibility. As Peter Thorslev defined this stance in *The Byronic Hero*, it meant balancing "the tension that results from the conflict of two contradictory drives, one toward total commitment, toward loss of self in a vision of absolutes, the other toward a skeptical and even aggressive assertion of self in a world which remains external and even alien." [32]

This Byronic tension, itself a variation on Machiavellianism, was evident to contemporary observers also, as Watson projected an image as a Prometheus-Satan or as a saintly man of feeling, by turns. In 1896, for example, a *New York Herald* reporter described him as a stranger to fear. The writer described him physically as lean and hungry-looking with a firm jaw, severe mouth, and dangerous eyes. Watson, the reporter continued, has "dark eyes that repel and attract." He is a man of sincerity, "tragically earnest in everything." Another reporter, this one from *The Progressive Farmer*, visited Watson just after the election of 1896 and found him playing his fiddle. A bright chord could fill him with hope, he said, and remind him of the vanity of pride. The reporter left, professing to be disconcerted over the question of how a man "with a butcher knife as principal political weapon, who is full of vitriol and intensely bitter and bitterly intense," could have a soft spot in his breast for such refinements as music. And, even Watson himself, in a prescient moment of self-reflection just two years before his death, commented to a reporter that the most important influences on his life were Napoleon and *Don Quixote*. [33]

Woodward was quite correct in recognizing a tension in Watson's personality and political actions upon which, though ultimately unsuccessful, he attempted to construct his interpretation of two Watsons and two Souths. (It should be noted, however, that he has more recently revised this interpretation using the phrase "Jekyll-and-Hyde," an allusion to Stevenson's novella of 1885, which carries Thorslev's Byronic tension within its plot.) Woodward was equally correct in focusing upon the eight-year period of intensified writing that followed upon the defeat of Populism as a time of profound change in Watson's life and values. For if Watson made no distinction between his life as a man of letters and as a political activist before 1896, afterwards he began to do so. To a reporter in 1904, he denied that he was either a statesman or a politician. He was a Southern man of letters, "who by a freak of fate has been carried into the political vortex and is being whirled whither he knows not." In another instance the same year, Watson refused to answer a reporter's questions about a political speech because he said he strictly divided his day and evening, the one for politics and the other for history.[34]

This suggests that the pattern of Watson's self-destructive personal history reveals not a dualism between an early and a later Watson but his own dawning personal recognition of the dualism at the heart of romantic republican values themselves. Though Watson remained loyal to those principles the rest of his life, his relation to them changed dramatically after 1896 because they became as sterile for him as they already were for Turner when the Populist insurgency began. Watson's satanic disillusionment—or Promethean defiance—after that date followed from his practical recognition that Populism, as a political movement, had been his last hope for expressing his own virtù while also restoring the virtue of the South and of the nation.

Something of the nature of Watson's Machiavellian moment may be gathered from a *New York Journal* article he preserved among his papers. It was written by James Creelman in 1900 and titled "Is Macaulay's Terrible Prophecy to be Fulfilled?"[35] The occasion of the article was the coming national election and the author's contention that the life of the republic was at stake in it. At such a time, he said, "it is well to recall a prophecy concerning the destruction of American institutions written by Lord Macaulay in 1857 to Henry S. Randel [*sic*], the biographer of Jefferson."

Macaulay wrote H. S. Randall that he did not have a high opinion of Jefferson and that he did not believe in majority rule. "I have long been convinced that institutions purely democratic must, sooner or later, destroy liberty or civilization or both," said Macaulay. Although Randall might have the mistaken notion that his country enjoys an exception from such evils, Macaulay warned, he himself saw it differently:

Either some Caesar or Napoleon will seize the reins of government with a strong hand or your Republic will be as fearfully plundered and laid waste by barbarians in the twentieth century as the Roman Empire was in the fifth, with this difference, that the Huns and Vandals who ravaged the Roman Empire, came from without, and that your Huns and Vandals will have been engendered within your own country by your own institutions.

Thinking this, of course, I cannot reckon Jefferson among the benefactors of mankind.

Watson had himself long used similar words to defend the order and values of the Jeffersonian tradition itself. The defeat of Watson's political party and platform in 1896 and its hopeless division in 1900 confirmed the practical possibility that Macaulay's judgment might be right. If so, it called the whole fabric of Watson's life into question, for it suggested that he had invested his life and hopes in a misdirected, even destructive, crusade for justice. Such a possibility could not have been easily discounted by Watson, because aside from present conditions, he had long been attracted to Macaulay as a great historian. In his school days at Thomson, Georgia, Watson's mentor and model, the Reverend E. A. Steed, had recommended Macaulay to the adolescent student. Watson recorded in his journal that he liked Macaulay's history better than any other that he read. He was particularly drawn to the persuasiveness of his rhetoric and his concern for style. Watson was, however, distressed to read Macaulay's critical attitude toward Byron, denigrating his dramatic genius. The aspiring young poet-historian who had already taken Byron as his ideal protested that Macaulay had shown Byron too little mercy for his faults.[36]

A more direct portrait of Watson's perspective during this period may be seen in a sketch he wrote, titled "In the Mountains," in which he invoked the poetic sensibilities of Keats to bring aesthetic meaning out of a lifeless historical landscape.[37] Lost in pastoral reveries about Indian chiefs who had passed by the place he was standing on their way to Peter Jefferson's for advice, he then imagined the pathetic pleas for justice young Thomas Jefferson must have heard and how the last Indian warrior must have "stood and gazed in despair over the land he had lost."

Watson said that he saw the ruins of an ancient tavern and amid them ancient bricks, which while still freshly made had received the imprints of a deer's hooves and the paws of pursuing hounds. Here they are, he continued, "curious mementos" for "another Keats" to gaze upon. The "foot prints of the deer, which is now a shade; the pack which chased it, also a shade; and the hunter who followed a pack, likewise a shade—all gone, save this tablet, which tells of the lust of pursuit and the glory of flight—could even match the almost matchless 'Ode to a Grecian Urn.'"

Watson turned to look at the ridge on the horizon and saw seven semicircles of earth thrown up at wide intervals. These were remnants of the Civil War, standing on the horizon of Jefferson's gateway to the West. "When the pioneers passed through the gap going from Virginia, no redoubts confronted them; only the Indian with his bow or rifle." But who were the devastating invaders who forced their way back from the West through the Gap, only to be met with gun and battery? "They were the children of those who had gone from the South to the winning of the

West; and from the conquered West, they came through the Gap which their fathers had worn deep in the soil—Come to conquer and devastate the South."

Clearly, at this moment in his life, Watson could not turn defeat into a premonition of victory to come. "He will not reach the heights," he concluded, but he could still "dream dreams and see visions." Out of this pressing need to restore a balance between his aesthetic sensibilities and the political ambitions upon which his heroic identity rested, Watson turned intently to writing history in the dying years of the nineteenth century, a time when the country was once again at war and political virtù and virtue were fatally divided.

Watson first directed his literary efforts to France because he believed it was a laboratory for the study of politics in general. In the first volume of his *Story of France*, published in 1898, he described the country as "the epic poem of modern history." Like the American South Watson portrayed in *Bethany: A Story of the Old South*, a fictional treatment of his own family that he produced a few years later, France was the scene of betrayed opportunity and lost initiative. The history of France, like that of the South, was a history of a tragic disaster.[38] Watson followed the trajectory of modern French politics as monarchical absolutism gave way to constitutionalism, which, in turn, yielded to radical communism and finally to military adventurism by 1896.

Watson began his study of France by implying a parallel between Southerners before the Civil War and the Celts and other tribes of ancient France. In Watson's story, these tribal people were independent, open, and hospitable; they worshiped neither material goods nor sexuality. He admired their decentralized and democratic tribal structure as well as their bravery, yet he also saw these virtues to be at cross-purposes with their virtù as a people. Lacking money, they could not develop a true civilization. As tribes, they could not develop national greatness. The inability of the Celts to unite made them vulnerable to "the despotic tyranny of the priests and the selfish brutal policy of the chieftains" which kept them from developing a splendid civilization of their own. It also led to oppression by the Romans. Although Watson considered Julius Caesar a ruthless agent for centralized Roman economic greed, he admired his virtù and his ability to defeat the Gauls, who were better warriors than his Roman troops.[39]

The second volume of *The Story of France*, published in 1900, concentrated on the French Revolution. Watson claimed to have had a freer hand to express his own interests in this book and he focused on the problem of personality as a dynamically creative and destructive political force.[40] Virtù was revealed, at least to Watson's satisfaction, as the essential form of all political power: "There were critical periods when the whole movement hung as by a hair and it seemed to be a mere toss up as to which way it would go. At such times, audacity wins; the power of initiative conquers. This audacity the court never had, the power of initiative the Revolution always had, and thus it won."[41] Great individuals may exhibit such change-producing virtù, according to Watson, but the average citizen is a slave to the system in power. "The year 1791 gave every indication from the beginning of being one of struggle politically, for the three principles of government stood face to face, each saying to the other two: 'I am better than you and stronger.'" In the year 1795, he wrote, "The democratic spirit is slain in the house of its friends." The republic was betrayed by those who praised it in the loudest voices. The people sank into monarchical and priestly slavery.[42]

Chaos reigned in the aftermath of the betrayed revolution until Napoleon, showing greater ambition than his rivals, took over the power of the nation. In *The Story of France,* Watson expressed ambivalence about Napoleon. He improved trade, removed the burdens of taxation, and restored the currency, but "the great commoner," as Watson called him, made the mistake of grasping for kingly power through aristocratic pretensions. It was Napoleon, military adventurer and man of ambition, who rescued the revolution and destroyed it at the same time. Napoleon battled against the despotic order of kings and special privilege, but he also made alliances with the despotic Roman Church and with aristocrats. Those alliances served to compromise all that he had accomplished. Watson felt that the compromises had failed to provide security; they only weakened the nation internally and made Napoleon more vulnerable when the kings combined to destroy him. Thus, though Watson revered Napoleon, he also saw these expressions of virtù as self-defeating of the nation's virtue.[43] By the time his biography *Napoleon* was published in 1902, however, Watson had largely overcome this ambivalence. He praised Napoleon's ambitions and accomplishments as he would soon praise Andrew Jackson's, and he attributed failures like the reestablishment of church power to Napoleon's personal ambition. That form of virtù led Napoleon away from the road of public service, a theme Watson repeated in his study of Jackson.[44]

Watson's aristocratic grandfather had sparked his lifelong hero-worship of Napoleon by giving him, as a child, John S. C. Abbot's biography of the leader. Watson once said that he knew Napoleon even before Washington.[45] It may be in this context that Watson's initial post-1896 writings, which centered on Napoleon and were written for young people, embodied the threat to memory and meaning that life's vicissitudes had brought with them. It may also be significant that in later years Watson dismissed Abbot's life of Napoleon as a "Romance" with "no sense of Napoleon's real character"; he thought his own journalistic style was superior to both such romances and academic history "written for professors."[46] Here, Watson would seem to have regained a measure of balance through a literary identification with realism, while having successfully preserved the sanctity of personal and republican memory. It was a doubtful victory, however, for this attachment to memory limited him to a pastoral formula; he railed against not being sufficiently recognized for his soulful effort and felt satisfaction that he had succeeded in resurrecting nearly forgotten facts of history from the kind of books, as he put it, that one sometimes finds on the shelves of old farmhouses.[47]

A confessional editorial Watson wrote in 1905 offers some insight into the inner struggle Watson had undergone in his effort to find a new balance between virtù and virtue as a Byronic hero and as a Jeffersonian republican.[48] It hints that his escape from his ambivalence concerning Napoleon's virtù and virtue was won at a price of permanently separating the two within himself and, perhaps even more important, that he knew it to be the price.

After recovering from a life-threatening illness, Watson wrote morosely of his failure to achieve a personal sense of accomplishment and to provide dynamic leadership for a successful regeneration of national political life. Watson wrote that he was surprised to find himself without a will to live. With Romantic *Weltschmerz*, which Thorslev associates with heroic egoism and the failure of a quest,[49] Watson wrote of being aware in his delirium of a cherished photograph of himself that stood in his sickroom, "a souvenir of the days when the world was young to you and none of the illusions were lost." He went on to recount how he had lost touch with his children in "study, labor, anxiety, ambition." His political ideals had been stolen and later denounced, and "the dream of your boyhood was at an end." He had quit the contest "a disgraced and ruined man": "Then you shut the world out of your life, buried yourself to all but the very few, called around you the serene companionship of books, breathed the atmosphere of the past, entered into the lives, the hope, the struggles, the sufferings of the sublime reformers to whose courage and sacrifice we owe all that makes the world tolerable—all that gives us liberty of person, of conscience, of speech."[50]

Watson went on to say that every word was written in inspiration and through tears. "Always, always, your soul was in the pen and you wrote no word that did not come from the heart." Again, he felt his efforts went unrecognized (though he did receive several positive reviews in national periodicals). Quite unself-consciously, he said that he then turned to making money, the only activity at which he was successful. With "disgusting facility you could heap thousand upon thousand." "Were you glad?" he asked himself, in finding that he had survived his illness. "Not particularly so." A reason for living was not as clear as it used to be. "The horse goes back to the treadmill and the dull march around the circle goes on as before."

The striking thing about this *Watson Magazine* editorial of 1905 is that Watson's assessment of his life's meaning is presented in terms of personal and political virtù in tension with the virtues he sought to defend. The ambition of his life was to "work manfully" to escape poverty and to fulfill his desire "to be a Tribune of the People, leading them upward and onward, cheered by their applause, made happy by the blessings of those whom your life-work elevated." At the same time, he regretted losing touch with his children in his ambitious efforts to reach his goals, and he expressed a kind of prideful self-disgust for being capable of making great sums of money with no effort. Making money was a kind of virtù, but Watson found it inferior to being "useful, a power for good" and a "leader of public opinion."

The dark shadow that fell over Watson's virtù, leaving him "disgraced and ruined" politically and personally, was that Classical nemesis, Fortune. "Perhaps you had come to realize," he wrote, "that you were one of those men with whom Fortune deals grudgingly, one of those whom Hope deceives . . . one of those who *always* has the wind and wave against him, and who never by any sort of chance finds himself in league with Luck."[51]

Since Watson's republican political culture, like Machiavelli's, was rigidly patriarchal in form and feminine in aspiration, his language, whether political or aesthetic, public or private, was riddled with the internal contradictions of virtù and virtue. Much of Watson's success as well as much of his personal anguish may be attributed to the conscious and unconscious skill with which he manipulated those contradictions for his public and perhaps also for himself.

Virtù to Watson, as to Machiavelli, was a masculine dynamic, always

seeking to shape Fortune to its own ends. Most important for understanding the common formula shared by Watson and Machiavelli, their
sexual metaphors of virtù were violently pornographic in form while remaining chaste in ends. This made their sexual imagery ambiguous and
their politics flexible. For example, Machiavelli used the language of
brutal sexuality as he advised the prince that since Fortune is a woman,
she must be beaten.[52] Because young men are "less circumspect and
more violent" with her, they are more frequently successful than are the
overcautious. But Machiavelli used the language of gentle harmony and
concord in relating to Fortune as well. Indeed, the language of virtù and
its relation to Fortune was deeply contradictory about gender rather than
simply antagonistic. To win Fortune, one must "importune and beat
her." Like a woman, Italy was "beaten, despoiled, lacerated," because
that fickle woman, Fortune, abandoned Cesare Borgia in his moment of
weakness, after smiling upon him as he ruthlessly trampled upon virtue
in his pursuit of masculine power. The contradiction was inherent in the
language of political striving because Machiavelli described such action
as entirely masculine. But the ideals for which the man of true manliness
was asked to strive, as well as the qualities of virtue placed on a pedestal
for him to admire, were all presented as feminine principles. In Watson,
too, virtù as ambition was unambiguously masculine but the alternative
ends of personal power or public service were not. In Watson's editorial,
it was Fortune who had betrayed him. But that other woman, his wife,
understood and continued to stand by him in his distress.

Watson's single-minded struggle to defend Jeffersonian republican
conventions by balancing virtù and virtue was enormously difficult to
maintain, given the scale of power invested in the corporations, government, and military, as well as the changing conventions of gender relations inherent in a culture moving toward a self-defined consumer's democracy. But in the first decade of the twentieth century, Watson's lonely
personal struggles could draw upon the vitality of a palpable sense of
public urgency. Despite the defeat of 1896, there remained a heady scent
of reform filling the polluted air of New York City and the mortgaged
cotton fields of the South, precisely because of the pervasive cultural turmoil in Anglo-Protestant republican America. Watson remained popular
in the South, but he was also lionized in New York City, the boiling center of American greed and reform. There, on the basis of his literary
successes as much as for his muckraking spirit, Watson was asked by
W. D. Mann, the promoter of *Smart Set*, to edit his own magazine. *Tom*

Watson's Magazine appeared in March 1905. Watson quickly became alienated from the business practices of his publisher and returned to the South, where he published *Watson's Jeffersonian Magazine* beginning in 1907. Watson's short-lived New York magazine contained literature and political commentary. The new Realist literature of Theodore Dreiser, Edgar Lee Masters, and Maxim Gorky, plus sentimental poems and romances, filled the space remaining after Watson's long collection of muckraking editorials, which took up a full quarter of each issue.[53]

The single theme that permeated these early editorials was the conundrum of virtù and virtue. Nearly every editorial described the oppression of weakness by power. Law, Watson observed, is considered to be for the weak, while the strong have no need to obey it because the corporate mentality knows only greed without limit. The railroads find it cheaper to pay damages for loss of life than to pay for safety measures for avoiding accidents. When a child-labor law is nearly passed to "liberate the children from the slavery which is grinding up their tender limbs into dividends," a misguided or corrupt Southerner rushes to the legislature to quash the bill.[54]

Yet this rehearsal of the reformist's plea for defense of the weak from the oppression of power was unmistakably Machiavellian in its implication. Watson's editorials ambiguously inverted the relation of power to value, and he consequently appealed to sexual metaphors for the purpose of defending a problematic social order—that is, one he wished to uphold and challenge at the same time. Therefore, despite his liberal-sounding themes of trust-busting, regulation for public safety, and equal treatment under the law, these editorials from 1905 actually anticipated his future crusade against Catholics, Jews, and blacks. As such, they show that Watson accurately read the true character of Progressive reform and that he may have hoped to play Machiavelli to the prince of Hearst, or Bryan, or Roosevelt on a national scale, as he later settled for being boss of Georgia's Democratic machine when faced with Wilson's national victory. Watson was a Jeffersonian of the heart, however, and the necessity of hoping to play the fox to men of lesser political integrity must have galled him—especially following his brief reunion with the heroic memories evoked before the 1904 presidential election when the mid-roaders (as the antifusionist wing of the Populist party was known) briefly appeared to have taken back control of the remnants of the Populist party. Watson energetically answered their call. He stumped all over the country for the hopeless crusade, in the course of which he made his first speech for disfranchisement of blacks so that they could not be used against the beleaguered remnants of Populist reform in the shifting power struggle of Georgia politics.[55]

This, then is the context in which Watson's fiery reform writings of the following year must be read. In one representative 1905 editorial, Watson exposed the brutality of the Pittsburgh Steel Trust in razing the humble home of a poor widow. The trust simply took the dwelling, he wrote, "as the lion takes his prey, as Tammany Hall took New York, took it as the ravisher takes the helpless victim of his lust." Watson went on to say that "a brute who violates an unwilling woman and is lynched for it, commits in morals precisely the same kind of wrong upon the victim which these mighty men of the Steel Trust committed upon the Widow Lot." Then, in equally Machiavellian style, he offered a conservative defense of the patriarchal values he had just called into question. He pointed out that the deceased husband of the Widow Lot had been a laborer, and yet, who was it who did the heartless deed? The outrage was perpetrated by a thousand union laborers who were supposed to be organized in solidarity with the victim![56]

In another instance, Watson exposed the brutal enforced labor of a group of Martinique Negroes. They had been recruited to labor on the Panama Canal, but when they saw the inhuman work conditions, visible from the ship, they refused to disembark. Then, with the unlawful assistance of the U.S. government customs officer, the Negroes, "bleeding from ugly wounds and in a pitiable condition," were driven to shore. And yet, said Watson, these were the very people for whom the United States, "in a burst of spectacular philanthropy, sent charitable gifts" only a few years earlier following a natural disaster. But, Watson wanted to know, where was Booker T. Washington? Where were the northern philanthropists? Why did they not cry out as they would have done had the deed been done in the South by Southerners?[57]

In another editorial, still from 1905, Watson anticipated the New Criticism with a review of Upton Sinclair's muckraking novel, *The Jungle*. Watson judged it "a great book; possibly the greatest book of its kind that any American has written." But Watson, though a defender of the socialists at the time, rejected the message that Sinclair had overlaid upon the story: "Did you harrow up my soul with all those pathetic details," remonstrated Watson, "just to make a socialist out of me?" Could not Sinclair have allowed the novel to do its own artistic work without "a treatise on socialism tacked on the end?" he asked. Why did not Sinclair, like Stowe, let the plight of the victim be given the place of "rousing the passion of men against the system"? [58]

Over the next two or three years, editorials in *Watson's Jeffersonian Magazine* largely maintained this balanced division between political editorializing and literature. Watson wrote twice, at length, about the neglect of southern writers, and of literary genius that was lost to the world because of the indifference of southern readers and northern critics.[59] He could offer genuine praise for one poem of Paul Dunbar's, despite a prejudice that blacks were generally outside the pale of the Anglo-American poetic tradition. Byron remained his ideal poet and self, for when ridiculed by the critics, Byron did not turn his face to the wall to die as Keats was said to have done (Watson hoped the story was untrue for, appreciating Keats's work, it was painful to think the man was so structurally weak). Rather, identifying himself as a less aesthetic "*modern*" than Keats, he preferred "My Lord Byron," who "gulps down a few bumpers of wine, seizes his grey goose quill, and goes after the whole tribe of English Bards and Scotch Reviewers." Before that event, "Byron hadn't written a worthwhile line, *The lash of the reviewer roused him.*" [60] At the same time, Watson began to write that the fame of the artist, like that of the political reformer, was a roll of the dice, the work of Fortune. Great work upon which the author may have expended his or her most gifted efforts might be ignored while a trifle, thrown off in a moment, might make him or her famous. Talent, especially if it came from the South, might be ignored, while a talent no greater but coming from New England would be immortalized. What was true of poets was equally true of orators. William Jennings Bryan was a less gifted orator than a half-dozen speakers Watson had known, "but by the caprice of Fame the crown has been placed upon his head, and he will wear it to the end." In Promethean rage against an intractable Romantic fate, which an equally Romantic ideal of his heroic self was powerless to change, unable to inspire public acclaim sufficient to his noble ends while lesser men prospered, Watson began both to distance himself from his aesthetic ideal and to plunge helplessly into it. In November 1908, in an editorial titled "The Oddities of the Great," Watson quoted Lamartine that "genius bears within itself a principle of destruction, of death, of madness." He suggested that the poets—perhaps even Byron, along with the rest— were less than whole men. He poked fun at "our hero-worshipping souls" for overlooking their weaknesses, and not admitting that poets tend to become unbalanced and "lack mental symmetry and poise." Yet as he wrote such phrases from his mansion at Hickory Hills, he was infamous in the neighborhood for falling into insane rages over the sound of a farm bell, or a cow's lowing, or a neighbor-child's piano banging—all patterned after stories he had read as a youth about Carlyle.[61]

Could the episodes of violent and unbalanced behavior for which Watson became increasingly notorious over the last several years of his life have been a way to live out an identity in which he could no longer find hope? To say that Watson was always an actor, playing the role of a Romantic hero, does not mean that he was pretending; it merely suggests that the character roles he had left for himself were narrowed once he lost hope of balancing virtù and virtue. Indeed, given the Romantic conventions out of which Watson had created himself, Prometheus or Satan were the only roles he could still play.

Watson's descent into hopelessness did not occur overnight or because of any one event or set of events. It accumulated out of the failure of his expectations built upon his faith in Jeffersonian republican values, but those values themselves defined the terms upon which his inevitable failure would come. Trapped within the conventions of Machiavellian republicanism, *precisely because he believed in them,* Watson became increasingly obsessive as time went on, but he remained within the Machiavellian conventions of Anglo-Protestantism. The fear that virtue was finite and subject to the combinations of the apparently unlimited virtù of corporate greed led Watson to believe that aesthetics and religion were being co-opted by the forces of centralized power. Therefore, in 1909 he began to publish warnings against the Catholic Church and Protestant foreign missions. If the first of these offered a threat of superstition and primitive virtù, controlled by a secretive hierarchy, the second represented the foolish overextension of limited Protestant virtue into an unlimited eastern space, without a regenerative frontier line, and ruled by Fortune, not Providence. Taking both together, virtue was certain to diminish in America, while the degrading virtù of Catholic primitivism would fill the vacuum.[62]

Watson had long harbored fears of Catholic tyranny. Though it was only from 1908 that he began earnestly warning that the Catholic population was about to overwhelm Protestantism, he had saved some articles on that theme from the 1870s.[63] Anti-Catholicism was, of course, a longstanding prejudice associated with republican ideology, but it seemed not to worry Watson much personally before the breakdown of his ability to balance aesthetics and politics as virtue and virtù. At that point, with increasing bellicosity, he pressed the traditional Protestant crusade against the pornography of the Catholic Church to fanatic extremes. "Chemise-wearing bachelors" who were "foot kissers," Watson alleged, raped Catholic women. The priest, who "is often a powerfully sexed man," was alone with beautiful women in the confessional. These women, he explained, believe the priest can forgive their carnal sin and have been taught to believe that a woman obeys God by obeying priests. The contradictions of virtù and virtue were given even greater tension in Watson's litany because Catholics were seen to "worship a woman" and because priests were characterized as effeminate in dress and full of masculine power at the same time.[64]

The Protestant foreign mission movement, on the other hand, seemed to Watson to be a capitulation to the forces that were weakening American democracy at home and supporting the growth of corporate power abroad. The missionaries were spending millions of American dollars, ostensibly to spread the gospel. But in reality they were merely capturing foreign markets for business. These new markets, in turn, made it possible for corporate business interests to tighten the protective system against American consumers. The foreigners themselves were being corrupted because conversion to Christianity was the price for the benefits of the missionaries' aid. As in the case of northern philanthropy to Martinique Negroes or, for that matter, to American Southerners, Watson felt that the real aim was not Christian charity but economic and political exploitation.[65]

However, Watson expressed his fear of the increasing imbalance between virtù and virtue equally in his concern over the exodus of idealistic young American men and women to help people in other lands while American women and children were being destroyed in American factories. He was incensed that white missionary women went to China to save rich Chinese women from the deformation of bound feet while their American sisters ruined their health by binding their bodies in fashionable corsets.[66]

While American Protestants squandered their virtue and virtù abroad, the dynamic power of corporate corruption escaped from the limits imposed on it by Protestant moral values and democratic political ideals. This trend was intensified because the Roman Catholic Church, which represented autocratic values and a retreat from modern progress into pagan tradition, was brought from the outside world into America by cheap immigrant labor. In this struggle between innovation and tradition, the terms of inversion could not be made into a new balance that might provide hope for an optimistic Anglo-American future. Progressive corporate economics and regressive Catholic religion together subverted any escape through inversion within the *republican* conventions to which Watson continued to look for deliverance.

Similarly, the "lecherous Jew" Leo Frank represented the corruption of southern innocence by the centralized virtù of the corporations, as well as another form of the fatal inversion of the Machiavellian balance of innovative violence and tradition as law.[67] In Watson's view, the big money power of the North, in the person of the factory manager Frank, raped young southern girlhood, in the person of Mary Phagan. According to Watson's rhetoric, she had been abused economically in Frank's northern-owned factory before being murdered in sexual exploitation. Following the commutation of Frank's sentence in 1915, Watson wrote in a display of rhetorical heat, "Our grand old empire has been raped, we have been violated, and we are ashamed." In effect, he then called for the virtù of the people to be established by lynching Frank so that "the next Jew who dares what Frank did is going to get exactly the same thing we give to Negro rapists." Home rule and the defense of womanhood were wedded in this diatribe; the masculine threat of Frank's virtù to the feminine values of the South required southern virtù to rise up in masculine wrath against him.[68]

Fourteen years earlier, however, Watson had defended a Jewish shopkeeper who had accidentally killed another man in self-defense. At that time, he had appealed to the jury to recognize the virtue behind "the godly tears flowing from a morally incorruptible Jew possessed by his people's love of life." Watson rested his case successfully with the reminder that the Jews were virtuous because they were the recipients of the Law, the descendants of Moses, David, and the prophets. For this reason, he concluded to the jury, "No Jew can murder."[69]

If the failure to find a balance between virtù and virtue brought Watson from a defender to a persecutor of a Jewish defendant on trial for murder, it resulted from his consistent defense of republican values in each case. Similarly, if Watson appeared to eschew sectionalism and reject racism before 1896, it was for reasons that were entirely consistent with his later reputation as a sectionalist and race-baiter. Watson's campaign literature and his famous *Arena* article of 1891, in which he laid out his Populist principles for a national audience, were really straightforward calls for home rule by white southern men.[70] For Watson in

1891, black freedom was a political reality that needed to be addressed. It was a simple fact of the post–Civil War nation. If the ex-slaves had been fewer in number, "the Anglo-Saxon would do as he pleases, right or wrong the weaker would go under." But, wrote Watson, when blacks number more than eight million and are intermingled in the society, they must be considered as a part of a political solution.

For Watson, the Negro presented the problem of competing virtù between the races. He saw no evidence for the belief that black racial virtù was diminishing and that blacks would disappear in a hundred years, as many contemporary observers of the "racial problem" argued. Watson's primary concern, however, was not biological purity, but civic virtue. He professed a lack of concern about declining numbers of white births; he poked fun at Theodore Roosevelt's fears of race suicide and his exhortation of white women to breed more children. Nor was Watson particularly bothered by race mixing, which he felt was probably decreasing.[71] He feared not a black threat, per se, but the role blacks might play in the struggle between antagonistic white aspirations. Watson believed the drive for self-preservation was an elemental animal passion. Consequently, should southern blacks and whites find themselves at cross-purposes, he foresaw "results which the imagination shrinks from contemplating." A horrible future could be averted only by "an honest attempt at solution." To Watson, this meant a new political alliance that could break the deadlock of the old political forms. The races could never get along until both sides agreed to leave the old parties and cast their lot in a common movement against corporate corruption and for republican virtue.[72]

In Watson's view, black and white interests were compatible and even mutually dependent, but the dominance of a white South was not questioned. Only in the southern white agrarian response to the dual evils of expanding modern capitalism and the "lower" race's lack of initiative could virtù and virtue be balanced and create the conditions for universal political and economic harmony for all races. The same logic applied to regions. Watson's rejection of sectionalism (in his *Arena* article and in *The People's Party Paper* before 1896) was as compatible with his goal of home rule as his call for black cooperation was compatible with white supremacy. Watson believed a national alliance would bring the "money power" to heel and return the nation to the values of Jefferson's southern vision. In his rhetoric of antisectionalism and black/white cooperation, Watson argued from the perspective of a Jeffersonian quarrel with Hamilton's antidemocratic industrialism and not from that of a racial or sectional liberal. Watson argued, like Jefferson, that the South did not initiate slavery, but inherited it from corrupt British commercialism. The South did not free the slaves and unleash the disruptive conditions of political equality. Instead, he said, the South had been victimized by these acts. That victimization, however, was not attributable only to the greed of the English kings and northern corporations; it was a catastrophe visited upon the South in part by other Southerners who exploited the race issue to gain selfish political advantage. The corporation and the black man were linked in Watson's mind because northern Republicans had used black equality to control southern political and economic life. But just as important, white southern Democrats had used an appeal to the "solid South" as a means of exploiting all the southern people, white and black, in northern capitalistic terms.[73]

In his 1904 novel *Bethany* Watson depicted antebellum white Southerners aimlessly squandering their own virtues in drinking, knife fights, and political squabbling.[74] Harmony reigned only in the enclosed plantation world, separated from the divisive virtù of other whites. He portrayed blacks as peaceful and emasculated. Because they were under control, relations between the races were harmonious. Far from celebrating a plantation labor system based on the Protestant work ethic, Watson celebrated his grandfather's plantation as an island of balanced calm in a sea of irrational particulars, a republican utopia in which virtù and virtue could still remain in balance: "It seems to me there was neither feverish haste upon it nor vagrant leisure, fretful exaction nor slipshod looseness, miserly gripping nor spendthrift waste. Everything was systematic. A man of settled thrifty habits, my grandfather had drilled his slaves to his orderly methods and thus the old routine went on from year to year."[75]

Watson described his grandfather, who died when he was only nine, as a dignified and self-contained man in whom virtù and virtue existed in complete balance. Yet this grandfather, who had introduced Watson to Napoleon and had become entwined with the French conqueror in Watson's mind, was broken by the Civil War. This man of inner strength had been destroyed by a conflict that was undertaken to defend a tranquil way of life. For Watson the betrayal of Populism by white Northerners and Southerners repeated the tragedy of the Civil War, but on a more advanced scale of political corruption. In this new world, the "Negro question" appeared to reflect the advancing degeneration of political vir-tuc in a society dominated by corporations. Neither slavery nor Reconstruction, Watson said, had made blacks a threat to southern life. "I knew the Negro and found him very, very human—sometimes good, sometimes bad, sometimes indifferent," he wrote in 1907. Even in Reconstruction days, blacks had not impressed him "as a storm cloud hanging over the South." Blacks were swept out of political power with the end of carpetbag rule and would have remained politically neutralized had not white Southerners themselves called them back into the political arena. The result of this cynical grab for power was that it gave "blacks a better political position than the carpetbag emissaries of Thad Stevens had ever been able to give them." [76]

Beginning with the hopeless Populist campaign of 1904, Watson perceived a worsening crisis in the southern balance of power, which in turn rested on the greater failure, nationally, of 1896. After 1904 he perceived that events had turned blacks into a threat to preserving what remnant of southern virtue remained. But removing blacks from the political equation, as he acknowledged in the *Arena* article of 1891, was an act fraught with dilemmas of its own: "If the South proclaims that the Negro shall not vote, and at the same time lavishes her millions in educating him, will she not be pouring out her treasure, wrung from her white tax-payers, to increase the number of the negroes to whom the denial of the franchise is an intolerable wrong?" he asked. The better educated blacks become, Watson charged, the more they will desire the political privileges denied them. All thoughtful men must know this, said Watson, "and yet the South is developing two radically antagonistic policies: she is doing all she can to elevate the negro to the height where he will be wretched without the ballot, and at the same time she is throwing up barriers to keep him away from the polls!" [77]

Colleges built for educating blacks, said Watson, were "masked batteries which will open upon your Constitution—inevitably." The result could only be bitter antagonism and discord between the races. On the other hand, the black masses, ignorant and incapable of cultural development, growing poorer and less healthy, also posed a threat. According to Watson, blacks had never been capable of producing a civilization. When left to themselves, as in Santo Domingo and Haiti, they had forgotten the values of white civilization and returned to barbarism. But white civilization pushes most blacks upward: "In America *he* swells the ranks of civilization's advancing army, and he has to go forward." [78]

In his widely quoted editorial from 1905, Watson called on Booker T.

Washington to recognize "that the only portion of his race which has ever made any development is that which has the vast advantage of being sustained, encouraged, taught, led and *coerced* by the whites among whom they lived."[79] On this basis, Watson said, the South was vindicated for saving blacks from their own natural barbarism; yet, by this same logic, the South had created the conditions for the emergence of black leaders who were demanding social equality and political power. Watson was conscious of this contradiction inherent in southern race relations. He rejected both colonization and enfranchisement for educated blacks as equally unworkable escapes from this dilemma. Concerning the latter, he wrote, "They will not thank you for what you conceded, and will hate you for what you withhold," and "you would simply be putting a deadly weapon into their hands, after having given them a provocation which they could never forgive." The South had gone too far to take a step backward. Its safety in the future depended on making good the position it had taken. "Let us say frankly," he wrote, "that self preservation requires that we disarm the black of his ballot, and close the door of office to him, as far as lies within our power."[80]

Watson's last stand in defense of southern virtue was far from a triumphant announcement of white supremacy on the march. Instead, Watson offered a limited possibility for restoring the political and social balance of the Old South of memory, in the light of the debacle of 1896. Blacks, he said, should be forced into a "condition of recognized peasantry." How would the aspirations of black Americans be contained? Watson's answer reflected the defeat of his heroic hopes for national political regeneration and his acquiescence to a sectional position as the limit of southern potential: "The negro politician would migrate; the over-educated negro gravitate to the other side of the Mason and Dixon's line; the more ambitious and restless of the race would leave the South; and their places would be taken by desirable white immigrants . . . and thus the negro would cease to be a peril."[81]

In many ways, socialism presented a combination of what Watson saw as these expanding conditions of corruption. At first he was sympathetic towards socialist criticism of the evils of capitalism and assumed that those abuses were the source of socialism's appeal. But as a republican who associated private property with personality and both with political virtue, he ultimately was driven to oppose socialism for the same reason he opposed the corporations. The substance of his opposition was distilled in the following comment: "Communism, at least has consistency but socialism is a hopeless confusion between the two systems."

It wars upon individualism while rejecting communism, endeavors to obliterate the distinction between that which is public and that which is private, confuses the relation of man to state, ignores the profound human instinct and craving for self and for individual ownership, strikes at the mainspring of human action, saps the foundation of the home and threatens the integrity of the marital tie.[82]

Watson was particularly scandalized by the threat to the marriage bond, because by linking property to personality in republican terms, he also linked marriage to property. Arguing from a republican point of view, he denied the socialist contention that this association led to the exploitation of women. On the contrary, he argued, by defining property in terms divorced from personality both socialism and capitalism justified systems of abstract wealth, which made exploitation inevitable.[83]

Socialism, however, was an even greater threat to the home, the embodiment of personality and property, than was capitalism. For according to Watson's republican logic, socialism's confused attack on property and partial denial of personality would require women, like property, to become common to all—including the lowest members of the community.[84] That meant, to Watson, that black men would get white wives. Because he believed that competition and the savage protection of selfish ends are basic to human nature, and that the greatest virtù always dominates, socialism would leave the virtuous producer just as vulnerable to organized rapacious expropriation as would corporate capitalism. But in addition it would leave him vulnerable to combinations of men with neither virtù nor virtue—that is, an underclass of parasites who would demand equal shares of the community's produce. Socialism became an even greater threat when the masses of unachieving parasites who would claim the producer's property in the form of goods and daughters seemed certain to be Negroes. And the dilemma would only be compounded, as Watson understood it, if they were not.

Unlimited sexual freedom, like unlimited greed for money, equally threatened to create a frenzy of unsatisfied lustful striving that would destroy civic values. The twin poles of socialism and capitalism left republican conventions of universals and particulars hopelessly confused, leading Watson ever deeper into the contradictions of power and value. Just as Andrew Carnegie's particular extra share of the universal wealth of the land was seen as theft from the available shares for his work force, socialist collectivism appeared to be a universal that threatened the liberty of the individual producer.[85]

In heroically confronting the dilemmas of race, religion, and economics after 1895, Watson found himself trapped within a whole series of self-augmenting and interrelated double binds. For example, his belief that blacks were tools of political corruption exacerbated his fear of Catholic, socialist, and corporate tyranny, but required him to defend two black draft resisters against Wilson's tyrannical usurpation of the right of conscription in 1917. Like Jefferson, Watson attributed the presence of the Negro in America to a specifically modern form of the corruption of power: expansive commercialism. Northern corporate power had then loosed the restraining bonds of slavery through the Civil War.[86] When a national political leader from the South, Woodrow Wilson, finally regained Jefferson's national office, he turned out to be an agent of expansive commercialism and imperialist pretensions. Then, with conscription, this Anglophile president who had sold out his own birthright proceeded to reintroduce servitude. In repeating the original sin, Wilson revealed himself as a traitor not only to his section but also to the nation's republican heritage. His centralized usurpation of liberty, euphemistically called "the new freedom," was even more devastating than slavery, in Watson's view, because it turned whites and blacks equally into tools for a war effort that had been unleashed to make the world safe for corporate greed.

Through the dying promise of republican reform, Watson remained as stalwart as Alexander Stephens, whose position he championed against Wilson's Conscription Act, or Thomas Jefferson, whose memory he preserved against Wilson's Espionage Act. In his own mind, he stayed a hero until the end; if he could not be Napoleon he would be Don Quixote.[87] And yet in 1910, the year his editorials lost all balance in headlong battle with the forces of corruption, he had honored the memory of his first hero, the man who had introduced him to Byron, Carlyle, Tennyson, Macaulay, and Gibbon—his late teacher, Epenetus Alexis Steed. This brilliant young teacher who had provided the foundation for all his ideals, Watson revealed, had told the adoring student that ambition, fame, and the heroism that brought them together were not worth pursuing. Watson honored him for saying so, revealing Watson's deep ambivalence about the value of his whole life's direction. But he could not resist portraying Steed as an unsung hero, a true Romantic champion, for having transcended personal ambition.[88]

There is a certain symmetry between Watson's frontier of the heroic personality and Turner's geographical frontier of heroic nation building, which transcends their very different paths toward fame. Both men followed the well-worn path of Romanticism, self-consciously defining themselves as artists, for whom politics served as their field of expression. Though weighed down by a sense of the death of their republican heritage, neither could escape a duty and a genuine affection towards the memory that continued to live on in their dreams of personal and national heroism. Holding fast to memory, like the pastoral elegists of the poetry of their youth, they drew their own self-destructive forms of responsibility from an aesthetic and political balance in the process of dissolution.

However, if Charles Beard was able to substitute a positive promise of a Progressive industrial future for the failed agricultural frontier eulogized by Turner, his own categories were even more successfully exploited in 1938 by the young southern biographer of Tom Watson. For Woodward was able to translate Watson's tarnished past of discredited agrarianism and racism into a formula for generating a positive new interpretation of the South. Woodward honored a fallen hero who was also an anti-hero; he wrote a brief against the entropy of southern political virtue, which doubled as a celebration of the region's rich and vibrant potential for indigenous reform. In this sense, Woodward's revision of southern historiography closely paralleled Reinhold Niebuhr's revision of the American jeremiad. As we shall see, Woodward's biography of Tom Watson was a variation on the family romance, a genre Woodward both laid to rest for southern historiography and revitalized by transposing it into a new Machiavellian key.

However, before considering Woodward's successful Machiavellian synthesis, we must turn to the family romance itself. For it is there, at the mediation of self and society, and natality and death, that we may view the aesthetic foundations of the transformation by 1945 of republicanism, as a pastoral elegy, into liberalism, as a Romantic one.

CHAPTER FOUR

The Southern Family Romance of
Thomas Dixon, Jr., and W. J. Cash

The family romance, as a genre, dominated Anglo-American literature through the nineteenth century. From Parson Weems to James Fenimore Cooper, to the antebellum plantation-legend writers of the old South, to Henry Adams's *Democracy* and Ellen Glasgow's *The Descendant* the problematic themes of self-created heroic individuals contending with the tensions of family and social legitimacy were obsessions for American writers. Beginning in the 1890s, however, the critical pattern for viewing the family romance genre has been to dismiss the earlier mode as hopelessly sentimental or uncreative, while extolling the more realist tone that replaced it as the twentieth century approached.[1] Much of the praise for the Southern Renaissance rests upon this realist/romantic division, symbolically broached with the end of the agrarian frontier and its patriarchal conventions. A second critical theme in relation to this literature has been its susceptibility to Freudian interpretation, an avenue pioneered by Freud and Rank in their choice of the term *family romance* to describe a fantasy built upon the resentment created in a child at the stage when the parents no longer appear perfect and all-powerful.[2] Through Freud's own application of the Classical Oedipus story to life, critics gained a ground to dismiss their Romantic antecedents and to confirm the Realism or Modernism of those writers who dismantled the older aesthetic resolution to the problem of history.

Perhaps the earliest and most effective blend of these two strands of criticism was formulated by W. J. Cash. Cash was an enthusiastic follower of H. L. Mencken, who imitated the Sage of Baltimore's insider assault upon southern provincialism when it was in fashion during the 1920s.[3] However, in *The Mind of the South*, which he completed in 1941 after eleven years of anguished effort, Cash put aside the acerbic style he had copied from Mencken and attempted to distance himself from the tired fad of South-baiting. Instead, he wrote an anguished, personal challenge to the empty legacy of the plantation legend. He could not, however, resist baiting the New Agrarians, whom he singled out for attack for attempting to rehabilitate a mindless and utopian fantasy. Yet, even as he did so, he simultaneously embraced their New Criticism.[4]

Espousing New Critical standards, Cash dismissed the romantic literature of Reconstruction as, on one hand, too sentimental, and on the other, too ideological. Though he himself had written an unpublished potboiler set in the exotic South sea just before undertaking his debunking of the southern legend, he applauded the Southern Renaissance writers for resisting the urge to travel to a "Never-Never Land" and for standing more or less outside the legend. Cash applauded Ellen Glasgow, in particular, for rejecting propaganda for art, and he expressed ambivalence toward Margaret Mitchell's ambiguous blend of the two.[5] Personally about to put aside his long bachelorhood when *The Mind of the South* was being completed, Cash made it plain that he had himself participated in, but wished to step away from, romanticism in sexual matters. In doing so, he offered Freudian explanations for the southern preoccupation with the cult of true womanhood and paranoia over rape. Once more, he tied such romantic conventions, as defined by Freud, to the fear and hatred of blacks. Cash was made uncomfortable by "strutting Negroes," but he also recognized that racial hatred had poisoned white southern society and left its members victim to economic exploitation. And finally, he rejected the "demagogues" of the 1920s and 1930s. Instead, though deeply distrustful of centralized government, Cash looked forward to a more humane industrial future of rational progress by embracing the New Deal and Roosevelt's leadership in restoring southern prosperity.[6]

Cash's book was generously received in the South, as well as in the North; a surprising sign, to many critics, of a new attitude dawning in the South. That positive reception itself seemed to confirm Cash as a true prophet—a son of the South calling forth a spirit of change through the severity of his denial that change had ever been produced during all the South's long past. His tragic death in Mexico, soon after the book's publication, promoted his image as an anguished crusader for rational and humane values. His passionate opposition to the forces of social violence, though contradicted by his own violent language and celebration of the purifying virtue of heroic self-sacrifice, immediately became associated with his intense anti-Nazism, rather than being traced to an older republican division between virtù and virtue.

Though Cash's preoccupation with the Nazi menace to civilization may have led him to his own death—he came to fear he was being followed by Nazi agents and hanged himself—his paranoia was politically correct in 1941. It did not, therefore, serve to undermine the realism of his analysis of the South or his role as a prophetic voice of Modernism. To the contrary, with the exception of Donald Davidson and Richmond Beatty, commentators uniformly praised him for being a liberal southern spokesman on the side of change.[7] At that time, and subsequently, critical opinion forgave him his own romanticism because he championed heroes of realism, those choice southern men and women who were in the process of liberating themselves from a dysfunctional and violent past. Distinguished historians, such as Joel Williamson, Winthrop Jordan, and still later, Bruce Clayton and Richard H. King, applied Cash's Freudian interpretation to the history of the South, with fruitful results. Bertram Wyatt-Brown and Michael O'Brien drew upon Cash as well for their views of the South within the context of his critique of southern romanticism in both its political and intellectual forms. Indeed, as Wyatt-Brown has acknowledged, Cash's presence within the historiography of the South in the latter half of the twentieth century has been both pervasive and largely uncited.[8] It has become part of the fabric of southern reality. However, as part of the American studies canon, which includes Perry Miller's *New England Mind* and Henry Nash Smith's *Virgin Land,* Cash's work has had influence far beyond the field of southern history since 1941.[9]

As with Miller, who wrote both before and after him, and Smith, who wrote after him, Cash's appeal lay in his ambiguous narrative of hope in despair. Like them he wrote with an intensely personal mission to describe the decay of a redemptive community of promise until, through time, it had been transformed into its opposite. In each of these roughly contemporary cases, the specific identification of the authors with the failed tradition—of the South, of New England, of the West—was central to their ability to transform mere history into an elegiac narrative of personal heroism in the face of loss.[10] Miller, Smith, and Cash wrote as if they knew they were heroes of realism, whose individual quests for clear-eyed truth had penetrated the "cloud of patriotic obscurantism," hidden by New England piety, Western myth and symbol, and the southern "savage ideal." [11] Each seemed convinced that following the trajectory of a failed romantic past could prepare Americans to live in an uncertain and alienated future. Though the precise relationship of the failed histories of their proto-American communities to the national future could not be known, they thought they heard echoes reverberating in their own individual experiences of lost innocence. Their romantic realism led them to recognize their own lives as focusing a crisis of personalism and of consciousness in the twentieth century, a crisis that was created by the very "frontier experience" that was supposed to have been the source of their defense. In each of these writers, frontier violence as a form of innovation was ambiguously juxtaposed with the decadence of the frontier as it existed over time. For each, the birth implied the death of the Anglo-American cultural tradition.

For Perry Miller, the nonconformist errand that gave birth to the New England mind led to mindless conformism, as the mind of Newton led to the mindlessness of atomic annihilation at the new frontier of modern physics. For Smith, the frontier myth of the peaceful garden made the backwoodsmen the standard bearers for industrial progress and then led to a violent and expansionist foreign policy when agrarian economics came to its inevitable end. For Cash, the natural innovation of the frontier continuously thwarted the redemptive artificiality of true aristocracy, a condition that could only grow over time. For Cash, the frontier legacy of the romantic hedonism of sensuous blacks and poor whites ensured that the primitivism of the frontier would turn budding aristocracy into the decadence of the southern legend. [12]

The historian of old New England, Perry Miller, like Cash the historian of the Old South, was emboldened by Mencken in his quest to debunk outmoded forms in the 1920s. Miller may or may not have derived from Mencken a passion for the writing of Joseph Conrad, as Cash reported that he himself had. Nonetheless, it certainly colored his conceptualization of the "savage ideal" as the intersection of European honor and the primitive frontier. [13] Miller, therefore, may or may not have first conceived his mission to describe the slow destruction of his own ancestral line during a romantic voyage to the banks of the Congo. His life project may or may not have suddenly occurred to him, as he said it did, while he was unloading the oil drums of capitalist expansion in "that barbaric tropic." He may or may not have been thinking of the failure of

Turner's frontier, while sitting alone along the same Congo River that Conrad's biographer, Jean-Aubry, had just identified in 1926 as the site of the Romantic elegist's personal epiphany and of his horror tale of frontier decadence, *The Heart of Darkness*. But by 1956, in his preface to *Errand into the Wilderness*, Miller himself linked Smith's Turnerian frontier as metaphor with his own assaults upon the New England tradition, when he described to his readers the origins of his *New England Mind* of 1939.[14]

Whatever else the classic elegiac histories of Miller, Smith, and Cash represented to their authors and readers, then and now, they were expressions of the terrors and the promises locked within the conundrum of continuity and discontinuity in Anglo-American history. And, though W. J. Cash may have lacked the enormous erudition of Perry Miller and the aesthetic distance of Smith from his region and past, he more directly addressed the contradiction of time as innovation and simultaneously as tradition than did either of his great contemporaries. His attack upon the southern legend and its constituent elements of paternalism, "gyneolatry," and racism was developed within the context of the dualism of frontiers that repeatedly frustrated the maturing of alternative aristocratic traditions in his region. However, according to Cash's own interpretation of southern history, this was due to the contradiction of time at the heart of Machiavellian political and aesthetic values. Thus, W. J. Cash was not a harbinger of some new world of modernist rationality, mysteriously emerging around his birthdate in 1900, then maturing in tandem with his own life history, and finally blooming on his grave, as it were, in the new realist world of post–World War II America.

Quite to the contrary, Cash was groping toward a new variation on the Machiavellian romance that he shared with the local idol of his boyhood in Gaffney, South Carolina: Thomas Dixon, Jr. Like the elderly and now unfashionably romantic Dixon of the 1940s, whom he sought to exorcise through mockery, Cash was fatally tied to the republican political and aesthetic conventions from which he sought to remove himself. Like the once fashionable Thomas Dixon of 1900, against whom Cash's Freudian interpretation was so useful for repressing distressing parallels to himself and to Modernism itself, Cash was preoccupied with balancing the contradiction between virtù and virtue, a balance that the southern plantation legend had failed to preserve aesthetically. For as Michael Kreyling has shown in his study, *Figures of the Hero in Southern Narrative*, the literary genre of the southern plantation legend was not merely a stock formula imitation of Cooper or Walter Scott, as critics like William Dean Howells began to charge in the 1890s.[15] Cash's dual purpose of separating himself from the failed literary hero of his youth while preserving his own role as a defender of Modernist literary heroism in the South made it possible for him to see this and to take sentimental stories set in "Cloud-Cuckoo Land," "Never-Never Land," and "Happy-Happy Land" very seriously indeed. Therefore, though Cash accepted the critical judgment that the plantation legend was simple and mindless, he also promoted a Freudian interpretation of its appeal, which anticipated Kreyling's view that no narrative form is ever simply mindless imitation.

However, finding a universal heroic mythos in crisis in the southern legend, as Kreyling does, depended upon being able to excavate "the literary remains" of a dead cultural form. Cash, who insisted the southern legend was only a dangerously sentimental myth, was actively engaged in trying to finish it off. Therefore, a contemporary study of the southern legend, such as Kreyling's *Figures of the Hero in Southern Narrative,* reflects—or refracts—Cash's role in burying the legend in *The Mind of the South.*[16] Perhaps more important, it reveals Cash's pivotal service in turning the southern legend into a purely aesthetic myth, which could then be offered as a paradigmatic literary formula for escaping change as history. Thus, through the interpretive power of the New Criticism and with Cash's service in identifying the southern heritage as a myth, Kreyling has been able to restore formal meaning to a heroic narrative which he recognizes as having died. Kreyling clearly is able to address this particular narrative form of heroic meaning in a creative but personally detached way, which was not available to Cash in 1941, when he explains that "a cultural group accepts its narrative form, and rejects others, because that form alone embodies the group's nearest image of itself as its most truthful and accessible scripture."[17]

Figures of the Hero in Southern Narrative is a literary history, treating more than thirty texts that fall into the pattern of the southern family narrative as it existed between the plantation legend and the 1970s, when Kreyling says it died. The earliest of these narratives include George Tucker's *Valley of the Shenandoah; or, Memories of the Graysons* (1824), Beverley Tucker's *Partisan Leader* (1856), and William Alexander Caruthers's *Cavaliers of Virginia; or, The Recluse of Jamestown* (1834). In each case, he notes, the hero is a handsome male, of refined manner, immediately recognizable as having a spiritual or other-worldly character. The hero faces two challenges in his dual effort to sustain personal dominance and to confirm social conventions of morality. One of these is the villain who must be warred against, without compromising the hero's virtue. The other is the discovery and wedding of his female cognate, who must be wooed and not simply conquered by his virtù.[18]

Typically, the villain, who is a physical and spiritual opposite of the hero, imposes himself on a closed rural or small-town community from outside the fold of the social family. He is often a Yankee who symbolizes commercial greed and lustful sexuality. The mate, on the contrary, must come from within the family group and exude purity and steadfast loyalty. The challenge, on both sides of the hero's quest, is that of legitimacy. Only by defeating the villain without compromising his own standards may the hero publicly pass on his values, and those of the narrative itself. To preserve the difference between the dominance of the hero's virtù and that of the villain, the hero's triumph of the spirit must flirt with the triumph of the flesh—that is, with moral corruption or physical death. On the other hand, the wife-mate must so perfectly match the hero as to approach sisterhood and to flirt with incest. Indeed, the heroine is often a cousin. She is found as close to home, physically and psychologically, as is possible. The villain not only comes from as far away as possible, geographically and culturally, but is opposite in body type and manner as well. The perfect wife-mate must be such a pure and complete reflection of the heroic ideal that she may be unmarriageable and the transmission of heroic virtue may be rendered impossible. Alternatively, crossbreeding must lead to tragic death and the shaking of the very foundations of the community's harmony. This may occur if the hero marries the wrong mate, or if a female's natural passion results in her failure to distinguish the hero's selfless ambition from the villain's selfish ambition. On the positive side, when the hero finally weds the heroine, rather than the exotic outsider whose temptation confirms his virtù, he marries within type and therefore escapes history.

Clearly, the anxiety being exorcised in the southern family romance revolved around the requirement that like marry like in order to preserve the universals of tradition as they were being assaulted by the particulars of time.[19] What is true about the southern family romance as a positive and satisfying public convention for expressing and resolving a republican culture's anxiety over a Machiavellian moment of change, however, was necessarily true in reverse. It was a natural vehicle for undermining the hold of tradition, when it came to be viewed as an outworn and ineffectual literary form, evoking critical groans and public laughter.

The changing attitude of public and critical acceptance of the family romance genre between 1890 and 1940, therefore, must be recognized as a political as well as an aesthetic reorientation of Machiavellian political culture in the North as well as the South. For until the 1890s the southern family romance was generally accepted in all sections of Anglo-America. The disavowal of the form resulted when it failed to offer a credible avenue for confronting the relation of continuity to change in history. That is, it began to lose favor at a moment in aesthetic time in which "traditional" formulas for escaping history no longer served to deliver readers and writers from their contradictory culture, but instead gave them into its hands.

W. J. Cash, who saw the nativity of Jesus as pointing to the mystery of birth, "and the mystery of life which is contained in birth, and the mystery of death which is foreshadowed in birth," was at once a self-consciously alienated product of, and an unconsciously conservative rebel against, that very condition. He secretly wrote romance while extolling realism, because, as he wrote publicly in 1936, real men and women are romantic creatures. "There is a strange aspiring and upward reaching in him; that, condemned to death and inevitable defeat in the flesh, he can and does (and wholly apart from theological determinations) assert his spirit as immortal and incorruptible—a shining sword and a flame against which Time and the grave may not prevail." He revered the memory of Napoleon, and loathed the diminished "rat-like man" who strutted obscenely about "the great man's" grave—proof, in 1940, that "in the world there was nothing certain save that, after his brief span, he slept and would sleep—and that the empires fragile man raises are fragile things.[20]

Characteristically, then, Cash opened *The Mind of The South* with an admonition to historians of the South for ignoring the central importance of time in shaping frontiers and aristocracies. He went on to describe the paradox of a tradition of frontier replacing frontier, first as primitive land, then as plantation, and finally as the frontier of industrial progress. Cash described the opposition between aristocracy and these successive frontiers within the classic conventions of republican ideology; though from his own perspective, he clearly thought he was approaching an apocalyptic break with the past into a final frontier of Modernism. However, when Cash's use of Modernism is closely examined, it may be seen to be a conservative rebellion in the effort to reassert a problematic legitimacy for southern cultural and political leadership. Once more, it is an aesthetic and political challenge to Romanticism as a form of unreality, mounted heroically in the name of defending a submerged Romanticism as a new form of Realism. Finally, because Cash found promise as well as despair in the destruction of tradition, his Modernism illustrates the continuity between nineteenth- and twentieth-century Anglo-American culture as one Machiavellian "tradition," preoccupied with balancing the internal contradictions associated with time as innovation and duration.

In the beginning of it all, said Cash, "little clumps of colonial gentlemen" of virtue existed, but not in any meaningful numbers. Their refinement, however, undermined their ability to compete against the virtù of their rougher neighbors. "The odds were heavy against such gentlemen—against any gentlemen," he wrote, for "the land had to be wrested from the forest and the intractable red man." This was a "harsh and bloody task," not at all suited "to the talents which won applause in the neighborhood of Rotten Row and Covent Garden." The robust convicts and rough and rowdy frontiersmen who began as servants soon surpassed the refined and languid gentlemen who hired them.[21]

During the first frontier stage, according to Cash, there were no aristocracies, only the undifferentiated relation of man to man, which replaced the fading remnants of a sparsely distributed European culture. In the backcountry, this pioneer breed became frozen into an unchanging but crude dualism of thievery and industry, swindlers and strivers, the vulgar and the unpretentious. For Cash, this unholy mixture of humanity at its crude best and worse, this raw virtù, might have been transformed into virtue by time, since aristocracy is a product of duration.[22] However, Eli Whitney, the Yankee serpent in the post-Edenic garden, initiated change by interesting himself in extracting the seed from the fiber of the cotton plant. In doing so, he brought a new frontier to the South, the plantation.[23] As trees fell, soil eroded, and wildlife disappeared with the advance of the plantation, the most industrious and ruthless men, the quick and the simply lucky, developed greater power and more land, while their fellows were pushed into poverty. An aristocracy was developing, but as it did so, it walled the old frontier into a decaying physical landscape of dirt, malnutrition, and poverty. The natural world of the peasant and his natural biological condition, under the innovative violence of the plantation, combined to leave the poor backwoodsman a hopeless victim of the continuity of time in nature, that is, of decay. Even the simple heritage he had brought from Europe faded away in the heat of the quivering, sultry southern air, and ideas that had shaped his slim stock of knowledge steadily evaporated into the creeping languor of southern summer days. The process of inner destruction was, therefore, not only inherent in the economic centralization imposed from without by Yankee dynamism; it was equally a part of the physical reality of the southern environment itself. It was imposed from within. The sexually profuse and fecund foliage, the voluptuousness of color and smell, even the summer heat evoking images of passion and death formed "a sort of cosmic conspiracy against reality in favor of romance."[24]

"What the frontier had begun," Cash explained, "the world which succeeded it—that world which was the creation of the plantation—was admirably calculated to preserve and even greatly to extend." For the effect of the plantation system was "to perpetuate essentially frontier conditions long after their normal period had run—to freeze solid many of the aspects of the old back woods."[25] This meant that as the powerful plantation owner grew self-sufficient and isolated, waxing paternalist over his domain, poor whites did the same on their meager leavings as romantic individualists. The unfortunate result was that law and government—like true aristocracy the fruit of duration—grew far too slowly to have made much progress before the Civil War destroyed the plantation frontier forever.

The Civil War and Reconstruction, for Cash, represented a Yankee application of force to sweep the South into the American mainstream of commercialism. But Cash, who also laid much of the blame for southern sensuousness and romanticism on the internal presence of blacks, quite unconsciously identified a feminine South with the black woman in the Old South in his anti-Yankeeism: "Torn from her tribal restraints and taught an easy complaisance for commercial reasons, she was to be had for the taking." Boys on and off the plantation "inevitably learned to use her, and having acquired the habit, often continued it into manhood and even after marriage."[26] Like the South, the black woman's naturalness associated her with the decadence that flows out of passion, destroying the basis of institutional order in marriage and family. Meanwhile, not only did puritanical Yankees mount an increasingly bellicose attack, depicting every Southerner as "a Turk wallowing in lechery," but the Southerners themselves turned to "gyneolatry" to show the Yankees that "southern virtue" was superior to any on earth, as proven by the purity of their women.[27] The mutually self-destructive republican conventions out of which Cash confronted "the southern mind" become even more evident on closer inspection. While identifying the South of the Civil War and Reconstruction, in form and substance, with the plight of the black slave woman on the plantation, Cash wrote as if the Southerner were always male and described the woman he held up to the evil Yankee's derision as "puritanical" in her values.

Through the devastation of the war that Yankee commercial interests initiated in their greed when political force proved inadequate, the South was "stripped and bled white—made, indeed a frontier once more," he wrote. Reconstruction policy was aimed at assuring that the new frontier would be both "absolute and continual."[28] With the destruction of the aristocracy, such as it was before the war, and the burden of an imposed Yankee frontier, southern development of a new aristocracy and of law was blocked forever. Despite surviving elements of virtù, the aristocracy of the Old South could not flourish in the hard third frontier of progress. There were "individuals of unusual latent energy, who, while holding more or less fast to the better part of their heritage, managed to ride triumphantly through by sheer force." But for most, "they were too firmly bound within their pattern, were at once too soft and too fine," so their virtue succumbed to decay.[29]

Thus, the remaining vestiges of virtue among yeomen were directly destroyed when, as was natural given their long frontier heritage, they adjusted to the crass new Yankee frontier of commercialism. The immature aristocracy of plantation culture, on the other hand, declined either by slow adaptation to the new order or through direct and immediate decay, in the case of the "young and more malleable." For the older ones who were more fixed in the aristocratic tradition, the new order meant falling into bankruptcy or diminished status, and finally, over time, into oblivion.[30]

With the resurgence of the vulgar frontier, and the sense of loss, terror, and withdrawal that accompanied the decline of the aristocrats, the legend was frozen into place in "the great haze of memory . . . , poised somewhere between earth and sky." Every Southerner, rich or poor, could now freely trace his family to aristocracy, since virtually all Southerners were related. The Yankees as people of the frontier were equally drawn to the romance of the plantation legend. In a bright and shining fantasy, set in "Cloud Cuckoo-Land," as Cash called it, everyone found their romantic heart's desire.[31]

Cash's jeremiad against the Yankee frontier followed the pattern that Sacvan Bercovitch has attributed to Perry Miller's study of the Puritan jeremiad. It is the pattern of a stylized complaint that runs from promise to decline to a prophesy of return.[32] Therefore, as Cash considered more recent history, he repeated the same pattern of looking for an avenue for a prophesy of return as a salvation from a declension that became more desperate with each frontier cycle. The paternalism of the plantation owner had given way to a more destructive paternalism in the mill owner. The helpless confinement of a walled frontier, which the plantation had made of the backcountry, had given way to an even more literal walled frontier in the diminished opportunity provided by the absentee-owned mill. The romantic individualism and lazy sensuousness of the backcountry frontiersman had given way to the strike-breaking individualism and lack of resolve that locked the mill worker into industrialized misery.[33]

But since Cash's realist description of a doubtful aristocratic past was rooted in his present hope for Modernism, it was Modernism that provided his lens for viewing all past possibilities for deliverance of the South, by history, from a history that had failed. Consequently, Modernism was the best as well as the last prophetic promise of return to political and aesthetic virtue. Modernism, he emphasized to his readers, was different from Yankee progress, though it seemed similar in its methods and aims and carried similar dangers where the frontier mentality held sway. Modernism, however, unlike industrial progress, directly challenged Puritan values, setting Marxism against capitalism, as it set Freud, Adler, Jung, Nietzsche, Dewey, Veblen, and John Watson against bourgeois standards. As these Modernists—along with sociologists, such as Howard Odum and his associates; historians, such as those from W. A. Dunning's school and John Spenser Bassett; and writers, such as James Joyce, T. S. Eliot, Irving Babbit, and Ellen Glasgow—leavened American attitudes after the turn of the century, they created a genuine if limited weakening of the hold of Romanticism, and with it, the "savage ideal." Cash saw evidence for this prophetic return of the sacred—as his European contemporary, Walter Benjamin, put it—in the rejection of Romantic literary forms. (Cash was indebted for this perspective to the New Critics.[34]) Yet, personally identifying with the southern family he criticized, he feared that the sentimentality and frontier romanticism of the New Agrarians were only tentatively being replaced in the New Critics. He feared that the "barnyard morality" sparked by the breakdown of Puritan mores as a result of Modernism was only tentatively being overcome by the example of great Modernist authors, political leaders like Franklin Roosevelt, and southern liberals of conscience, such as William

Poteat, president of Wake Forest University. The institutions of law and government, and the European cultural tradition embodied in education, stood as the only checks against a far more ingrained frontier tradition of violent romanticism. This made the degenerate European Hitler's barbaric destruction of civilized European culture into a threat against the very ground of Cash's hopes for the South, for America, and for the world.[35]

The march of Nazi storm troopers may well have shattered the ground of Cash's messianic hope in Modernism and have kept him from being able to complete his manuscript for so long. Perhaps, too, his inability to conceive of time in any other way capable of fulfilling the requirements for southern redemption turned the prospect of completing *The Mind of the South* into a depressing burden in the late 1930s, so that his delay may have been due to more than personal fears of southern family criticism or feelings of inadequacy. Cash intimated that this was the case when he ascribed his inability to complete the book to the feeling that there "was no way out" and frequently fell into tirades over Hitler.[36] Besides, as an editorial writer and essayist for Mencken's *American Mercury*, Cash frequently confronted public opinion. His concern over criticism or censure reveals how closely he still identified with the South of his childhood, as does his concentration on mill-town economics and North Carolina history, from which he extrapolated interpretations on the whole region. But it seems doubtful that these ties to his community alone explain his shaken will as he tried to write the last third of a book that had been intentionally provocative in the first place.

If his own disillusionment with the redemptive possibilities of Modernism was at the root of Cash's despair, this suggests a tragic parallel to Walter Benjamin, another prophet of Modernism, who took his life within a few months of Cash's suicide. Benjamin, of course, took his life because he was being hounded by real Nazis. He was trapped at a border between Spain and France, which was also a border between safety and arrest, when he killed himself. But Benjamin had earlier rejected escape to America because he could not bear living in America as "the last European." Cash's Modernism, balancing innovation and tradition, was deeply conservative in its rebellion as well. The memory of European values was the only real substance behind his conservative aristocratic ideal, just as it was the basis of his avant-garde hope in Modernism. Cash, the Modernist who bicycled all over Europe in 1927, weeping at the beauty of Chartres Cathedral, viewed himself as a last European in

America, even as he viewed the South as the last decaying outpost of European culture in America.[37]

Cash's suicide after completing a personal mission to expose the holy of holies, the sacred temple of southern honor and virtue, to public ridicule, also calls up associations with Perry Miller's death in alcoholic despair almost a quarter-century later. But Cash's resigned despair and detachment from the South resembled more Benjamin's response to bourgeois Germany than Miller's defiant resolve to go down with his Puritan heritage like a lion at bay. Cash's messianic faith in Modernism, like Benjamin's faith in the angel of history, allowed him to separate modern values from progress, gaining a positive hope for political renewal in deconstructing a failed aesthetic form.[38] As a Southerner, Cash was prepared to separate modern values from Yankee faith in progress, as the New England historian Perry Miller could not or would not separate Yankee values from their Puritan roots.

Miller described the failed Puritan errand as one in which "New England did not lie, did not falter," but after doing all that Winthrop demanded, "then found that its lesson was rejected by those choice spirits for whom the exertion had been made." He remained squarely within the pastoral elegiac tradition of identifying autobiographically with the failed hero or tradition.[39] However, for Cash, the South, not Western civilization, had failed, and the fact of that failure released him for a new hope through Modernism. Had not Hitler intervened, Cash, like Benjamin, might have been able to present a guardedly hopeful vision of the future through ambiguity, as Reinhold Niebuhr and the New Critics were able to do. That is, each might have fully entered into the Romantic elegiac style because each tried to use memory as a bridge to the past in order to lay it to rest and then embrace a messianic future through a redemptive new aesthetic.

But Cash's bid to resolve the problem of continuity and discontinuity in history was blocked by history itself. He had argued that European civilization offered a redemptive form of discontinuity from the continuity of the American frontier. For the continuity of degeneration that had led to Yankee rapacity established Reconstruction, which in turn established "the savage ideal" in the South. The paradoxical innovation and continuity of this history, as understood by Cash, may be seen in his use of the adjectives *violent* and *puerile* to describe a *tradition* that was seemingly condemned to eternal youth.[40] But this history of youth could be interrupted—made discontinuous—by the innovation of age. How could such a paradox be accomplished? The answer was through Modernism, because it was at once iconoclastic and rooted in age-old European culture. Yet, in Cash's own words, the savage ideal that had "paralyzed Southern culture at the root" but had otherwise been banished from the West since "the decay of medieval feudalism" was now established in Fascist Italy, Nazi Germany, and Soviet Russia.[41]

Inevitably, for the Cash of *The Mind of the South*, this meant that Reconstruction had become the blueprint for the future of not just the American South, but the whole West. His Romantic elegy for the southern legend had not provided an escape from the "savage ideal," but rather had paralyzed him within it and with no possible hope for a day of redemption. His aesthetic formula for escaping the implications of the pastoral elegy, and with it, identification with a failed history, had been revealed as merely a variation on the same literary convention that lay behind the family romance itself.

At this point, it should be clear that Reconstruction—understood exactly as the one-time Johns Hopkins University graduate student of history, Thomas Dixon, learned it—constituted the central motif of Cash's book. Indeed, it was from Dixon that Cash first learned the tale of Reconstruction that his book retells.[42] After all, Cash grew up in a mill town where Dixon was a local hero extolled by friends and relatives and where Cash and all his boyhood chums were regaled on Saturday afternoons by *The Birth of a Nation*. Cash even chose to attend Dixon's alma mater, Wake Forest University. There, the Dixon family name still retained its formidable presence in the 1920s, when Cash was a student, even if Thomas Dixon's aura was beginning to fade.

Clarence Dixon, a conservative older brother who clashed with the more worldly Thomas, had been offered the presidency of the institution in the 1880s. Later, in 1920, when Cash was a sophomore, he heard Clarence, an influential Baptist minister, chastise his hero William L. Poteat, then president of Wake Forest, for permitting the teaching of evolution. But if Clarence Dixon reminded Cash uncomfortably of his own father's grim Baptist fundamentalism, it also happened that his hero, the liberal William Poteat, was admired and cultivated as a friend by Thomas Dixon.[43] Just as Cash defended the early Ku Klux Klan and denigrated its later revival, defended Modernism against Yankee progress, and supported Roosevelt in 1932, so, in each of these cases, did Thomas Dixon. But in the mid-1930s, Dixon had returned home to North Carolina, both financially broken and out of aesthetic and even political style. The old man who had enthusiastically supported Roose-velt in 1932 had become disillusioned with him—not only because Dixon thought communist agents were infiltrating the government, but because he feared Roosevelt was taking the nation into war.[44] By 1937, Dixon had finally run out of the energy to rebuild his fortunes as he had done previously. Unsung and ill, he provided a very different sort of presence in North Carolina from his romantically heroic image during Cash's youth.

Just as Cash's quarrel with the southern family romance was a family quarrel carried on by an ambivalent son, so his quarrel with Dixon was a family argument between generations. For all the difference in style, their pattern of disillusionment—first with the southern legend and sec-ond with Modernism—followed the same form. Each sought to escape failed republican values and disillusionment with democracy, which, as we have seen, an older contemporary of Dixon and near-contemporary of Cash, Tom Watson, had tried to defend through loyalty to the roman-tic heroic ideal. Dixon tried to detach himself from Watson and Agrari-anism in 1900, as Cash tried to detach himself from the New Agrarians in 1940, by cultivating an aesthetic political romanticism which was nei-ther pastoral nor entirely within the Romantic elegiac mode. Though each was a critic of Agrarianism and southern provincialism, neither es-caped his self-identification with southern exceptionalism. Each, there-fore, transcended a pastoral style within classically Machiavellian terms, but neither could follow his faith to a full belief in the purifying violence of deconstruction, from which he could create a new romantically heroic self-narrative.

One reason that it has been difficult to recognize the continuity be-tween Dixon and Cash is that the Freudianism Cash used to distance himself from a failed ideal of his own youth fit seamlessly within the larger aesthetic formula for submerging republicanism as a failed politi-cal faith in the early twentieth century. Just because Freudianism pre-sented so many advantages for describing and illuminating forms of per-sonal and political disillusionment, it could be an effective method for hiding them as well. Since Dixon was drawn to the same psychological dualisms of human conflict as Cash, he was readily pigeonholed simply by turning this similarity into a case study for proving the applicability of Cash's hypothesis about the pathology of the southern legend. From this perspective, Dixon's early Freudian psychological interests seemed to il-lustrate how the excesses of the "savage ideal" formed a pathological mind, while Cash's own later application of Freud to the same Reconstruction paradigm as Dixon's only served to prove the prescience of Cash's insight into southern culture. This Freudian equation, which Cash and the Swedish sociologist Gunnar Myrdal helped conventionalize in the 1940s, naturally had the effect of abstracting racism from its cultural context, and then projecting it back onto history—a self-reinforcing description of prejudice when applied to a Dixon or a Watson, which made any careful consideration of their thought or values appear unnecessary because they were by psychological definition historically irrelevant.[45]

The Freudian interpretation of the family romance was an attempt to offer a normative description of a historical process from outside of history. It atemporally traced the discovery of mortality by a romantic heroic self, in flight from a timeless and perfect authority to a new and more realistic role in the context of a shared adult community. But rather than codifying a universal scientific law of change, beyond aesthetic conventions and mythic narrative, the Freudian interpretation was actually firmly embedded within a particular cultural history. It had been derived by Freud from a Classical narrative, the Oedipus drama of Sophocles, in the context of a passionate reaction against romanticism and in quest of the culturally stabilizing values of realism.[46] As a Classical and therefore timeless aesthetic, *Oedipus Rex* confirmed a temporal pattern of tension between savagery and order which could be unlocked and healed if exposed through an atemporal method for interpreting language.

In other words, Freudianism successfully submerged its own romantic-heroic aesthetic by dividing Classicism and Romanticism from each other as if they were real space-time events instead of aesthetic conventions, rooted in specific political tensions. Freudianism, therefore, subverted the conventions of the Romantic heroic narrative itself, through a claim to a higher realism. This was, of course, a variation on the quest romance, which Kenneth Bruffee has shown is closely attached to the formula of the Romantic elegy.[47] As such, the appeal of Freudianism soon became inseparable from the fashionability of the Romantic elegiac style at the turn of the twentieth century. During the 1930s, 1940s, and 1950s, when Cash, Miller, and Smith were writing, these aesthetic innovations for preserving order within a failing republican Anglo-American culture were being reflected and refracted in numerous but self-reinforcing ways. These included the process by which New Deal liberalism successfully challenged first the republicanism of the New Agrarians and then Charles Beard's industrial democracy, associating the former with violent romanticism and the latter with utopian fantasies of anticapitalist sectarianism and political isolationism. In both cases, by ahistorically promoting the aesthetic distinction between Classicism and Romanticism as if it were a real division within historical space and time, a transfer of power steadily proceeded in the direction of corporate capitalism. By the time of Niebuhr's *Irony of American History* (1952) and Richard Hofstadter's *Age of Reform* (1955), Progressivism and Populism were being defined as two sides of the same unrealistic past, and a corporate capitalist future was being promoted as realism.[48]

Historically, however, no stable cultural or parental authority, from which a romantic flight had been taken, ever existed, or at least there had been no such authority since Machiavelli's Renaissance. There had been no ideal heroic Revolutionary generation, nor aristocracy of culture, nor southern ethos from which standard a history of decay could have been historically traced. Neither was there, historically speaking, a timeless and classically rational perspective that could be applied to the historical record and did not participate in the prejudices of aesthetic style, in which it was, as a cultural particular, inextricably bound.

Therefore, the decayed or pathological quality, which seemed so advanced in a figure like Dixon and so healthfully escaped by Cash in 1941, largely reflected a particular crisis of style. Cash's then-fashionable use of Freudian language to separate himself from an unfashionable Dixon was culturally acceptable without requiring historiographical conventions for viewing Reconstruction, or blacks, or women, or economics that were different from those supplied by Dixon. A comparison of Dixon's writings with Cash's *Mind of the South* reveals that most of Dixon's stereotypes were still there in Cash; the black man as sensuous, mindless, arrogant, and violent; the black woman as natural, and therefore both a passionate victim and a victim of passion; the puritanical white woman separated from her sexuality; the horsefaced, bespectacled do-gooder/fool of a Yankee schoolmarm; the rough and degraded frontier yeoman; the model factory as modern, but without having Yankee values, and so on.[49]

If Cash's Freudian and New Critical attack on Dixon and the southern family legend repeated Dixon's own tale of Reconstruction, Cash's negative relation to the author of *The Leopard's Spots* and *The Clansman* must have been more complex than he acknowledged. If Dixon himself was not really celebrating the vitality of the southern legend, as historians since Cash have assumed; if Dixon was actually groping toward an early form of the Romantic elegy through which heroically to escape its failure he must be seen as having far more significance than Cash's Freudian anti-Romanticism has encouraged historians to accord him. This enlarged cultural role for Dixon, beyond that of a simple and vicious propagandist, does provide a perspective that may make sense of the internal contradictions in Cash's narrative, his own fall from critical grace since the 1960s, and the role of the Romantic elegy in revitalizing Machiavellian political values. But, to do so requires that Dixon's life and writings be given serious study for their insights into the aesthetic and political crises that were hidden in the officially optimistic rhetoric of the Progressive-era America in which he lived and wrote.

Dixon is of course most infamously remembered for his screenplay, *The Birth of a Nation,* directed by D. W. Griffith in 1915, a film unsurpassed at the box office until *Gone with the Wind* two decades later. Margaret Mitchell acknowledged that she had grown up on Dixon's books, as did Cash.[50] That Margaret Mitchell's book, on which the film was based, had roughly the same relation to Dixon's work as did Cash's presents a formidable argument for placing Dixon near the center of any analysis of Anglo-American culture in the first half of the twentieth century. But Dixon's shared success with Griffith in *The Birth of a Nation* was only the capstone of a career that had remained remarkably tuned to the public pulse since Dixon turned himself into one of the most popular preachers in America, in New York during the 1880s.[51] By the 1890s Dixon, as one of the most sought-after lecturers in the history of the chautauqua circuit, had lectured all over America to more than five million persons in a five-year period. It was not until after the turn of the century that he embraced a racist message. But when he did so, he was once again in touch with the public pulse. He watched his first novel sell one hundred thousand copies in its first few months and eventually over one million copies. He repeated that phenomenal record of sales in his next three books, two of which were conceived as part of one projected trilogy—on southern life under Reconstruction and one as part of another projected trilogy on modern urban social life. Yet it must be remembered that, despite all the years of acclaim, Dixon consistently denied the efficacy of his public roles, abandoning each in turn. Dixon rejected public careers in politics, law, and the ministry before turning to fiction because he found that rhetorical skill could as easily justify immoral purposes as galvanize public opinion for the good. He, therefore, was as critical of the public acclaim gained through the emotional sway of rhetoric as was Cash, only

Dixon felt that this was not a southern form of weakness but one as visible in the North as in the South. He gave voice to that distrust of rhetoric in *The One Woman: A Story of Modern Utopia* (1903), written immediately following *The Leopard's Spots: A Romance of the White Man's Burden, 1866–1900* (1902), in which the hero's oratorical triumph served as the climax of the narrative:

Yes, you fellows are all orators. You must affirm else the crowd will leave you. You never have doubts and fears. You always know. Only affirm a thing enough and never try to prove it, and thousands of fools will accept it at last as the word of God. That is the secret of the power of all demagogues and emotional orators. The slickest horse-thief that ever operated in the West was a revivalist who migrated there with a tent. While he held the crowd spellbound with his eloquence, his confederates loosed the horses in the woods and got them to a safe place. Oratory is one of the cheapest tricks ever played on man, but an everlastingly effective one, because it is based on affirmation. Any man who is too hard-headed and honest to affirm a thing he don't know and can't know never leads a mob. They will only follow a man who speaks with the sublime authority of knowledge he does not possess.[52]

Though he continued to strive for that public acclamation and initially reveled in finding himself a sensation as a novelist, Dixon began to distance himself from writing even before the public's enthusiasm began to wane following his three great popular successes: *The Leopard's Spots, The One Woman,* and *The Clansman* (1905).[53] Nor was Dixon ever able to regain an audience for his subsequent films that remotely approached that of *The Birth of a Nation.* Indeed, Dixon had sufficiently faded from the public's consciousness between 1905, when *The Clansman* was staged, and 1915, when the film was released that Griffith garnered most of the public attention from the film. Similarly, Walter Hines Page had been enthusiastic and anxious to publish *The Leopard's Spots* in 1902, but by 1913, Page found Dixon's style embarrassingly outdated. Apparently a significant transformation in American tastes and sensibilities occurred over less than a decade, which brought Dixon's popularity into rapid decline.[54]

Dixon's earlier public role in leading a reform-oriented church of social progressivism, his nationwide lecture tour challenging provincial Americans with the problems of modern urban values, and finally, his racist call to save civilization from collapse from within were all successful formulas for revivals. All were forms of rhetorical display that placed the crisis within republican values before great popular audiences all over the country. Indeed, it might be said that Dixon was a true revivalist who found his métier in religious, political, and finally literary forms of a naturalist-romanticism, at a time when other, more traditional forms of cultural revivalism seemed to have fallen into disarray. Yet his increasing inability to hold his crowds and his continuous effort to find new ways to reach them—from pulpits and lecterns, and in plays, novels, and films—suggests a public becoming restive with his call for moralistic reform, more interested in being entertained than in hearing his message for restoring the republican virtues of a fading democracy in an increasingly urbanized and centralized nation.

During his years of popularity, Dixon was highly adept at identifying and speaking to the anxieties of his varied audiences, concerning the speed and finality with which that republican producer's democracy was being transformed into a consumer's democracy. However, Dixon aspired to being more than a popular artist. He wished to be a moralistic reformer. His obsessive concern in his novels, as in his ministry and lectures, was power—the power of religion, of love, and of Tammany Hall; of ideals, of money, of socialism, and of mobs. But, Dixon recognized that it was the categories of gender and race within which the forces of centralized economic and political power and the disintegration of the republican standards of the personal moral life would be confronted in the twentieth century.

Within the republican tradition to which Dixon was heir, all social relations were defined as manifestations of power. Yet within republicanism the exercise of power was seen as divisive and an invitation to Fortune to enter into civic affairs. Gender, therefore, had a dual significance. On one hand, it witnessed to the brutal reality of an elemental physical order of male dominance over female subservience. On the other hand, it paradoxically necessitated an artificial and contextual, that is, a political, balance of power and value, for the preservation of public harmony.[55] The mediating institution for balancing this contradictory set of binary oppositions—male virtù and female virtue, coercion and co-operation, expansion and stability, particulars and universals—was the idealized household of the Classical *polis*. In the Jacksonian variation on this political tradition, the Classical ideal of the *polis* had been redefined from a dynamic American republic into a dynamic democracy, to balance the rise of urban capitalism with the ideal of Jefferson's agrarian arcadia. American democracy as a spiritualized political ideal was reified into a physical institution, which alone could promise to mediate human equality and liberty. In Jacksonian America it appeared as a universal movement toward social harmony. Democracy stood, literally, between God the timeless, absolute ruler of the cosmos and the particular lives of millions of human beings. If neither God nor the masses was accessible to human understanding because He was infinite and they were all too finite, democracy could reveal a providential plan, fulfilling cosmic meaning in human time. Concretely, democracy appeared miraculously to resolve all the republican contradictions of power. It theoretically included everyone and perfectly balanced the universal natural law of evolutionary change with the particulars of individual aspirations.

From this perspective, the growing loss of religious faith at the end of the nineteenth century may have derived less from the rationalism of science or new intellectual doubts about God's existence than from a crisis of faith in Jacksonian democracy. This, at least, appears to have been the case for individuals otherwise so different in style and sensibility as Thomas Dixon and the New England historian, Henry Adams. Though Adams was a generation older than Dixon, he began to express his disillusionment with democracy at about the same time as did Dixon, in the early 1880s.[56] Once more, Adams expressed his disillusionment with democracy at that time by using the southern family romance as an ironic vehicle for exploring its failure. He did so in a novel appropriately titled *Democracy*.[57] This in itself provides evidence that the southern family romance was already being used in a far more sophisticated way by the 1880s than William Dean Howells, W. J. Cash, or the New Agrarian critics recognized when they characterized it as simple and sentimentally escapist literature. Clearly, the southern family romance had become a formal and publicly recognizable challenge to the legitimacy of the heroic ideal, at the same time that the genre had already become ersatz and uninspiring as a serious aesthetic formula for defending it. And it was in this ironic atmosphere, when moralistic Realism was itself under attack by the followers of Naturalism for failing to extricate itself from Romantic values, that Dixon, having lost faith in politics, law, and preaching, decided to plunge into a writing career.

As David Noble has explained, Dixon's perspective on history had been drawn from the republican New England historians: Bancroft, Prescott, Motley, and Parkman.[58] Much as the New Englander Henry Adams experienced a contradiction between their narratives of the triumph of American democracy and the loss of his own family's exceptionality after the Civil War, Dixon came to believe that the defeat of the South and the horrors of Reconstruction presaged a national history of greed and corruption, which had been increasing since that time. For Adams, the mounting contradiction between the inevitable triumph of the ideal of democracy, embodied in George Washington, and its apparently equally inevitable self-destructiveness had created a crisis of personal and political legitimacy. Adams considered democracy a rotten plank, "floating in a shoreless ocean," but it had provided the only support for political progress. Washington was the "polar star," the father-founder, balancing Federalist aristocracy and Jeffersonian democracy. It was he who "alone remained steady, in the mind of Henry Adams, to the end"; but Washington was also the summation of wickedness. This was true for Adams, not only because Washington came at the end of the road of slavery, which his New England father and father-founders had insisted explained the corruption of the South, but because that road of democracy also led to Tammany Hall.[59] Adams looked to Europe for civilizing values out of which he might escape the contradiction of order and anarchy in American history but found only a mounting tension between them. His vitriolic anti-Semitism reflected Adams's loss of belief that democracy could be controlled by patrician values. He could find no basis for unity in the scientific world of physics or the political world of history but the unity of chaos. For Adams, chaos appeared to be the only common principle that could link order and anarchy—tradition and innovation. As he looked at conditions in Europe between 1880 and World War I, he saw chaos everywhere winning out over individualism and tradition. Supporting the trusts and the Jews against church and state, he feared, would lead to America's being swallowed by the socialists. Supporting church and state against the Jews and trusts might lead to the opposite fate of being swallowed by the capitalists. "You and I," he complained sardonically to his brother Brooks in 1899, "come in and say: What does it matter; it will come to the same thing anyway." The collapse of Europe and the resulting accretion of financial power into America seemed to Adams a negative frontier offering only a march of degradation, not progress. The coming collapse of Europe, which to Adams seemed a certainty, meant inevitably the transference of the money center from London to New York. "Westward the course of Jewry takes its way!" Even the form of Adams's racism pointed to a westward movement of progress toward a democratic future of degradation, moving from the Russian frontier in the East, through Europe, and then to America.[60]

Adams's themes were composed against a social revolution and a neo-Copernican revolution in space and time in which, after the pattern of Machiavelli, he made himself central by making himself peripheral. He defined that self as an object to be pitied and mocked, much as Machiavelli mocked and promoted himself in his plays and in his advice to *The Prince*. Adams's *Education of Henry Adams* (1907), was a family romance gone absurd, in which he cast himself as a man separated from his society and his time.[61] His political *ressentiment*, and his inversion of religious piety, were signs that he had consigned the role of Providence to the periphery. Indeed, rather than an anguished will to believe, there were echoes of Machiavelli in the privy in Adams's confession that "in my view, Hell was all there was to make life worth living. Since it was abolished, there is no standard of value. Hell is the foundation of Heaven, and now costs nothing and measures nothing."[62] Adams mocked himself as the diminished son who was unable to harmonize Mount Vernon with Boston or himself with his father's world. He conservatively challenged the legitimacy of a corrupt national government in *Democracy*, noting that Washington's deification was probably as false as Robert E. Lee's effort to emulate it. Yet through the figure of the sensitive southern hero, John Carrington, with whom he as a culturally displaced New Englander ironically identified, Adams nevertheless tried to preserve an aristocratic ideal against the corrosive effects of democracy. But Adams's ironic identification with aesthetic conventions symbolized by Carrington did not lead to a marriage with the hero's female cognate, according to the rules of the southern family romance. Instead, the woman, Madeleine Lee, finds the strength to repel the villain named Ratcliffe through the spirituality and refined self-control of Carrington. But she does so only through a complementary repelling of the heroic Carrington. For he is only able to mate with her spiritually, when he is physically absent. He can prove his worthiness to her and therefore sustain her life force, but only through the act of returning to his southern home alone. At the end of the novel Sybil, Madeleine's sister, writes Carrington to tell him that he should try again for Madeleine's attentions with more than a hint that she hopes to make the match herself. There is a postscript from Madeleine, as well, keeping a door open to an eventual consummation between the hero and his female cognate, but her last words to Carrington, like her last words to Sybil, are expressed as *ressentiment* towards democracy and not as intimations of marriage.[63]

The same application of the family romance as an ironic attack upon itself is found in Adams's companion novel of 1884, *Esther*.[64] As Carrington in *Democracy* was portrayed as the perfect spiritual mate who cannot be joined physically, Stephen Hazard, the young clergyman-hero in *Esther*, is compared to the church, which is spiritually uplifting, but only from a distance. Esther Dudley, an innocent young woman from the West, may not directly represent democracy, for she carries her own symbolic baggage as a female principle of natural force in search of a male principle with which her spiritual and physical life may find consummation. But given the feminine implications of republican ideals of civic virtue in complementary and contradictory relation to male forms of virtù, the title character at least shares in the problem of democracy as a woman desiring to submit to the male virtù of religious dogmatism or science. As was Madeleine Lee in *Democracy*, Esther is repelled from the antagonist—in this case George Strong, a dispassionate scientist—by the spiritual force of Hazard. But once again, the unfulfilled female cognate repels the antagonist, though more bleakly than in the first novel, through a break that also repels the hero, in Esther's case, sending Hazard back home to his church.[65]

Esther, however, makes explicit Adams's ironic use of the mediating role of art, as at once a theatrical illusion and a means of expressing a deeper truth through dramatic analogy. For in this apparently romantic formula novel, Adams mocked himself and justified himself at once. Adams was the anonymous author of a dramatic narrative, which offered a heroic challenge to the determinism of his own publicly acknowledged historical narrative of the death of Jeffersonian democracy. The central figure of that dramatic narrative is a dramatic artist, Wharton, who is alienated from the theatricality of religious ritual. As an artist, Wharton is alone capable of teaching Esther how to live without innocence or attachment. He binds Hazard's spiritualism and Strong's objectivity. But he confesses to Esther that he is incapable of painting innocence without suggesting sin. He has learned from his suffering to adore purity and repose but cannot grasp them. The artist Adams, like the artist Wharton, points the way to dissolution and madness at the same time that the historian-scientist points to unity and rationality, because the unrealized dramatic imagination cannot be realist, it can only be theatrical and romantic. "Wharton's real notion of art" is a volcano, says Hazard to Esther. "You may be a volcano at rest, or extinct, or in full eruption, but a volcano of some kind you have got to be."[66]

Adams's inability to sustain his faith in the unity of an authority in which democracy could be grounded forced him to separate politics from value and aesthetics from science. This, in turn, left in doubt his own life quest as a historian. Was he promoting anarchy or order through the process of his education? He acknowledged this post–Civil War crisis of legitimacy by writing Machiavellian romances in which he anxiously struggled with the terrors of solipsism, his family's national loss of legitimacy, and his own frustrated desire to act heroically for something, anything.

Thomas Dixon, too, wrote Machiavellian romances in which he tried to contend not only with the southern family's loss of national legitimacy and the failure of the heroic southern ideal, but with the failure of democracy itself. Despite his melodramatic style, it is not unreasonable to place Dixon's writing within the same framework as Adams's cool and ironic, though occasionally equally melodramatic, romantic narratives. Lincoln remained the fixed pole of Dixon's commitment to the nation, for much the same reason that Washington remained Adams's central symbol. Dixon treated Lincoln piously in his novels. He seemed to take pleasure in portraying him in Walt Whitman's staunch Unionist terms, as he claimed him as a Southerner and a true champion of democracy.[67] In doing so, Dixon distanced himself from the defense of the Lost Cause, and yet made the South's claim to legitimacy real, despite the North's victory in the Civil War. But he also could not avoid Lincoln's responsibility for the Civil War policy of emancipation, which doomed the South to the horrors of Reconstruction even as it established "the first true democracy in the world." According to Dixon, in *The Clansman* (1905) and *The Southerner* (1913), Lincoln's fate of suffering and death linked him to the oppressed South of Reconstruction and made it possible for Dixon to use Lincoln to repudiate slavery while embracing a policy of black disfranchisement. The innovative violence of Lincoln's creation of the union was balanced for Dixon by Lincoln's repudiation of social and political equality for blacks. This was a doubtful standard for political legitimacy because it was contradictory to democracy as a dynamic ideal and because it was a defense of the Anglo-Saxon family that was itself created through family violence. Dixon acknowledged as much when he had the hero of *The Southerner*, John Vaughn, decide to assassinate Lincoln as a tyrant after tragically killing his own brother during a battle. As a Southerner, of course, Lincoln in his military victories by definition suffered the same tragedy as John Vaughn each day. If the rise to the presidency by a backwoods rail splitter confirmed the promise of democracy, his execution of the office equally confirmed its demonic implications.[68]

In the novel, Lincoln confesses to his would-be assassin that "I had my ambitions, Yes—as every American boy worth his salt has." The humblest of the humble, he had dreamed of the White House as a child in a log cabin. "My dream came true," says the penitent President, "and where is its glory? Ashes and blood." Lincoln tells Vaughn that he envies the dead on the battlefield their rest. Then he asks Vaughn to risk his life on a secret mission, having found new hope by convincing him that he, Lincoln, is not really a tyrant, after all. In telling the truth, the President has turned a murderer into a friend and restored legitimacy to his government. However, while Lincoln's subsequent death absolves him from direct responsibility for the policies of Reconstruction, it also initiates the advent of those policies which, according to Dixon, turned democracy into a self-defeating contradiction.[69]

The tragedy behind each of Dixon's novels is his conviction that the Civil War and Reconstruction were at once necessary and self-defeating manifestations of democracy. These manifestations included race, but were not confined to it. Instead, they were rooted in the intersection of the public and private realms of political and social meaning in the *polis*, and the contradiction between power and value that Machiavellianism located within the private household.[70] This may be seen by the fact that Dixon's other early novels, which ignored race or only incidentally included it, such as *The One Woman* (1903), *Comrades* (1909), and *The Root of Evil* (1911), were concerned with other forms of modern life than Negro equality as a threat to the sanctity of the family, which was the source of private and public virtue.[71] In these novels of modern life, Dixon warned against the evils of socialism and capitalism as complementary corruptions of democracy, much as did Henry Adams. But, unlike Adams, Dixon repudiated anti-Semitism and anti-immigrationist prejudices because he associated outsider status and a history of suffering from oppression with southern history.[72]

However, given the central place of Reconstruction for Dixon's view of American history as presented in *The Leopard's Spots* (1902), *The Clansman* (1905), and *The Traitor* (1907), he believed that the success of democracy, which made the integration of such outsiders into one national household a possibility, portended disaster when applied to blacks. For Dixon, the law of democracy sweeping over the earth inevitably destroyed slavery, but by that same law of development, democracy must lead to the "Africanization," and therefore the primitivization, of the nation. Just as the nation could not exist half slave and half free, he had Lincoln say, it could not exist half white and half black. The racial virtù of Anglo-Saxons, as the Civil War proved, was capable of horrible violence within its own household. How much more terrible would the violence be when the household itself was challenged by an alien people? Even under monarchical and aristocratic forms of society, he said, two antagonistic races had never been able to live peacefully. "How could it be done," he asked, "under the formulas of Democracy with Equality as the fundamental basis of law?" Yet that was the very program expressed in the modern age by democracy itself. If Anglo-Saxons succumbed, the principle of biological degradation by which "one drop of Negro blood makes a Negro" would assure that the proud race of Anglo-Saxons would be turned into vicious animals. If they resisted, as Dixon thought they surely would, their unleashed virtù would destroy their own virtue as well as physically destroying blacks. So long as there was a black presence in America, according to Dixon's tragic dilemma, no resolution of the republican contradiction of virtù and virtue was possible.[73]

This double bind rendered heroic action, as a revitalization of political virtue, necessary but self-destructive for Dixon—a point that becomes more clear when *The Leopard's Spots, The Clansman,* and *The Traitor* are placed together. For in the course of that trilogy, Dixon portrays the Klan as having degenerated from a sacred fraternity into a mob over the course of time. The Judas-like betrayal of the original heroic clan ideal by a traitor, Fred Hoyle, in the third book in this Reconstruction trilogy destroys the public life of the true hero, John Graham. As the legitimate leader, Graham resisted the temptation to use the Klan to avenge his private wrongs and officially disbanded the Klan in obedience to law. Not only does the traitor, Fred Hoyle, usurp an illegitimate leadership to use the Klan to further his own illicit passions, but he goes on to prosper in the public realm by becoming a federal judge. Graham finds his legitimation as a hero only in the private realm. As the book ends, his female cognate has recognized and married him while in prison, but there is no hint, despite his vindication, that he will ever return to a public leadership role. The Graham family mansion, a symbol of the values of the Old South, is torn down as the innovative forces of progress triumph over southern tradition.[74]

This same structure was already present in the first of Dixon's Reconstruction novels, *The Leopard's Spots,* as well. After the brutal lynching for rape of Dick, the son of his father's body servant, the hero Charles Gaston broods upon the tragedy. "Now," he reflects, "scarcely a day passed in the South without the record of such an atrocity, swiftly followed by a lynching, and lynching thus had become the punishment for all grave crimes." Yet, under the democratic conditions of Reconstruction, "the insolence of a class of young Negro men was becoming more and more intolerable." With horror, he thought of the result awaiting them, once "they roused that thousand-legged, thousand-eyed beast with its ten thousand teeth and nails!" Gaston heard Reverend John Durham's "fateful" words, recalled from his childhood, echoing in his ears: *"You cannot build in a Democracy a nation inside a nation of two antagonistic races. The future American must be an Anglo-Saxon or Mulatto."* This scene is placed after the rape and the lynching but just before the hero's resolve to compel the respect of his lover's father. "I'll take my place among the leaders and masters of men," Gaston vows. "I will compel the General's respect; and if I cannot win his consent, I will take her without it."[75]

However, this private violence, which threatens the successful completion of the family romance, is avoided in the narrative because the young Anglo-Saxon has an avenue in public leadership through which he can win the father's respect. After Gaston has defeated the father, General Worth, through a rousing speech for white supremacy at the state convention, the General replies, "My boy, I give it up. You have beaten me. I'm proud of you. I forgive everything for that speech. You can have my girl." But since Sallie had disobeyed her father, recognized the greatness of Gaston at his lowest ebb, and married him secretly in prison, his vindication is her vindication, her virtue is rewarded by his triumphant virtù. When elected governor, he acknowledges the applause by bowing "to his bride, not to the crowd."[76]

General Worth is, of course, angry when he discovers that his daughter had disobeyed him, but he quickly relents. "It is no disgrace to surrender" to the "youngster" because, he says, "I've fought a foeman worthy of my steel." He surrenders the house to Gaston, telling him he may now run it as he sees fit, just as he will run the public household as the new governor. "Come to think of it," concludes General Worth, it was quite a brave thing for his daughter to march into a jail and marry her lover in prison. "By George, she's a chip off the old block! I don't care if the world does know it." Thus, the ineffectual father is defeated by the insolent young innovator, "with the power to mould a million wills in his, [and] change the current of history," restoring to the public and private households a state of peace and harmony. Only in Gaston's subtle contempt for the false values of popular acclaim is the worm in Dixon's faith in democracy allowed to show itself in the heroic narrative. Dixon closes *The Leopard's Spots* with the young governor's confession that he would "rather be the husband of such a woman than to be ruler of the world." [77]

In the novel, however, Dixon also presented a counter–family romance and a counter–heroic narrative through George Harris, the son of Eliza of *Uncle Tom's Cabin.* [78] George Harris falls "deeply and madly in love" with Helen Lowell, the daughter of his patron, the Honorable Everett Lowell, a Republican congressman from Boston. Like Gaston, he worships his "white robed-angel" from afar with "a secret passion he had kept hidden in his passionate soul." As Gaston's powerful oratory was an expression of his own devotion to Sallie Worth, Harris's musical compositions with a "cadence that held the imagination of his hearers in a spell" were the breath of his secret love for Helen. When he asks for the hand of his inspiration he is contemptuously dismissed by her father. Though the congressman had extolled the principle of equality as the soul of democracy, he would not accept a Negro as worthy of marriage to his daughter. Harris protests that social and political equality cannot be separated because politics is but a manifestation of society that rests upon the family, which is in turn the unit of civilization. "The right to love and wed where one loves is the badge of fellowship in the order of humanity. The man who is denied this right in any society is not a member of it." He is outside its bounds, like a beast of the field. He ceases to exist as a person to those who have so removed him, says the disillusioned Harris.

Unable to gain the respect of Lowell, despite his having a Harvard degree, intelligence, and talent, Harris recognizes himself to be the victim of a hypocritical double standard, which he cannot heroically overcome. His principled rejection of this hypocrisy eventually leads him to desperation when he is faced with the cruelty of racial hate, which denies him even the lowliest employment in the exploitive new mill economy. He ends his life as a criminal in the control of the same Simon Legree, now a corrupt businessman, from whom his mother had escaped forty years earlier.

These counter–family romances merge when Gaston, who will ascend with the speed with which George Harris will fall, initiates an ominous ride of intimidation by the Klan to reassert Anglo-Saxon manhood. This ride is defended by Dixon in the novel precisely because "there was no violence except the calm demonstration in open daylight of omnipotent racial power and the defiance of any foe to lift a hand in protest." The

Anglo-Saxon race stood together as one, "fused into a homogeneous mass of love, sympathy, hate, and revenge." This triumph of Gaston is predicated upon the despair of George Harris, though not, as is often suggested by Dixon's interpreters, on the lynching of black rapists. This, however, can be seen only in the context of Dixon's whole work.[79] In that larger context, it is evident that Dixon genuinely was opposed to violence as self-destructive of the virtue of Anglo-Saxons but considered it inevitable under the conditions of democracy after Reconstruction. Therefore, in *The Clansman,* the Klan was necessarily required to act more aggressively to fulfill its mission to preserve Anglo-Saxon virtue than it had in *The Leopard's Spots.* The Klan nearly turned into a mob when members were outraged by a black man's rape-murder of a white woman. But it was saved from degeneration into brutishness by self-restrained leadership and the rule of order. Vengeance was exacted, but through the ritual killing of the guilty Negro by the executioner's sword rather than the animal passions of the men. *The Traitor* of 1907, however, featured the triumph of division within the Klan, violence against an old Jewish immigrant, and the murder of the governor. All these terrible consequences resulted from the degeneration of the Klan into a mob, with private passions running wild.[80]

In the developing context of his novels, Dixon portrayed a bleak personal vision of an unrelenting movement away from political meaning into chaos, a movement that systematically proscribed the efficacy of every available avenue of heroic action, not only in relation to race but to gender as well. In the matter of race, Dixon insisted he was writing with scrupulous attention to historical accuracy as he pursued, after 1900, a single-minded mission to disabuse the public of a false belief in sentimental evolutionary hopes for democracy. He sought to do so, despite a failure to transcend identifiably romantic language, through a brutally realistic reappraisal of the forces that made moral uplift and racial tolerance impossible. In his first novels, *The Leopard's Spots* and *The One Woman,* Dixon gave the preachers the central role of confessing the failure of those idealistic views of democracy in the modern world which he himself had championed a few years before. In substance as well as in literary form, this mission of public education was much like Adams's literary efforts to cast doubt on his own earlier hopes for evolutionary progress. Dixon embraced an aesthetic pattern similar to the one pursued by Henry Adams for transforming the successive deaths of each of his efforts at public education into a personal aggrandizement. In each case, the outer failure of an authority or tradition revealed the narrator's inner loss. The heroic standard was invoked within the text, but only to transform that inner loss into a victory over the self and failed standards of meaning.

The central theoretical construction behind *The Leopard's Spots* and *The Clansman* (which John Hay, Adams's friend and alter ego, read in proof and endorsed),[81] and *The One Woman* and *The Root of All Evil* was that modern conditions had fatally transformed the delicate balance that Western civilization had fashioned between the volatile private passions of the isolated individual and communal harmony. Dixon believed that an order could not be refashioned through the acts of the lawless individual's passion, but only through the rebuilding of a republican ideal of citizenship. He believed that feminine virtue could provide such a basis, though ultimately Dixon despaired of separating the problems of gender from those of race under modern conditions.

Dixon's more hopeful perspective on gender, in relation to race, was essentially presented in *The Leopard's Spots.* In the story of Allen McLeod, a Populist who is branded a southern traitor, and Mrs. Durham, the minister's wife, Dixon not only presented his view on gender, but presented a third counter-variation on the southern family narrative formula.[82] The satanic McLeod has lost his soul in his ambitious desire to rise out of poverty and superstition. Thus, his Populism is identified by Dixon with the demonic side of democratic ambition. He owes his education to the minister's wife, Mrs. Durham. Her unfulfilled life had found an outlet in teaching needy children. Now an ambitious politician, her former student recognizes and seeks to use the sexual frustration that he knows is just below the surface of her maternal affections. "All women are born slaves and choose to remain so through life," says McLeod. "It is curious to see you, a proud, imperious woman, born of a race of unconquerable men, staggering today under the chains of four thousand years of conventional laws made by the brute strength of men. And you, if you struggle at all, beat your wings against the bars that the slave-holding male brute has built about your soul, fall back at last and give up to the will of your master."[83]

But Mrs. Durham turns aside this cynical effort to use her frailties to get at her husband, McLeod's real motive, and thereby preserves her own virtue as well as her husband's. She does so by turning scientific rationalism to the service of her ideals, much as Dixon had used the atheism of Robert Ingersoll in the 1890s as a back-handed confirmation of religious faith. Quoting the argument in *The Natural History of Love*, a book McLeod has given her to break her spirit and cause her to surrender to sensuality, she says: "Love finds its satisfaction in the child, its ardour cools, and it dies, unless kept alive by the social conventions of the family, which are not based merely on violent emotion, but also on unity of tastes, which produce the sense of comradeship. For these reasons it is possible to fall violently in love more than once, and there are dozens of people who possess this magnetic power over us."[84] But Mrs. Durham goes on to explain that she deduces freedom from this law of necessity, not slavery. In the union of her first great love, she recognizes, she was actually bound not by contract or convention, but more universally, in Nature's law which is also God's law.

This nonconventional use of the family romance in *The Leopard's Spots* is significant first because it parallels the Naturalist formula for attacking Naturalism, which Dixon used in *The One Woman*. Instead of race conflict, however, the central concern of that novel was gender, and its location was not the Reconstruction South but Dixon's contemporary New York. Socialists and capitalists take the place of Populists and carpetbaggers. And the main protagonist is a New York minister, drunk with his own social theories of democracy on the march—a closer autobiographical sketch of Dixon than the Reverend Durham in *The Leopard's Spots*, who rejected a call to a Boston congregation out of love for the South.

Second, McLeod's words of temptation to despair, which he addressed to Mrs. Durham, were later voiced by Dixon himself in an article he published in the *Saturday Evening Post* in 1905.[85] But Dixon applied them to the condition of black Americans with ambition and intellect, and not to white women. W. E. B. Du Bois, Dixon wrote, exemplified the hopeless situation of blacks possessing ambition and intellect; his was "the naked soul of a Negro beating itself to death against the bars in which aryan society has caged him." Similarly, Booker T. Washington's aims of educational reform were laudable, Dixon admitted, "resting on eternal truths," with which "only a fool or knave could find fault." Yet he opposed Washington's efforts because educating blacks was creating "a nation within a nation" between two hostile races.[86]

Why did Dixon believe that despite the formal similarities in the positions of white women and blacks, the former could achieve personal freedom and participate in preserving the virtue of their community, while the latter could not? Why could brutal male power result in "love licks" that would make female subservience soul-enriching, while it nec-

essarily led to ominous hatred among blacks toward their natural masters? Why could the frustrated sexuality of Mrs. Durham's teaching escape surrender to sensuality, while blacks could only be driven into its
violent embrace by Washington's teaching?

The answer to this question, for Dixon and apparently for his readers,
lay in the republican resolution to the inherent instability of the private
household, the foundation of the public household. As a crossroads of
male virtù and female virtue, of the private realm and the public realm,
and ultimately, of the self and the community, the household stands at
the center of the Machiavellian problem of innovation and stability. According to Dixon, the danger of passion as a corrupting force in a modern world reflects a loss of boundaries in all aspects of democratic
American life. Dixon considered the implication of this loss of limits for
economic corruption and the corruption of private life under both socialism and capitalism in *The One Woman, Comrades,* and *The Root of Evil.*
Like Tom Watson, Dixon considered socialism to be the greater threat to
republican values among two evil systems because it attacked the legitimacy of the economic independence of the home and the ideal of personalism upon which marriage is based. "The home is the basis of modern
civilization," Colonel Worth tells his idealistic rebellious son Norman in
Comrades. "If you destroy it, the home will not survive. If the home sur-
vives it will kill socialism. The two things can't mix."[87] But when the socialist leader chooses Barbara, the hero Norman's cognate, to be his mis-
tress as co-regent of the revolutionary socialist household, Norman
rebels against the false father of the commune, reunites with his true father, and wins Barbara, who has surrendered her ideas of free love.

The Root of Evil, as the title suggests, criticized corporate capitalistic
greed, as *Comrades* emphasized the evils of socialism. *The Root of Evil,*
however, presented Dixon's growing doubt about the possibility of retaining the heroic ideal through a natural affinity recognized by the hero
and his true mate.[88]

According to the convention of the southern family romance, the
beautiful leading character of the novel, Nan Primrose, should be the
female cognate of Jim Stuart. He is a handsome, young southern lawyer
who struggles valiantly against the greed and cynicism of New York City.
Stuart feels a passionate desire for Nan in his soul, knowing she belongs
to him by destiny—as she knows also. But Nan has actually transgressed
the ultimate taboo of the southern family narrative: She has married the
wrong man, a small, furtive, and dark Southerner named John C. Cal-

houn Bivens. His wealth gives Bivens a status in New York he could never have pretended back home in North Carolina, where his father had been a coward in the Confederate army.

In the South, it would have remained obvious to Nan that he was inferior to the hero, Jim Stuart. But in the North, his millions give Bivens an image that bedazzles and finally corrupts her noble spirit. Dixon draws Bivens as a doubtful villain, rather than as a symbol of alien values. He is a product of the modern age, at once an oppressor and a good husband, friend, and church member. Bivens came to New York from within the southern family, but has lost his boundaries, so he is a mixture of "sobriety and greed, piety and cruelty, tenderness and indomitable will, simplicity of tastes with boundless ambition."[89] The hero is Bivens's friend and his enemy, and fulfills his life quest by resisting his own natural heroic urge to take Nan from Bivens. Instead, he comes to love a child-woman who becomes his wife, confirming Dixon's naturalistic rejection of the traditional southern family romance, while revitalizing the promise of heroic transmission at the same time. She may not have been born to share his destiny, but the "little pal," whose father had been destroyed by Bivens's power, grows slowly in Stuart's affections. The epilogue tells the reader that the cottage he built for the love of his life, Nan, is now no longer rented to others. "The lawn is a wilderness of flowers and shimmering green." Roses cover the house, framing a window where Jim and Harriet, now a "little mother," live in domestic bliss. But if Dixon has laid to rest the southern family narrative in order to restore its fecundity on naturalistic grounds, he has also warned that money and power without limit have challenged the heroic ideal, blurring the difference between the natural leader and the natural criminal.[90]

Similarly for Dixon, the commercial expansion of European imperialism had long ago transgressed the natural boundaries of the races, established by God and defended by the natural instincts of racial aversion. But slavery did more than unseat God and his natural law through the arrogance of economic virtù. It introduced a volatile new element of instability into the Anglo-Saxon household.[91] Through the institutionalized structure that developed under slavery, however, the complications it caused within the private household were contained and even somewhat ameliorated. This was accomplished through the forging of paternalistic bonds of responsibility, much as the effects of exploitation and the cruelty of political domination were avoided in the Roman Republic by defining client cities as children. For, as children, the weaker cities could be considered as fortunate recipients of benevolent protection, rather than victims of despotic control. Under republican values, such rule over children could be ennobling, while the rule over other adults must initiate a process of corruption.[92]

Dixon carried this republican convention to one conclusion in his novel *The Sins of the Father*, which was first presented as a stage play in 1912.[93] Dixon succinctly stated his case: "Even under the iron law of slavery, it was impossible for an inferior and superior race to live side by side for centuries as master and slave without the breaking down of some of these barriers." Yet "the moment the magic principle of equality in a democracy became the law of life," all social and racial barriers "must melt or democracy itself yield and die." Given the history of the South and of slavery, Dixon explained, a paradox was inescapable: In a biracial society, democracy must destroy democracy. Race relations presented an unresolvable problem: "Every road of escape led at last through a blind alley against a blank wall." Even a limited mixture of races, Dixon warned, was sufficient to "put out the light of intellect and light the fires of brutal passions."[94]

The central figure of *The Sins of the Father* is Tom Norton, Sr., who is modeled after Charles Gaston, the hero of *The Leopard's Spots*. A fearless newspaper editor, Norton had led the effort to overthrow Negro rule. Like Gaston, he fulfilled his political role with great skill, forcefulness, and integrity. But unlike Gaston's, Norton's life is portrayed as a failure that ends with the bullet he places in his own head. Norton's downfall results from the gulf between his political activity, which would purify the *polis* by removing the Negro from political life, and his personal passions, which have led him into the arms of Cleo, a beautiful mulatto woman. "It's enough to make the devil laugh to hear you politicians howl against social and political equality while this cancer is eating the heart out of our society," he is told.[95] Though Norton, the leader of the white democracy, had subdued the mob and rallied a defeated people to take back their political birthright, he was forced to face defeat in his own home, as he "watched his boy's tiny arms encircle the neck of Cleo, the tawny young animal who had wrecked his life, but won the heart of his child." The "age-old disease of the *Beast*" was being passed on before his very eyes. The proximity of the races inevitably destroyed virtue and turned the whole society into a tissue of lies. This was not only evident in the passions of men like Norton, according to Dixon, but in the innocent fragility into which white southern women had been trained to hide from the sins of their husbands and sons.[96] The presence of blacks attacked the family structure of the nation, sapping it of its inner strength and trust. Norton contemplated this implication of racial contact until he awakened in shock to "the gradual wearing down of every barrier between the white and black races by the sheer force of daily contact under the new conditions which Democracy had made inevitable."[97]

The self-defeating paradox that Dixon contemplated through Norton was that he, like most of his Anglo-American contemporaries, believed the purification of southern politics depended upon the disfranchisement of Negro voters. Yet also like them he was heir to a political tradition that recognized no basis for the restraint of the private passions outside of the *polis*.[98] Ironically, therefore, the purification of the political process meant that any form of contact between whites and blacks must necessarily corrupt whites and drive blacks toward a violent effort to escape their condition. While this was true in every forum of racial interaction, it was especially the case in the intense passion of sexual relations. In this context, the animal attraction that the mulatto women of Dixon's novels were able to exercise over white men resulted from their ambiguous position of being both black and not black, yet never white. These women hate their blackness and therefore live a purgatorial existence between two worlds. In order to escape being condemned to life and marriage with blacks, which is made onerous by white prejudice, these women attempt to save themselves in the only way open to them as women. Their white features and intelligence, coupled with their Negro animality, make them irresistible: therefore they are prepared to use their sexuality to wrest a place in the white society for themselves and their children.[99]

According to the conventions of republican ideology, women are associated with the private passions. Therefore, women as the centers of the private household necessarily threaten the stability of the public household. However, within the complementary roles of gender relations, codified within republicanism, a virtuous woman may inspire a fallen man to reform or to channel his virtù in a politically responsible direction. A weak man may learn to accept his political responsibility by her awakening of his virtù through his passion for her. There are many examples of this kind of redemption in Dixon's novels, especially among immigrants, who lack education and are new to the ways of democracy.[100] However, by the definition of the situation, the mulatto woman cannot inspire such political virtue and therefore cannot be virtuous. Her sexuality must always lead away from political responsibility and toward the antipolitical realm of private passions.

The heroines in Dixon's novels, whether black or white, are always described as child-women. They are pure potentialities. Their greatest power for good resides in their renunciation of their personal talents or careers to become mates who will transmit the heroic legacy into a new generation. This self-sacrifice, as a form of self-realization, is deemed necessary by Dixon because the heroic male's virtù must conquer to realize itself, while he may be tamed of arrogant self-aggrandizement only through the influence of feminine virtue. For Dixon, as for Machiavelli, the virtues are necessary for social and political harmony, but they require virtù to bring them to fruition. In turn, however, feminine virtue must tame masculine virtù because it threatens the stability necessary for the values associated with civic life to survive.

Dixon's melodramatic name for the untamed and unregenerate virtù of the true man is "the Beast." In *The Sins of the Father,* for example, Norton is aroused in a moment of passion: "The Beast . . . had been bred in the bone and sinew of generations of ancestors, willful, cruel, courageous conquerors of the world. Before its ravenous demand the words of mother, teacher, priest, lawgiver were as chaff before the whirlwind—the Beast demanded his own." [101] In the presence of a desperate mulatto woman, this virtù, always morally doubtful but necessary for the defense of virtue in a hostile world, becomes a disastrous flaw. The particulars of race and every other social responsibility are swept away as the "universal" animal passion in him "finds its counterpart in the universal in her." In the unnatural conditions created by human manipulation of the boundaries between the races, universals destroy the particularity of individual experience instead of confirming it. Universal passion overwhelms the critical faculties of particular men and women. In terms that appear both datedly "romantic" and ironically anticipatory of Hannah Arendt's republican jeremiad in *The Human Condition,* Dixon says that "two such beings are atoms tossed by a storm of forces beyond their control." [102]

Despite the melodramatic form of Dixon's novels, his message is the classical political convention that separate and incompatible peoples must necessarily live in a state of violence because they are incapable of creating a *polis* together. Without a *polis,* human beings can only live in enslavement to their passions or under the power of others. The private household is the foundation of the public household, but it is also the seat of the private world of needs, which may distract the citizen from his public responsibility. Only when the private self and the public community are in harmony does balance prevail, and with it peace and harmony of interests. The "Beast," as Dixon described it, is simply virtù without a *polis* to tame it. Sex between blacks and whites, though portrayed with lurid sensationalism, is not the only form of "the Beast's" presence within modern society, according to Dixon in his novels. He described it as having a thousand heads and legs. He characterized it as the source of crowd behavior, which may as easily avenge a Negro's rape of a white woman or turn on a virtuous white man once its passions have been aroused. Dixon warned that both capitalism and socialism pander to it. The anarchists who long for the individualistic solitude of the forest, and the socialists who are drawn to the life of the herd, are equally responding to "the Beast," and are for that reason, he insisted, interchangeable. "The Beast" can spontaneously generate itself within urban mobs of any color, he warned.[103]

But if such patterns of behavior can only be controlled within institutions that are themselves threatened by lawless passion, a spiral into a maelstrom of violence becomes unavoidable. As a result, Dixon, in his novel *The Fall of a Nation: A Sequel to the Birth of a Nation* (1916), voiced apocalyptic threats from European kings towards American democracy in exactly the same terms as he had earlier warned of the Negro menace to democracy.[104] The hero of the novel, John Vassar, a Polish-American congressman, recognizes the false idealism of the peace movement, very much as Dixon's earlier hero in *The Leopard's Spots* came to realize the false idealism of racial harmony. Charles Gaston told General Worth, "I believe that government is the organized virtue of the community, and that politics is religion in action." That may be a poor sort of religion, Gaston admitted, "but it is the best we are capable of as members of society." Vassar similarly challenges the foolish virgin, Virginia Holland, naive leader of the peace movement. "I am only assuming the facts of modern life: That force still rules the world; that government is force; that there are two forms of government and only two, and that they are irreconcilable." Though Vassar was referring to government by imperial masters, rather than mulatto or Anglo-Saxon dominance, the "irreconcilable conflict" appeared in exactly the same terms.[105]

Once more, though Dixon remained true to the family romance formula of resolving the tale with the marriage of the hero and his cognate along with the restoration of the nation from occupation by foreign powers, Dixon no longer claimed that the "one woman" could make the disjointed world right again. By his final novel, *The Flaming Sword*, Dixon could offer neither marriage nor a reprieve for a defeated democracy.[106]

Instead, Angela Cameron, the granddaughter of Ben Cameron, hero of *The Clansman*, finds her entire family murdered by a black rapist. In the last paragraph of Dixon's last novel, set at a moment of utter defeat for the democratic forces of the nation, he warns his readers of "a malignant, contagious, mental disease now sweeping the world as the Black Death swept Europe in the Middle Ages." In 1939, the danger to the nation was no longer the black republicanism of Booker T. Washington, which could be removed through colonization at the cost of a mere ten million dollars and a twenty-five-year program, as Dixon had advocated in 1905. The new disease sweeping the world to its inevitable destruction was communism, created by "the collapse of the human mind under the pressure of modern life." The Negro threat was now the black communism of W. E. B. Du Bois. Colonization was still Dixon's only solution, but now at a cost of one hundred million dollars and a one-hundred-year program. And that was a solution without potential even for Dixon himself.[107] For in the novel, colonization had but one sponsor, and that sponsor was doomed to defeat because he was Marcus Garvey. "A powerful conspiracy had been formed by his enemies," according to the novel's hero, a Southerner named Phil Stevens, "to drive him from America and destroy his work." As Dixon knew, Garvey had been deported by the U.S. government in 1927.

Why would Dixon persist in advocating a scheme for colonizing American blacks over nearly four decades, when he clearly stopped believing in it himself long before 1940?[108] The answer seems to be that it provided the only resolution available to him for the republican conundrum of the contradiction between private and public households. It became an aesthetic escape from a democratic history that was inevitable and inevitably corrupting. It was Thomas Dixon's own literary formula for escaping the despair of a Jacksonian Machiavellian moment.

It is quite true, as Maxwell Bloomfield noted some years ago, that Dixon developed a stock set of phrases and ideas between 1887 and 1899, which he used over and over again for the rest of his life.[109] But rather than attributing this to simple shallowness or opportunism, we may see Dixon as trapped within the dualism of at once defending and rejecting the heroic southern ideal of his youth. Dixon did not write a pastoral elegy to that past, nor could he free himself through composing novels on the Romantic elegiac model. Instead, as his autobiography reveals, Dixon seems to have struggled all his life with an ambiguous self-identification with his uncle, Colonel Lee Roy McAfee, who was a fit figure for elegiac fantasy since he was a bright and dashing leader of the Klan during Reconstruction, but who died at the age of twenty-nine of tuberculosis.[110] In 1922, Dixon even tried to raise a statue in full Klan regalia to McAfee's honor in Shelby, North Carolina. Then, after a great public controversy over the issue, he vigorously attacked the new Klan as renegade, self-appointed judges who were wrong to hound Negroes and foreigners. Though it might be argued that this stand was less paradoxical than simply opportunistic, given the surprising amount of sentiment against the statue, it must be kept in mind that this was precisely the pattern Dixon had already established towards the Klan between 1902 and 1907 in his trilogy on Reconstruction.

After serving as a heroic public figure, McAfee became a lawyer, and a young Thomas Dixon swept his office, ran errands, and basked in the aura of that pillar of Shelby society. However, when the twenty-year-old Thomas Dixon made a similar effort to embrace public service as a legislator and then as a lawyer, he found a very different reality than his fantasies had prepared him to expect. In the first instance, he found himself not among selfless heroic leaders but only "prostitutes of the masses." In the second instance, after a brief attempt to establish a law practice, he again became disillusioned because his considerable persuasive powers were being used to no greater purpose than to "befog the minds of a jury" in the interests of some client's fee.[111] By the time Dixon was old enough to vote, he had already lost faith in the republican universal of public service and had tried to find a heroic ideal in religion. For the first time in his life, wrote Dixon, "I became conscious of the spirit of God expressing omnipotence in nature—of the infinite mind in action." He felt at one with "the power behind the glory of the sweep of the sun and tide."[112]

This was a dramatic identification with the positive movement of history, which Dixon would try to recapture again and again through his life, though each effort would lead only to a curiously regenerating experience of disillusionment. Long after abandoning his ministerial career. Dixon declared that in film "we had not only discovered a new universal language of man, but that an appeal to the human will through this tongue would be equally resistless to an audience of chauffeurs or a gathering of a thousand college professors." Still later, in 1925, he turned to his last universal scheme after his disillusionment with film and the death of his brother, Clarence. He decided to build a great complex of residences and lecture halls in the pristine mountains of North Carolina, as a rcfugc for authors, actors, musicians, and lecturers. It was to be a great international chautauqua, dedicated to the democratic discussion of all great Western ideas.[113]

By 1889, Dixon had been installed in the massive Twenty-Third Street Baptist Church, in the heart of New York City. The young minister spoke before overflowing crowds, quickly gaining national recognition. John D. Rockefeller attended a service and was favorably impressed. Dixon soon convinced him to fund a great temple in the center of Manhattan, so that Dixon could preach salvation to the throngs in the center of the greatest city in America. But the rivalry of a still larger church than Dixon's sabotaged his ambitious plans, much as the establishment pols had combined against him to frustrate his effort to win the speaker's chair of the North Carolina state legislature in 1883.[114]

A few years later, Dixon unleashed a diatribe against the Protestant establishment, at least in part because of this incident. In *The Failure of Protestantism in New York and its Causes*, Dixon castigated the New York churches for permitting provincial denominational politics to stand in the way of the poor and spiritually unnourished.[115] But expressing his ever-present dualism over his own heroic aspirations, he also wrote bitterly of the personal ambitions that had brought him to New York in the first place. "New York is the greatest graveyard of Protestant preachers in America," he declared. "Toward the dazzling light of its metropolitan life they eagerly flock from the smaller cities. Against its adamantine surface they dash their brains out like bewildered birds around a lighthouse."[116]

Early in 1895, Dixon abandoned denominational religion and briefly opened a Universal Church of the People. It was this effort to establish a universal form of religious socialism which he portrayed as pure hubris in his novel *The One Woman: A Story of Modern Utopia*. The new church, he said, was to be built upon the twin ideals of unity in all essentials and liberty in all nonessentials, bound together through the ideals of charity. Dixon's sermon-lectures were strongly tinged with political oratory. From his new pulpit, he attacked the corruption of Tammany Hall and the Populist message of the Democratic party under William Jennings Bryan. He passionately supported Cuban independence and war with Spain. His messages were received enthusiastically by the largest congregation in the nation. People queued for blocks before the services. The police were needed to route the traffic. As the turn of the century approached, Thomas Dixon was at the height of his power. Yet once again Dixon resigned in disillusionment. His reason was that the idea of an organic universal Christianity now appeared to him to be a false ideal. It attracted great crowds, he explained, but its superficial popularity could not foster a "vital force." "Belief in the old religious authority is gone," Dixon made his social gospel minister confess in *One Woman*, written a few years after he left the church: "Our church is thronged because of a peculiar personal power with which I am endowed. I could wield that power without a church, society, creed or Bible. Esthetic forces now draw people to non-ritualistic churches that once came for prayer and preaching. The preacher must secularise his sermon or talk to vacant pews. Historic Christianity has been destroyed by Criticism."[117] Denominationalism now seemed to him to be "the personal equation in religious life." Its loss, he warned, would harm and not help the spread of Christianity. Dixon declared his intention of returning to the Baptist ministry. He never did so.[118]

Meanwhile, Dixon repeated the same pattern in his domestic life. In 1897 he left New York to live in a restored tidewater plantation. The railroads made such a long commute possible and also allowed Dixon to range far into the Midwest to give lectures at a rate of one thousand dollars a night. In an article published by Dixon in 1902, he contrasted the purity and natural abundance of his new home with the expensive squalor of New York.[119] He wrote that some of the craftsmen who so cheaply and elegantly restored his mansion, Elmington Manor, had never seen a railroad, and he hoped for their sakes that they never would. Dixon went on to contrast his lifelong desire for such a tranquil and beautiful home with his other lifelong passion, "the hopes of life in a great metropolitan city." "I dreamed of its giant boulevards . . . its palatial homes, and gleaming lights." Its "myriads of people," he wrote, "filled the horizon of my youth with the glory of an endless sunrise." And so, he confessed, "in the natural course of events, New York swallowed us!"[120]

As Dixon became disillusioned in turn with each avenue for ushering in the democratic millennium, he looked to the South to find a source for renewed political vitality. He found, instead, a double bind in race that poisoned his hope for achieving democracy and retaining republican ideals at the same time. For this reason, Dixon was no more capable of finding a lasting solace in a romantic southern landscape than he was in returning to the Baptist ministry. By 1905, Elmington Manor had completely lost its attraction. Dixon declared that he was ready to reenter the life of the "great herd," to try to recapture the excitement of life in New

York City. Indeed, Dixon admitted that he had secretly kept his New York apartment all the while he had been denigrating the northern city for the idyllic southern plantation life to which he had escaped.[121]

Dixon's vacillation between the materialism of New York and the spirituality of the South reflected his effort to refashion a balance between Modernism and nature as a way to restore continuity with his past but to achieve discontinuity from the tragic history that threatened its memory. Stylistically, therefore, Dixon was critical of Realism in the name of defending the memory of his own southern family romantic ideal. Romanticism, he insisted, stood as a shield and a sword against degrading materialism. Yet, he found it necessary to challenge the conventions of the southern legend in his depictions of racial and sexual themes, because his message of reform required just such realism. Dixon railed against the separation of art from politics—a division he associated with the Naturalist school—but he could not offer a hopeful resolution of the division between aesthetics and politics for the reading public, or establish his own heroic role, except through laying to rest the heroic ideal he championed.[122]

The romance and historical writing, since Machiavelli, have shared a similar crisis of discourse for confronting the problem of cultural legitimacy and the transmission of meaning over time. Literary expressions may not have families, but they do exist within genres, and over the history of any genre, an individual text or style may either fall into oblivion or attain a respected place within a cultural canon. So long as it continues to be read, over generations, a text remains available for the formulation of cultural meanings. It does so, however, not only in the "timeless" form of subsequent editions of the original text, but inescapably in the web of "marriages" out of which new literary modes are continuously being generated.[123] Within a Machiavellian perspective, this means that the authority of the text (or genre as a whole) may fail if the latest form of the narrative tradition does not sustain the reader's ability to identify with its redemptive personal and public message. This of course, was the crisis within the genre of southern family romance that was shared by Dixon and Cash, a crisis that simultaneously called the scientific foundations of the Dunning school of Reconstruction historiography into question as well.[124]

Dixon was not able aesthetically to escape the Machiavellian contradictions of his romantic republican values through a detached irony, after the manner of a Henry Adams. On the contrary, Dixon's disappointed hopes, his prejudices, and his heroic aspirations were all rendered transparent through his Romantic style, without providing any way to resolve or transcend their pessimistic implications for public action. Indeed, his passionate quest romances increasingly turned him into an embarrassment to his once-enthusiastic fans, who outgrew his message. For urban consumers after the turn of the century gained myriad opportunities, within a burgeoning market of mass entertainment forms, for transforming their own memories into Romantic elegies. As consumers, they flocked to ever more sophisticated Machiavellian romances, such as *Gone with the Wind,* a film that might be described as having preserved in amber Dixon's message in *The Birth of a Nation.* Even Dixon, who repudiated the effort to reissue the film with a modern soundtrack and who complained against the death of Romantic fiction, seemed to recognize that a new synthesis for reasserting his heroic ideals was beyond his grasp by the end of the 1930s.[125]

For the same reason, W. J. Cash could not turn his disillusionment with Dixon into a creative new Machiavellian synthesis. He remained trapped within the continuity of Dixon's disillusionment with the historical legacy of Reconstruction. Nor, as we have seen, could Modernism provide an escape from history for Cash, once Adolf Hitler, Joseph Stalin, and Benito Mussolini provided a European end to his own hopes for the continuity of history.

As a result, especially since the 1960s, Cash's reputation as a literary stylist and critic of the South has been in decline. His legitimacy now rests on his role as a pioneer, anticipating the new realism of southern historiography, though not fully liberated from the romanticism he is thought to have brought to an end. Given the Machiavellian pattern of defining outworn syntheses as romantic and replacing them with new "realistic" ones, however, Cash's place within the American studies canon appears to be moving downwards, towards a final resting place near the untended grave of Thomas Dixon.

CHAPTER FIVE

Ironic Inversions: Pastoralism in C. Vann Woodward and Langston Hughes

In 1938, C. Vann Woodward garnered a front-page endorsement in *The New York Times Book Review* for his biography of Tom Watson from conservative historian Allen Nevins.[1] Nevins approved of *Tom Watson: Agrarian Rebel* as much for Woodward's allusions to Huey Long and Ben Tillman as for his analysis of Populism and the origins of the New South. That same year Woodward was awarded the prestigious Charles Sydnor Award for historical scholarship from the Southern Historical Association. The accolades bestowed upon this rebellious young historian, in whom his biographer, John Herbert Roper, found a pattern of being both willing and able to "use the advantage of one in the center to help him press toward the periphery," provided him with the position and the fulcrum to move southern historiography into a confrontation with nationalism and the failed promises of economic Progressivism in post–World War II America.[2] Like Reinhold Niebuhr, upon whom he came to rely for his ironic interpretation of history in the 1950s and 1960s, Woodward at once challenged the legitimacy of American national culture and reaffirmed a redemptive mission for it, finding moral poverty in its ostensible success but a wealth of cautionary wisdom among its defeated and despised. Like Robert Penn Warren, whom he came to know in the 1930s, he learned to write southern history as a creative paradox, an inversion of piety and progressive hope, as he wrote in 1956, to "penetrate the romantic haze of an older generation as well as the cynical stereotypes of our own." In doing so, as Woodward claimed with a bow to the Southern Renaissance writers, the New South was endowed with "the sense of tragedy and dignity which history had hitherto reserved for the Old Regime," consciousness of the past was brought into the present, and the Negro was made intelligible "without the glasses of sentimentality." [3]

It was, above all, from the writers of the Southern Renaissance and in the years before the Depression, certainly long before he formally began to study history, that Woodward began to develop the perspective that would later shape his study of Tom Watson. As an undergraduate at Henderson-Brown College, a small Methodist institution in Arkansas, Woodward voraciously read both political fare and the new fiction. According to his biographer, he edited the *Oracle,* the school newspaper, and participated actively in the Garland Society for Literature. [4] This last group was a left-leaning gathering of students who regularly commented and wrote on political affairs and college issues. As for so many young intellectuals of the period, H. L. Mencken served as model and as inspiration.

Mencken identified himself with Baltimore, a border city that was neither southern nor northern. Mencken thus lived at the crossroads of literature and politics as the self-appointed champion of culture against nostalgic sentimentality and calculating philistinism. Because he was not of the South, he could be more southern than the South, a defender of the old aristocratic *kultur* of the past against its degeneration into religious fanaticism and mental and physical torpor. Because he was not a New Englander, he could coldly admit to the failure of Puritanism through its degeneration into the crass pretense of a triumphant cash nexus. He used mockery to deflate its claims of moral superiority in the name of Emerson, Hawthorne, and Melville.

Mencken loved to play New England off against the New South in criticizing the conditions of American life, just as he played each section off against itself, and much as he enjoyed inverting Anglo-Saxon claims of superiority by pointing out the degraded racial stock of Anglo-Americans in the very language they themselves used against blacks. His own personal biological claim of Nordic superiority doubled as an ambiguous prodding for reform of the degenerated culture of Anglo-Saxons and as an equally ambiguous support for black intellectuals in their challenge to a rotting civilization and their own quest for self-expression. [5]

For this reason, the Old South that Mencken extolled was not the Old South of popular sentimental nostalgia, but a vital center of classical American civilization which had degenerated through the ravages of time. Consequently, as Fred C. Hobson has observed, Mencken's famous essay of 1920, "The Sahara of the Bozart"—the essay usually credited with launching the southern literary reawakening—was very much elegiac in form. But it was also crusading in intent because criticism was, to Mencken, a catalyst capable of reinvigorating tradition into new, living forms. To this end, Mencken carefully cultivated a role for himself in the 1920s as a father to dissident young artists in both the Harlem and Southern Renaissances. He used his influence as a public figure to legitimate complementary revolts against failed forms of cultural authority by figures as divided and diverse as Howard Odum and Allen Tate, W. E. B. Du Bois and Wallace Thurman. But he always did so in the name of a classical standard that stood outside of time, in a universal realm of aesthetic truth. Therefore, "The Sahara of the Bozart" marked out Mencken's Machiavellian identification with a classical past, which his subsequent efforts as a vituperative critic would try to restore through a support of innovative cultural rebellion among admiring young writers.

In the essay, Mencken mourned the South as a shriveled civilization which had been the "main hatchery of ideas" for the nation down to the middle of the nineteenth century. It had been a civilization of "manifold excellences—perhaps the best the Western Hemisphere has ever seen." But in the fall of the South from greatness, he said, it was "as if the Civil War stamped out every last bearer of the truth, and left only a mob of peasants on the field." Mencken declared the Leo Frank case to be "a natural expression of Georgian notions of truth and justice," and characterized "the mind of the state" of Virginia to be such that a Lee or a Washington was no longer imaginable as one of its citizens. Indeed, Anglo-Saxons had so degenerated from their cultural and biological standard of the past, he said, that they now approached the savagery of African blacks. Meanwhile, American blacks as the recipients of the best blood of the old southern aristocracy, gained through Anglo-American degradation, offered the one aesthetic alternative to a condition of paralyzing cultural stagnation in the arts.[6]

Mencken's theme was that the failure of idealism that led to World War I and catastrophe could serve as a compost out of which might emerge vibrant expressions of cultural renewal. The degradation of black life was, for him, a case study in the sociological possibilities of aesthetic regeneration. His interest in black writers, like his interest in white Southerners, flowed from his conviction that aesthetic creativity was possible only when a civilization or a people was about to recover from its cultural wounds, or to displace those superior specimens who had been weakened by some intense conflict, such as war.

This was the Darwinian argument Mencken advanced in his essay from *Prejudices: Forth Series,* "The American Novel," to express hope for an American literary revival out of the despair wrought by World War I in Europe.[7] Practically gloating over the destruction of the European culture he revered, Mencken intuited that because America had been spared such a devastation by virtue of its privileged place, a national flowering of American culture could be predicted. "It seems to me," he wrote, "that, in the face of this dark depression across the water, the literary spectacle on this side takes on an aspect that is extremely reassuring, and even a bit exhilarating." He continued, "For the first time in history, there begins to show itself the faint shadow of a hope that, if all goes well, leadership in the arts, and especially in all the art of letters, may eventually transfer itself from the eastern shore of the Atlantic to the western shore." In the rebelliousness of the young postwar American writers, Mencken saw neither a disrespect for tradition nor the corruption of foreign influence. Quite the contrary, he said, their "goatishness" was really a proof of a rising nationalism, "perhaps of the first dawn of a genuine sense of nationality." Writers like O'Neill, Dos Passos, and Lewis, he wrote, were pioneers of literature, faithfully reflecting American life by showing its defects rather than its virtues. They were leading a national awakening that would "turn on the light" and make it possible to escape romanticism and "to think things out anew and in terms of reality."

This was a highly ambiguous interpretation of progress. It permitted Mencken to defend American nationalism conservatively through innovative ideals of aesthetic creativity that offered renewal through the process of deconstruction itself. It was an ambiguity that flourished in the contradictions of American racial values. Was Mencken a gruff but honest realist with a heart of gold, a champion of the aspirations of black Americans who were excluded from genteel literary society? Or Was he a Ligurio, the manipulative friend from Machiavelli's drama, *Mandragola*—the matchmaker who uses everyone for his own ends of self-aggrandizement, and who, incidentally, resolves everyone's needs through his deceptions? Was this the private role of Mencken's literary criticism in manipulating the sectional division between North and South? Or did he pursue it for other ends of arbitrating a higher nationalist-oriented aesthetic? After all, Mencken was convinced that aesthetic vitality was essential to political greatness. Evidence from Mencken's writing including his recently published diaries, could be offered for any of these interpretations. However, Mencken's studied effort to remain morally neutral but aesthetically honest in relation to blacks and toward racism itself is revealing of his larger intentions.

Mencken never wavered from his ambiguous position on race, despite prodigious knowledge of the black experience, gained from years of close scrutiny. From that detached perspective, he could refer to blacks as "darkey," "coon," and "niggero," and identify them with primitive degradation. For example, in his review of Howard Odum's *Black Ulysses*, Mencken wrote, "For the first time the low down coon of the South—not the gaudy Aframerican intellectual of Harlem and the universities, but the low down, no-account, dirty and thieving, but infinitely rakish and picturesque coon—has found his poet."[8] Such Realism from Mencken's pen, however, simultaneously opened the doors to black writers. Mencken urged them to create themselves in their own image, according to their own aesthetic as, he said, every other ethnic group should also do.[9] On the other hand, Mencken was unable to maintain such Ligurio-like neutrality between use and affection in relation to the white South. Mencken's Machiavellian sociology broke down when it came to incorporating disillusionment with faith in the creativity of American national exceptionalism, as F. Scott Fitzgerald would express it in *The Great Gatsby* of 1925. That was the year of the Scopes trial, in which Mencken shed ambiguity for a fervid defense of Enlightenment rationality and the scientific faith of progress, as his hope for a re-awakened South. The following years saw the publication of Thomas Wolfe's *Look Homeward, Angel,* and Faulkner's *The Sound and the Fury* and *Sartoris* (1929), and Ransom's *God Without Thunder* and *I'll Take My Stand* (1930)—none of which could be integrated effectively within the rubrics of Menckenian satire.[10] These novels and New Agrarian essays, which were somehow focused—but not created—by the Scopes trial, presented an inversion of Mencken's own call for an iconoclastic southern literature. They were more detached from the romantic myth of the Old South than was Mencken, who had appointed himself as the guardian of the memory of its lost aesthetic virtù. Conversely, they were more attached to the continuity of a despised and degraded Southern virtue in opposition to the same Yankee Puritanism Mencken had tried to undermine in his support of southern writing.

Mencken either remained silent or missed the intent of these works in his critical writings. The reason was not that Mencken had become too detached from the South in which, between 1925 and 1929, writers were turning to its defense. Quite the contrary, in the years between the Scopes trial and his marriage to a patriotic southern woman, Sara Haardt of Montgomery, Alabama, in 1930, Mencken had established friends among the southern clergy and frequently expressed disillusionment with northern "standardization." The acerbic Mencken had become critically vulnerable by guilessly admitting to his attachment. "Once known as the South's bitterest detractor," Donald Davidson wrote of Mencken in 1932, he has come "to look almost like a disguised Confederate raider who had chosen his own methods of devastating a too-Yankeefied civilization." A few years later that assessment was echoed by Lambert Davis, the editor of the *Virginia Quarterly Review*. In soliciting an essay from Mencken for the *Review*, he characterized Mencken as at once the South's "severest critic—and a sentimental Southerner at heart." Lambert went on to tell Mencken that "you are considered in many quarters the father of the South's literary renaissance." Therefore, "you ought to pass judgment on whether your offspring are legitimate or not."[11]

In 1927, when C. Vann Woodward was still a college student, the irreverent Mencken would not have been viewed as anyone's cultural father figure, only as a champion of or panderer to the new turn to Naturalism in the arts and sciences. Even the New Agrarians remained circumspect about whether to claim or criticize him, maintaining an ambiguous distance. Nor did Mencken overtly enter into any economic or political debates over how to create a new social order in practical terms until his disillusionment with the New Deal.[12] For despite his Modernist rhetoric, Mencken was fighting a rearguard action to restore republicanism in a corporate consumer democracy. As the once aloof Fugitives *cum* New Agrarians who shared his anguish acknowledged, Mencken had provided them with a bridge between aesthetic rebellion against Romanticism and political awareness by revitalizing a degraded and ridiculed southern culture against Yankee Puritan dominance. At the same time, northern critics of Romanticism and capitalism, such as Charles Beard, Edmund Wilson, and James T. Farrell, who attempted to translate republican values into a new urban context, lauded Mencken's *American Mercury* for, in Beard's words, its "smashing, stinging audacity."[13]

As a member of the collegiate generation contemporary with the height of Mencken's iconoclastic popularity, Woodward brought a number of these themes together in a speech he presented to the Garland Society in the fall of 1927. The speech was entitled "Romance and Reality." The occasion was Woodward's recent return from a summer trip to Europe and the Soviet Union. It reflected his restive impatience with the oppressive cultural atmosphere of Henderson-Brown as much as a desire to seek out vital, new sources for political and cultural reform.[14]

Drawing parallels between post–World War Europe and the post Civil War South, and enthusiastic about the Russian experiment, Woodward called for a new realism to replace the discredited romanticism of an earlier era. Pretending that the traditions of the old plantation South were still adequate to new realities was as false as the European effort to hold onto equally romantic traditional values after the changes wrought by war. Only realism, he assured his listeners, could respond adequately to the challenge of freedom, urbanism, and industrialism in a new era.

The following year, Woodward transferred to the more cosmopolitan atmosphere of Emory University in Atlanta, where he majored in philosophy and literature, and after graduation he accepted a position at Georgia Tech, teaching English composition. In 1931, Woodward traveled to New York City, where he earned a master's degree in political science from Columbia University. The young Southerner in search of cosmopolitan adventure found himself drawn to the theater and to the writers of the Harlem Renaissance, still the creative center of northern black urban culture in the 1930s, yet largely the product of the intensive black migration out of the rural South in the 1920s.[15] As such, despite its internationalist and cosmopolitan image and its cultivation of primitivism and African roots, the Harlem Renaissance was an extension of the same movement to revitalize alternative possibilities for social democracy through aesthetics that gave rise to the Southern Renaissance. Like Woodward and other young white southern intellectuals, young black intellectuals in Harlem were reading Mencken and fashionably patterning their own styles upon his. They too, were seeking freedom over southern stereotypes and were in search of a life-giving history, recoverable through art. Political conceptions of community and agrarian idealism pervaded their social consciousness, particularly after 1929, but earlier as well, much as it did for southern white writers. An exotic Africa, rather than an idealized Europe, provided a classical standard against which to challenge both a rural southern past of oppression and the painful dislocations of northern urban life.

During his first year at Georgia Tech, Woodward had met and developed a friendship with the poet, novelist, and critic J. Saunders Redding, then a young assistant professor of English at Atlanta University and a talented actor who was playing the title role in Eugene O'Neill's *Emperor Jones* to southern audiences. Redding offered Woodward an opportunity to experience a personally committed response to racism that was rooted in both a passionate sense of justice and an artistic vision of a truly integrated South. Though Redding had only recently arrived in Atlanta from Brown University, his perspective had been prepared by his appreciative reading of Jean Toomer's *Caine* (1923), with its themes of social protest against racism, the alienation of northern city life, and the promise of redemption through a folk experience deeply rooted in the southern soil. Redding was also impressed by Sterling Brown's similar but less lyrical message when his *Southern Roads* (1932) appeared the next year, and by his friend Langston Hughes, whom Woodward was to meet the following year in New York.[16] Until that time, Woodward has written, he had never dealt with a black person on an equal basis, though he was already troubled by racism in southern society.[17] Arriving at Columbia University without any very definite academic plans, Woodward soon gained access to the world of the Harlem Renaissance through Langston Hughes, and he was even invited to perform with an amateur Harlem theatrical group. Woodward approached W. E. B. Du Bois about a study of Du Bois's ideas for his thesis. As Woodward remembered, "an interview in his editorial office at the *Crisis* got nowhere, however, after he heard that deep South accent of mine."[18] The thesis that Woodward did write turned out to be a rehearsal for *Tom Watson: Agrarian Rebel*—a study of Tom Heflin, the Alabama "demagogue" of the 1920s. Clearly, the later conception of the early Tom Watson as a racial liberal owed something substantial to the Harlem Renaissance and the themes of black and white equality that were being sounded in the 1930s by Langston Hughes, Sterling Brown, Saunders Redding, and other artists of the "New Negro" movement. It was ultimately that perspective which Woodward projected back onto Watson and the Populist South, for it could not have been derived from the historical record of Georgia politics at the end of the nineteenth century. It could not have been found in Tom Watson's own values, or even Woodward's own universe of thought, before the indirect and direct influence of the Harlem Renaissance.

The Harlem of this "New Negro Renaissance" had been created by the massive demographic movement of blacks out of the American South following World War I. It has been estimated that this great urban migration was undertaken by more than five hundred thousand blacks between 1910 and 1920, and that another eight hundred thousand followed during the 1920s.[19] Harlem was transformed into the largest urban concentration of black Americans when more than one hundred thousand middle-class whites fled their community in the 1920s, ironically providing in their own flight a new urban frontier for Afro-American social, political, and aesthetic experimentation.

As the name implies, the "New Negro Renaissance" was a far more widespread phenomenon than what was concentrated within Harlem alone. Nor were Harlem's refugees and emigrants all drawn from the American South. Jamaica, South America, Africa, literally the whole world mingled in the streets, bars, and literary salons of Harlem. Yet the dominant demographic pattern out of which the Harlem Renaissance was born, and the cultural forms through which it was viewed by white observers and by most participants themselves, were established by the great migration of black folk out of the rural South. The anthropologist/novelist Zora Neale Hurston, for example, remained aesthetically and physically linked to Eatonville, Florida. Though educated in Wisconsin, the Washington, D.C.–born Jean Toomer identified with Sparta, Georgia, and Arna Bontemps identified with northern Alabama. Even those writers who emigrated from Jamaica or the Barbados, such as Claude McKay or Eric Walrond, had grown up in rural agrarian environments, which continued to shape the content of their writing.[20]

Consequently, the new world of which the artists of the Harlem Renaissance dreamed was as much an effort to imagine another agrarian South, as were the contemporary aesthetic visions of such southern white authors as Ellen Glasgow, Harry Harrison Kroll, Elizabeth Madox Roberts, or Allen Tate before the Depression and, far more ironically, Erskine Caldwell or William Faulkner in the 1930s. For all were similarly attempting to construct other Souths than the failed South of history, by rejecting Romanticism and establishing a classically timeless aesthetic pattern through which that history could be exploded into its elements, purged, and finally deprovincialized. Indeed, their search for a usable past reveals the continuing frustration for those who had seemingly emancipated themselves from an unusable one. For southern black and white intellectuals of the period alike, this search for aesthetic frontiers ordained that, as Robert Bone has observed of the Harlem Renaissance, they would predominantly explore pastoral themes in their works.[21]

Pastoral themes are associated with the frontier convention of two worlds that must be kept in tension with each other.[22] These may be the two worlds of childhood and adulthood, of a rural past and an urban present, or the duality of the white Southerner as American citizen or of the black American who is self-divided in a white society. Once more, this doubleness of experience may be complementary rather than adversarial. One example is the way rural white Southerners and urban blacks responded to being defined as primitives by a powerful and condescending modernist consumer culture in the 1920s.

This mixture of cultural condescension and fascinated exoticism expressed at once an attitude of social domination over "unsophisticated inferiors" and a hunger for personal moral regeneration through a return to simplicity. That dual definition, in turn, provided a weapon for gaining a position of superiority over the dominating culture and a trap of defining opposition to that dominating culture in its own terms. In this way, rural white Southerners and urban northern blacks found new avenues of aesthetic creativity through embracing an *imposed* definition of their own cultural superiority. In the case of the Harlem Renaissance, the descent into primitivism provided a claim to an aesthetic birthright of cultural creativity for blacks against the lifeless standardization of white society. Simultaneously, the descent into primitivism for white tourists promised to be a rite of purification, a return to the origins of creativity from a decadent bourgeois society. The pastoral form, characteristically an ironic convention of inversion, could offer the redemptive possibility of rising by declining. Therefore, blacks who embraced the idea of their own primitivism could follow it to a purified taste for cultural refinement on one side, while white elites could ascend by descending into a subterranean jazz den, on the other. In Robert Bone's words, the Harlem writers "acted on the precept, common to all pastoral, that a descent in the social scale will be rewarded by a gain in spiritual stature." [23]

This same narrative formula was simultaneously finding expression in a number of aesthetic and social movements throughout the 1920s and 1930s among white rural Southerners as well as among black urban Northerners. For example, without proclaiming racial equality, the segregated South of the 1920s had been broached aesthetically by Southern Renaissance writers influenced by Mencken, such as Julia Peterkin, writing of Gullah blacks in *Green Thursday* (1924); T. S. Stribling, writing of an educated black man's rejection of the South in *Birthright* (1922); and DuBose Hayward, who wrote *Porgy* (1927). [24] In a very different vein, the famous Scopes trial of 1925 concerning the teaching of evolution in rural Tennessee literally and symbolically captured the essence of this pastoral inversion for lettered Southerners, such as the Fugitive poets. For a cultivated writer, such as John Crowe Ransom, that event captured the challenge of the vital religious primitivism of myth against scientific industrialism, which informed his defense of religious and poetic fundamentalism in *God Without Thunder* (1930). This same inversion of values was provocatively flaunted in the title of Andrew Nelson Lytle's essay for *I'll Take My Stand* (1930) in which he described the heroic challenge to a leviathan industrialism by the harried southern farmer in the metaphor of "The Hind Tit." "Squeezed and tricked out of the best places at the side," explained Lytle, "he is forced to take the little hind tit for nourishment; and here, struggling between the sow's back legs, he has to work with every bit of his strength to keep it from being a dry hind one, and all because the suck of the others is so unreservedly gluttonous."[25] If the pastoral formula served Lytle's design for offering a moral and aesthetic alternative to a rationalized money economy, for Donald Davidson it meant that "the despised hinterland" was the begetter of artists rather than the megalopolis to which they migrate "at considerable risk to their growth."[26]

Similarly, sociologists such as Charles S. Johnson of Fisk and Howard Odum of the University of North Carolina were just as committed to a pastoral perspective as were the Southern Renaissance and Harlem Renaissance writers. It is true that, as social scientists, they saw themselves as laborers against the cultural lag of the southern agrarian past. But, more important, they saw themselves as having personal missions to preserve the natural world of folk culture as it was being transformed into the artificial world of civilization. The folk represented for them the vital nurturing source of social stability. They viewed the dynamic changes of economics and technology as forms of progress leading to civilization but also, especially after World War I, as harbingers of chaos. The role of the social scientist, they believed, was to mediate the natural and the artificial, and the traditional and innovative conditions of social life. In doing so, they would assure that the stabilizing values of the folk culture would not be "blown away with changing environment," but that it would remain "to enrich the soil from which it sprang."[27]

Charles S. Johnson's mentor was Robert E. Park, onetime ghostwriter for Booker T. Washington and founder of the Chicago school of sociology. Park viewed race relations as a form of frontier experience and was fascinated by the idea that the primitivism of the Negro and other "marginal peoples" was a lingering vestige of universal human history. In his view, as he wrote in his introduction to Johnson's ethnographic study, *Shadow of the Plantation* (1934), folk culture persists only where there is not yet a written history. It exists "for the most part in unrecorded ballads and legends which, with its folklore, constitutes a tradition which is handed down from generation to generation by word of mouth rather than through the medium of the printed page." Such "marginal people" represented for Park and Johnson living, breathing frontiers of society.

They embody the vitality of the frontier because they are suspended "somewhere between the more primitive and tribally organized and the urban populations of our modern cities." The ethnologist, not the historian, explores this human territory and in so doing witnesses the inevitable destruction of the originally zestful folk-culture as it is transformed into the realism of history and of fact. Once the fluid, half mystical life of the peasant enters into history, once he has been pulled into the maelstrom of urban civilization, the joyous peasant becomes a proletarian, without memory or in many cases without even a will to live.[28]

According to this formulation, the "marginal man" stands poised between the memory of a vital and stable folk culture in the past, and the proletarian tragedy of shattered culture at the gateway of civilization. Park, who was careful to universalize this condition by applying it to women and to all racial groups, defined the social scientist as a "marginal man" as well.[29] But for Park and Johnson the social scientist's marginality is the direct inversion of the marginality of the folk he or she studies. The scientist's self-conscious marginality within civilization complements but does not actually repeat the tragedy of the folk. Where the folk are unlettered and unindividuated, the social scientist is educated and highly individualized. While the folk still hold the secret of harmony and social balance but face the alienation that is the price of progress, the marginal social scientist is alienated but faces the prospect of harmony and social balance through learning the secret of folk-life and applying it through social planning to heal the scars of progress. The marginal folk do not know that their confusion and despair are temporary since the city presents a new kind of frontier of opportunity. The social scientist, less obviously a powerful father than a wise shepherd, knows that in the intermingling and eventual amalgamation of disparate peoples the lost harmony of the folk will be restored at the level of a more nearly universal civilization. And the social scientists will be partners with the unconscious folk themselves in preserving knowledge of that harmony and applying it through social planning. Only then will their true roles as life-giving fathers become manifest.

This same theoretical, indeed one might say mystical, perspective lay behind Johnson's editorial policies in *Opportunity Magazine,* the single most influential forum for the promotion of the Harlem Renaissance between 1923 and 1927. Johnson used literary competitions to attract and promote the development of black talent and to put black writers in contact with white publishers. He did so, he wrote, to bring Negro writers "into contact with the general world of letters to which they have been for the most part timid and inarticulate strangers."[30] At the same time, Johnson used *Opportunity*, the official organ of the National Urban League, to publish sociological studies of black migration and the problems of poverty and discrimination associated with urban life. Through these two complementary sides of his magazine's mission—the promotion of literary culture as "a great liaison between the races" and the dissemination of relevant sociological data on black social conditions for reform— Johnson tried to usher folk culture into a new urban civilization, a promised land of cultural vitality just beyond the present.

Charles S. Johnson's work in social science paralleled Howard Odum's, and the two sometimes served together on professional boards. A student of race relations, Odum's interest in the black experience predated the Harlem Renaissance days, but his professional work in the 1920s and 1930s was deeply affected by the literary pastoral themes he shared with the writers of the two renaissances. This may especially be seen in his explorations of the primitivism of southern blacks in the 1920s, organized around a living folk legend, a "black Ulysses," whom Odum came to know in that decade. Odum's titles, *Rainbow 'Round My Shoulder* (1928), *Wings on My Feet* (1929), and *Cold Blue Moon* (1931), reflected the reciprocal influence of the Harlem Renaissance on the literary interests of the popular reading public, as well as on the new southern sociological theory itself.[31] Odum, however, also used pastoral themes borrowed from Southern Renaissance writers in his study of the rural South, using his own family history as well. In *An American Epoch: Southern Portraiture in the National Picture* (1930) and *Southern Regions of the United States* (1936), Odum combined the "poetic with the scientific." It was, he explained in *American Epoch*, "as if a new romantic realism were needed to portray the old backgrounds and the new trends and processes."[32]

In these books, Odum wrote portraits of southern life that lovingly recreated an agrarian past yet poignantly and personally criticized its folkways for failing to offer a viable vision for the future. The personal anguish in these studies by Odum, whose father was a loyal follower of Tom Watson, surfaced most strongly in his discussion of the folkways of white southern politics, which he described as a romantic savage ideal. His greatest optimism was expressed in direct juxtaposition to his discussion of politics, and he found it in the "significance of the new realism" characteristic of the southern literary awakening. "In all this new literature there was vitality and promise," he wrote in 1936, "an ever increasing evidence of regional maturity protesting against the older decadence and the current immaturity." [33] As this quote from *Southern Regions* suggests, Odum and his influential journal *Social Forces* were deeply influenced by H. L. Mencken, who strongly supported Odum in return. Odum's work at the Institute for Research in Social Science at Chapel Hill provided many of the sociological underpinnings for, among other studies of the period, W. J. Cash's *Mind of The South* and C. Vann Woodward's *Tom Watson: Agrarian Rebel.* [34]

Ironically, despite their objective style and use of statistical tables, the frontier interpretations of cultural creativity behind the modernist sociological theories of Park, Johnson, and Odum closely paralleled the form and function of the Romantic literary theory of the critic and novelist of the Old South, William Gilmore Simms. Following Romantic aesthetic conventions of pastoralism, Simms viewed the artist as a marginal person, "a *seer!*" who must preserve, and yet make useful, the past for the future. "He must be able to discover that which is hidden from all other eyes—which other minds have not conjectured—which other persons have not sought." If the writer fails in this, said Simms, "he is not the man to preserve a nation's history." For Simms, romance requires the dimension of obscurity if the writer in search of truth is not to be deprived of the vitality of inspiration. The author's pastoral responsibility cannot be fulfilled within the rigid categories of historical fact. "There must be a faith accorded to the poet equally with the historian, or his scheme fails to effect. The privileges of the romancer only begin where those of the historian cease. It is on neutral ground, alone, that differing from the usual terms of warfare, as carried on by other conquerors, his greatest successes are to be achieved." [35]

The artist who would preserve and employ the materials of American history for his own purposes, Simms wrote, must be a serious student of its lore. For "there are no absurdities in a time, when a people is alive and in action, which the true philosopher can despise." Indeed, Simms continued, the artist must "seek to imbue himself with all the workings of our spiritual nature—what they hoped and what they dreaded—how deep were their terrors, how high their anticipations." Through his investigations, Simms's author gains the elements necessary to create "*vraisemblance* which is his aim." How can we doubt the legitimacy of the romance, Simms asked, when it "conforms, in its delineations, more decidedly than any other, to the various aspects of man, and nature, and society?" [36]

This same pastoral responsibility, seen as the liaison between the natural and artificial, required Park to locate the province of folk culture in ethnography, rather than in history. The sociologist uses the tools of his investigation like a magnifying glass, explained Park, making the obscure visible; or, again, he may record a casual remark, which "like a ray of light through a keyhole, will illuminate a whole interior, the character of which could only be guessed at as long as one's observations were confined to the exterior of the structure." Praising the sophistication of Johnson's studies of the local tenant farmers in Macon County, Alabama, Park found them so "pregnant with human interest, that they might have been written by Julia Peterkin or DuBose Hayward, whose stories of Negro life exhibit an insight and 'acquaintance with' the life they are describing that is unusual even in the writers of realistic fiction."[37]

For a social theorist such as Charles S. Johnson, who actively brought creative literature and sociological research together in the Harlem Renaissance, folk culture and aesthetic imagination were really two expressions of one pastoral struggle aimed at creating a "New Negro" culture equal to, and fully integrated with, other American cultural groups in the urban frontier. Though Johnson believed that a separate black American culture was not possible, he was apparently unwilling to accept Park's parricidal theory of inevitably increasing assimilation, of the blurring and then the disappearance of racial identity. Park's prophecy of progress, as he acknowledged, assumed a very high cost in wasted lives, but they were lives he did not identify with in a directly personal way, as did Johnson.[38] Park's sociology, born as much out of his old love for Goethe's *Faust* as from Darwinism, was very near to a formal expression of the Romantic elegy. Johnson and Odum remained too personally committed to their folk cultures to embrace Park's resolution. Instead, they identified with the communities of their youth and affected a pastoral elegiac style of writing throughout their careers.

Simms's theory of narrative, however, like the sociologists' theory of folk culture, was based upon a pristine and innocent American past. Like Park, Simms was prepared to detach himself from his cultural past in the conservative interest of preserving it against the consequences of history. The past could only be recovered as a source of aesthetic vitality, for Simms, through an act of literary parricide against English culture. Simms did not offer an Enlightenment faith in science as an instrument to penetrate the necessity of history, or to find vitality in an obscure world of innocence or the chaos of modern alienation, as did Park. Instead he promoted a classical style of timeless art, capable of revealing its truth in the obscurity of dawning history and the complementary obscurity of the present moment. Like Park, Simms believed historical periods of transition were the most creative and hopeful. "Commotion, though in storm, is the proof of a new and more hopeful life," Simms wrote, explaining that progress by its own internal dynamic assumes agitation. It is calm, he said, which should be feared.[39]

Simms's version of creative possibility through pastoral inversion found the perfect romantic subject in the Satanic figure of Benedict Arnold, rather than in the coldly virtuous Washington. Indeed, Simms went so far as to suggest that the principle of pastoral inversion could serve to reveal the ambitions and jealousies of Washington and transform Arnold into a tragically sympathetic figure in the future. Eventually, Simms predicted, "Washington himself shall be made to do justice upon the head of the traitor,—as by a similar license, Richmond slays Richard, and Macduff the usurper of Scotland, in the presence of the audience." For Simms, following Shakespeare, Arnold's degeneration became the proof of his virtues while simultaneously leveling Washington. For Simms, too, it was a forthrightly Machiavellian resolution to the problem of creativity and authority.[40]

The pastoral mode shared by Simms and the New Sociologists is one possible manifestation of the cultural tension between the artificial and the natural, the collective and the personal, or tradition and innovation. Indeed, the pastoral appears almost archetypal in the great variety of ways in which it may appear. However, the Machiavellian form of pastoralism we have been considering represents a specific aesthetic and political response to the problem of power and value through inversion, specifically through an ethically compelling use of fraud.

According to Machiavelli, contrary to our expectations, cities founded on barren sites are most environmentally suited for hardening men into virtù and uniting them in common purpose.[41] Fertile soil makes men lazy and saps their virtù, while delivering them from the necessity of working together and developing their virtue. Unfortunately, however, any city in a position to maintain a static balance between virtù and virtue will be unable to grow strong enough to expand or properly protect its interests against others. Therefore, for Machiavelli, the father-founder must subvert the natural to preserve the artificial. He must subvert the natural because it exists only within the particulars of time, which makes it at once necessary and destructive for the artificial, and therefore timeless, realm of the public household, the *civitas*.

In Harringtonian terms, the natural realm had to be preserved, if domestic virtue was to be assured.[42] At the same time, the artificial exercise of virtù leading to progress could only be won through heroic expansion abroad. The contradictory relation of these political and economic ends resulted, as J. G. A. Pocock has explained, not from their antithesis but from the fact of their inescapable interpenetration with each other. That fundamental contradiction revealed itself, said Pocock, "at the moment of conceptual time in which a republic was seen confronting its own temporal finitude, as attempting to remain morally and politically stable in a stream of irrational events conceived as essentially destructive of all systems of secular stability."[43]

However, as I have suggested, the Machiavellian response to such a moment is not an automatic dissolution into some new political realism or into some romantic cultural void. Instead, a stylistic transformation takes place, quite undramatically and even predictably, through which a continuing aesthetic and political balancing of contradictions may be reestablished. In the image suggested by Wayne Rebhorn in his study of Machiavelli's aesthetic, the exposure of a confidence game does not reform the confidence artist, it merely provides the occasion for another confidence trick.[44] Indeed, the trust engendered by the realism of the exposure may be used by a facile confidence artist as the ground for a more ambitious trick. The frequent success of confidence games, however, is not due to a universal cause. The continuing gullibility of the "mark" is not ordained by human nature, though demonstrably it is not contrary to human nature either. Rather, the confidence artist appeals to a particular lust or attachment in the "mark," which the artist recognizes in himself or herself but is consciously prepared to exploit for other ends. It is, of course, the ambiguity over just what his ends were that makes Machiavelli such an intriguing artist and political thinker. But whether writing as a confidence man, a shrewd judge of human nature, or both, Machiavelli suggested that such lust or attachment is usually linked to some form of power. It is rooted in the desire for autonomy and claimed at the expense of another's. If the "mark" does not identify with the ends of the confidence artist's scam, or if he or she has additional values that are contradictory to such ends, the game may not be completed or may be only partially completed.

It is, therefore, important to recognize the link between the white Anglo-American culture and the black urban culture of the Harlem Renaissance as a mutually Machiavellian one. Thus Robert Bone's interpretation of the role of pastoralism in the Harlem Renaissance as an ironic inversion of power could be drawn from the same New Critical interpretation of the pastoral that was developed in the 1930s by William Empson, and this same pattern of ironic inversion could be visible in cultural critics as formally dissimilar in time and style as the New Sociologists and William Gilmore Simms.[45]

However, for the same reason that the New Criticism, as a Machiavellian convention, could offer such a penetrating analysis of a Machiavellian political culture, it is easy to miss the significance of alternative uses of pastoral forms, which may exist alongside them, and even challenge their validity. Since Machiavellian inversions of pastoral themes are rooted in a conservative identification with a tradition of doubtful legitimacy on the part of the artist or critic, a failure to identify with the tradition or to defend its legitimacy may well offer other cultural possibilities than Machiavellian ones. For example, Machiavellian conventions shared by the modernist Park, the ambivalent Odum, and the Romantic Simms, as we have seen, were less applicable to a figure such as Charles S. Johnson, despite his close relation to both Park and Odum.

The black experience in America, as Michael Kreyling notes, has never been compatible with the southern heroic narrative, because from Simms to Styron, the southern hero has consistently enacted or embodied black enslavement. Similarly, despite the close association between the Southern Renaissance and the Harlem Renaissance, black writers did not envisage a harmonious relationship between themselves and a historical community of agrarian simplicity. They were physically and geographically alienated from any ground for a conservative defense of southern tradition through innovation. They neither could nor would romanticize a rural South of lynching and enforced migration or the northern urban commercial culture that exploited them while liberating them. Therefore, despite many influences, including their own use of Machiavellian pastoral formulae to advance themselves in a white society, black writers such as Langston Hughes, Sterling Brown, Arna Bontemps, and Nela Larsen, among others, never entirely embraced a Machiavellian perspective. Instead, they sought a transcendent, shared humanity in ordinary experience. They attempted to identify with, not detach themselves from, their folk culture as they understood it. The Harlem artists emphasized themes of fundamental human solidarity in suffering, even while longing for personal autonomy. They recognized the ground of such solidarity as at once political and aesthetic. Art might help heal divisions of class and race, they believed, but it could not be appealed to separately from class and race as persistent historical realities.

This perspective may be seen most clearly and consistently in Langston Hughes, whose poetry, stories, novels, and dramas spanned the spectrum from jazz to social protest between 1920 and his death in 1967.[46] Hughes rejected the spirit and the letter of the New Criticism, which he derisively called "the lily ponds" because they are beautiful on the surface but decadent underneath. Instead, consciously blending concerns for social action and aesthetics, he tried to develop alternative pastorals, even anti-Machiavellian pastorals, in the 1920s and 1930s. Predominant among these was his use of the blues tradition. One example of this approach and its divergence from Machiavellianism may be seen in Hughes's collection of short stories, *The Ways of White Folks* (1934), previously published in such magazines as *Opportunity* and *American Mercury*.[47] Among these was one titled "Cora Unashamed." Hughes did not shy away from social protest, even as he offered a blues description of the life of an aging, lonely domestic, Cora, existing but hardly living in small-town Melton, Kansas. Having had a child with a passing white carnival roustabout, the first long dead and the second long gone, Cora is portrayed as long suffering but not as conventionally saintly. Nor does the pastoral rural setting of her hometown evoke the slightest image of vitality. Her one link to human affection is with her employer's daughter, Jessie, about the age her own daughter would have been had she lived. But Jessie, whose mental impairment isolates her from her white family as Cora is isolated as a person of color, dies from the effects of an abortion. She loses her baby and then her life to preserve the false bourgeois honor of her family who are scandalized because the young father was a foreigner and not from a legitimate, established family.

At the funeral, Cora confronts the family with their deed, and she is forcibly removed from the room and from her position. Somehow, Cora and her less-than-ideal parents eke an existence from their garden and junk collecting, we are told. Hughes's concluding affirmation of life through the character of Cora is not based on the picaresque promise of escape to the city. Nor is it based on a pastoral image of agrarian vitality gained from establishing harmony through her forced return to the land. Rather, for Hughes, it rests upon a moral integrity woven into the fabric of her life, graciously persevering in the face of misery.

Another of the stories, "Poor Little Black Fellow," ironically exposes the hidden exploitation behind charity and exposes the arrogance of the Pembertons, "one of New England's oldest families," who decide to raise the child of their deceased servants as if "it" were their own son. Hughes subtly shows the reinforcing humiliation the kind Pembertons visit on

Arnie, and the collusion between these actions and the social racism to which they expose him, even as they provide him with a special trip to Europe. Though the tone of the story is maudlin, it moves to a conclusion of black revolt, as Arnie's eyes are opened to his true situation by a black entertainer living the high life in Paris. They are opened, not by ideology, but by happiness: "Somebody had offered him something without charity," the narrator explains, "without condescension, without prayer, without distance, and without being nice."

Like any number of young writers suffering what Robert Bly has termed the "boy-god" complex, Hughes has Arnie walk out on the Pembertons and out of his golden cage into the freedom of the Paris streets.[48] But in doing so, Hughes does not simply repeat the heroic abandonment of a dull social conformity for picaresque adventure. More important, he rejects the Machiavellian convention that the nurturing form of the parent-child relation, whether applied to cities or people, may be used to circumvent the inevitable corruption born of power and dependency. He does not give his protagonist a new identity through a solipsistic escape from society but promises that Arnie will find another society in which color does not separate him from others or from himself.

Much of Hughes's other writing, particularly in the early 1930s, was preoccupied with confronting the problem of legitimacy in a pastoral context, but that context was clearly anti-Machiavellian in orientation. In 1922, Hughes wrote a poem called "Mulatto," but he did not pursue that theme of legitimacy again until 1931, when he confronted the issue in a play by the same name. *Mulatto* was not performed until 1935, when it opened on Broadway to hostile reviews.[49]

Set in Georgia, the play, like the original poem, was an effort to confront the tragedy of interracial hatred as a form of family destruction. Hughes linked class oppression to racism in the play, as a small-time county politician, Fred Higgins, wishes "the South had more men like Bilbo and Rankin." But Hughes's central theme was the moral corrosiveness of racial exploitation. Higgins chastises Colonel Norwood, the white father of four unacknowledged Mulatto children:

Nothing but blacks in the house—a man gets soft like niggers are inside. (*Puffing at cigar*). And living with a colored woman! Of course, I know we all have 'em. I didn't know you could make use of a white girl till I was past twenty. Thought too much o' white women for that—but I've given many a yellow gal a baby in my time (*Long puff at cigar*). But for a man's house you need a wife not a black woman.[50]

Colonel Norwood is killed by his son as a tragic consequence of failing to acknowledge their true relation, despite being bound by it. Bert, the son, is pursued by a mob of angry whites, and kills himself to avoid being lynched. Before his death, his mother and Norwood's unacknowledged mate, Cora, berates the father's corpse: "Col. Tom, you hear me? Our boy out there runnin'. (*Fiercely*) You said he was ma boy—*ma* bastard boy. I heard you . . . but he's yours too . . . but yonder in de dark run- nin'—from yo' people, from white People." In failing to recognize his common humanity with his mate and son, Norwood brings tragedy and forfeits his own legitimacy as a father. Hughes could offer no resolution but death for the abandoned son and madness for his twice-abandoned mother. But there is no effort to preserve paternal or white authority in the play's conclusion.[51]

The character of Hughes's criticism of American economic and racial values reflected in these writings was profoundly affected by the Scotts- boro case of March 1931. Eight young blacks were accused of raping two white women after an interracial fight on a freight train in which all were riding illegally. Both the NAACP and the Communist party vied in representing them, galvanizing Negro opinion across the country. Hughes wrote a number of political protest works that fall, including two appre- ciations of John Brown, which he linked to the Scottsboro case, and a one-act play, *Scottsboro Limited.* He became highly critical of the efforts of black leadership in defending the Scottsboro boys, and gained a con- trastingly positive impression of the Communist party's militant stand. However, he continued to remain personally close to W. E. B. Du Bois, who was being denounced by the League of Struggle for Negro Rights, the communist-oriented group with whom Hughes sympathized, and of which he was later named an honorary president.[52]

Harlem, then, was ablaze with indignant protest against southern rac- ism and economic injustice during 1931–32, the year the young South- erner, C. Vann Woodward, came north to discover a more cosmopolitan world than his own mundane South. At the time Woodward met Hughes, the poet was already planning an extensive reading tour through the American South, which was to begin during the first week in November.

Five years before, after deciding to accept the patronage of a wealthy widow, Charlotte Mason, Hughes had toured the South for the first time. Then, sexually pursued by Alain Locke, the classical scholar and cultivator of primitivism through whom he was introduced to Mason, Hughes spent the summer in search of the peasant joy of the primitive folk with the author and student of anthropology, Zora Neale Hurston.

By 1931, however, Hughes was deeply alienated from the aesthetic primitivism of Locke, Mason, and Hurston. He could find little joy in the fate of the Scottsboro boys or in fulfilling Mason's desire to direct him through an enforced innocence to a formally beautiful primitivism of pure art. Perhaps in part to put that old life behind him and to rebel against the subtle destructiveness of Locke's and Mason's oppressive blend of academicism and primitivism, Hughes felt compelled to return to the South in 1931. Hughes clearly had a very different object in mind from cultivating the primitivist folk wisdom of simple harmony with nature. "I want to create an interest in racial expression through books," he had written to Walter White in August, "and do what I can to encourage young literary talent among our people." Hughes believed that a tour of the American South "would do a great deal to link the younger writers with the black public they must have, if their work is to be racially sound." [53] Once more, Hughes seemed to court controversy, taunting white sensibilities and black professors alike.

The tour was met with enthusiasm by students across the South and confirmed Hughes's belief that Negro leadership was both too cautious tactically and too timid morally. It was very much a shoestring operation, and Hughes had only one firm commitment, which was at the University of North Carolina. He got that single commitment from a white school by writing to Howard Odum, whose *Rainbow Round My Shoulder* had been given a favorable review by Hughes in *Opportunity* a few years earlier.[54] Odum had passed the letter on to his colleague Guy Johnson. Johnson was outraged by the sensation Hughes created when, before his arrival, he contributed an essay and poem on the Scottsboro case to *Contempo,* the campus literary magazine. The poem, "Christ, in Alabama," provocatively ended: Most holy bastard / Of the bleeding mouth / *Nigger Christ / On the cross of the South.*" [55] In Nashville, Allen Tate found Hughes to be an interesting writer whom he would have been pleased to meet in the North or in Europe. However, Tate refused to attend a party given for Hughes, out of respect for southern tradition. Only in Mississippi, according to Hughes's biographer, Arnold Rampersad, did Hughes find himself cordially accepted by a member of the Southern Renaissance, William Alexander Percy. Percy introduced Hughes to an audience of blacks and whites in an African Methodist Episcopal Church in Greenville, referring to him as "my fellow poet." Percy corresponded with Hughes for some years afterward. "But," Hughes commented later, "I met less than half a dozen such gentlemanly Southerners on my winter long tour. Instead I found a great social and cultural gulf between the races in the South, astonishing to one who, like myself, from the North, had never known such uncompromising prejudices."[56]

Soon after Hughes's return from the South, Woodward was graduating from Columbia and off for a tour of his own, a summer's visit to Europe and the Soviet Union. Still drawn, as ever, to the literature of revolt against provincialism, Woodward soaked up the culture of the Left Bank and came away with a Black Sun edition of James Joyce's *Ulysses.* He then traveled to Berlin, where he observed another kind of revolt from discredited tradition in the intense political rhetoric of committed young fascists and communists. From there he went on to Moscow, still with robust hope for the Russian revolution, but he was given pause by the processes of industrialization and of agrarian collectivization being undertaken by Joseph Stalin. Through it all, he kept hearing questions from the French, Germans, and Russians concerning the fate of the Scottsboro boys.[57]

Woodward was doubly stung by his recognition that this injustice was a source of shame for him not just because he was an American, but more particularly because he was a Southerner. He vowed to challenge the next racial incident he would encounter upon his return to the States. But his Soviet-inspired Progressivism was deeply eroded when he found that his efforts to defend a young black Communist party organizer, Angelo Herndon, were cynically used by the party for selfish propaganda purposes. Woodward continued to be active in reform activities, but he increasingly found himself frustrated by his own dualistic desire at once to affirm and to exorcise his southern identity. Woodward, who doubted the seriousness of Roosevelt's New Deal as well as the intentions of the communists, felt that same ambivalence as a Southerner toward such public figures as Huey Pierce Long, the contemporary boss of Louisiana, and Tom Watson, dead less than a decade and still a presence in Georgia. Such men were blessed with the personal courage and ambition to take action for the poor and oppressed in their region, but they were also cursed with the hubris to grasp for personal power that went beyond the limits of political virtue. As a college student, Woodward had been drawn by the tragic tale of Dr. Faustus and by such anti-heroic dramas as *Emperor Jones,* and he was similarly drawn to and repelled by the realism and romantic heroism of the Longs, Watsons, and Heflins in the hard times of the early Depression years. In fact, even while Woodward was still at Columbia and writing a thesis on Tom Heflin of Alabama, he began to

consider expanding the study into a book that would confront the paradoxes of a number of similarly flawed giants of southern democracy as
Classical tragedies.[58] Undoubtedly, Odum's *An American Epoch*, which
had been published in 1930 and which emphasized the same theme of
paradox in southern culture, was an important influence on his thinking.
Stylistically, Odum acknowledged the need to resolve the division between a romantic pastoral past and a realist scientific future by combin-
ing the two forms in his writing. Thematically, he described the South as
many Souths, yet one; "preeminently national in backgrounds, yet provincial in process," it was at once romantic and realist in character. The
South was both better and worse, Odum explained, as it paradoxically
unfolded its national destiny from the past to the future. "From high estate came low attainment, and from dark places came flashing gleams of
noble personality."[59] But Woodward saw another paradox in Odum's own
ambiguous defense of a continuing pastoral vitality in the regional South
through the nationalist economics of the New Deal. Woodward's criticism
was similar to the paradox the Agrarians had identified in Mencken's defense of scientific rationalism at the Scopes trial and which they pilloried
with Agrarian militancy in *I'll Take My Stand*.

The very title of Woodward's projected epic, *Seven for Demos*, hints at
his iconoclastic use of Classical symbolism to attack a decadent social
order of exploitation based on "the double-think of worshiping the symbols and myths of the Lost Cause" while "simultaneously serving the
masters of the new plutocracy."[60] Eventually, however, Woodward began
to flounder in the enormous range of his study. He sought out the support of Howard Odum, through family connections, and Odum helped
Woodward win a Rockefeller Foundation research grant. Then, favored
by a fortunate encounter with Georgia Watson, the Populist's granddaughter, Woodward decided to limit the projected book to an examina-
tion of one anti-heroic reformer, Tom Watson. He decided as well to
enter the University of North Carolina where Odum taught and where
Watson's papers had just been deposited.[61]

Perhaps Woodward's most important debt to Odum's *American Epoch*,
however, may be found in Odum's characterization of Watson as a pathetic victim of southern defeatism, a leader who missed greatness because he succumbed to personal bitterness.[62] Similarly, beyond the accidents of their meeting, and his fortune in finding her willing to open
sensitive family papers and memories to his probings, Georgia Watson
and Woodward shared a similar sense of dissociation between the South

as an idea and as a political and social reality. Woodward (and presumably Georgia Watson) wished simultaneously to assault the false patriarchal authority of the institutions and values of the New South and conservatively to rebuild a foundation for relegitimizing the southern family romance through realism. Woodward's study of Watson, therefore, promised to provide a historical source for a legitimate line of southern dissent, which could then be used to delegitimize the currently dominant South as defined by northern nationalists and by their New South supporters, including Odum.

In other words, rather than anxiously weighing the dilemmas of objective research versus partisan service to change, Woodward was preoccupied with the more fundamental dilemma of how to establish discontinuity from the past while finding in it a usable basis for effecting change in the present. How could he establish a frontier line between continuity and discontinuity, between a compromised past that needed to be escaped and a legitimizing past upon which to ground a new future? Woodward's historiography of the frontier, an ambiguous line between aesthetics and politics, which he called a "crossroads," was his meeting ground for fashioning an answer to the dilemma of continuity and discontinuity in the southern past and future. It was here that Woodward found his appreciation of both the officially segregated Southern Renaissance and the Harlem Renaissance; the New Regionalist sociologists and the New Agrarian poets; Mencken's literary aesthetic of inversion and the political inversion of republican industrialism championed by Charles Beard. As Woodward explained in his autobiographical essay, *Thinking Back: The Perils of Writing History*, "there was a Chapel Hill–Atlanta–New South liberal axis, and a much dimmer Chapel Hill–New York–Union Square radical axis. Meanwhile, a Nashville–Baton Rouge Agrarian axis was shaping up, taking form eventually in the *Southern Review*. Between Nashville that was alleged—with exaggeration—to be bristling with hostilities and practically impassable: Vanderbilt Agrarians *vs.* Tar Heel Liberals."[63]

Woodward approved Allen Tate's definition of the Southern Renaissance as "a glance backward," and as a literature "conscious of the past in the present, shaping, haunting, duplicating, or reflecting it.[64] The Southern Renaissance was a mediating ground of history and imagination, in which Woodward recognized a new framework for southern historiography. Without defining the Southern Renaissance as a "crossroads," he wrote in 1975, "there is no satisfactory accounting for powerful inner conflicts of these writers, the unrelenting tensions between what [Robert Penn] Warren once called 'the Southerner's loyalties and pieties—real values, mind you' and his religious and moral sense, equally real values." In struggling between "a traditional society and a modern one," a conflict was engendered that "necessitated a coming to terms with the past." The "crossroads" and the "backward glance," Woodward concluded, were "necessary conditions" to what happened. However, Woodward emphasized, "necessary conditions" do not constitute historical explanations. Any number of possibilities may exist as necessary conditions, but historical events that make those possibilities actual may not necessarily occur.[65]

Woodward learned this perspective directly from Charles Beard, whose essays in the 1930s emphasized the political implications of all historical writing and the necessity of finding a way to master relativity as a part of the historian's moral and professional responsibility. From Beard, too, Woodward gained the insight that the fundamental problem of history is not found in the struggle between objectivity and subjectivity, or commitment versus scholarship. Rather, Woodward recognized it to be a peculiarly personal problem that he, as a disaffected Southerner, experienced even more acutely than did Beard himself—the problem of continuity versus discontinuity in time.

The student of history "who tries to penetrate the pageant of politics to the economic interests behind the scenes," Beard insisted, "is not any less interested in truth than the so-called objective scholar, who feels superior because he ignores economic interests and eschews interpretation, which defends other interests." "We may shut our eyes to the abyss of thought that yawns at our feet, so perilous," he wrote in the defense of the practice of historiography, but "the abyss remains."[66]

Beard's most complete statement of this argument appeared in *The American Historical Review* in January 1934, "Written History as an Act of Faith."[67] In that address, Beard defined history as "thought about past actuality, instructed and delimited by history as record and knowledge authenticated by criticism and ordered with the help of the scientific method." According to Beard, there is an inevitable discontinuity between history as thought about the past and history as the actual past. Therefore, unavoidably, "the pallor of waning time, if not death, rests upon the latest volume of history, fresh from the roaring press." This suggests that the crisis of history is a crisis of reference, because neither space nor time may be fixed with certainty if historians cannot know actualities but can only place them within a particular frame. This frame is constructed, quite arbitrarily, between the poles of those events deemed necessary and those deemed desirable by the particular historian. The former may be the facts of history as they are apprehended, selected, and arranged within the subjective mind of the historian. The latter are the values, hopes, and ideals that motivate the historian's researches. Within these poles, Beard explained, only three possibilities are available to the historian: history is chaotic, or it is cyclical, or it is directional. Finally, said Beard, whether broadly or narrowly defended, each historian makes a choice on the basis of an act of faith.

Beard provided Woodward with the intellectual framework that made the establishment of a historical alternative to the present necessary as a founding possibility for another future than offered by the present. He also, with Mencken, traded the legitimacy of outworn narratives of heroic romanticism for the Progressive promise of finding creativity in discontinuity. Happily for Woodward, Beard's Progressivism fatally undermined the appeal to tradition upon which the legitimacy of the Bourbon South depended. For Mencken, who idealized the Old South, the balance between innovation and tradition was lost with Roosevelt's New Deal. The progress he had championed at the Scopes trial had turned into standardization, and in Mencken's eyes, this form of realism was a fate as tragic in its implication for culture as was the violence of chaos or the dullness of repetition.

Charles Beard, unlike Mencken in the 1930s, still retained faith in democracy and, therefore, in the possibility of finding a direction to progress. He preserved that direction, as Turner had been unable to do, by surrendering the romantic pastoralism of Jeffersonian agrarianism for the realism of modern industrialism. However, despite his professed realism, Beard depended for this resolution on the heroic leadership of Franklin Roosevelt to use the opportunity of the Depression to defeat capitalism and avoid war. But Roosevelt's values and his policies for a national interest, which had become entwined with those of corporate capitalism, diverged into different actualities from Beard's hopes. History, like a dead weight, precluded any realistic future for Beard's republican ideals, once Roosevelt began to repeat Wilson's movement toward participation in the chaos of another world war.

For Woodward, however, as a Southerner and critic of the New South, the defeat of Beard's faith in progress by the Depression opened a hopeful avenue for inverting Beard's failed realism into a new form of romanticism, to be challenged by a new pastoral realism. Thus, wrote Woodward, "in the post-depression editions of the first two volumes of *The Rise of American Civilization*, that glowing conclusion about 'the dawn, not the dusk of the gods' was replaced by something a bit vaguer." Woodward saw a still further diminution of Beard's faith in Progress in the third volume, as "the optimistic title of the series is relegated to microscopic type on the title page," and the new title, *America in Midpassage*, merely "implies a course steered, an eventual landing." Reading Beard, Woodward went on to say, sometimes gave him the feeling "that American culture is something produced in New York, and American politics something determined in Washington." Odum's regionalism, he pointed out, offered a contrasting realism to Beard's future of "superurbanization, bigness and technological civilization."[68]

The aesthetic power of Woodward's biography of Tom Watson, originally titled *The Political and Literary Career of Thomas E. Watson*, depended upon the failure of corporate capitalism in 1930, after its defeat of Agrarianism in the 1890s. It depended, too, on the inversion of failure into success, possible only within the literary formula of pastoralism. In his intentionally provocative choice of Watson as an ironic hero, Woodward could at once tweak the nose of Progressive liberalism and avoid committing himself to a failed romantic agrarian ideal. He could stand critically yet ambiguously between the Regionalists, like Howard Odum, and the New Agrarian poets, such as Allen Tate. He could stand just as critically and ambiguously between the facts of science and the imagination of literature. In doing so, he was able to exercise his taste for the ironic, a taste he would later refine through Reinhold Niebuhr's influence, by standing Charles Beard's historiography on its head. For Beard's narrative of national history was predicated on his hope that a new industrial republicanism was emerging from a discredited romantic agrarian past. Woodward's forward-looking Populists, however, reversed the equation and so challenged the optimism behind the same corporate Progressivism that fashioned the New South. The root of the post–Civil War southern tragedy as portrayed in Woodward's tale of agrarian betrayal was an ironically regionalist microcosm of the national tragedy of the triumph of corporate capitalism as drawn by Beard. Through that irony, Watson's qualities—both good and evil—served Woodward's dual purpose: to challenge national conventions of Progressive superiority wielded over the people of the "provincial" South with which he identified, while loosening the cold fingers of a dead southern past of betrayed ideals with which he could not identify.

Watson, as a political and literary figure, represented the creative possibility of social and political change, focused at the frontier line where the contradictory implications of time as continuity and as discontinuity meet. In life, Watson and the Populist values he championed failed. Continuity in history, therefore, offered both hope—because racial equality and republican virtue really had once lived in the South—and despair—since they degenerated into hate after 1896. Continuity meant that Watson and Populism were foundational facts and actual traditions. Discontinuity offered the possibility of change: the escape from outworn conventions, but also the danger of chaos, as in the later life of Watson. While Watson's effort to establish a Populist democracy may have failed actually, as a historical fact of record, it still provided the necessary condition for the possibility of redemptive change, as well as for organized violence. Such promise for balancing piety and murder, ambiguous as it was, could be constructed neither from the formalism characteristic of the constraints of objective facts, nor the chaos threatened by the free play of the imagination. Rather, for Woodward, the promise existed only as a possibility, suspended between the realms of past and present, fact and fiction, pedestrian reality and the creative realm of the mind.

The aesthetic imagination and political reality, according to Woodward's "crossroads" formulation, are at once continuous and discontinuous with each other. To sustain such a precarious balance between chaos and order, the historian must mediate the two—an act closer to the creative possibility of the novelist than to the scientist's classification of facts. Indeed, Woodward has called the novelist and the historian "siblings," a social-scientific classification for a relation that is as close as possible to being exactly the same while remaining separate. "Both sprang from a common parentage of storytellers," he has explained. Both use a similar vocabulary, both require imagination, both put evidence together in a similar fashion in order to "create" the truth.[69]

"Over the years, as I have watched my novelist friends at their work," Woodward explained in 1969, "as I have read their books and talked with them about their problems. I have learned to appreciate more and more how much we have in common in our uses of the past, our interest in it, our demands upon it, our concerns with it." [70] History as a discipline may provide the mediating role between actualities and possibilities just because it lacks unique categories that would clearly separate it from fiction. Consequently, all novels are really forms of historical literature, seeking "to understand, describe, to recapture the past, however remote, however recent." If this is so, however, why has Woodward reacted so negatively to novelists such as E. L. Doctorow, Alex Haley, and Gore Vidal in recent years?[71] Why has he chosen a Classical conceit of claiming they have sinned against Clio, the muse of history? Why has their sin of writing fictional history instead of historical fiction unleashed the forces of chaos, "denying any significant difference at all between history and fiction"?

The answer would appear to be that, like all Machiavellian formulations, Woodward's must face the inescapable presence of Fortune at the juncture of creative change, the frontier between continuity and discontinuity in time. The historian working ambiguously on the border between what might have been and what might yet be must discover and safeguard the actual ground of the past, if Fortune is to be tamed and directed toward human meaning. This, in Woodward's own phrase, is the historian's "priestly role."[72] For without an apprehension of past actuality, there can be no alternative possibility to legitimate some other future from a repetition of what is or from the chaos of arbitrary change. Frustratingly, the historian is unable prophetically to evoke the appearance of the alternatives he or she makes possible in the present through scholarship. That ability belongs only to the realm of the creative imagination. However, for Woodward, this makes it essential that historians and novelists or poets should retain their separate offices. Otherwise, the particulars of history lose their relation to the universals of art. The actual can exist only as a particular, while the possible is to be found only in the universal. Therefore, despite the close association of history and fiction, only the historian, as priest, ensures that the actual retains its particularity and, consequently, allows the imaginative to fulfill its universal role of transcending time, without plunging into chaos.

Woodward the historian has shared this common religious purpose with Robert Penn Warren, the poet and novelist, since they first became acquainted in the 1930s. Indeed, this complementary attachment became even stronger with the emergence of the civil rights movement, when they found themselves together as southern exiles at Yale in the 1960s. *Tom Watson: Agrarian Rebel* and *All the King's Men* are, as Richard King has suggested, the same kind of book.[73] This is so not just because the Huey Long phenomenon served as a background for both works, but precisely because Warren steadfastly refused to call his novel a history of Long and because Woodward suppressed the extent to which his biography was written like a novel by avoiding the psychological dimension of Watson's actions. In Warren's words, "the big difference between history and fiction is that the historian does not know his imagined world; he knows *about* it, and he must know all he can about it, because he wants to find the facts *behind* that world." On the other hand "the fiction writer must claim to *know* the *inside* of his world for better or worse." [74] For Woodward and Warren, as close intellectual collaborators and friends, their common concern is not to preserve some abstract code of scholarship but to preserve the balance between actuality and possibility as a political and aesthetic balance of continuity and the discontinuity of time. The form of that balance, as we shall see more fully in the final chapter, has been accomplished through a complementary political and aesthetic use of the Romantic elegiac form.

Perhaps the clearest example of this anguished effort to preserve such a balance, for Woodward, may be seen in his response to W. J. Cash's *Mind of the South.* In 1941, Woodward wrote a generally positive review, in which he catalogued Cash's "attacks upon the imponderables of the intangibles of southern history." These included the South's romanticism, its violence, and "its paradoxical combinations of hedonism and puritanism." Woodward considered such problems to be more amenable to the methods of the novelist than to those of the historian, and "Mr. Cash has fortunately chosen a literary and imaginative rather than a scholarly approach." Woodward recognized that the question of continuity and discontinuity was the central concern of *The Mind of the South,* and he considered Cash's emphasis on continuity to be a valuable corrective that would challenge both the romanticizers and the professional historians. For, said Woodward, "with their 'period books' and courses," they "must share the blame for neglecting the important themes of continuity." But Woodward thought that such a corrective was of limited value, because it deflected discussion from his own concerns of discontinuity in the past, most particularly during the 1890s and more recently the 1920s and 1930s. Nowhere was that analysis of continuity less useful for recognizing the "artificial unity of southern society," than in the change of mentality that occurred concurrently with the breakup of the old agrarian economy and the triumph of the New South. Woodward, for one, could hear no echo of Stuart's cavalry as he looked at skyscrapers on southern skylines, despite the associations of skyscrapers with hierarchy, social organization on the bureaucratic model, and corporate loyalty—all the conditions Tom Watson warned against and failed to defeat in his own political career. [75]

In 1966 Lester Maddox was elected governor of Georgia, a crowning blow to the collapse of the *continuity* of the New Reconstruction of the civil rights movement, which Woodward had helped to establish with his study of *discontinuity* in the first Reconstruction, *The Strange Career of Jim Crow* (1955). Woodward wrote a stunned letter to his long-time friend, Glenn Rainey:

Is it really as bad as it looks? Or is that possible? Or is it some nightmare about the ghost of Tom Watson? Or can half a century roll back and Georgia suddenly revert to the Leo Frank days of howling mobs led by grinning goons? Or does history really go backward? I feel like Rip van W. in reverse. Where have I been anyway? Maybe [southern liberals] were dreams and Tom [after 1900] the only reality. . . . Hell of it is that it does not look like a local phenomenon. West Coast, East Coast, Midwest. All closing in fast. . . . Looks much like 1877 from where I sit. Chaos and old night.[76]

Not only had the civil rights movement splintered, but Woodward's faith in a southern president who aspired to earn Roosevelt's mantle by fulfilling the promise of the New Deal had collapsed, presenting an ironic mirror image of Beard's tragedy. Woodward, the historian of paradoxes, had dared advance the prophecy in 1964 that Lyndon B. Johnson would fulfill the promise of a new South. He did so in the dedication to a book he edited, titled *A Southern Prophecy: The Prosperity of the South Dependent upon the Elevation of the Negro.*[77] The dedication was affixed to a new issue of a book by a bona fide southern gentleman, Lewis Harvie Blair, who in 1899, had ironically presaged the civil rights movement by attacking the doctrine of white supremacy at the high point of its power. But Woodward's dedication mocked its author by 1966 through a reverse irony. In an inverted repetition of Roosevelt's policies, Johnson had abandoned the fight against poverty at its high-water mark to engage in a disastrous civil war in Asia for the corporate nationalist ends of American economic power.

It is hardly surprising, then, that the historian whose dedication to Johnson had been "in hope of fulfilment of a southern prophecy" responded defensively to a 1967 biography of W. J. Cash by Joseph L. Morrison that was entitled *W. J. Cash, Southern Prophet: A Biography and Reader.*[78] In his review of Morrison's book, Woodward scored Cash for his reliance on Mencken's style of *Kultur* criticism, which was an inadequate and dated basis for writing history. He repeated his charge that Cash had blurred the distinctively "un-American traits of Southern history—its *dis*continuity." Morrison's book, he said, was the occasion, not the inspiration, for his remarks since it was wholly laudatory, extolling Cash not for his novelistic gifts but as a historian. As a labor of love, Woodward said, Morrison's book "tells us all we need to know (and perhaps a little more) about the obscure struggles of the modest, neurotic, but rather appealing and courageous writer," but "the much needed critical reevaluation of *The Mind of The South* remains to be done."[79]

In the waning days of 1969, after the fall of Johnson, the deaths of Martin Luther King and the civil rights movement, and the personal family tragedy of his son's death from cancer, Woodward weighed in with the first sustained historical criticism of Cash's *Mind of the South*.[80] He began his essay in the *New York Review of Books* by confessing his own responsibility for failing to call Cash's immensely popular book to task for its failure as history, whatever its aesthetic successes. But Woodward could not accept Cash's "Menckenian buffoonery" as a legitimate formula after Perry Miller's formidable revision of its aims. He did not appreciate the irony of calling a book *The Mind of the South* while denying the existence of mind among Southerners, notwithstanding Henry Adams's famous quip to that effect in *The Education*. But the center of Woodward's attack on Cash's reputation, as anticipated in his 1967 review, was the issue of continuity and discontinuity, unity and fragmentation.[81]

Cash, for example, had placed blacks in the center of his story of the unity and continuity of southern romanticism. But in integrating them into the scheme of unity through which he viewed southern culture, Woodward complained, Cash had failed to give them a separate and independent existence. There was neither a black mind, in Cash's account, nor an acknowledgment of the separate legacy of slavery for black Americans—a past that was quite different from that of white Southerners. Cash had turned black Americans into an affective presence only and neglected the significance of their own cultural origins.[82] Woodward's criticism in part reflected his lessons in the humanity of blacks gained through the Harlem Renaissance and his civil rights activities. But beyond these experiences of education into humanity, Woodward also found a separate black experience useful for a post-Menckenian defense of southern exceptionalism, an exceptionalism—or distinctiveness— gained through the white South's failure rather than its success. The fall of the South served as an ironic challenge to the hubris of national exceptionalism. Black culture, as independent from white southern culture, offered Woodward one more source of discontinuity for sustaining hope in another South that would be redeemed by its own prophetic witness to the nation. Yet to escape the problem of fragmentation, Woodward could not accept black power. Finally, given the Machiavellian pattern of his quarrel with the South of history and possibility, Woodward had to use the independent existence of black aspirations to defend conservatively the legitimacy of his white southern fathers, to show *they* had bequeathed the possibility of another South. He could not embrace Langston Hughes's unity of the blues.[83]

Similarly, Woodward criticized Cash for creating a false unity in southern culture. The bluegrass country, the delta, the Gulf Coast, the Ozarks, Texas, Louisiana, and Arkansas, for Woodward, were discontinuous, as was the southern economy. Only discontinuity could account for the distinctiveness of the South and its history. Nationalist history is continuous history, but a regionalist history must be a discontinuous history. The South's history was again and again broken by discontinuity, "slavery and secession, independence and defeat, emancipation and military occupation, Reconstruction and Redemption." In contrast, Woodward said, "Unbroken continuity has been persuasively suggested as a characteristic that accounts for the uniqueness of American National history. With the oldest constitution of any nation, with political parties, executive office, legislative bodies, and judiciary, along with basic institutions and traditions dating continuously from eighteenth-century origins, the United States does indeed enjoy a history of uniquely unbroken continuity."[84]

Woodward countered Cash's defeated Modernism with a standard Machiavellian formula in which he posited a classical national past challenged by an innovative regional rebellion. That rebellion, justified by its ability to provide a new basis for a purified realism, followed the same conventions as the challenges to monarchical authority in republican politics and Romantic challenges to Neoclassicism in art. In formulating a new Machiavellian pattern to replace republicanism on one side and Modernism on the other, Woodward redefined Cash, the antiromantic Menckenian, as himself a "bemused" Romantic. It was Cash, not blacks or the fictitious "man in the center," who was trapped within his own Romantic literary conventions by inadequate historiography. "After some years in the profession, one has seen reputations of historians rise and fall," Woodward wrote, "The books of Ulrich Phillips and later Frank Owsley began to collect dust on the shelves, and one thinks of Beard and Parrington. In America, historians like politicians, are out as soon as they are down. There is no comfortable back bench, no house of Lords for them. It is a wasteful and rather brutal practice, unworthy of what Cash would agree are our best Southern traditions. I hope this will not happen to Cash." Cash did have something valuable to say about the continuity of being a Southerner, Woodward admitted, it was just that "he rather overdid the thing." But, he continued, extravagance is a trait shared by Southerners and he himself might well be as guilty of it as Cash. If so, he concluded, "Jack Cash would have been the first to understand and not the last to forgive. Peace be to his troubled spirit."[85]

Despite, even because of, its gracious closing, Woodward's historiographical critique of *The Mind of the South* was written as a Romantic elegy for Cash. Like any Romantic elegy, Woodward's gained its expansive magnanimity at the price of committing the fallen heroic challenger to his silent grave. And it was in doing so that the troubled elegist himself experienced the hope of renewal.

However, within the tragic conventions of Machiavellian aesthetics, no elegiac triumph over the deconstruction of meaning may be long preserved. Woodward's own ground for preserving the meaning of southern history has lately been tainted with charges of romanticism by revisionists who challenge his views on the radical discontinuity of the early and late Watson, Reconstruction and Redemption, and the first Reconstruction and the second. The promise of an ironic transformation of the nation through the tragic self-discovery of the South appears to be fading, and with it the literary Southern Renaissance that gave it life. Woodward's autobiographical writings, in turn, reveal his growing preoccupation with his own continuity as a historian and make visible the ironically dreadful implication of discontinuity when applied to one's own life's work.

For many years, Woodward has skillfully staved off those who would engage in historiographical parricide through a willingness to adjust his old interpretations to meet the conclusions of changing scholarship, and by parrying with his critic with the weapons of irony and ambiguity. Still, he has written in *Thinking Back,* anyone who has been writing since the 1930s has a great many "thin" and "emaciated" positions that may haunt their author, and he finds himself no exception. It has become, therefore, a full-time vocation for him to stave off those young scholars who would, as he says, engage in "gerontophagy," that is, "the primitive ritual of eating one's elders."[86] Perhaps, within the conventions of a Machiavellian criticism, no other fate is possible, no matter how long delayed or cheerfully resisted. For it is essentially a Faustian bargain that a Machiavellian culture makes with its favored critics when it offers them accolades, as bold young professionals, for exposing contradictions and building new syntheses, only to subject them, as aging professionals, to the same pattern of deconstruction at the hands of a new generation. To appropriate a favorite metaphor of Allen Tate's and Robert Penn Warren's, this pattern mirrors the character of Machiavellian cultural forms themselves, not just the individuals who creatively shape and promote them for the larger public that consumes them.

CHAPTER SIX

A Romantic Elegy
for Republican Virtue: Allen Tate,
Robert Penn Warren,
and the Machiavellian Cycle

As New Englanders living at the turn of the century, Henry Adams and his old friend and student of history, Henry Cabot Lodge, had found themselves uncomfortably suspended between the romanticism they attributed to the isolated rural South and the realism they attributed to the new northern urbanism, wrought by imperialism. These men considered themselves patriarchs of a diminished generation. They believed they were part of a remnant of Puritan culture that retained the sacred memory of a once-heroic generation but had lost the capacity to translate its values into an increasingly centralized economy and decentralized culture.

Adams, of course, had no children, unless one were to count his platonic fatherhood of George Cabot Lodge, Henry's son. Bay, as he was nicknamed, was a genteel poet who, according to Henry Adams's eulogy, was unable to resolve the division between artist and citizen in the new commercial ethos of the early twentieth century. That is to say, he was unable to resolve the tension between his attraction to "effeminate" culture and his duty to distinguish himself through "masculine" forms of power—the complex responsibility to preserve both virtue and virtù expected of the heirs to the leadership class in Progressive New England. He was unable to resolve them, Adams said, just because "society was not disposed to defend itself from criticism or attack," and therefore, the poet in revolt was paralyzed because his society seemed to care sincerely about nothing:

The Bostonian of 1900 differed from his parents and grandparents of 1850, in owning nothing the value of which, in the market, could be affected by the poet. Indeed, to him, the poet's pose of hostility to actual conditions of society was itself mercantile,—a form of drama,—a thing to sell rather than a serious revolt. Society could safely adopt it as a form of industry, as it adopted other forms of bookmaking.[1]

If Bay's surrogate father urged him to revolt against the New England culture of 1900 as "a conservative Christian Anarchist," Bay's actual father, Henry Cabot Lodge, tried to provide Bay and his generation with a heroic standard in George Washington, a conservatively patrician hero who was at once an Anglophile in culture and an Anglophobe in his politics. He succeeded, however, only in inspiring his son's tragic identification with Cain, the title of Bay's verse-drama of Promethean rebellion against authority, published in 1904.[2] But for the Lodges, father and son, Washington's authority could not be separated from Cain's rebellion because tradition and innovation are as inseparable within Machiavellian cultural conventions as are piety and murder. The resolution to this tragic dilemma turns on the conservative Machiavellian insight that Washington and Cain must be inverted into each other as complementary symbols for necessity and contingency. The loss of a ground for classical authority and the need for innovative violence to restore it could be resolved, according to Machiavelli, by admitting that Fortune, not Providence, holds the world order together. According to Henry Adams's principle of contradiction, upon which Bay's artistic and personal philosophy was based, Washington was admitted to be Cain, but Cain could also become Washington because "order and anarchy were one." The price of that resolution, as Adams perceptively admitted in his own post-Darwinian version of Machiavellian Fortune, was that the unity behind his synthesis was chaos.[3]

Stated in terms of actual social practice, this meant that the fathers to Bay's generation bequeathed their sons an onerous responsibility. They were born to a station and were heirs to a training that charged them with the duty to find an aesthetic redemption for their New England Brahmin culture and to take it to the masses in order to save democracy from itself. They were expected to use their talents and privileged status as premier Anglo-Americans to reinvigorate a fading heroic claim to national political leadership. They were expected to do this in the name of a selfless civic religion of disinterested service because the national American culture of the first half of the twentieth century was still dominated by the conventions of the New England jeremiad. However, for Bay and his generation, as for Henry Cabot Lodge and Henry Adams in theirs, the dominant national culture was crumbling apart. Its breakdown was becoming increasingly visible in its internal moral capitulation to commercialism and in the increasingly effective cultural challenges from without, especially those brought by the combativeness of a reawakening South and the steady influx of immigrants from Eastern Europe.

The effort to balance the pressures of innovation and tradition in Bay Lodge's self-identification as a conservative Christian Anarchist was part of a larger movement among young New Englanders of his generation. Macdonald Smith Moore has dubbed them the centennial generation because these elite young men were born about 1876.[4] Moore suggests that the symbolism of the nation's centennial worked as a catalyst in forming a sense of destiny in these youths and that the character of their sense of vocation may be usefully illustrated through such Yankee musical composers as Charles Ives and Daniel Gregory Mason. These young men, who attended Yale and Harvard in the 1890s, shared many of the attitudes of literary artists like Bay Lodge. However, as composers they were convinced they could serve an integral role in formulating a new musical language for the national culture.[5] Composing seemed to them to be at once an expression of pure aesthetics, a counter-force to consumerism, and a communal and democratic service for binding the Anglo-Saxon racial identity of the nation against the urban innovation of Jews and blacks. Each of the centennial generation composers whom Moore describes in his book *Yankee Blues* felt he had a personal mission to meet national spiritual needs and to preserve the cultural ascendancy of New England as the source of American identity. As composers, they were mediators of the spiritual and the social, the formal and the functional. Therefore, they thought that above all other artists, they were in a position to rescue the religion of national culture from the degradation of romantic sensuality on the one hand and the grim naturalism they associated with an increasingly urbanized landscape on the other. They felt they were men of a new frontier with an "errand into the wilderness," creative links between the civilizing culture of Europe and the raw energy of America. They tried to balance the contradictions of Anglo-Protestant identity by being virile and muscular in their musical forms while leading genteel life-styles of cultured respectability befitting their station. They tried to balance the requirements of virtù and virtue by becoming successful at masculine pursuits, such as business in Ives's case or editing and public lecturing as a professional critic in Mason's case, while fulfilling a role of spiritual education as composers.[6]

These, then, were strangely conservative "Modernists," using difficult rhythms, dissonances, and innovative timbres to challenge and revitalize the New England culture of their fathers. Through their musical rebellion against sentimentally repeating purely classical forms, while rejecting the musical claims to Americanism of blacks and Jews, the Yankees hoped to inaugurate a positive American cultural future by reinvigorating the spiritual legacy of New England.

Even to themselves, it was clear they they were failing in their mission during the 1920s. By the 1940s, their cultural heirs had completely lost their bid to lead an aesthetic revival of Anglo-American values. They were never able to persuade musical audiences with their republican message that art should be organic, that it should nurture virtue and bring forth the fruit of the indigenous American spirit from the soil of New England, the sacred site of the nation's temples of liberty. This mission had placed Yankee composers, as artists, in tension between classical music as pure sentiment and vernacular music as pure entertainment—an aesthetic distinction of high- and lowbrow culture that followed the emergence of a consumer democracy on the heels of the Yankee victory in the Civil War. Once the first generation of Yankee composers, such as Ives or Mason, had graduated from college, they put aside the youth culture of frivolous entertainment and took up the high seriousness of their calling as ministers of cultural reform. They attempted to bridge the gap between themselves and their audiences by educating the masses up to a cultivated democratic taste, resisting sentimentality and mechanical repetition, and offering instead a redemptive form of education.

But the masses preferred the high jinks of ragtime and the excitement of jazz to the "highbrow" culture from which they had already been excluded by the economics of taste, itself part of the new legitimacy of the social hierarchy of the corporate order. Once more, the redemptive mission of the Yankee composers was undermined by the apostasy of many of their own Protestant elite brethren. During the 1920s, critics such as Gilbert Seldes, John Hammond, and Carl Van Vechten led a revolt of taste that helped legitimize the new music. These impresario/critics of the New Negro Renaissance saw black vitality as a new, subversive pastoral form, an aesthetic resource that whites must mine and exploit for their own uses if blacks could not or would not. For jazz, and the jazz culture of the Harlem Renaissance, seemed to them a perfect foil to the cold moralism of the official redemptive culture of New England. Indeed, their argument for embracing jazz was similar to H. L. Mencken's defense of black writers as a leaven for American literature (though Mencken hated jazz).[7]

The Yankee project of cultural redemption was also undermined by the defection of European critics to the aesthetics of jazz. Many European critics saw jazz as quintessentially American because it seemed the essence of primitivism, evoking rhythms of new worlds of redemptive energy for an overcivilized Old World, a world battered by a sense of defeat but yearning to believe that a utopian future was emerging from the ashes of the war. This European attitude made it difficult for the Yankees, as heirs to a superior European civilization, to defend the canon against the onslaught of "barbarian" Negroes and Jews. Consequently, faced with public apathy and the rejection of a New England identity as the source for American musical values, successful younger composers were less and less likely to be Yankee, and less likely to accept conventional standards of social respectability. Successful young composers like Aaron Copland, Ernst Bloch, or George Gershwin were not trained in New England universities (Copland and Gershwin did not even attend college). Socially defined as neither white nor black, young Jewish composers straddled the worlds of musical taste as mediators between "white sophistication" and "black Primitivism."[8]

The battle to retain leadership over national musical culture, according to Moore, was not lost by New England's sons overnight. Indeed, the Yankee effort to shape American national culture through musical form was not entirely relegated to the periphery of American musical culture until World War II. However, in the context of that cultural struggle between the wars, music criticism took a central stage in cultural politics, along with literary criticism. The Yankee musical critics, as innovators who were conservatively loyal to their heritage as New Englanders, considered jazz to be a far more insidious expression of social and cultural disintegration than ragtime. It ambiguously mocked respectability while celebrating its own sophistication. Its evocation of the natural was disturbingly sensual, and its urban rhythms were provocatively, even passionately, alienated. Not surprisingly, the Yankee critics inveighed against jazz when it exploded upon the consumer scene following World War I, characterizing it as mindless commercial music that would sabotage the civic virtue of the nation.

Considering H. L. Mencken's inversion of Progressive antisouthern criticism, which he used to defend an ideal of a classical Old South, his parallel role in supporting the war against jazz, waged quite independently of the centennial composers, was less paradoxical than it might appear. Mencken, like the Yankees, was a loyal defender of both Realism and classical European culture against consumerism and standardization. Though he was as virulent a critic of Puritanism as he was of southern romanticism, he shared the Yankee composers' war against jazz because he believed it to be a degradation of classical sentiment and aesthetic form. Indeed, according to Mencken's ear, jazz was *not* sensual at all but was like "the sound of riveting" in its mechanical formalism. On the other hand, the defenders of jazz associated it with the jungle devolution into the anarchic degradation of black sensuousness or oriental (Jewish) exoticism, a formula of creativity Mencken was himself committed to in principle, if not in taste.[9]

As a powerful formula of inversion, the new jazz music was then both sophisticated and primitive. It was conceived as sensuous and romantically undisciplined but also, inversely, as metallic and regimented. It subverted martial music and classical music at the same time and yet reinvigorated both these forms for public consumption. Therefore, its critical defenders could claim continuity and discontinuity with Western musical forms at the same time. Thus, while jazz was associated with black romantic sensualism, bursting the bonds of a repressed and standardized white society, a critic such as Daniel Gregory Mason heard jazz as cold, mechanical and commercial. The early twentieth century, he complained, "looks disturbingly like a Gilded rather than a Golden Age, an age seeking quantity for the sake of joy, in short, a mechanised age." Mason then issued his own pastoral challenge to the public's attraction to jazz. He asked Americans to lift themselves out of the decadent passive consumption of music. To that end, he said, "it is high time for us, sternly putting away the pipedreams of business romance, to use a little of the realism of the artist, and soberly begin thinking out ways and means."[10]

However, to the despair of Mason and the other Yankee composers, it was the jazz culture of the New Negro, centered in the Harlem Renaissance, which captured the national imagination, not their own offering of a morally spare aesthetic of republican virtue. Jazz, as "primitive jungle music," offered a pastoral inversion of a decadent consumer culture, not an attack upon it. It therefore promised to infuse the animal energy needed to revitalize the dying Anglo American republican ethic of democratic production, without sacrificing the self-absorbed ideal of a burgeoning consumerism. The critical community of Yankee music critics, very much in contrast, looked in desperation for a source of folk vitality through which to challenge jazz as a redemptive democratic art form; they found it in the culturally despised Midwest. Many critics saw in the raw-boned, "self-educated" farmer-composer Roy Harris a last hope for translating the soul of the folk culture into a national community. Especially in the light of the Depression, Harris appeared as an agrarian hero of culture who might lead an aesthetic renewal that would defeat the commercial ethos and with it, perhaps, the decadent urban consumerism his supporters believed was embodied in jazz. In the words of his centennial-generation teacher, Arthur Farwell, Harris had come "from old Anglo-Saxon stock, with Scotch Irish ingredients, he arises not out of the mechanistic tumult of the times, but out of the broad metaphysical movement which gave birth to Emerson and Whitman." In the 1930s, it could not be admitted that Harris, a mythic hero of culture, studied in Paris with Nadia Boulanger, as had Aaron Copland and other young American composers. Harris was "America's great white hope," sprung pure and unsullied from the rude frontier, as Moore characterizes his image for most of the decade between 1930 and 1940.[11]

However, after briefly wearing the mantle of Cincinnatus, Harris fell from critical grace to become the subject of mockery for his hollow musical heroics just before World War II. Harris failed to achieve a redemptive national revival through his musical compositions, in part because his tragically impossible burden of personal responsibility for that redemption amounted to a double bind for himself, as well as for those elites who had awarded him his status. In conventional Machiavellian terms, sustaining his role as a life-giving hero of culture required him to find an aesthetic balance between the conservation of a civilizing tradition and the heroic conquering of competing barbarian contenders. He was, in other words, expected to conserve an exceptional American musical identity at the same time as he was supposed to be on the cutting edge of innovative musical creativity. Harris's effort to find a legitimate balance between cultural virtue and virtù was fatally undermined—as were the efforts of other Yankee composer/critics of his time—when he was forced to contend with the consequences of the emergence of a dubious European ally in Nazism. Suddenly, the beleaguered Yankees shared an odious but pedigreed claimant to the mantle of heroic preserver of European virtue against cultural corruption. German Nazi moralism was officially opposed to the decadence of jazz.

The ground melted away beneath the ideal of an exceptional Yankee-American musical culture after World War I, as it melted away from an exceptional American political culture founded upon an Anglo-Protestant jeremiad. The redemptive culture of white Protestant New England could not survive World War II and the demonically racist nationalism that had rent the holy land of the Reformation and its rationalist culture, which had once been mediated through liberal Protestant theology. But the elements of an impending breakdown of Anglo-American national culture along racial and economic lines were already visible before the war to perceptive critics such as Reinhold Niebuhr and W. J. Cash, who warned that the crisis in Germany must reverberate to American shores.

Though Perry Miller became prominent only after the war, he shared Reinhold Niebuhr's sense of crisis in the national American culture, which he believed was rooted in the failure of New England's jeremiad. Unlike Cash and Niebuhr, Miller did not concern himself with the implications of the German cultural crisis as he constructed his elegy for New England's dominance in the 1930s. However, like Niebuhr, Miller had read Max Weber's *Protestant Ethic and the Spirit of Capitalism* and believed that it captured the tragedy of New England's progress into decadence as well as Germany's. Each responded similarly to a growing sense of defeat, from within and without, of liberal American Protestantism.

Miller's elegy for Yankee culture, *The New England Mind*, written on the eve of the war, captured the sense of decay of New England's redemptive culture from the disillusioned perspective of the leading American writers of the 1920s. His study of the origins of the decline of New England and his own identification with that decline on a personal and scholarly level, Miller later insisted, grew out of his contemplation of the defeat of Yankee civilization on the banks of the Congo.[12] By this Miller seemed to mean both the expansion of capitalism into the paradox of "unintended consequence," as presented by Max Weber, or irony as Niebuhr called it, and the corrupting sensuality of the black Africa of his imagination. Similarly, W. J. Cash, in his elegy for European culture and its last frontier outpost in America, *The Mind of the South*, lamented the triumph of black sensualism over Anglo-American rationality. For both Miller and Cash, the triumph of the jazz age over the redemptive pastoralism of Anglo-American artists signaled the end of an exceptional America between the world wars.

But the exhaustion of Machiavellian republican culture by the eve of World War II merely defined the national war of redemption that soon followed. Neither Reinhold Niebuhr nor Franklin Roosevelt claimed—as Washington, Lincoln, and Wilson had—that one last redemptive act of bloodshed would usher in a stable heritage of peace and harmony. Each, instead, offered a new realism that assumed murder and the struggle for power would remain a constant within American history for the future. An American crusade of redemptive political violence against the democratic racialism of the Third Reich, therefore, could only be justified afterwards (particularly when facing the tarnished redeemer-nation claims of a militant Soviet Union) by a new Machiavellian formula for slaying and affirming the ideal of political exceptionalism at the same time.

That formula was put together between 1945 and 1960 with such powerful symbolism that its fragility did not become visible before the 1970s. Only quite recently have the seams in the postwar synthesis of corporate power and individual rights become visible, as the liberal defense of capitalist democratic realism and the defense of civil rights have become increasingly antagonistic towards each other. Americans have been forced to recognize economic, political, and technological limits amounting to loss of a frontier of the imagination and not just of the environment. Indeed, only with the unredemptively tragic deaths of Malcolm X, in 1965, Martin Luther King in 1968, and ultimately, of the civil rights movement itself under Lyndon Johnson's shattered presidency has the implication of the collapse of post–World War II liberalism begun to become a popularly recognized crisis of meaning among Americans, regardless of racial, gender, or ethnic background.

Looking back upon the breakdown of Reinhold Niebuhr's potent formulation of the postwar Machiavellian synthesis in the 1960s, its elements stand out quite clearly. For example, Niebuhr's writing in the 1940s spoke powerfully to the disillusioned Marxist Will Herberg, who later authored the sociological study of American religious culture, *Protestant, Catholic, Jew* (1951).[13] Herberg decided to affirm his nominal Jewish background rather than convert to Protestantism only because Niebuhr influenced him to do so. In the 1950s, Herberg consciously and quite successfully patterned his chosen role as a Jewish prophet to American civil religion after Niebuhr's role as a voice of spiritual realism for the nation. During the 1960s, Herberg appealed to the authority of Reinhold Niebuhr in justifying his attack upon Martin Luther King's legitimacy in the pages of the *National Review,* even as King had appealed to

Niebuhr to justify civil disobedience against racism from the Birmingham jail. In the 1960s, too, the liberal Protestant clergyman Robert McAfee Brown appealed to Niebuhr's ideas and example to defend a left-liberal critique of the existing society, while Michael Novak, a conservative Catholic and critic of ethnic assimilation, simultaneously appealed to Niebhur to justify a right-leaning rejection of utopianism.[14] This was a clash of redemptive visions within American religious and political culture, which in the 1970s and 1980s turned into a still deeper division among "neoconservative" intellectuals, many of whom were Eastern European Jews with socialist pasts who tried unsuccessfully to reaffirm Niebuhr's balance between economic liberalism and the politics of racial justice.[15]

During the period between 1945 and 1965, Niebuhr's synthesis had permitted him to mount an effective moral and political challenge against the idea of an exceptional Protestant America, while he conservatively defended an exceptional American mission to preserve world freedom, through irony. This same Machiavellian inversion of political and cultural exceptionalism brought Niebuhr and C. Vann Woodward together intellectually after the war in Woodward's collection of essays, *The Burden of Southern History*.[16] In the title essay and in "The Irony of Southern History" in the same volume, Niebuhr's inversion of a failed New England jeremiad into a positive affirmation of democracy was complemented by Woodward's positive inversion of a similarly failed southern agrarian heroism. Niebuhr and Woodward stood in ambiguous relation to their own Anglo-Protestantism and detached themselves from the Yankee vision of industrial progress. However, at the same time, each preserved an aesthetic convention of irony which, like progress, traveled only on one linear moralistic and redemptive plane, either from hubris to destruction or from humility to glory. Woodward even suggested that Henry Adams's cynicism had found resolution in a hidden redemptive vision of the South in *Democracy* and *Esther*.[17] Neither Niebuhr nor Woodward, nor those influenced by them in post–World War II America before 1965, seriously considered the possibility that irony may confound *all* such moralistic expectations. That thought *had* occurred, however, to Frederick Jackson Turner's student, the historian of revolutions Carl Becker.[18]

According to Becker, writing in the 1930s, irony is not a political law of moral redemption, as Niebuhr and Woodward later suggested. Rather, Becker defined irony as an aesthetic description of the transformation of space and time in history from the point of view of relative human experience. Irony, he suggested, cannot be utilized to resolve the problem of grounding action because it is itself an expression of the unresolvable contradiction inherent in all such Enlightenment dualisms as subjectivity and objectivity, eastern civilization and western frontier, continuity and discontinuity in time.

Becker's most complete consideration of irony, *The Heavenly City of the Eighteenth Century Philosophers*, was a historiographical challenge to the same scientific method that Charles Beard was attempting to reformulate and preserve.[19] It was written within the context of shifting notions about the character of space and time, which artists, scientists, philosophers, and even disillusioned American communists were creatively debating through the 1930s in an effort to find a new foundation for faith in progress. Though Charles Beard had been influenced by Becker in his formulation of "history as an act of faith," Beard, unlike Becker, retained his belief in progress and in American exceptionality despite the inescapable contradictions that relativism posed for his hope for political renewal during the Depression decade.[20]

Becker, in contrast to Beard, and perhaps because he was a student of Turner's, did not seek to explore new frontiers. Instead, he turned to the study of Europe and to the history of writing about history. Becker believed that culture was inescapable; therefore, there could be no frontier line of progress marking a creative and destructive clash of civilization and savagery from which revolution might spontaneously create a new order. American exceptionalism could no longer have appeared viable to Becker once he came to view it as an extension of the European culture it was supposed to have escaped. Becker, therefore, suggested that there is transformation in history because space and time are always changing relative to observers, but there is no justification for calling that transformation either progress or, as Henry Adams had done, its opposite—degradation.[21] For Becker, the logic of this rejection of the objectivity of the idea of progress humanized it into a cultural convention, expressing the elemental longing for meaning and shelter in an unfeeling universe, shared as a tragic fate by all human beings.[22] Taking this historiographical view, Becker could not reasonably have divided science from art, politics from religion, or, especially, past from present.

Becker's interest in the eighteenth century as a focus for understanding irony, and his refusal to abstract history from culture or knowledge from the knower appealed very much to Allen Tate, who in the late

1920s and early 1930s was attempting to detach himself from Progressive New England standards and recover a regional identity.[23] Tate differed from Becker at that time, however, in his belief that irony, as an aesthetic category, could be controlled by artists and used to challenge the world of science and secular politics that the eighteenth-century philosophers and their legacy of the French revolution had created. Like the *philosophes*, Tate was searching for a principle that could release him from the paralyzing contradiction between abstract, relativized time and committed action. As Louis P. Simpson notes, Tate later claimed that he thought of the Agrarians as new Encyclopedists when he and John Crowe Ransom were providing the theoretical underpinnings for the movement.[24]

Tate may have developed that particular characterization after reading Becker, but long before 1933 he had come to believe Western culture had taken a disastrously wrong turn by separating aesthetics from science during the Enlightenment. Tate's appreciation of Becker's historiography was prepared for through his immersion in historical studies of the Civil War in the late 1920s. Together, these studies reveal that he was not hostile to applying a historical perspective to aesthetics, as some students of the New Criticism have suggested. Rather, as Tate himself reported, he opposed the false objectivity of abstract scientific history in the interest of establishing a historical grounding for a revolution against modern scientific-industrial culture, a culture that had been established on the foundations laid by the *philosophes*, as active men of learning.[25] The modern vehicle for his counter-Enlightenment Agrarian movement to restore Western unity was to be a republic of letters, with a reverse mission to that of the *philosophes*. Instead of moving on a wave of progress into an alienated, secularized state, as Becker described the consequence of Diderot's scientific relativism, Tate wanted to harness relativism to reverse that process and restore the unity of Dante's medieval vision of political and religious harmony.[26]

It is necessary, however, to recognize that the ambiguity so characteristic of Tate's views between the late 1920s when he became politically active and 1950 when he converted to Catholicism reflected his growing despair of finding a positive resolution to his quest. Already at the beginning of his most politically active phase, with the publication of *I'll Take My Stand* in 1930, Tate affirmed the need for a corporate Catholic religious tradition to replace the Protestant individualism of the South he championed. Such a faith, he said, would allow the Southerner to bore into society from within to effect a secular revolution. If the Southerner could not bore from within because the contingencies of history had deprived him of tradition, his only recourse was to bore from without.[27] In essence, this meant that Tate was searching for a way to restore a classical traditional society but could conceive of no avenue for doing so outside of the romantic individualism derived from the same degenerated standard he was attempting to replace.

By 1936 and *Who Owns America?* Tate, at least on the surface, appeared to have found a blend, not just of the political and the spiritual, but of the agrarian Protestant South and Catholic Europe, in his new Distributist-Agrarian coalition. But instead of celebrating a political unification of classical and romantic values, Tate found himself both disgusted with the narrow provincialism he encountered among his fellow Agrarians and sharing their fear of being swallowed up by combinations of other interests, centered in New York. He withdrew his active support. No sooner had Tate achieved the balance between civic and spiritual values for which he had so desperately struggled, than he admitted defeat. He had worked politically to achieve a redemptive synthesis of time as tradition and space as political economy, but even in 1930 he had complained that as a Southerner, he faced "a paradox," which he could not say how to resolve: "He must use an instrument, which is political, and so unrealistic and pretentious that he cannot believe in it, to re-establish a private, self-contained, and essentially spiritual life."[28] The heroic reformer, this statement suggested, must be a confidence artist, but how could a confidence game have established a legitimate and stable basis for community in the first place?

Unable to resolve that dilemma, Tate turned more and more towards the negative ideal of withdrawal. His transformation from political activist as an Agrarian into an aesthetic contemplative, by way of the New Criticism, marked a melancholy defeat for Tate, which finally led to his conversion to Catholicism in 1950.[29] As Tate said in 1952 having long since surrendered political activism, "While the politician, in his cynical innocence, uses society, the man of letters disdainfully, or perhaps even absentmindedly, withdraws from it." The man of letters simply renders the image of the man of his time like a mirror, and "what modern literature has taught us is not merely that the man of letters has not participated fully in the action of society: it has taught us that nobody else has either." In a society in which means have no ends, everyone acts his part in a plotless drama, Tate said, a drama of withdrawal.[30]

Tate's disillusionment culminated in a conversion—perhaps less to an actual Catholicism than to an aesthetic image of it—because Tate resigned himself to the inevitability of withdrawal in the context of some corporate form of society. Tate's hope was that modern writers would establish a political and spiritual reprise of the medieval jeremiad. In 1930, he wrote of the Old South as a "profoundly European community" that "could entertain the biblical mythology along with the Greek, and it could add to these a lively mediaevalism from the novels of Sir Walter Scott."[31] In 1945, he still hoped to find a way to build "the kind of unity prevailing in the West until the nineteenth century," which was "a peculiar balance of Greek culture and Christian other-worldliness, both imposed by Rome upon the northern barbarians." According to Tate, "It was this special combination that made European civilization, and it was this that men communicated in the act of living together. It was this force which reduced the regional heterogeneity to a manageable unity, or even sublimated it into universal forms." This civilization, Tate continued, is almost gone. Rather than asking what is right, contemporary men and women ask if it will work. "In our time," he complained, "we have been the victims of a geographical metaphor, or a figure of space: we have tried to compensate for the limitations of the little community by envisaging the big community, which is not necessarily bigger spiritually or culturally than the little community."[32] Like his famous metaphor of the modern civilization having only half of a whole horse—the mechanical power of an abstracted internal combustion engine instead of the whole, grass-eating horse—Tate complained that humanism had ended up defending only half a tradition. Contemporary humanism, he said, "has ended up as only half of a half: it stands for only half of the Greek spirit, the empirical or scientific half which gives us our technology. Technology without Christianity is, I think, barbarism quite simply: but barbarism refined, violent and decadent, *not the vigorous barbarism of forest and the soil.*"[33] Even before 1936, when he still believed in the possibility of republican virtue, Tate's solution to bringing about a return to vigorous culture was never a direct and simple return to Dante's heavenly vision but its inversion. Tate wanted to preserve the Christian half of the dual culture of the modern West, but he believed that would end in a disavowal of life. He wished to be one with nature, experienced as living and worldly history, but he believed science had corrupted naturalism, turned it into mere process, and emptied it of internal meaning. Therefore, he sought to preserve spiritual order and natural passion, universal truth and particular experience, by using each negatively against the other. Once he became disillusioned with the possibility of using politics and economics, which he believed were mirrors of religious values, to create the ground for a redemptive society, he attempted to shape a positive message of his own by showing the absence of meaning in each side of modern experience. Tate believed he could negatively construct a positive truth about the human need for the wholeness that modern experience could not provide, as a kind of reverse mirror image of reality.[34]

Since Tate believed his poetic vision rested upon a dissociation of sensibility in modern man, to use the phrase Tate borrowed from Eliot and made famous, he cultivated his own sense of dissociation.[35] Throughout the 1930s he counterbalanced his deeply felt urge to convert to Catholicism and to embrace a universal Western religious heritage with a particular historical identity as a white Protestant Southerner. In doing so, Tate closely followed T. S. Eliot's lead in embracing a negative way to truth.[36] Though ostensibly devoted disciples of Dante, Tate and Eliot quite forthrightly admitted that, as moderns, they were alienated from Dante's angelic or spiritual mission because each wished to balance will and community—that is, Machiavellian virtù and virtue—and not just accept religious orthodoxy. Therefore, Tate's decision as an Agrarian to throw himself into a southern identity through a reactionary act of will, taking on its entire ethos down to a justification of lynching, was actually complementary to his simultaneous desire to surrender his will through conversion to Catholicism.[37] That is, Tate's was a form of Machiavellian ambiguity toward the relation of will and acceptance, and the individual and the universal, adapted to a moment of crisis within Anglo-American Protestant culture. As Craig Cairns has written in reference to Eliot, who expressed his admiration for Machiavelli more directly than did Tate, order was the central virtue he wished to sustain, and a good religion was one that guaranteed order by maintaining continuity with the past. Thus, says Cairns of Eliot, "the politics of Machiavelli and the bridge to the past of the Anglican Church come to be identified with each other."[38]

On one hand Tate followed Eliot's lead when he complained in his essay on southern religion in *I'll Take My Stand* that southern Protestantism could not serve its purpose in preserving civic order, because as a religion it lacked the capacity to enlist science in its cause. "Since there is in the Western mind, a radical division between the religious, the contemplative, the qualitative, on the one hand, and the scientific, the natural, the practical on the other, the scientific mind always plays havoc with the spiritual life when it is not powerfully enlisted in its cause."[39] Allowing science to go its own way, Tate said, had disastrous consequences for community and personality. Had the South had the right kind of religion, more in tune with its aristocratic European culture, it would not have lost the Civil War, and a different social ethos would have gained ascendancy than New England's. On the other hand, in 1929 Tate faulted Eliot for converting to Anglicanism because he believed Eliot had surrendered his poetic voice in doing so. According to Tate, who was then resisting conversion to Catholicism, Catholics were as internally divided as any other moderns.[40] He therefore believed that conversion could not resolve the problem of restoring a balance between particularity and universality. Tate believed, however, that through art, the dissociation that Dante positively confronted within a fourteenth-century crisis of religion and economics could be balanced negatively, to reveal a positive social and spiritual ideal by its absence. The persistent problem for Tate with this formulation, however, was similar to Machiavelli's or Henry Adams's: the problem of grounding action upon a negative foundation in order to bring about a redemptive transformation of time and space without Dante's sustaining positive faith in providential history.

Tate explored this dilemma in a number of contexts during the 1920s and 1930s, in both his New Agrarian and New Critic roles. As commentators on Tate's work have noticed, he did so by setting up a classical East versus frontier West dichotomy instead of a South versus North dichotomy, since he believed both the North and South lacked cultural and political unity.[41] Also, he recognized how interrelated the dilemmas of his southern identity were with those experienced by New Englanders. Tate complained that a once classical and stable civilization had spawned the romantic will of the western frontier. Using Neoplatonic conceptualization and echoing Yeats and Baudelaire, as a modern Dante and his double, Tate described this frontier as classical Western civilization's own anti-image in a hellish New World. The Civil War was the last great conflict in that struggle between the East and West. It pitted the South as the last outpost of European civilization against the industrial North. With the defeat of the South went the last check against northern acquisitiveness and compulsive organization. But as a fratricidal war, the War Between the States was an expression of a divided history of internal conflict, which the South shared with its northern Protestant brothers and sisters, and which was the self-divided legacy of European civilization itself since the sundering of medieval unity with the Reformation.[42]

Tate had first confronted this dual legacy of alienation and attachment to a self-divided history in his biographies of Stonewall Jackson and Jefferson Davis, the former hero being classically stable but incapable of surviving modern chaos and the latter self-divided and incapable of preserving tradition. He equivocated between these two tragic conditions in his poetry during the early 1930s, turning them into the basis for his aesthetic creativity.[43] For example, in the companion poems "The Mediterranean" (1932) and "Aeneas at Washington" (1933), Tate contrasted the Classical harmony of the center of the Western tradition with its degeneration at its western frontier in modern times. The failure of the latter, his Aeneas shows, represents a degeneration into a fallen condition, brought about because his modern descendants either were not wise enough to preserve tradition or were the victims of its internal contradiction. In either case, the poet laments that "we've cracked the hemispheres with careless hand!" Only through the relativity of the historical imagination may the artist return to the original harmony of the classical hero. In doing so, the artist reminds modern men and women of their potential for living with the integrity of the ancients. Yet by that same relativity he or she is barred from remaining within their company and may return only as an act of piracy. As he explained in his 1936 essay "What Is a Traditional Society?" the very effort to revive the past hastens its destruction if it is only picturesquely restored. "For the moment the past becomes picturesque it is dead."[44]

Similarly, Tate's *The Fathers* (1938) is a tragic confrontation between Major Buchan, a classical hero who is incapable of surviving in the context of modern chaos, and George Posey, the alienated romantic hero who successfully acts but cannot preserve social order. As Arthur Mizener and Thomas Daniel Young have both observed, *The Fathers* charts the "terrible conflict between two fundamental and irreconcilable modes of existence," which shatters the unity between the private and public as well as between the past and the modern worlds.[45] As such, the novel, which grew out of Tate's stalemated biography of Robert E. Lee, may equally be read as a confrontation of the unresolvable tension between necessity and contingency. Tate's message in *The Fathers*, as in his poetry, is that art must mediate such unresolvable tensions at the center of human experience. As the metaphysical poet begins at one end of human experience and the romantic symbolist begins at the other, Major Buchan's classicism contrasts with George Posey's romanticism. Lacy Buchan, like the critical reader, must find a moment of balance between the two extremes. The innocent reader, Tate explains in his 1938 essay "Tension in Poetry," wishes to live in the past but cannot do so. The reader is forced to live in the contingencies of the present. The critical reader, like Lacy Buchan, must experience the past along with the present. By doing so, "he makes present the past, and masters it; and he is at the center of the experience out of which the future must come."[46]

Lacy Buchan's mastery of the past reveals that *The Fathers,* like "The Mediterranean" and "Aeneas at Washington," was an unsuccessful attempt to formulate a Romantic elegy that would aesthetically deliver Tate from the personal guilt that he believed was an inescapable condition of modern life—a guilt he could not avoid, since his role as critic required him to recognize his own limitations, fixed by the relativity of history. "Criticism may isolate the imperfect, and formulate that which is already abstract; but it cannot formulate the concrete whole," Tate wrote in 1934. Later, in 1951, after his conversion, Tate would say that even Dante's poetry, and not just criticism, must be tragic, for if Dante had actually seen the Beatific Vision, he would not have written a poem about it. But in 1934, in "Three Types of Poetry," he still had hope for salvation through literature and therefore said only that the third type of poetry, exemplified by *The Divine Comedy,* remained the transcendent promise of aesthetic redemption, beyond the tragic dissociation of modern sensibilities.[47]

Consequently, Lacy Buchan's elegy for both fathers was actually the occasion for Tate to mourn his own lost innocence, asking why life cannot change without "tangling the lives of innocent persons?" Why, asks Lacy, must innocence be lost, leaving guilt as the price of survival?[48] This was, of course, Allen Tate's anguished question as well. Finally, Tate's Romantic elegy remained incomplete. His own attachment to the southern myth left him unable to resolve the "terrible conflict between the two fundamental and irreconcilable modes of existence," which the two fathers represented for Lacy within the narrative.

In each of his works from the 1920s and 1930s, Tate made clear his belief that the condition of modern consciousness of time and space alienated the modern artist from Dante's unity. Anglo-American writers, he said, had fallen away from the standard of Dante, just as Western culture had fallen away from its vital source by becoming a frontier without a center. The inability of artists to maintain a unity between fact and meaning through the poetic form of the allegory, he said further, was indicative of the loss of that cultural unity. "I allude here to Dante's ability to look into a specific experience and to recreate it in such a way that its meaning is nowhere distinct from its specific quality," he wrote in "Three Types of Poetry" in 1934.

The quality and intention of the allegorical will are the intention and quality of the will of science. With allegory the image is not a complete, qualitative whole; it is an abstraction calculated to force the situation upon which it is imposed toward a single direction. In the sixteenth century science proper had achieved none of its triumphs. The allegorist had before him no standard by which he could measure the extent of his failure to find the right abstractions for the control of nature. He could spin out his tales endlessly in serene confidence of their "truth." But by the end of the eighteenth century his optimism had waned; it had passed to the more efficient allegorist of nature, the modern scientist.

Divided from natural experience, the poetic will became divided from society and itself, creating the romantic will of revolt. "We find here two assertions of the erring will diverging for the first time," Tate concluded, "science *versus* romanticism." [49]

Tate's view of a post–Dantean world as divided demonically between forms of human creativity, resulting in a contradiction between different forms of knowing and also between different forms of living, was conventionally Machiavellian, as was his solution to it. Aspiring to bring about a new political and aesthetic order, Tate as a founding father of the New Agrarian movement had heroically mounted a conservative defense of a tradition he believed was neither legitimate nor recoverable. Tate held that without the forms of "the higher myth of religion and the lower myth of historical dramatization," men had "lost the forms of human action," and he hoped to restore them. But Tate recognized the indispensability of religion and history as myths, not as truths. He wrote that he did not wish to restore the Middle Ages, or any other age. "I do not want to restore anything whatsoever. It is our task to create something," Tate protested against his critics in 1936. [50]

But, of course, Tate wanted to conserve something as well as to create something. He wanted to conserve the southern family romance and his own quarrel with himself, through which his poetry became possible. In linking the continuity of the southern legend to his mission to create a national form of cultural criticism, Tate placed himself at a transitional point between the pastoral and the Romantic elegy. He described his own southern society as creatively poised on the edge of destruction, as was feudal England in the sixteenth century, or as taking a backward glance as it entered the twentieth century.[51] In emphasizing the temporality of history, and of the Southern Renaissance itself, he underscored the relativity of all transitions perceived in time without a fixed standard. This permitted Tate to offer a prophecy of return to Western unity in the future as well as an elegy for a dying traditional world of the past. His was a southern prophecy and elegy that could find kinship in the poetry of Emily Dickinson, whose creativity Tate linked to New England's imminent fall, on the eve of the Civil War.[52] He praised and identified with her for simultaneously fulfilling and betraying New England culture. For Tate, Dickinson's greatness was evoked by her role in presiding over the death of Puritan culture, and she also approached the Romantic elegist's ideal for him because her poetry "comes out of an intellectual life towards which it feels no moral responsibility. Cotton Mather would have burnt her for a witch."[53]

Tate's profound sensitivity to moments of transition permitted him to read the signs of New England's fall from cultural power, just when its role as a center of "highbrow" culture had reached its height. He saw this fall, exquisitely framed in the poetry of Dickinson and Robert Frost, as an opportunity for southern provincialism to be turned into a pastoral force for a *rinnovazione*, a renewal of virtue through a stoic conflagration, not through Christian apocalypse.[54] Therefore, Tate's idea of cultural renewal had to be temporary, existing only in the smoldering ashes of the old world destroyed, not any new, utopian future. Within this context, Tate was drawn to the aesthetic power of the elegiac form because it achieves aesthetically the stoic ideal of autonomy, the end so highly prized by Machiavelli as an artist of political culture. However, the great difference between stoicism and Machiavellian republicanism is that the latter found autonomy neither wholly good nor bad, but deeply problematical. Therefore, the elegy raised to the moment of balance in Frost or Dickinson, at least as Tate read them, was an ideal that eluded his grasp as a patriotic Southerner. Perhaps for that reason of being unable to balance both memory and detachment, he finally converted to his personal monastic vision of Catholicism and ceased to write poetry in the 1950s.

Robert Penn Warren, echoing his mentor and friend, Allen Tate, once said that all his fiction had been preoccupied with Dantean themes, particularly those of the mirror and the problem of true and false fathers.[55] Warren, however, read Machiavelli with as much care as he read Dante, and by returning to the origins of American political culture, he went

beyond Tate to fashion successfully what is perhaps the most sophisticated Romantic elegiac aesthetic in twentieth-century American literature. Though his early novels, such as *Night Rider, At Heaven's Gate,
World Enough and Time, Band of Angels,* and even *All the King's Men,* were
somberly equivocal about the possibility of redeeming historical time, his
last novel, *A Place to Come to* (1977), successfully established a positive,
darkly humorous, even exuberant, foray into the redemptive possibilities
of death.

In *A Place to Come to,* Warren's protagonist, Jediah Tweksbury, is introduced through the absurdly ribald death of his father, who was pitched
from his wagon while drunkenly relieving himself. The burden this death
puts upon the young man's life is the burden of finding a meaning to his
own existence in its elemental entanglement with vulgar nature. He is
caught up in another form of this same contradiction during World War II,
in "the great checker game in which America, with its murderous innocence, was busy pushing and pulling, hither and yon, its millions of little
checkers." Tweksbury is sent to south-central Italy by the "brass-bound
Blind Doomsters" of Washington, D.C., to fight with partisans.[56] During
this assignment he personally executes a cultured Nazi officer who will
not surrender his absurdly irrelevant idealism and face the truth of violent reality. Then, following the war, Tweksbury enters the University of
Chicago, where he encounters the cultured and erudite Dr. Stahlmann,
who commits suicide because he *does* see the violence of Hitler's Germany and is unable to live in the face of its shattering contradiction to
Dante's spiritual ideal. The lesson that Tweksbury learns from all this is
that anything may become a way of life, even death: "Even the question
why death should become a way of life could itself become a way of life.
That question was there continuously and inevitably, like the air you
breathe or the bread you eat, but in its inevitability it had long since
ceased to demand an answer. It had become, as it were, purely rhetorical."[57] Reading over and over again his battered copy of *The Divine Comedy,* Tweksbury tried to keep his sanity through Dante's all-embracing
meaningfulness. "The trouble here," says Tweksbury, "was that, while
this was my program for keeping sane, the book's vision of all-embracing
meaningfulness, in the midst of the incessant violence and perfidy depicted there, aggravated, by fundamental and ironic contrast, my awareness of the blankness of spirit that was then my way of life." Tweksbury
considers what he might be willing to die for, including his own hometown, but feels only alienation. "Was I ready to die for the Confederate

States of America?" he asks, and answers himself, "They were already dead." Finally, he decides that "all the dying I was prepared to do was die laughing." Yet one problem remained to keep him from surrendering to an ironic existence; he was not willing to accept the insensitivity of a naturalistic world as the alternative to Dante's spiritualism.[58]

Having entered the academic world, however, and finding himself caught up in the Dante industry, Tweksbury makes a bargain with Hell, which results in establishing his reputation as a scholar of medieval literature. He writes a critically acclaimed essay arguing that in Dante's *Divina Commedia*, death defines life. Tweksbury considers this a pact with the devil because he achieves this insight as an accident of association, when his new wife Agnes, a Lutheran pastor's sexually repressed daughter, dies of cancer of the uterus while he completes his dissertation.[59]

On one level, *A Place to Come to* is written as a long elegy in which Tweksbury finally achieves separation from Agnes and allows life to define death instead of the other way around. On another, Tweksbury and his high-school girlfriend, Rozelle Hardcastle, are linked together as Paolo and Francesca, Dante's illicit lovers who suffer in the second circle of Hell. The pair find a this-worldly salvation by the close of the narrative because Warren reads their foolish and poignant story as an attempt to find love. Tweksbury, by the end of the novel, achieves a liberation, even a participation in blessedness. Warren is careful not to claim too much for his character, who confesses he "had not been found worthy to sit on the placeless, sunlit lawn of Dante's vision and listen to the blessed music that was the language uttered by the saints and sages—or at least, I had brought back no fair report to open the ears of others." However, a short space later he permits Tweksbury to use the word *blessed* in a letter to Dauphine, the mother of his son, who was only briefly present in the novel. As he uses the word, asking for "your company for what blessedness it is," Jediah Tweksbury—who signs the letter "Your (whether you like it or not) Jed"—achieves a quite unequivocal redemption. Ironically, Warren is able to communicate his character's sense of resolution only when he has fully subverted Dante and rendered his spiritual romanticism into the terms of realism through the formula of the Romantic elegy. After years of being tempted to accept Tate's religious answer, Warren escapes Dante's influence over him, as he told Peter Stitt in 1977, by coming to view Dante as merely another Protestant, who rejected this world for a transcendent one.[60]

Warren's ambivalent need to pattern himself after Dante's example and yet to transcend the power of Dante's influence in order to achieve spiritual autonomy reflected his comprehension that he, as a man of letters, personally mirrored a fundamental contradiction within Western culture itself. Since Machiavelli, nature and history have become the ground of human depravity in a radically contingent world, and yet, in a world deprived of Providence, they have also been the only grounds upon which redemption can be conceived. Within this context, Dante's *Divine Comedy* has aesthetically represented both a Classical ideal of a lost world of virtue and an inspiration for revolt against decadence to restore a lost innocence through violence.

Warren recognized that the inherent contradiction within this Machiavellian resolution is the same contradiction that divided the North from the South and himself from his southern heritage. For the terms of Warren's own quarrel with Dante may be seen in his deep attraction to Dante as a source of spiritual criticism of the mechanical world of crude naturalism, on one side, and in his uncomfortable conviction that Dante was a father of the Puritan hatred of this world, on the other. Before Warren could achieve autonomy from Dante's vision of spiritual unity, therefore, and claim his own acceptance of the world as it is, he first needed to lay to rest his southern identity. He did this in his 1963 novel, *Flood*, subtitled, *A Romance of Our Time*.[61] In that novel, Warren violently destroyed the pastoral elegy by which he had formerly preserved his identification with the South and rejected the aesthetic formula he had defended so tenaciously since he joined the New Agrarian Critics and the New York intellectuals in helping to create William Faulkner's literary reputation during the Cold War.[62] In *Flood*, he detached himself from what appeared to him to be a failed aesthetic and a failed political ideal of a nostalgic South, and he thus made possible the successful application of a Romantic elegy to Dante as a mirror of Western culture itself in *A Place to Come to*, published a decade later.

As Lewis P. Simpson observed in 1975, the second-generation Southern Renaissance writers, led by Warren, shifted from a preoccupation with memory and history to a detachment from the South and a concern with the isolated, existential self. He suggested then that this change represented an act of dispossession of Faulkner's and Tate's generation, and perhaps of the Southern Renaissance itself.[63] Though Simpson mistakenly assumed that *Flood* was the summation of Warren's artistic career, he was not mistaken in reading *Flood* as an antipastoral elegy.

Flood is a mournful, but, for Warren, an ultimately liberating admission that the southern identity is merely one of loneliness: "Hell," says Brad Tolliver, the figure whose personal torment forms the core of the narrative, "no Southerner believes there is a South. He just believes that if he keeps on saying the word he will lose some of the angry lonesomeness." Only the colored folks are not lonesome, Tolliver concludes. "They may be angry but they are not lonesome."[64] In contrasting black identity with the emptiness of southern white denial, Warren makes it clear that he speaks a Faulknerian truth that must disappear in the same flood of change that is destroying the white South. The black American as "a fundamentalist of Western Culture," he explained two years later, mirrors the white society in reverse. It is true, for Warren, that this black role "is to dramatize the most inward revelation of that culture," but "in the end, everybody has to redeem himself." Significantly, Tolliver's existential loneliness is mirrored by a young black man named Mortimer Sparlin who, in search of his racial identity, discovers only his own emptiness.[65]

Warren juxtaposes Tolliver, as a troubled and bitter writer, with a serene, almost mystically joyous counter-figure, Yasha Jones, a famous filmmaker who has come to record the flooding of Tolliver's old hometown, Fiddlersburg, Tennessee. Jones's earlier brush with mortality is the root of his acceptance of life, which allows him to fall in love with Brad's sister, Maggie. Brad Tolliver, on the other hand, has become trapped in his own unconfronted past, from which he fled as a young man. In headlong flight from himself, he follows a reverse image of Beatrice in a blind Leontine Purtle. Tolliver believes she will provide him with an inner vision of life's meaning, but she instead mocks his sentimental romanticism when she turns out to be a frequent guest at the "Seven Dwarfs Motel." Instead of bearing a cosmic message of spiritual light, she is the living mirror of the sign that lights up the sky above the motel. It shows "a young woman whose endowments were not obscured by a virginally white nightdress," who "was waking to the kiss of Prince Charming." Beneath the sign are the words:

BREAKFAST SERVED IN COTTAGE
TENNESSEE SMOKED HAM AND RED GRAVY
YASSUH, BOSS!

Tolliver fails to find a sexual epiphany when his sentimentalized journey with "Beatrice" takes him to the center of Hell instead. Or, to exchange Cervantes for Dante, Tolliver discovers his Dulcinea is linked spiritually

with the false and sentimentalized South to which he is returning quix-
otically on his white charger, a Jaguar that bolts "like a thoroughbred ig-
nominiously stung by a horsefly," as he pulls into the motel.[66]

While waiting for the flood that will destroy the town, Tolliver will be
deluged by the breaking loose of a flood of memories, through the redemptive and damning violence of change. Brad Tolliver will not find his
own peace with the world until, at the novel's conclusion, he risks death
to preserve the lives of others. Only then does he accept the death of the
hold of the past upon him, freeing him to search for the still unknown
connection between the past and present that may reveal "the human necessity" that still eludes his grasp.

For the present, he must take his quest out into the world, though later
he might return to his past, which has been submerged in the chaos and
baptism of its watery grave—or rather, as he corrects himself, he cannot
return to Fiddlersburg, but only to the shores of its memory. The pastoral elegy has been elegized, and left behind with the southern past:
"But then, even as he felt a sudden, unwilled, undecipherable, tearing,
ripping gesture of his innermost being toward those people over yonder,
who soon now would eat the ham and chicken and cake and chess pie,
and after the goodbyes and weeping, would go away, he thought: *There is
no country but the heart.*"[67]

Beyond his private experience as an artist, resolving a series of paradoxes and contradictions in his own life, Warren's journey as a public
man of letters paralleled a similar transformation in American political
culture. In moving from the pastoral elegiac form as he learned it from
Tate and Ransom at the beginning of his literary career to the Romantic
elegy, which he perfected over a long period of time, Warren fashioned a
strategy for resolving the tensions in his own relation to a corporate capitalist society and an individualistic consumer ethos. In that process, Warren helped to define aesthetics within the conventions of a new Machiavellian economic and political milieu for Cold War America. And in
doing so, he participated in removing racism as a barrier to the completion of twentieth-century America's shift from republicanism to democratic consumer capitalism, and at the same time, he participated in
bringing an end to the Southern Renaissance itself. For this reason, Warren's work in the 1930s and 1940s toward a new Machiavellian synthesis
may best be seen from the perspective of its completion in *Flood* and *A
Place to Come to.*

Warren's transformation from a somewhat detached younger associate of more serious and senior New Agrarians to a leading theorist of the New Critics to the Romantic elegist for the South and its legend began with his decision to move west in 1925, after graduating from Vanderbilt University. He studied at the University of California–Berkeley until 1927, when he moved to Yale, and then in 1929 attended Oxford on a Rhodes scholarship. During that period, Warren's sole contact with the old Fugitive circle was through his former college roommate and friend, Allen Tate, with whom he sometimes stayed and also corresponded. In 1928, after Tate had immersed himself in southern historical biography and influenced Warren to do the same, Tate helped Warren obtain a contract for a biography of the abolitionist revolutionary, John Brown. The result was Warren's first published work of prose, *John Brown: The Making of a Martyr,* which appeared in 1929.[68]

Whatever the shortcomings of *John Brown* as history, Warren accurately read the aesthetic politics of the time. His biography of the northern Protestant abolitionist was an assault upon *both* the standards of New England moralism and the legitimacy of black liberation. As Warren remembered it in 1974, he was then immersed in the study of the Irish patriot Yeats and the Elizabethan poets and saw in Brown an example of the dualism that permeated Anglo-Protestant culture.[69] Brown intrigued Warren both as a historical symbol and as a personality because he was a man of the border between morality and murder, the East and the West, and the Promethean hero and the Satanic villain: "On the one hand, he's so heroic, on the other hand he's so vile, pathologically vile. . . . Brown lives in the dramatic stance of his life, rather than in the psychological content of it; he lives in noble stances and noble utterances, and at the psychological and often *the factual* level of conduct was—it's incredible—brutal. Perfect self-deception—yet, 'noble'."[70]

Warren took the facts of Brown's life from a number of existing biographies. Not surprisingly, with the exception of Alan Nevins, most reviewers were unimpressed with the results. What is surprising, however, is how closely *John Brown* paralleled Thomas Dixon's interpretation of Brown in *The Man in Gray: A Romance of the North and South,* published eight years earlier in 1921.[71]

Warren never mentions Dixon, either in his curiously discounted footnotes, which he says were only for his private use and were printed by mistake, or in his bibliographical note at the end of the narrative. Indeed, Warren may not even have read Dixon's novel or remembered that he had. However, considering Warren's subsequent rise to prominence and

Dixon's decline towards oblivion, the similarity in their views at this stage of Warren's career provides a useful insight into the role of race in constructing his Romantic elegy for republican political values and his successful translation of Machiavellianism into a new era of Cold War capitalism, as Dixon failed to do.

Like Dixon's, Warren's interpretation of John Brown's life leaned toward an interest in the psychological duality of Brown as both a moralist and a cunning self-advancing fraud, a perspective Warren reported he found lacking in the standard biographies by Oswald Garrison Villard and H. P. Wilson. For both Dixon and Warren, Puritanism was at the heart of this dualism. Brown's was "a soul at war with the world," wrote Dixon, "a soul at war with himself. He was the incarnation of repressed emotions and desires." Warren's Brown suffered from that "psychological mechanism for justification which appeared regularly in terms of the things which friends called Puritanism and enemies called fanaticism." Brown, for both writers, was a self-appointed god who used casuistry to justify turning other men into living machines. For Warren, Brown's Puritan fanaticism led him to the attempt to create "the birth of the nation," as he designated chapter 9, through violent insurrection at Harper's Ferry. Brown's martyrdom, Warren suggested, was an echo of an earlier martyr, John Brown of Kent, who died in 1511 in insurrection against Catholic tradition—anticipating the Protestant Reformation as the later Brown anticipated the Civil War and the triumph of the Protestant North. For Dixon, the Puritan found violence against the witch or the Indian "an outlet for his repressed instincts": "The only holiday he established or permitted was the day on which he publicly thanked God for the goods which He had delivered. Through him the New England Puritan Thanksgiving Day became a national festival and through him a religious reverence for worldly success has become a national ideal." [72]

John Brown functioned for both writers as a representative symbol, a *figura*, who expressed cultural tragedy as focused in his particular life. In Dixon's view, John Brown was the historical embodiment of Jacobin leadership. He was the demagogic manipulator who used his own role as a martyr as an advertisement for himself. He was the representative leader for a diminished age of the new, modern collective mind, produced by the newspapers and turning individuals into mobs with "as little originality in them as in the machines which printed the editions." [73]

For Warren and Dixon both, John Brown was a cunning manipulator of this new audience. "The paranoiac had been transfigured now into the

Hero and the Saint through the worship of the mob which his insanity had created," Dixon explained. According to Warren, Brown convinced his followers by giving them "of the same insane root which he himself had eaten years before; he taught them the meaning of ambition and the meaning of imagination." Both Warren and Dixon contrasted this violence with the "feeling of a man like Lincoln, humane, wise and fallible, but learning from his own failings," in Warren's words; the "gentlest, broadest and sanest man" among the republicans, in Dixon's. Warren's "Stonewall" Jackson prayed for Brown's deliverance as the crisis of civil war waited in the wings.[74]

For Dixon, once more like Warren, the futile death and maiming of "eight thousand of our noblest sons," in a "hopeless tragedy, pitiful, terrible"; was made all the more horrible by the fact that "every issue could have been settled and better settled without the loss of a drop of blood." Dixon and Warren professed to have learned the same lesson from the Civil War—that only compromise, through the agency of law, stands between moralism and fanaticism in an era of mob rule. Therefore, the reasonable and measured Robert E. Lee, who brought Brown to justice at Harper's Ferry, was the hero in both accounts, illustrating the folly of an ethic of a romantic revolt based upon a "higher law," as espoused by Brown.[75]

Just as Dixon and Warren interpreted the significance of Brown and the centrality of the Civil War in American history similarly in this instance, they also considered themselves responsible for offering a southern challenge to New England's redemptive myth about the freedom that supposedly emerged from the bloodshed of the Civil War. Warren's biography ended at the moment of Brown's lawful execution, ominously anticipating the wages of Brown's violent Puritan moralism, which were about to be paid by Northerners and Southerners alike. Dixon's novel continued in time until the end of the war, when he had Lee forewarn of another crisis on the horizon. Slavery had been brought to an end, Dixon's Lee explained, but only by the accident of war's necessity, not on principle. The suddenness of the slaves' emancipation must finally bring a calamity worse even than the war itself, if the former slaves are not removed. "It must create a Race Problem destined to grow each day more threatening and insoluble."[76]

This prophetic warning, which Dixon felt called upon to deliver in defense of the southern family romance, marked the point where his interpretation diverged from Warren's. Warren did not raise fears about black freedom for white southern society in his biography. The reason for this was not a greater sensitivity to racism in Warren, who described the typical southern black as a happy and mindless creature, "who never bothered his kinky head about the moral issue," and who was incapable of working without white supervision.[77] Once more, Warren soon raised similar fears to Dixon's in his essay "The Briar Patch," his contribution to *I'll Take My Stand*, which he completed while at Oxford, soon after *John Brown*.[78]

In that essay, Warren advanced the then-standard view of Reconstruction provided by the Dunning school, in which blacks played the role of buffoon, the role Dixon gave them in his novels. During Reconstruction, the Negro was given "big talk and big promises," Warren explained wryly, and "sometimes he got an office out of it all and smoked cigars in the chair of a legislature." The political training he gained was in "corruption, oppression, and rancor," and when the Yankees left, he discovered he had paid a heavy price for his legislative seat and cigar. After centuries of oppression, he was briefly used as a tool, sacrificing his only real capital, the goodwill of the white man who controlled his fate. But unlike Dixon, who saw the removal of blacks as the only avenue for avoiding self-destructive violence on the part of the white community, Warren assumed that blacks were inevitably part of the southern landscape. As potential scabs in an industrial order, blacks needed to share in the prosperity of the agrarian economy, or both white and black Southerners would suffer equally. In both *The Leopard's Spots* and his autobiography, Dixon had registered his disillusionment with an Agrarian future for the South, and felt that a southern industrialism might replace it if black scab labor could be removed. Warren still defended an Agrarian future for the South in 1930. Therefore, like Tom Watson rather than like Dixon, he urged "an enlightened selfishness on the part of the Southern white man," in which blacks and whites would organize together to resist industrial exploitation while socially remaining separate, with blacks in an inferior position.[79]

Yet, at almost the same time that Warren was echoing Dixon in his biography of John Brown and Watson in his "Briar Patch" essay, he was detaching himself from Agrarianism in his first short story, "Prime Leaf," which he later expanded into a novel, *Night Rider* (1939), a tale of the "Black Patch" tobacco wars in Kentucky. Warren refused to call *Night Rider* a historical novel because he witnessed the tobacco war as a child, and he denied that it was an elegy for Agrarian politics. Instead he categorized it as a "philosophical novel," concerned with the plight of modern human existence.[80] In the novel, Warren described the corruption that finance capitalism brought into the agrarian community. But that abstracted violence of corporate economic greed, so often the subject of New Agrarian polemics, remained very much in the background to the purpose of his narrative. The story instead took the reader through the slow devolution of the farmers' tobacco cooperative into a fanatical darkness of murderous terrorism as they resisted finance capitalism. However, Warren's next novel, *At Heaven's Gate,* used the character of Bogan Murdoch, a ruthless finance capitalist, to explore many of the same concerns as *Night Rider.* Warren left the question of evil ambiguously suspended between economic exploitation and romantic idealism. His solution is the balanced life of the border between the two, a pragmatic stance he later espoused in *The Legacy of the Civil War* (1961), where everything is subject to revision in the interest of maintaining the individual's autonomy and social order.

Night Rider presented a Dantesque consideration of a descent into Hell for southern farmers, which mirrored John Brown's slide from Puritan moralism into fanaticism. The protagonist, Percy Munn, is a lawyer, who is trapped by his lack of self-knowledge and the fraudulent and corrupt interests that have tainted the Association of the Growers of Dark-fired Tobacco, as a part of the corruption of all that exists in time. He has an illicit love interest in Lucy Christian, the daughter of a failed father-figure named Bill Christian. He blindly leads Percy Munn into the web of fraudulent moral choices. This reveals the setting of *Night Rider* to be in the second circle of Hell in which each of the protagonists is equivocally damned. Percy Munn and Lucy Christian are Paolo and Francesca, Dante's frustrated lovers who are tragically bound and yet separated by their sin of lust. They exist in agnostic balance between suffering on their way towards ultimate damnation and suffering towards some final and terrible expiation, which may release them from their sin—or confirm them irrevocably in it. Illicitly driven to each other through their alienation, and seeking warmth in forbidden romanticism, their secret is revealed when Percy's entanglement in the tobacco growers' association spreads new forms of violence into the world around him. Munn and Lucy are discovered by her father when he rouses Munn to tell him that Munn's barn of tobacco has been burned to the ground. The horror of the betrayal by his daughter and friend causes Bill Christian to fall victim to a stroke that will lead to his death.[81]

The arsonists in Warren's second circle of Hell, in which everything is connected to everything else, are members of a reconstituted Klan who had threatened to burn out landowners keeping black tenants on their lands at the expense of white ones. Disgusted by the violence that the association, secretly led by Munn, has unleashed, Mr. Grimes, his white tenant, decides to go west for a new beginning. The Klan mistakenly assumes that Munn had defied the warning. Warren's conviction of the universality of guilt in this sequence points beyond Munn's vigilantism toward the story of Willie Proudfit, whose own effort at a new beginning in the West seemingly led into a still deeper circle of Hell instead of redemption. However, it also points back to an earlier scene in which Munn's altruistic effort to prove a client innocent of a murder led directly to a black man's execution for a crime he did not commit.[82] The Negro's innocence is the innocence of nature, not of moral purity. Nevertheless, Munn's moral implication in this death results in Munn's personal fall into, or knowledge of, his guilt. It also reveals the corruption of the southern agrarian world, on a deeper level than the capitalist nexus of tobacco cropping. Without ever giving the Negro a name or the status of personhood, Warren uses the existence of racism to transcend the pastoral ideal of the southern family romance. In doing so, he effectively neutralized the ideal that Tate was unable to escape because he felt required to defend the southern family romance in order to challenge northern cultural dominance.

That scene concerns Munn's legal defense of a farmer named Bunk Trevelyan, accused of murdering a neighbor over water. Convinced of his innocence, Munn is finally driven to organize an illegal search for the murder weapon among the black sharecroppers. "They's a cabin in the far side of these-here woods," Munn is told by a deputy leading the search:

"Old yaller, wall-eyed nigger man lives there, used to live on the Burdett place. You remember, Burke"—and he turned to the other deputy—"that old, yaller, wall-eyed nigger's name?"

"It doesn't matter," Mr. Munn said.

"Naw," the first deputy agreed, "it don't matter what he calls hisself. This ain't exactly what you might call a social visit."

The nearly bare boughs of the trees "made a web like pattern of shadow on the road," as one deputy remembers going coon hunting with friends in these woods as a boy, and another makes a crude racial joke, sniggering, "You might say as you're coon-hunting tonight, too." Munn is oblivious to the implication of this banter. After rousing the Negro, they discover the murder weapon in his kitchen. When Munn asks him to explain his possession of the knife, the Negro gives an absurdly lame answer—a hopping bullfrog led him to it.

Using the most vulgar naturalism, Warren compares the plight of the Negro, trapped in the web of circumstances, to a fat old bullfrog and links Percy Munn's moral fall to the same naturalistic plane of contingencies that led to the destruction of the frog and the Negro:

'Fore I knowed hit he hopped right up under that-air cawn-crib, right up under whar the log wuz a-setten on the hunk of lime-rock, and I retched up under and grabbed holt of his laig and pulled him out, and 'fore-God-a-mighty, he drug out that-air knife, . . . so I taken hit and cut off his laigs and put 'em in my pocket and thowed that ole frog in the dirt, then I say, naw, I'll give him to my shoats, so I picked him up and put him in the slop. He kept on a-sloshen round in the slop, but he could'n swim none to speak of, and I thowed him to them shoates. Hit was that big ole red shoat got him, I seen him when she done hit. She done taken him—

Munn cuts the unnamed Negro short in self-righteous disgust. The next day, in court, expert empirical evidence proving the date of manufacture and sale establishes the knife as the murder weapon. Trevelyan is declared innocent and the Negro is hanged for murder. Eventually, the unfolding story reveals that everyone but Munn recognized the crime had been pinned on the Negro. Warren permits the reader to know that this act was irrelevant to winning the case. It was an accidental result of Munn's effort to prove—not Trevelyan's innocence, but—his own moral innocence.[83]

The naturalistic revelation of the possibility of idealism through its absence, which Warren achieved in this sequence of events in *Night Rider*, provides a key to his later work; it is a perspective that Warren has attributed to his reading of Machiavelli and Dante.[84] In *All The King's Men*, which Kenneth Bruffee has interpreted as a form of the Romantic elegy, both Jack Burden's and Cass Mastern's stories follow the negative symbolism of Dante's journey into Hell, which Percy Munn followed in *Night Rider*.[85] Though race had, at least formally, only a peripheral role in Munn's and Mastern's confrontations with guilt, and none at all with Burden's, Warren did take it up as a specific theme in *Band of Angels* (1955), and in *Segregation: The Inner Conflict in the South* (1956). In the latter book, which consisted of a series of interviews—a formula he repeated in *Who Speaks for the Negro?* (1965)—Warren directly addressed the relation of race to the southern family romance.[86] Those who support segregation and those who support desegregation, he wrote in that context, are caught in a paradox: "in seeking to preserve individualism by taking refuge in the vision of the South redeemed in unity and antique virtue, they are fleeing from the burden of their individuality—the intellectual rub, the moral rub." To state it differently, Warren said, the desire to retain continuity in social form is to accept a world of frozen values, when "the essence of individuality is the willingness to accept the rub which the flux of things provokes, to accept one's fate in time."[87]

John Burt has characterized Warren's writing as so perfectly balanced among ambivalences and ambiguities that he leaves us guessing whether we live in a neutral territory in which life is possible, or whether we are just caught between the devil and the deep blue sea.[88] This quality reflects Warren's attraction to, as well as horror of, John Brown, as his archetypal image of the individual who lives his life on the border of violence and morality. Warren's literary explorations have been in the ambiguous border space between Naturalism and Romanticism, where appeals to higher laws of right lead to murder, because they are not sufficiently grounded in the necessity of a social code based on realism about human evil. Nevertheless, as a writer of the border, Warren sympathetically identifies with his romantic heroes, such as Brown, Willie Stark, or Jeremiah Beauchamp, because Realism itself threatens to destroy all aspirations for human meaning by reducing every human impulse to "the great twitch," as Jack Burden calls Naturalism.

This division, which Warren has linked to the tension between the space of freedom as defined by the Declaration of Independence and the traditional stability through time associated with the U.S. Constitution, forms the "paradox of democracy, one recognized by Jefferson and Washington."[89] Like Parson Weems, Warren made his life's work the confrontation with and resolution of the paradox that American history embodies at once a movement toward democracy and a disintegration of the spirit of democracy into fanaticism and the corruption of self-interest. The West to which John Brown travels to find his millennialist mission— like the West to which Jefferson's nephews travel only to be undone in the brutal murder of a slave, or the West in which Willie Proudfit becomes a destroyer of nature—is a place in which the self is lost, rather than fulfilled. But the act of losing the self initiates a crisis of self-awareness that makes a redemption of that self possible.[90] By offering an aesthetic link between Realism and Romanticism, Warren offered a new lease on life for the Romantic novel, and for the political mission shared by Anglo-American writers as diverse as Warren and Parson Weems, or Woodward and W. J. Cash. Perhaps most significantly, beginning with Jack Burden in *All the King's Men,* Warren successfully fashioned a paradigm for replacing a failed heroic ideal through the narrator's own sense of loss, leading to a final stage in which a confused and undistinguished minor character can achieve central status within the narrative. Warren's hero for a nonheroic age becomes the skilled practitioner of aesthetic politics, capable of transforming death into a personal resurrection.

For this reason, despite its originality in balancing Machiavellian dilemmas of space and time, Warren's message necessarily remained very much within the same tradition as that of Parson Weems, who was both a master of aesthetic politics and a moralist in search of a way to distinguish true fathers from false ones. Like Weems, whose aesthetic and political vision was centered in the impending tragedy of civil war, Warren looked back to the Civil War as a key to the American identity. For Weems, that division within the nation framed his crusade against drunkeness, gambling, and adultery, a mission revealed in the "Drunkard's Looking Glass," one of his popular pamphlets. Personal vice, for that ambiguously Protestant clergyman, exuberantly embracing this world, revealed a deeper civic corruption, threatening the health of the nation itself. The failures of personal responsibilities mirror political dissension in a world of interconnected consequences. In Warren, "all the self-division of conflict within individuals becomes a series of mirrors in which the plight of the country is reflected, and the self-division of the country a great mirror in which the individual may see imaged his own deep conflicts, not only the conflicts of political loyalties, but those more profoundly personal." [91]

Until his death in 1989, Robert Penn Warren was a writer who remained closely tied to Shakespearean conventions for balancing Machiavellian dilemmas of power and value. His aesthetic mission was found in holding a mirror to his readers' eyes to bring them to an awareness of the consequences of living in a society without the bonds of community. He explored the contradictions of being trapped within a self-destructive social web of power without legitimate authority but not without redemptive possibilities within its own conventions. Robert Penn Warren successfully bridged the divisions between aesthetics and politics for Cold War Americans and for that feat he will almost certainly retain an important role—whether acknowledged or not—in the future narratives of historians of Anglo-America in the twentieth century. Warren's prescient reading of the necessity of rejecting segregation as well as Agrarianism in the last half of the twentieth century and his accompanying description of the necessity of enclosing the self against a society that must fail because it lacks community have made him a compelling witness to the transformation of Anglo-American political culture in our time. Above all, Warren excelled as both a historian and novelist in his ability to identify those "special qualities of the South, or what may be thought of as such," which "are really qualities that simply belong to old America, qualities that can still be observed in back country New England," and which are both good and bad.[92]

Whether Robert Penn Warren achieves a secure niche in the American aesthetic canon is more problematic. The apotheosis to literary immortality depends on a far more doubtful combination of fashions, interests, and influences from publishing houses, the academy and those who continue to write in the genre-tradition that Warren has bequeathed to his heirs, than does acceptance into the historiographical canon. In Warren's role as a twentieth–century American artist, as for all who aspire to a prophetic office within a Machiavellian culture, continuity of influence is a function of time, power, and fortune, and not simply a matter of talent or message.

The success or failure of Warren's post–New Critical Romantic elegy for merging aesthetics with politics remains an open question for the future. Whether he will achieve aesthetic immortality through the Classical heroic formula of revitalizing the political order by instilling a new sense of moral autonomy in his readers also remains an open question for the future. But Warren's reformulation of Machiavellian aesthetics and politics in literature does share an ironic dilemma with C. Vann Woodward's similar effort in southern historiography and Reinhold Niebuhr's theological reformulation of the American jeremiad. None of these historian-critics gained his status by pandering to public approval or institutional power. Yet as artists in flight from being judged guilty of Romanticism, they desired to be relevant producers who were useful to their audiences. They wished to discover redemptive answers for healing a society in crisis. Ironically, therefore, in their early works they mediated a sense of personal and public loss only to discover that by embracing that loss they had gained professional self-advancement and powerful positions as critics. Once more Warren, Woodward, and Niebuhr read each other's works and intuitively welded themselves into a mighty cultural triumvirate that has outlasted the challenges of critics who have identified them individually with liberal Anglo-Protestantism at the end of its long decline.

However, with the death of Warren, the unraveling of Niebuhr's legacy, and increasing challenges to Woodward's new southern historiography, the question of whether or how long their versions of the aesthetic frontier will remain in fashion has entered upon our cultural horizon. That frontier and its Machiavellian conventions have long been associated with a male world of power in contradiction with value. But given the great adaptability of Machiavellian solutions to revelations of its own internal contradictions, there is no reason the next favored servants of Machiavellianism should not be found among women or intellectual heirs to a non-Anglo-American tradition.

That possibility reflects a twentieth-century experience of irony that has failed to serve as a redemptive law of political transformation as Warren, Woodward and Niebuhr tried to use it. Instead, as Carl Lotus Becker suggested, irony must ultimately remain elusive even if it does sometimes coincide with our desires or needs. It cannot be controlled or directed by Southerners against Northerners, nor can it be harnessed by moralists to ethical ends. Nor can irony be used as a bridge between aesthetics and politics, nor between versions of romanticisms and realisms. Irony is not redemptive. It is the inescapable experience of limits as shaped by our public and private lives.

But if irony holds no inner secret of redemption but only mirrors us in our cultural constructions, ordinary individuals may still choose from existing cultural alternatives to Machiavellian ways of living. Those choices do not require a redemptive irony to offer real possibilities of a future that is qualitatively different from the Anglo-American past; or to find the vision needed to live in rebellion against a society unwilling or unable to change. Such a personal response offers no frontiers of escape from history. It offers only a positive invitation to think creatively about what constitutes legitimate authority within the history we actually live; but it requires a moral refusal to conservatively defend cultural forms of power which our own history has failed to sustain.

NOTES

INTRODUCTION

1. J. G. A. Pocock, *The Machiavellian Moment: Florentine Political Thought and the Atlantic Republican Tradition* (Princeton: Princeton University Press, 1975).

2. David W. Noble, *The End of American History: Democracy, Capitalism and the Metaphor of Two Worlds in Anglo-American Historical Writing, 1880–1980* (Minneapolis: University of Minnesota Press, 1985). See particularly pp. 16–27.

3. Perhaps the most representative example of the disappearance of republicanism is Louis B. Hartz, *The Liberal Tradition in America: An Interpretation of American Political Thought since the Revolution* (New York: Harcourt, Brace, 1955).

4. In recent years there have been a great number of publications treating Shakespeare as a political thinker as well as an artist, and one who explored fundamental tensions within the context of Machiavellian cultural categories. See for example: Stephen Greenblatt, *Renaissance Self-Fashioning: From More to Shakespeare* (Chicago: University of Chicago Press, 1980); Stephen Greenblatt, *Sir Walter Raleigh: The Renaissance Man and His Roles* (New Haven, Conn.: Yale University Press, 1973); Harry V. Jaffa, "The Unity of Tragedy, Comedy, and History: An Interpretation of the Shakespearean Universe," in *Shakespeare as Political Thinker*, ed. John Alvis and Thomas G. West (Durham, North Carolina: Carolina Academic Press, 1981), 207–303; and John D. Cox, *Shakespeare and the Dramaturgy of Power* (Princeton: Princeton University Press, 1989), 67–90. On Shakespeare and popular culture, see Lawrence W. Levine, *Highbrow/Lowbrow: The Emergence of Cultural Hierarchy in America* (Cambridge, Mass.: Harvard University Press, 1988), 14–46. For Shakespeare and the South, specifically, see Peter C. Kolin, ed., *Shakespeare and Southern Writers: A Study in Influence* (Jackson, Miss.: University Press of Mississippi, 1985), 3–11; and Peter Kolin, ed., *Shakespeare in the South: Essays on Performance* (Jackson, Miss.: University Press of Mississippi, 1983), 3–8.

5. Thomas Dixon, Jr., *The Leopard's Spots: A Romance of the Whiteman's Burden, 1865–1900* (New York: Doubleday, Page, 1902) and *The Clansman* (New York: Doubleday, Page, 1905).

6. C. Vann Woodward, *Tom Watson: Agrarian Rebel* (New York: Macmillan, 1938).

7. Wilbur J. Cash, *The Mind of the South* (New York: Knopf, 1941).

8. Kenneth A. Bruffee, *Elegiac Romance: Cultural Change and Loss of the Hero in Modern Fiction* (Ithaca: Cornell University Press, 1983), 15–16.

9. Ibid., 43–47.

10. Ibid., 52–56. Bruffee traces this genre of the quest romance to Conrad, and treats Robert Penn Warren's *All the King's Men* as an example.

11. See the foreword to Bernard Bailyn, ed., *The Pamphlets of the American Revolution: 1750–1776* (Cambridge, Mass.: Harvard University Press, Belknap Press, 1965), vii–xii. Bailyn acknowledged his debt to J. G. A. Pocock's then-unpublished paper "Machiavelli, Harrington and English Political Ideologies in the Eighteenth Century"; later published in *William and Mary Quarterly* 22 (October 1965): 549–83.

12. Bernard Bailyn, *The Ideological Origins of the American Revolution* (Cambridge, Mass.: Harvard University Press, Belknap Press, 1967), vi.

13. Sören Kierkegaard, *The Present Age*, trans. Walter Kaufmann (New York: Harper and Row, 1962), 65–67.

14. Bailyn, *Ideological Origins*, 305.

15. Carl Becker, "The Spirit of '76," in *Everyman His Own Historian* (New York: Crofts, 1935), 47–80.

16. For a comparison of the implications of Becker's and Niebuhr's perspectives, see Richard Nelson, "Carl Becker Revisited: Irony and Progress in History," in *Journal of the History of Ideas* 48 (April–June 1986): 307–24, especially p. 329 and n. 79.

17. Bailyn, *Ideological Origins*, 319.

18. Ibid., xi.

19. Ibid., 1–2.

20. Ibid., 9–19. See for example, Alexander Karanikas, *Tillers of the Myth: Southern Agrarians as Social and Literary Critics* (Madison: University of Wisconsin Press, 1966), 209; and Frank Lentricchia, *After the New Criticism* (Chicago: University of Chicago Press, 1980), xii.

21. Lentricchia, *After the New Criticism*, 3–8.

22. Ibid., 35–39.

23. Ibid., 116, 192–93.

24. Ibid., 185.

25. Ibid., xiv.

26. Pocock, *Machiavellian Moment*, 545.

27. Henry Nash Smith, *Virgin Land: The American West as Symbol and Myth* (New York: Vintage Books, 1950); and Leo Marx, *The Machine in the Garden: Technology and the Pastoral Ideal in America* (New York: Oxford University Press, 1964). David Noble discusses this criticism of Smith and Marx in "American Studies and the Burden of Frederick Jackson Turner: The Case of Henry Nash Smith and Richard Hofstadter," *Journal of American Culture* 5 (1982): 34–44. See also the revisionist reassessments of Smith and Marx in the light of these

criticisms: Henry Nash Smith, "Symbol Myth and Idea in *Virgin Land,*" 21–35; and Leo Marx, "Pastoralism in America," 36–39, both in *Ideology and Classic American Literature,* ed. Sacvan Bercovitch and Myra Jehlen (Cambridge, Mass.: Cambridge University Press, 1986).

28. Russell Reising, *The Unusable Past: Theory and the Study of American Literature* (London: Methuen, 1986), 15–17, 163–73; and for a similar view from a Marxist perspective, see Robert Weimann, *Structure and Society in Literary History: Studies in the History and Theory of Historical Criticism,* expanded ed. (Baltimore: Johns Hopkins University Press, 1984), 134–40.

29. David W. Noble, *Historians Against History: The Frontier Thesis and the National Covenant in American Historical Writing Since 1830* (Minneapolis: University of Minnesota Press, 1965).

30. Pocock, *Machiavellian Moment,* 534–41.

31. Barry Marks, "The Concept of Myth in *Virgin Land,*" *American Quarterly* 5 (Spring 1953): 71–76.

32. Smith, *Virgin Land,* 126–35, 164.

33. J. G. A. Pocock, "Between Gog and Magog: The Republican Thesis and the *Ideologia Americana,*" 325–46, in *Journal of the History of Ideas* 48 (April–June 1987): 332–33; and Pocock, *Machiavellian Moment,* 551.

34. Pocock, *Machiavellian Moment,* 549.

35. See Thomas W. Cutrer, *Parnassus on the Mississippi: The Southern Review and the Baton Rouge Literary Community, 1935–1942* (Baton Rouge: Louisiana State University Press, 1984), 39–41. See also Smith's identification with the author as Romantic hero in Henry Nash Smith, *Democracy and the Novel* (New York: Oxford University Press, 1978), 13–15.

36. Smith's New Deal critique of Agrarianism appeared in Henry Nash Smith, "The Dilemma of Agrarianism," *Southwest Review* 19 (April 1934): 215–32.

37. Reising, *Unusable Past,* 167–72.

38. See David Levin, *History as Romantic Art: Bancroft, Prescott, Motley and Parkman* (Stanford: Stanford University Press, 1959), 36–37. In 1837, Bancroft received a letter from George Ripley praising him for attacking "the always ignorant and often petulant idolatry of Locke" (Levin, 240, n. 50). For a related discussion of Locke and republicanism, see Richard Nelson, "Liberalism, Republicanism and the Politics of Therapy: John Locke's Legacy of Medicine and Reform," *Review of Politics* 51 (Winter 1989): 29–54.

CHAPTER ONE

1. See William C. Widenor, *Henry Cabot Lodge and the Search for an American Foreign Policy* (Berkeley: University of California Press, 1980), 13–14, 120.

2. Henry Cabot Lodge, *George Washington* vol. 1 (Boston: Houghton Mifflin, 1898), 8–9.

3. Ibid., 4–5.

4. Ibid., 9.

5. Ibid., 10.

6. Ibid., 11.

7. Ibid., 10, 47.

8. Ibid., 43.

9. Ibid., 42–43.

10. Ibid., 42–45.

11. Ibid., 13, 87.

12. Ibid., 47, 169.

13. Quoted in Marcus Cunliffe's "Introduction" to Mason Locke Weems, *The Life of George Washington* (Cambridge, Mass.: Harvard University Press, Belknap Press, 1962), xxiv.

14. Ibid.

15. Dwight G. Anderson, *Abraham Lincoln: The Quest for Immortality* (New York: Knopf, 1982), 17–38; Jay Fliegelman, *Prodigals and Pilgrims: The American Revolution Against Patriarchal Authority, 1750–1800* (London: Cambridge University Press, 1982), 200–203, 304(n. 15); and Garry Wills, *Cincinnatus: George Washington and the Enlightenment* (New York: Doubleday, 1984), 35–37, 43–50.

16. For biographical details on Weems's life see Cunliffe, "Introduction," ix–xiii; Anderson, *Abraham Lincoln*, 17–20; and the main source for their material, Emily Ford Skeel, ed., *Mason Locke Weems: His Works and Ways*, 3 vols. (privately published, 1929).

17. See Skeel, *Mason Locke Weems*, 1: 259. Skeel estimates the date as 1791–92.

18. Ibid., 1: 150–56.

19. Ibid., 1: 155.

20. Weems, *The Philanthropist*, in Skeel, *Mason Locke Weems*, 2: 14.

21. Marcus Cunliffe ed., Mason Locke Weems, *The Life of Washington*, 1.

22. See William Gilmore Simms, *Views and Reviews in American Literature, History and Fiction: First Series*, ed., C. Hugh Holman (Cambridge: Harvard University Press, Belknap Press, 1962), 55–74, for a discussion of Benedict Arnold and Washington as Romantic inversions of the heroic in relation to the death of Andre. See also William Gilmore Simms, *Views and Reviews in American Literature, History and Fiction: Second Series* (New York, 1845) for essays on Major Andre and on "Weems, the Biographer and Historian"—both of which were highly positive assessments of their subjects.

George B. Forgie has linked James Fenimore Cooper's 1821 romance, *The Spy*, to Simms and Weems in *Patricide in the House Divided: A Psychological Interpretation of Lincoln and His Age* (New York: W. W. Norton, 1979), 208–25. He did not, however, emphasize that Cooper's spy, Harvey Birch, was a character created out of the public's familiarity with the Andre case both in England—where the novel was also very popular—and in America. I suggest that Washington was already a doubtful hero for Cooper, as he was for Simms and Weems. Consequently, it is Birch, not Washington, who is the actual hero of the novel because he alone successfully inverts the themes of darkness and light, permitting Washington to be, ultimately, on the side of the angels. For a more recent look at the Andre case and public attitudes towards it, see McConnell Hatch, *Major John Andre: A Gallant in Spy's Clothing* (Boston: Houghton Mifflin, 1986).

23. Fliegelman, *Prodigals and Pilgrims*, 218–19.

24. Weems, *Life of Washington*, 103–7, 173–75.

25. Ibid., 19.

26. Ibid., 95–96.

27. Ibid., 20.

28. Ibid., 2–3.

29. Ibid., 18.

30. Ibid., 181–82, 188–93, xxxvi, n. 43.

31. Ibid., 13–16, xxxvii–xlii; Wills, *Cincinnatus*, 50–51.

32. Skeel, *Mason Locke Weems*, 1: 40.

33. Cunliffe, in Weems, *Life of Washington*, xliv–xlv; Catherine L. Albanese, "Our Father, Our Washington," in *Sons of the Fathers: the Civil Religion of the American Revolution* (Philadelphia: Temple University Press, 1976), 143–81.

34. Albanese, *Sons of the Fathers*, 148–53.

35. Weems, *Life of Washington*, 182.

36. Ibid., 182–83.

37. Ibid., 159, 152 (emphasis added).

38. This is a particularly knotty problem for separating Lincoln from Washington, without positing a classical and timeless generation of founder-fathers, which Weems suggests never actually existed. This is a context that Freudian interpretations circumvent formally by positing a psychological experience of a mythic patriarchal Classicism. But that solution tends to break down when one tries to place these fathers in time and place, that is, in history. Compare, for example, George B. Forgie's assumption of 'a post-heroic age' in *Patricide in the House Divided* (3–14) with Anderson's, in *Abraham Lincoln* (9–12 and particularly 246–7 n. 19, 251–52 n. 11). Compare also Robert A. Ferguson, "'We Hold These Truths': Strategies of Control in the Literature of the Founders" (in *Reconstructing American Literary History*, eds. Sacvan Bercovitch and Myra Jehlen [Cambridge, Mass: Harvard University Press, 1986], 1–28), to Michael Paul Rogin, "The King's Two Bodies: Lincoln, Wilson, Nixon, and Presidential Self-Sacrifice" (in *Ronald Reagan, the Movie, and Other Episodes in Political Demonology* [Berkeley: University of California Press, 1987], 84–89). Perhaps all formalism, whether based on psychology or the New Criticism, fosters similar conundrums.

I suggest that considering republicanism as one genre of what has come to be called "Romanticism" since the nineteenth century may help us to recognize similar patterns in other forms of submerged romanticism, such as Freudianism, Marxism, deconstructionism, and the New Criticism itself. See also note 17 above.

39. Pocock, "Between Gog and Magog," 341–43.

40. Marilyn Butler, *Romantics, Rebels and Reactionaries: English Literature and its Background, 1760–1830* (New York: Oxford University Press, 1982); Robert Rosenblum, *Transformations in Late Eighteenth Century Art* (Princeton: Princeton University Press, 1967); Robert Rosenblum and H. W. Janson, *Nineteenth Century Art* (New York: Harry N. Abrams, 1984); Hugh Honour, *Neo-Classicism* (Baltimore: Penguin Books, 1968); and Hugh Honour, *Romanticism* (New York: Harper and Row, 1979).

41. Butler, *Romantics, Rebels and Reactionaries*, 18–19. The theory of "a stable eighteenth century classicism evolved in the nineteenth century," writes Butler, and adds that "it is the natural corollary of the concept of Romanticism, which was supposed to have superseded classicism." On the other hand, Hugh Honour says that the name "Neo-classicism" has become problematical because "it was invented in the mid nineteenth century as a pejorative term for what was then thought to be a lifeless, chilly and impersonal 'antique revival' style expressed in stillborn imitations of Graeco-Roman sculpture." This nineteenth-century reading of a quarrel between Romanticism and Classicism distorts the continuity between these rebellious aesthetic styles, he suggests (Honour, *Neo-Classicism*, 14).

42. Butler, *Romantics, Rebels and Reactionaries*, 6; Honour, *Neo-Classicism* 43–67; and Rosenblum, *Transformations*, 112–20, 170.

43. Butler, *Romantics, Rebels and Reactionaries;* Rosenblum, *Transformations,* 59–79.

44. Butler, *Romantics, Rebels and Reactionaries*, 8.

45. Albert Row, *Blake's Illustrations to the Divine Comedy* (Princeton: Princeton University Press, 1953), 30–31; Rosenblum, *Transformations*, 169–70 nn. 76–80; Rosenblum and Janson, *Nineteenth Century Art*, 60–62; Butler, *Romantics, Rebels and Reactionaries*, 50–51.

46. Butler, *Romantics, Rebels and Reactionaries*, 20.

47. Ibid., 22–26.

48. Ibid., 8.

49. Ibid.

50. Ibid., 9–10; Honour, *Romanticism*, 21–23, 46, 189; Steve Ellis, *Dante and English Poetry: Shelley to T. S. Eliot* (Cambridge: Cambridge University Press, 1983), 3–5; Stuart Y. McDougal, ed., *Dante Among the Moderns* (Chapel Hill: University of North Carolina Press, 1985), ix–xiii.

51. Butler, *Romantics, Rebels and Reactionaries*, 6; Rosenblum and Janson, *Nineteenth Century Art*, 62–63.

52. Butler, *Romantics, Rebels and Reactionaries*, 183–87, Rosenblum, *Transformations*, 172–77.

53. Rosenblum, *Transformations*, 64–95.

54. Butler, *Romantics, Rebels and Reactionaries*, 6.

55. Pocock, *Machiavellian Moment*, 486, 538.

56. See for example, Dante Alighieri, *Monarchy and Three Political Letters*, ed. and trans. Donald Nicholl and Colin Hardie, introd. Walter F. Bense (New York: Garland, 1972), ix, 3–7, 103–8; Ellis, *Dante and English Poetry*, 244. "What we may conclude with safety," says Ellis at the close of his study, is that "no poet seems to have been able to hold in a balance the 'two Dantes,' the Aristotelian Dante of the secular world, with his concern for the ordering of human society on earth, and the Dante who presents his Catholic visions of eternity." See also T. J. Jackson Lears, *No Place of Grace: Antimodernism and the Transformation of American Culture, 1880–1920* (New York: Pantheon, 1981), 155–59, for a discussion of the revitalization of interest in Dante among lettered Anglo-Americans in the 1890s.

57. Mason Locke Weems, *Three Discourses [Hymen's Recruiting Sergeant, The Drunkard's Looking Glass, God's Revenge Against Adultry]*, ed. Emily E. Ford Skeel (New York, 1929), 20. "I am very clear that our *Buckskin heroes* are made of, at least, *as good* stuff as any the *best* of the *beef* or *frogeating* gentry on t'other side the water. But neither this, nor all our fine speeches to our president, nor all his fine speeches to us again, will ever save us from the British gripe, or Carmagnole hug, while they can out-number us, *ten to one!* No, my friends, 'tis population, *'tis population alone*, that can save our Bacon." Weems then offered his readers wishes for a hearing ear, believing heart, "—and a saving antipathy to *apes*."

58. See for example, Mason Locke Weems, *God's Revenge Against Gambling*, 2d ed. (1812) in Emily Ford Skeel, ed., *Three Discourses*. What is sin, asks Weems, but the violation of law. And what is God's law? "What is it but LOVE. That divine sentiment, which beating first with strongest pulse towards wife and children, thence swells on to neighbors and relations, to country and all mankind, feeling for all a brother's solicitude, and with a brother's joy striving to do them good" (11). Man, he says anticipating in a Fourth of July oration in 1807 the message of his pamphlets on murder, drunkenness, adultery, and bachelorhood, is "a creature most selfish and arrogant—the slave of his passions—terrible in his hatred—and, when wrought to the pitch by a furious lust, ready to stab his mother; to sell his country; to kick at Heaven, and to hurl both soul and body into hell. . . . Look to history—Long before our time there were great republics in the world; why did not this boasted *knowledge* save them? They knew as well as we, that republics are better than monarchies; and that their own safety was bound up with that of the republic. Yet, we see, that did not do. Ambitious wretches among them strove for power, and because they could not succeed, they furiously destroyed the governments which they could not master." Only

love, says Weems, can preserve republics, because of the danger growing out of their freedom. "It counteracts the centrifugal and destructive tendencies of self-love, and, by causing republicans to study the good of others as their own, it makes them feel that '*each is to each a dearer self*;' and thus binds them together by a centripetal impulse, strong and indestructable as a rock of granite." Skeel, *Mason Locke Weems*, 1: 366 70.

59. See Cunliffe, "Introduction," xxiv–liii, lx–lxi.

60. Ibid., xiv–xv; Letter to Mathew Carey, his printer, January 13, 1809, Skeel, *Mason Locke Weems*, 1: 47.

61. This story related by Weems contemporary, William Meade, is quoted in Cunliffe, "Introduction," xxvii.

62. Mark Hulliung argues that interpretations of Machiavelli tend to ignore the subversive character of his writing in the interest of legitimizing a balance between idealism and realism that has been lost in the modern world (*Citizen Machiavelli* [Princeton: Princeton University Press, 1983], 219–58). Without attempting to comment on the merits of Hulliung's criticism of Machiavelli scholarship, two points may be raised in relation to his "quarrel" with the Enlightenment version of Machiavelli, which exhibits interesting parallels to the Enlightenment version of Faust. Both the real and the aesthetic anti-hero are tragic figures who legitimize a world of power by offering a doubtful balance between realism and idealism (or romanticism). See 219–22, and compare to a similar perspective in Erich Heller, "Faust's Damnation: The Morality of Knowledge," in *The Artist's Journey into the Interior and Other Essays* (New York: Random House, 1965), 3–45.

First, regardless of the original idea behind the Faust legend or the original identity of Machiavelli, a widely perceived cultural tension developed a "Faustian" quarrel between realism and idealism, just as it did a "Machiavellian" one. In each case that quarrel was codified as a crisis in the balance between power and value. That crisis, however, may not be separated from "our tradition," as Hulliung wishes to do, since it has formally come to define our view of what reality is (238, 255). However, Hulliung makes a second point which underscores how subversive Machiavellian categories for viewing reality are: "Machiavelli advised the politician to preserve the old names and symbols, even as he builds a new world," Hulliung writes, and "this is precisely what Machiavelli the political theorist does with our cultural heritage, our foundations. He tries to draw us into a position where every return to our cultural foundations, every conversation with the ancients, is a resurrection of Machiavelli and Machiavellism" (256). Machiavelli, of course, is in no position to do any such thing. But we do *experience* this tension both in our political institutions and in our efforts to interpret Machiavelli.

Together, therefore, these two points frame a tension between realism and idealism, or Classicism and Romanticism, which *we* find inescapable within the terms of the definition I have offered, but only so long as we identify with its ends and values. This suggests a narrower ideological formula, however, than is suggested by the concept of modernity. See Marshall Berman, *All That Is Solid Melts into Air: The Experience of Modernity* (New York: Simon and Schuster, 1982), 15–71, who also views the Faust legend paradigmatically.

63. See Hannah Fenichel Pitkin, *Fortune is a Woman: Gender and Politics in the Thought of Niccolò Machiavelli* (Berkeley: University of California Press, 1984), 57–63.

64. Niccolò Machiavelli, *The Prince*, Thomas Bergin, trans. ed. (Northbrook, Ill.: AHM Publishing Corp., 1947). chap. 2, pp. 1–2; Peter E. Bondanella, *Machiavelli and the Art of Renaissance History* (Detroit: Wayne State University Press, 1973), 140–41.

65. David Sices and James B. Atkinson, ed. and trans., *The Comedies of Machiavelli: The Woman from Andros, The Mandrake, Clizia* (Hanover, N.H.: University Press of New England, 1985). See, for example, *The Mandrake*, Act 5, Scene 4, lines 267–69; and *Clizia*, Act 5, Scene 3, lines 385–89. In both plays foolish fathers wish to maintain patriarchal power at the expense of their own sons' manhood. The old fathers must be humiliated, through deception, for their own good and that of everyone else—especially the ardent young lovers. For a discussion of these plays in relation to Machiavelli's self-identification as a fox, see Pitkin, *Fortune is a Woman*, 25–51. See also Sebastian de Grazia, *Machiavelli in Hell* (Princeton: Princeton University, 1989), 257–58.

66. Pitkin, *Fortune is a Woman*, 49–51.

67. Machiavelli, *The Mandrake*, Act 5, Scene 4, lines 1–32.

68. Hulliung, *Citizen Machiavelli*, 190–91.

69. See Wayne Rebhorn, *Foxes and Lions: Machiavelli's Confidence Men* (Ithaca: Cornell University Press, 1988), 1–11. Rebhorn argues that the "confidence man" may be traced to Machiavelli's innovative use of the trickster tale to provide a literary approach to reality that includes the narrator within the story. This new approach, he suggests, became paradigmatic for the Renaissance and has continued through Shakespeare, Milton, and Melville's *Confidence Man* (1857) to the present. It is important in using this metaphor to remember that a confidence artist makes an exchange with his or her victim, or mark, which is dependent on the mark's false sense of innocence, while Machiavelli assumes that all people deceive themselves. See also de Grazia, *Machiavelli in Hell*, 258–59.

70. Pocock, *Machiavellian Moment*, vii–ix, and Pocock, "Between Gog and Magog," 336, 345. Pocock has made it clear in both instances that he was not positing a monolithic "tradition," but an ambiguous form of contradiction and opposition which both shaped *and participated* in the dilemmas of Atlantic cultural moral and political thought. In that sense Machiavelli was the appropriate father for that culture. "If I had wanted to construct a "tradition" in . . . [the] sense of a legitimatory continuum, I would scarcely have started with Ma-

chiavelli, who must be one of the least legitimatory of political writers, or emphasized that the republic, taken as an ideal, was never *serenissima* and never legitimized itself" (336).

71. Pocock, *Machiavellian Moment*, 550.

72. Hannah Arendt, *The Human Condition* (Chicago: University of Chicago Press, 1958), 8–9, 177–79.

73. Ibid., 197–207.

74. See Catherine L. Albanese, "Our Father, Our Washington," in *Sons of the Fathers* 158–59; Pitkin, *Fortune is a Woman*, 79.

75. See Sacvan Bercovitch, *The American Jeremiad* (Madison: University of Wisconsin Press, 1978), xiv–xv, 7–10. See also Richard Nelson, "The Progressive Jeremiad, Critical Theory, and the End of Republican Virtue," *Clio* 16, no. 4 (1987): 360–79.

76. My interpretation of *The Divine Comedy* relies upon Joan M. Ferrante, *The Political Vision of the "Divine Comedy"* (Princeton: Princeton University Press, 1984).

77. Ibid., 5–7.

78. Ibid., 65–70, 302–3.

79. Ibid., 302.

80. Quoted in Bondanella, *Machiavelli and the Art of Renaissance History*, 135–36; Hulliung, *Citizen Machiavelli*, 213–14.

81. Pitkin, *Fortune is a Woman*, 49.

82. Machiavelli, Letter to Vettori, December 10, 1513, quoted in Ibid., 45; Ferrante, *Political Vision*, 236–39.

83. Machiavelli, *The Prince*, 75.

84. Ferrante, *Political Vision*, 367–74.

85. Ibid., 153–54.

86. Ibid., 378–79.

87. Donald Weinstein, *Savonarola and Florence: Prophecy and Patriotism in the Renaissance* (Princeton: Princeton University Press, 1970), 278–88. Cf. Pocock, *Machiavellian Moment*, 105–13.

88. Machiavelli, *The Prince*, 15–16.

89. Pocock, *Machiavellian Moment*, explains that *The Prince* is constructed on the need to balance innovation and fortune. "This seems to be the heart of the Machiavellian ambiguities. . . . The politicization of virtue had arrived at the discovery of the politicized version of original sin" (167). See also Arendt, *Human Condition*, 246.

90. Machiavelli, *The Prince*, 74.

91. Hannah Arendt, *Human Condition*, 28–37, 96–101, 196–200. Hulliung challenges the primacy of rhetoric in explaining republicanism, which he traces to Arendt's categories, in *Citizen Machiavelli*, 21–23. However, it is not self-reflexive speech which Arendt has placed at the center of republicanism, so

much as a contradiction born of history: the placement of eternal meaning in the finite space between birth and death, appearance and disappearance in time and space. As such the *polis* must escape its origin and divide the public realm from the private or perish in what Pocock calls a Machiavellian Moment. This self-destructive division is at the root of the separation of politics and aesthetics. Among its implications is a contradictory attitude towards gender, as Hannah Pitkin has seen (*Fortune is a Woman*, 304–6). It also leads to a similar contradiction with regard to race, as I attempt to demonstrate in later chapters.

92. Weems, *Life of Washington*, 222–23.

93. Ibid., 219.

94. Ibid., 224.

95. Ibid.

96. Ibid., 220–21.

CHAPTER TWO

1. Tension between farmers and city dwellers was clearly illustrated in the press coverage of the Chicago Exposition of 1893, where Turner read his famous paper on the closing of the frontier. *Harper's Weekly*, the *Chicago Herald*, and the *Tribune* all carried articles or cartoons that pilloried farmers as rubes, while the *Chicago Standard* and *Arena* included complaints about urban vice and ignorance. See Daniel T. Miller, "The Columbian Exposition of 1893 and the American National Character," 17–22, *Journal of American Culture* 10, no. 2 (Summer 1987), 19–20.

2. Stephen Kern, *The Culture of Time and Space: 1890–1918* (Cambridge: Harvard University Press, 1983), 239–40. "Technology tightened the skein of nationalism, and facilitated international cooperation," writes Kern, "but it also divided nations as they all grabbed for empire and clashed in a series of crises" (40).

3. See James Turner, *Without God, Without Creed: The Origins of Unbelief in America* (Baltimore: Johns Hopkins University, 1985), 128–29, 259–61. Turner suggests that it was not science that led to unbelief in the popular culture of nineteenth-century America, therefore Christian anti-religionism must have been the source. However, it is possible that one source of this new perspective may have been a failure in *political* faith in democracy, which led to unbelief towards both religion and science by many Americans in the 1890s. See also Paul Carter, *The Spiritual Crisis of the Gilded Age* (Dekalb: University of Northern Illinois Press, 1971), 136–43.

4. See Noble, *End of American History*, 13–15.

5. Pocock, *Machiavellian Moment*, vii–viii.

6. Ibid., 184.

7. Bondanella, *Machiavelli and the Art of Renaissance History*, 23–25, 140–41.

8. Noble, *End of American History*, 22–23.

9. See Nathan O. Hatch, *The Sacred Cause of Liberty: Republican Thought and the Millennium in Revolutionary New England* (New Haven: Yale University Press, 1977), 43–54; and Ernest Lee Tuveson, *Redeemer Nation: The Idea of America's Millennial Role* (Chicago: University of Chicago Press, 1968), 91–119.

10. Pocock, *Machiavellian Moment*, 535–39.

11. These examples are from Kern, *Culture of Space and Time*, 12, 212–13.

12. See, for example, Paul F. Boller, Jr., *American Thought in Transition: The Impact of Evolutionary Naturalism, 1865–1900* (Chicago: University of Chicago Press, 1969); Hamilton Cravens, *The Triumph of Evolution: American Scientists and the Heredity-Environment Controversy, 1900–1945* (Philadelphia: University of Pennsylvania Press 1978), 19, 63–73; and Dorothy Ross, *G. Stanley Hall: The Psychologist as Prophet* (Chicago: University of Chicago Press, 1972), 121–22.

13. Noble, *End of American History*, 16.

14. Frederick Jackson Turner, "The Significance of the Frontier in American History," in *Frontier and Section" Selected Essays of Frederick Jackson Turner*, ed. Ray Allen Billington (Englewood Cliffs, N.J.: Prentice Hall, 1961), 38, 42.

15. Ibid., 45–47; Frederick Jackson Turner "The Problem of the West," in *Frontier and Section*, 63–76, originally from *Atlantic Monthly* LXXVIII (September 1986): 289–97 (1896), 72.

16. Kern, *Culture of Space and Time*, 224–27; Ray Allen Billington, *The Genesis of the Frontier Thesis: A Study in Historical Creativity* (San Marino, Calif.: Huntington Library, 1971), 268 n. 35.

17. William Dean Howells, *A Hazard of New Fortunes* (New York: New American Library, 1965), 75–77, 66–67.

18. Ibid., 75.

19. Ibid., 66, 67.

20. Kern, *Culture of Space and Time*, 185, 214–16, 164. I am indebted to Kern for his theme of the negative use of space as an Atlantic cultural confrontation with the end of the frontier, which links Conrad's *Heart of Darkness* with Turner's "Significance of the Frontier in American History."

21. See Peter Dobkin Hall, *The Organization of American Culture, 1700–1900: Private Institutions, Elites, and the Origins of American Nationality* (New York: New York University Press, 1982), 17–19, 20–33; and for a more specifically economic and demographic overview, John J. McCusker and Russell R. Menard, *The Economy of British America, 1607–1789* (Chapel Hill: University of North Carolina Press, 1985), 33–34, 295–308.

22. George L. Mosse, *The Holy Pretence: A Study of Christianity and Reason of State from William Perkins to John Winthrop* (Oxford: Basil Blackwell, 1968), 17–33. Casuistry, as Mosse describes it, represents the sort of repressed borrowing from Machiavellianism that permitted the Atlantic culture's debt to him to remain so well hidden behind ambiguity.

23. McCusker and Menard, *Economy of British America*, 226–30. As Philip J. Greven noted in *Four Generations: Population, Land, and Family in Colonial Andover, Mass.* (Ithaca: Cornell University Press, 1970), the false notion that there had been a stable English family structure in seventeenth-century England has made the crisis of patriarchal legitimacy in New England at the end of the eighteenth century appear unique (262–68). See also Bernard Bailyn, with the assistance of Barbara DeWolfe, *Voyagers to the West: A Passage in the Peopling of America on the Eve of the Revolution* (New York: Vintage Books, 1986), 271–95; and Peter Charles Hoffer, *Revolution and Regeneration: Life Cycle and the Historical Vision of the Generation of 1776* (Athens: University of Georgia Press, 1983), 1–13.

24. This is the ambiguity inherent in the Renaissance project of "self-fashioning," which merges aesthetic form and political interest. See Wayne A. Rebhorn, *Foxes and Lions: Machiavelli's Confidence Men*, ix–x, 204; Greenblatt, *Renaissance Self-Fashioning*, 9; and Greenblatt, *Sir Walter Raleigh*, 50. This same ambiguity is shared by Robert Penn Warren, who, most successfully among the New Critics, translated these Machiavellian conventions in recent Anglo-American culture. See Mark Royden Winchell, "Renaissance Men: Shakespeare's Influence on Robert Penn Warren," in *Shakespeare and Southern Writers,* ed. Peter Kolin, 137–58; and John Burt, *Robert Penn Warren and American Idealism* (New Haven: Yale University Press, 1988), 1–9, 21.

25. Hall, *Organization of American Culture*, 79–87.

26. Noble, *End of American History*, 60–61. This is also a theme of Robert Penn Warren's writing, particularly in *Brother to Dragons: A Tale in Verse and Voices* (New York: Random House, 1953), 185–92, in which Jefferson's promise becomes a lie and he finds himself in complicity with his nephew Lilburn, who murdered a slave in the meathouse. "The burden of innocence is heavier than the burden of guilt," Lucy tells her brother, Thomas Jefferson. John Burt points out that this is not a brief for original sin, but an acknowledgment of the doubleness of experience. Ambiguously imbedded in that judgment against romantic optimism—the Declaration—is a promise of redemption by inversion. The evil loosed in romantic striving for the higher good is restrained by the realism of the Constitution. As John Burt notes, Warren retains both visions by taking the middle ground of ambiguity, balancing the two. See Burt, *Robert Penn Warren and American Idealism*, 199–218, especially 203–4. See also, Robert Penn Warren's introduction to Joseph Conrad's *Nostromo* (New York: Modern Library, 1951), xxxiii–xxxiv: "Man is precariously balanced in his humanity between the black inward abyss of himself and the black outward abyss of nature."

27. See Hall, *Organization of American Culture*, 254–65, for a discussion of continuity in the growth of corporations from the eighteenth-century patriarchal crises that spawned them. David F. Noble, *America By Design: Science, Technology and the Rise of Corporate Capitalism* (New York: Knopf, 1977), 3–20, 259–291, explicates the co-option of chemical and electrical engineers after the Civil War

by the corporations that employed them. Noble confirms the patriarchal nature of that corporate domination, though the "household" of the corporation had become far more abstracted than was the case in the earlier corporations, and technologically and economically far more powerful.

28. Robert Crunden, *Ministers of Reform: The Progressive Achievement in American Civilization, 1889–1920* (New York: Basic Books, 1982), 90–93.

29. See Lawrence Goodwyn, *The Democratic Promise: The Populist Moment in America* (New York: Oxford University Press, 1976); and David W. Noble, *End of American History*, 150 n. 10.

30. Charles and Mary Beard, *The Rise of American Civilization*, 1 vol. ed. (New York: Macmillan Company, 1930), 271.

31. Twelve Southerners, *I'll Take My Stand: The South and the Agrarian Tradition* (Baton Rouge: Louisiana State University, 1977).

32. Charles and Mary Beard, *Rise of American Civilization*, 271.

33. *I'll Take My Stand*, xxxviii–xxxix.

34. Donald Davidson, "A Mirror for Artists," in *I'll Take My Stand*, 49.

35. Ibid.

36. Charles and Mary Beard, *Rise of American Civilization*, 271.

37. Davidson, "A Mirror for Artists," 50.

38. Donald Davidson, *The Tall Men* (Boston: Houghton, 1927), 6–7.

39. Pitkin, *Fortune is a Woman*, 48–49.

40. John Crowe Ransom, *God Without Thunder: An Unorthodox Defense of Orthodoxy* (New York: Harcourt Brace, 1930).

41. Ransom, letter to Allen Tate, July 4, 1929, in *Selected Letters of John Crowe Ransom* ed. Thomas Daniel Young and George Gore (Baton Rouge: Louisiana State University, 1985), 181–82. Emphasis is Ransom's

42. Niccolò Machiavelli, *The Discourses*, ed. Bernard Crick, trans. Leslie Walker (Baltimore: Penguin Books, 1970), Chapter 2, line 2, 277–79.

43. Letter to Allen Tate, Spring 1927, in *Selected Letters of John Crowe Ransom*, 168. "The same logic which rejects the trite in art," Ransom wrote to Tate, "must right the systematic and formulary in religion. Actually—for you and me and the elite whom I know—art is the true religion and no other is needed. And for me—if not for you and others of the elite—this art must beware of cosmologies and the 'fixed points of reference' or it will sincerely become a merely systematic religion and scheme of valuation."

44. Allen Tate, "Ode to the Confederate Dead," in *Collected Poems, 1919–1976* (New York: Farrar Straus Giroux, 1977), 20–23.

45. Allen Tate, *Stonewall Jackson: The Good Soldier* (New York: Minton, Balch and Company, 1928).

46. Noble, *End of American History*, 43–45; Cutrer, *Parnassus on the Mississippi*, 197.

47. See the introduction to *I'll Take My Stand*, xxxvii–xlvii; and Lyle Lanier,

Andrew Lytle, Robert Penn Warren, and Cleanth Brooks, "The Agrarian Industrial Metaphor: Culture Economics and Society in a Technological Age," in *A Band of Prophets: The Vanderbilt Agrarians After Fifty Years*, ed. William C. Harvard and Walter Sullivan (Baton Rouge: Louisiana State University Press, 1982), 160–67.

48. See Noble, *End of American History*, 66–82. Noble makes the point that Niebuhr's training and writing were peripheral to the Anglo-American tradition while Beard's were within its mainstream. Beard, he says further, maintained a Progressive hero-worship in his hopes for Franklin Roosevelt, while Niebuhr offered an anti-heroic jeremiad against Hitler instead. In this sense, Niebuhr offered a negative, rather than a positive, vision of social redemption that defeated Beard's positive, "romantic" version of the escape from Romanticism.

49. Irony, for Niebuhr, was a formal law of oppositions that hold together two contradictory poles of human experience at the same time. Through irony, "absurd juxtapositions of strength and weakness; of wisdom through foolishness; of guilt arising from the pretensions of innocency; or innocency hiding behind ostensible guilt" could be balanced against each other. See Reinhold Niebuhr, *The Irony of American History* (New York: Charles Scribner's Sons, 1952), vii, 154–55. See also Richard Reinitz, *Irony and Consciousness: American Historiography and Reinhold Niebuhr's Vision* (Cranbury: Bucknell University Press, 1980); and Gene Wise, *American Historical Explanations: A Strategy for Grounded Inquiry* (Homewood, Ill.: The Dorsey Press, 1973), 300–303, 343.

50. Niebuhr, *Irony of American History*, vii, 154–55. Niebuhr's irony functioned in terms of a covenantal agreement; it therefore mediated political failure with the promise of spiritual redemption and mediated realist economic and political principles with romantic aesthetic ones.

51. Ibid., 368–69.

52. Bruffee, *Elegiac Romance*, 62–66.

53. See Alexander Karanikas, *Tillers of a Myth: Southern Agrarians as Social and Literary Critics* (Madison: University of Wisconsin Press, 1966), 171–88; Daniel Joseph Singal, *The War Within: From Victorian to Modernist Thought in the South, 1919–1945* (Chapel Hill: University of North Carolina Press, 1982), 198–231; and Paul K. Conkin, *The Southern Agrarians* (Knoxville: University of Tennessee Press, 1988), 89–126. All these scholars consider this aspect of the New Agrarians.

54. Karanikas, *Tillers of a Myth*, 209–10.

55. See, for example, Harold Bloom's appreciation for Robert Penn Warren, "Sunset Hawk: Warren's Poetry and Tradition," in *A Southern Renascence Man: Views of Robert Penn Warren*, ed. Walter B. Edgar (Baton Rouge: Louisiana State University Press, 1984), 75–79. Bloom notes that the ambiguous sign of the hawk has become "an inevitable sign of the truth." "Nothing," says Bloom, "is more dangerous for a belated poetry (and as Americans we can have no other)

than to establish a proper sign for the truth." Having achieved originality of vision and explicated himself, Warren has placed himself, in Bloom's eye, at the end of a tradition. He stands, "his face uplifted now skyward, toward sunset, at a great height." Bloom, in *Ruin the Sacred Truths* (Cambridge: Harvard University Press, 1989), describes an aesthetic, psychological, and cosmic trap in which "equal and opposed feelings, antithetical forces that are enemy brothers or sisters appear to be the emotive basis for the sublime." The artist cannot stay balanced between meaning and truth indefinitely, because "ambivalence increased to excess becomes irony, which destroys the sublime," 119.

See also Harold Bloom, *The Anxiety of Influence: A Theory of Poetry* (New York: Oxford University Press, 1973); and Richard Foster, *The New Romantics* (Bloomington: Indiana University Press, 1962).

56. Hall, *Organization of American Culture*, 21–22, 79–94. See Lawrence H. Schwartz, *Creating Faulkner's Reputation: The Politics of Modern Literary Criticism* (Knoxville: University of Tennessee Press, 1988), 77; and Christopher Lasch, "The Cultural Cold War: A Short History of the Congress for Cultural Freedom," in *The Agony of the American Left* (New York: Vintage, 1968), 63–116.

57. Cutrer, *Parnassus on the Mississippi,* 110.

58. Ibid., 83–90; Schwartz, in *Creating Faulkner's Reputation,* discusses the Rockefeller Foundation's role in supporting the rapprochement of the new Critics and the New York intellectuals in pages of the *Kenyon Review, Partisan Review, Hudson Review,* and *Sewanee Review,* and the role of these journals in American Cold War culture (73–141).

59. Cutrer, *Parnassus on the Mississippi,* 64–70.

60. Ibid., 81–82, 111.

61. Robert Penn Warren, *Night Rider* (New York: Random House, 1939); Robert Penn Warren, *All the King's Men* (New York: Bantam, 1946). See also Richard King, *A Southern Renaissance: The Cultural Awakening of the American South, 1930–1950* (New York: Oxford University Press, 1980), 231–41.

62. See, for example, Robert Penn Warren, "Pure and Impure Poetry," in *The Kenyon Critics: Studies in Modern Literature from the Kenyon Review,* ed. John Crowe Ransom (Port Washington, N.Y.: Kennikat Press, 1951), 17–41; John Crowe Ransom, "Criticisms, Inc." and "A Poem Nearly Anonymous," both in *The World's Body* (Port Washington, N.Y.: Kennikat Press, 1938); Allen Tate, "The Man of Letters in the Modern World," in *Collected Essays* (Denver: Alan Swallow, 1959), 379–93; Cleanth Brooks, *The Well Wrought Urn* (New York: Harcourt Brace, 1947); and Cleanth Brooks, *Modern Poetry and the Tradition* (New York: Oxford University Press, 1965).

63. Warren, "Pure and Impure Poetry," 18–19; and John Crowe Ransom, "Criticism as Pure Speculation," in *Selected Essays of John Crowe Ransom,* ed. Thomas Daniel Young and John Hindle (Baton Rouge: Louisiana State University Press, 1984), 137–38, 145–46.

64. See Louis D. Rubin, Jr., *The Wary Fugitives: Four Poets and the South* (Baton Rouge: Louisiana State University Press, 1978); Conkin, *Southern Agrarians*, 1–32; and John L. Stewart, *The Burden of Time: The Fugitives and the Agrarians* (Princeton: Princeton University Press, 1965).

65. Allen Tate, "What is a Traditional Society" (1936), in *Collected Essays*, 303; and Herbert Agar and Allen Tate, eds., *Who Owns America? A New Declaration of Independence* (Boston: Houghton Mifflin, 1936).

66. Quoted in Cutrer, *Parnassus on the Mississippi*, 127.

67. See Karanikas, *Tillers of a Myth*, 102–3.

68. Frederick Jackson Turner, "The Significance of the Section in American History," in Ray Allen Billington, ed., *Frontier and Section*, 115–35.

69. See Alan M. Wald, *The New York Intellectuals: The Rise and Decline of the Anti-Stalinist Left from the 1930s to the 1980s* (Chapel Hill: University of North Carolina Press, 1987), 121; and Schwartz, *Creating Faulkner's Reputation*, 204–8; and note 56 above.

70. Wald, *New York Intellectuals*, 139–45, 157–63, 217–25.

CHAPTER THREE

1. Gene Wise, *American Historical Explanations: A Strategy for Grounded Inquiry*, 187–211; and Noble, *End of American History*, 16–28.

2. Ray Allen Billington, *Frederick Jackson Turner: Historian, Scholar, Teacher* (New York: Oxford University Press, 1973), 75–76. See also Turner's letter of December 16, 1925, to Carl Becker in Billington, *Genesis of the Frontier Thesis:* "I had to tell Wilson about the neglected West, as he told me about the neglected South. Some of my stimulus to writing the article may have come from my attempts to put the case in those days" (235). Turner also viewed Jefferson and Washington as spiritual Midwesterners, rather than as Southerners. For example, in a letter to Edwin Alderman, president of Tulane, on February 19, 1903, he says: "I always think of Jefferson as deeply influenced by the fact that in origin he came from the interior of the South in the days when that interior region was essentially western in its characteristics, and that he was always moved by profound interest in western matters." Washington was national in character because of his experiences in the North and West, but John Randolph, whose experience was wholly Southern, was described as a romantic knight errant out of line with the mainstream of American development, Box 3, Frederick Jackson Turner Papers, University of Wisconsin Archives, Madison.

3. Billington, *Frederick Jackson Turner*, 434–37. Turner's contradictory balance between frontier and civilization was reflected in a similar one between anti-Populism and anticapitalism. Turner's anti-Semitism was a form of anti-urbanism, but he also expressed anti-Indian sentiments in his rejection of primitivism: "However you shatter the Jewish jar, the scent of the roses of Israel will

cling to it still, and socially I can't say that I ever found one I could be contented with," he wrote his fiancée in 1888. In 1906 he wrote to Charles R. Van Hise from the Grand Canyon, urging him to use his influence to keep Indian tribal names from being affixed to the points of the canyon. He was pleased that Moran's Point would retain its name, he said. But "Paiutte Point" would be a travesty since the Paiutes were "the most degenerate and disgusting and lo down [sic] aggregation of grasshopper eating savages that disgrace the West" (Box 8, Charles R. Van Hise Papers, University of Wisconsin Archives, Madison). Yet, in his lecture notes for his American history survey, he expressed mild criticism for the mistreatment of Indians (Ibid., box 4) and applauded stands against racial bigotry (Billington, *Frederick Jackson Turner*, 437).

4. Billington, *Frederick Jackson Turner*, 438.

5. Frederick Jackson Turner, "Section and Nation," in Billington, ed., *Frontier and Section*, 144–53.

6. Turner, "The Problem of the West," in Billington, ed., *Frontier and Section*, 75.

7. Ibid., 76.

8. Turner, "The West and American Ideals," in Billington, ed., *Frontier and Section*, 111.

9. Ibid.

10. Billington, *Frederick Jackson Turner*, 75–76.

11. Billington, *Genesis of the Frontier Thesis*, 277–78, and n. 68.

12. Noble, *End of American History*, 22.

13. Charles Beard, "Turner's 'The Frontier in American History,'" in *Books That Changed Our Minds*, ed. Malcolm Cowley and Bernard Smith (New York: Kelmscott Editions, 1938), pp. 66–71.

14. Tom Watson, "Imperialist Tendencies," *The People's Party Paper*, undated editorial, in the Tom Waston Papers, Southern Historical Collection, University of North Carolina Library, Chapel Hill. "The traditions of the fathers are being forgotten," wrote Watson. "The fundamental principles for which they risked life and property and earthly honor, are being uprooted by their degenerate sons."

15. Interview with Tom Watson, "Hon. T. W. Candidate for Presidency," clipping dated September 1904, Tom Watson Papers.

16. See Billington, *Frederick Jackson Turner*, 347–49; Billington *Genesis of the Frontier Thesis*, 188 and n. 15. Turner's lecture notes from his survey lay all blame for the Mexican-American War on the Mexicans: "*She wanted the war.* We could have avoided the war by not annexing Texas. Mex. thought she could win—very vain and high tempered," Frederick Jackson Turner Papers, "Lecture Notes," Box 4, Page 4.

17. Quite to the contrary of Turner, Watson opposed every official act of American military intervention. See, for example, Watson's editorials in *Watson's Jeffersonian Magazine* 3 (December 1905): 77.

18. Quoted in Woodward, *Tom Watson: Agrarian Rebel*, 334.

19. Ibid.

20. Ibid., Preface.

21. Daniel Bell, "The Face of Tomorrow: The Grass Roots of American Jew Hatred," *Jewish Frontier* 11 (June 6, 1944): 17.

22. Daniel Bell, "The Revolt Against Modernity," *Public Interest* 81 (1985): 56. See also Daniel Bell, "Our Country—1984," *Partisan Review* 51 (1984): 633, 637, where Bell states that his own political values and hopes for reform are based upon republicanism. He thus suggested an alternative to Watson and Populism that turns out to be based upon the same political values from which he was in desperate flight; Richard Hofstadter, *The Age of Reform: From Bryan to F. D. R.* (New York: Random House, 1955), 21, 62n, 81–83, and 91–92.

23. Lawrence Goodwyn, *Democratic Promise: The Populist Moment in America.*

24. Ibid.

25. Tom Watson, "The Character of Lee" (composed in 1871), vol. 2, Tom Watson Papers.

26. See such other scrapbooks as vol. 2, Watson's diary and commonplace book, vols. 3, 27, and 38, Tom Watson Papers.

27. Tom Watson, "The Fate of the Reformers" [1875?], vol. 3, Tom Watson Papers.

28. Quoted in Woodward, *Tom Watson: Agrarian Rebel,* 139.

29. Tom Watson, "Where is God?" *People's Party Paper,* October 16, 1891, vol. 27, Tom Watson Papers.

30. vol. 3, Tom Watson Papers.

31. Woodward, *Tom Watson: Agrarian Rebel,* 139–40.

32. Peter H. Thorslev, Jr., *The Byronic Hero: Types and Prototypes* (Minneapolis: University of Minnesota, Press, 1962), 141.

33. "Watson as Man and Politician," *New York Herald,* vol. 27, "Tom Watson's Fiddle," *The Progressive Farmer,* December 22, 1896, vol. 3. Reprint of interview with Agnes Perkenson, "Little Journey to Home of T. E. W.," October 3, 1920, in the *Atlanta Journal Sunday Magazine.* Tom Watson Papers.

34. Populist Nominee Privately Eschews Politics for Literature: Watson Tells of His Book." *Houston Chronicle,* September 1904, Tom Watson Papers.

35. Clipping from *New York Journal,* Sunday, July 29, 1900, 27 (vol. 27 of Tom Watson Papers). Henry Nash Smith discusses the original letter, which Macaulay sent Henry S. Randall, Jefferson's biographer. See Smith, *Virgin Land,* 243.

36. Tom Watson's written comments, vol. 3, Tom Watson Papers.

37. Tom Watson, "In the Mountains," reproduced in the *Columbia Sentinel,* Monday, January 29, 1923, Tompkins, Georgia, vol. 41, Tom Watson's Papers.

38. Tom Watson, *The Story of France,* 2 vols. (New York: Macmillan, 1898), 1: xiv; and Tom Watson, *Bethany: A Story of the Old South* (Washington, D.C.: Appleton Publishing Co., 1904).

39. Watson, *Story of France,* 1: 12–14.

40. Tom Watson, "Pages from a Lost Book," *Watson's Magazine* 2 (November 1908): 692–93.

41. Tom Watson, *Story of France*, 2: 409.

42. Ibid., 470–76.

43. Ibid., 1049–50.

44. Tom Watson, *Napoleon: A Sketch of His Life, Character, Struggles and Achievements* (New York: Macmillan, 1902). Watson serialized "Life and Times of Andrew Jacskon" from 1906 to 1910 in *Watson's Jeffersonian Magazine*. For Watson, Napoleon and Jackson were variations on the same theme of republican tension between personal virtù and civic virtue in a modernizing political structure. See Watson, "Life and Times," *Watson's Magazine* 4 (June 1906): 48–82. See also Pocock, *Machiavellian Moment*, 536, 648.

45. Tom Watson, "How I Came to Write Napoleon," *Watson's Magazine* 1 (November 1907): 1059–71.

46. Perkenson interview with Watson, "Little Journey to Home of T. E. W."

47. Interview, "Hon. T. W. Candidate for Presidency."

48. Tom Watson, "The Convalescent," *Tom Watson's Magazine* 2 (August 1905): 139–42.

49. Thorslev, *Byronic Hero*, 87–89.

50. Watson, "The Convalescent," 141.

51. Ibid., 140–42; and Pocock, *Machiavellian Moment*, 38.

52. Machiavelli, *The Prince*, 75.

53. See Woodward, *Tom Watson: Agrarian Rebel*, 366–69.

54. The editorial probably refers to Edgar Gardner Murphy, a southern Progressive who championed child-labor reform but who used his influence with Theodore Roosevelt to defeat the Beveridge Federal Bill outlawing child labor, on the grounds that it threatened states rights (*Watson's Magazine* 3 [January 1906]: 17).

55. Woodward, *Tom Watson: Agrarian Rebel*, 357–59.

56. Tom Watson, "The Widow and the Trust," *Watson's Magazine* 3 (January 1906): 257–61.

57. Tom Watson, "Peonage in Panama," *Tom Watson's Magazine* 3 (December 1905): 142–48.

58. Tom Watson, "Socialism and One of Its Great Books," *Watson's Magazine* 4 (May 1906): 321–30.

59. Tom Watson, "Some Random Talk on Literary Topics—And the Crowning of a Living Poet," *Watson's Jeffersonian Magazine* 1 (February 1907): 178–90; Tom Watson, "The Most Original Poem," *Watson's Jeffersonian Magazine* 1 (November 1907): 1041–44.

60. Ibid., Watson, "Some Random Talk on Literary Topics," 180–89.

61. Tom Watson, "The Oddities of the Great," *Watson's Jeffersonian Magazine* 2 (November 1908): 688–91; and Woodward, *Tom Watson: Agrarian Rebel*, 345.

62. See Woodward, *Tom Watson: Agrarian Rebel,* 418–20, for a brief discussion of the possible sources of Watson's anti-Catholicism. See also Barton Shaw, *The Wool-Hat Boys: Georgia's Populist Party* (Baton Rouge: Louisiana State University Press, 1984), 121–22. Those accounts, however, need to be supplemented by Fred D. Ragan's "Obscenity or Politics? Tom Watson Anti-Catholicism, and the Department of Justice," *Georgia Historical Quarterly* 70 (Spring 1986): 17–46. See also, for example, Tom Watson, "A Lady Missionary Defends the Present System," *Watson's Jeffersonian Magazine* 3 (September 1909): 664–65; and "Some Additional Facts About Foreign Missions," *Watson's Jeffersonian Magazine* 4 (March 1910): 195–96.

63. Watson had a number of anti-Catholic articles among his papers, including "Cardinal Antonelli" (undated), by Leroy M. Vernon, D.D., who died in 1876; and an article from the *Christian Advocate,* May 23, 1878, "The Irrepressible Conflict—Romanism," which predicted a 52 percent majority of Catholics in the United States by 1930.

64. Tom Watson, "The Roman Catholic Hierarchy, *Tom Watson's Magazine* 14 (April 1912): 942–43, 953. See also, for example, *Watson's Magazine* 15 (September 1912): 162, 331–37; *Watson's Magazine* 20 (January 1915): 135–38; and *Watson's Magazine* 21 (June 1915): 69–73.

65. Watson, "Some Additional Facts About Foreign Missions," *Watson's Jeffersonian Magazine* 4 (March 1910).

66. Watson, "Lady Missionary," 675.

67. The events of the Frank case are recounted in Woodward, *Tom Watson: Agrarian Rebel,* 379–89; and Leonard Dinnerstein, *The Leo Frank Case* (Athens: University of Georgia Press, 1987). Compare to Tom Watson, *Watson's Jeffersonian Magazine* 20 (January 1915): "The daughters of our best people," wrote Watson, "are continually intermarrying with Jews; and Gentiles are associated with Jews in fraternal orders" (140). But in "A Full Review of the Leo Frank Case," *Watson's Jeffersonian Magazine* 20 (September 1915): under photos retouched to accentuate Frank's features, the caption reads: "Note the horrible lips, the nose and averted eyes of Leo Frank—a typical pervert" (257). Yet further on Watson wrote, "In pressing the case against Leo Frank we have felt none of the fury of prejudice and race hatred" (277). See also *Watson's Jeffersonian Magazine* 22 (November 1915), 14. "As yet, the South has not been deluged by the foreign flood; as yet our native stock predominates, and the old ideals persist. . . . The mistake made by Jews, throughout the union, was that they made Frank's case a race issue." Republican ideology provides a basis for interpreting these juxtapositions, which are similar to ones found in Turner or in a figure such as Henry Adams.

68. Watson (untitled article), *Weekly Jeffersonian,* June 24, 1915, and July 29, 1915, quoted in Woodward, *Tom Watson: Agrarian Rebel,* 441–43.

69. See Louis E. Schmier, "No Jew Can Murder: Memories of Tom Watson

and the Lichtenstein Murder Case of 1901," *Georgia Historical Quarterly* 70 (Fall 1986): 453.

70. Tom Watson, "The Negro Question in the South," *Arena* 6 (October 1892): 540–50. See also *The People's Party Campaign Book: Not a Revolt It Is a Revolution* (Washington, D. C.: National Watchman Publishing Co., 1892).

71. Watson, "Negro Question in the South." See also George Fredrickson, *The Black Image in the White Mind* (New York: Harper and Row, 1971), 288–55. Frederickson also notes that the idea of black degeneracy predates Darwin and passed for "empirical common sense" (258). Republican ideology provided a framework for formulating and sustaining such views.

72. Watson, "Negro Question in the South."

73. Watson, "Populism," *Watson's Magazine* 2 (September 1905): 257–59; and Watson, *The Life and Times of Thomas Jefferson* (New York: D. Appleton and Co., 1903), 68.

74. See Woodward, *Tom Watson: Agrarian Rebel*, 353–54. Like much of Watson's material, *Bethany* was constructed of childhood memories of a lost heroic ideal. Stylistically, it is a strange mixture of naturalism against a false myth of antebellum harmony and an elegy for his own lost world, reconstructed from his childhood journals.

75. Watson, *Bethany*, 10.

76. Tom Watson, "The Negro Question," *Watson's Jeffersonian Magazine* 1 (November 1907): 1032–34.

77. Watson, "The Negro Question," 1037.

78. Tom Watson, "The Hearst Paper, the Egyptian Sphinx and the Negro," *Watson's Jeffersonian Magazine* 3 (February 1909): 101; and "Is the Black Man Superior to the White?" *Watson's Magazine* 1 (June 1905): 393–94, 397.

79. Watson, "Is the Black Man Superior?" 397; "The Negro Question" (1907), 1039.

80. Watson, "The Negro Question."

81. Ibid., 1040.

82. Tom Watson, "The Cow and the Socialist," *Watson's Magazine* 5 (August 1906): 178.

83. Tom Watson, "Socialists and Socialism," *Watson's Jeffersonian Magazine* 3 (December 1909): 9–11.

84. Ibid.

85. Tom Watson, "We are Growing Richer and We are Growing Weaker," *Watson's Magazine* 4 (May 1906): 385–93.

86. See, for example, *Watson's Magazine* 25 (September 1917): 324; and Watson, *Life and Times of Thomas Jefferson*, 68–70. In an unsigned copy of a letter to Dr. John Taylor on June 14, 1917, Watson wrote that the states have the right of conscription, not the national government. However, Watson doubted that conscription would end in 1917 as it had in 1866, because in 1866 the corporations

did not require a standing army and militarism had not infected the army and navy, Tom Watson Papers.

87. Perkenson interview, "Little Journey to Home of T. E. W."

88. Tom Watson, "An Incident in the Life of Epenetus Alexis Steed," *Watson's Jeffersonian Magazine* 4 (February 1910): 156–57.

CHAPTER FOUR

1. Michael Kreyling, *Figures of the Hero in Southern Narrative* (Baton Rouge: Louisiana State University Press, 1987), 8–10.

2. See Otto Rank, *The Myth of the Birth of the Hero: A Psychological Interpretation of Mythology,* trans. F. Robbins and Smith Ely Jelliffe (New York: Journal of Nervous and Mental Disease Publishing Co., 1914); and Richard King, *Southern Renaissance,* 27–29.

3. King, *Southern Renaissance,* 14; and Fred C. Hobson, Jr., *Serpent in Eden: H. L. Mencken and the South* (Chapel Hill: University of North Carolina Press, 1974), 111–20.

4. W. J. Cash, *Mind of the South,* 31, 389–94.

5. Ibid., 146–47, 430; and Joseph L. Morrison, *W. J. Cash, Southern Prophet: A Biography and Reader* (New York: Alfred A. Knopf, 1967), 114, 117–118. See also Fred Hobson, *Tell About the South: The Southern Rage to Explain* (Baton Rouge: Louisiana State University Press, 1983), 247–73.

6. Cash, *Mind of the South,* 116–20, 321, 252–59, 432–36, 371–77.

7. Morrison, *W. J. Cash,* 113–14, 119–30.

8. See Bertram Wyatt-Brown, *Yankee Saints and Southern Sinners* (Baton Rouge: Louisiana State University Press, 1985), 131–34; Michael O'Brien, *Rethinking the South: Essays in Intellectual History* (Baltimore: Johns Hopkins University Press, 1988), 169–79; Richard King, *Southern Renaissance,* 5–10; Bruce Clayton, *The Savage Ideal: Intolerance and Intellectual Leadership in the South, 1890–1914* (Baltimore: Johns Hopkins University Press, 1972), 1–3; Bruce Clayton, "A Southern Modernist: The Mind of W. J. Cash," 171–86 in Bruce Clayton and John A. Salmond, ed. *The South Is Another Land: Essays on the Twentieth-Century South* (New York: Greenwood Press, 1987); and Singal, *War Within,* 373.

9. Cash published an essay, "The Mind of the South," in *American Mercury* in October 1929, reprinted in Morrison, *W. J. Cash, Southern Prophet,* 182–97. Inevitably, however, Cash's book of 1941 was compared to Perry Miller's *New England Mind: The Seventeenth Century* (New York: Macmillan, 1939). As Woodward has noted, Cash himself would have been forced to consider his thesis in relation to Miller's. See C. Vann Woodward, "The Elusive Mind of the South," in *American Counterpoint: Slavery and Racism in the North-South Dialogue* (Boston: Little, Brown and Co., 1964), 264–65.

10. Smith was a student of Perry Miller's and therefore was applying Miller's categories as well as Turner's to the South and West of his own self-identified past, as did Cash. Cash's image of the mind of the South (or its absence) was on one side formally drawn from the New England criticism of Henry Adams, but on the other, it was an angry challenge to the Puritan-Yankee culture of New England, which had locked the South into a failed frontier ethos and economy. See Cash, *Mind of the South*, 101–5.

11. Each section of the country, therefore, produced between 1940 and 1950 a pastoral elegist for a dying heroic ideal, which was both identified with, and eulogized by, its author.

12. Perry Miller, "The Responsibility of Mind in the Age of Machines," in *The Responsibility of Mind in a Civilization of Machines*, ed. John Crowell and Stanford J. Searl (Amherst: University of Massachusetts Press, 1979), 8–14; Smith, *Virgin Land*, 216–19; Cash, *Mind of the South*, 61–65.

13. Perry Miller, Preface to *Errand into the Wilderness* (Cambridge, Mass.: Harvard University Press, 1956), viii; Morrison, *W. J. Cash, Southern Prophet*, 36, 139, 227.

14. G. Jean-Aubry, *Joseph Conrad and the Congo*, was first published in 1925–26. See Leonard Dean, ed., *Joseph Conrad's Heart of Darkness: Backgrounds and Criticisms* (Englewood Cliffs, N.J.: Prentice-Hall, 1980), 80. See also, Miller, *Errand into the Wilderness*, vii–x, 1–2.

15. Morrison, *W. J. Cash, Southern Prophet*, 13–14; Kreyling, *Figures of the Hero*, 9–11.

16. In this sense, Kreyling's detached perspective on the southern family romance parallels Sacvan Bercovitch's detachment from the American jeremiad. Kreyling finds Cash to be a heroic precursor to his own insight into the mythic meaning of the southern family romance through his heroic but ultimately self-destructive unmasking of chivalry (*Figures of the Hero*, 15, 65–74. Bercovitch sees the mythic structure of the jeremiad through Perry Miller's anguished historiography, making it into a purely literary form to which Bercovitch is related only aesthetically (*American Jeremiad*, xv, 5–12, 209–10). Each uses the Romantic elegiac formula to turn the defeated heroic scholarship of a Cash or Miller into a perspective for successfully escaping its tragedy.

17. Kreyling, *Figures of the Hero*, 11.

18. Ibid., 22–25.

19. Ibid., 20–25. That is, as an escape from history through history.

20. Cash, in Morrison, "Away In a Manger," *Charlotte News* (December 24, 1937), 232–34; "A Fantatic Menaces Civilization," *Charlotte News* (September 1, 1939), 257–60; "Realism and Romance: Southern View" *Charlotte News* (October 18, 1936), 224–27.

21. Cash, *Mind of the South*, 5–7.

22. Ibid., 8–9.

23. Ibid., 10–11.

24. Ibid., 47–49.

25. Ibid., 33–34.

26. Ibid., 87–88.

27. Ibid., 88–89.

28. Ibid., 108–9.

29. Ibid., 157.

30. Ibid., 158–59.

31. Ibid., 126–28.

32. Bercovitch, *American Jeremiad*, xi–xiv, 62.

33. Cash, *Mind of the South*, 208–9, 351–66.

34. Ibid., 392–93. Like Benjamin, Cash searched for redemption through deconstruction, a purified Romanticism through the destruction of sentimentality. See, for example, Walter Benjamin, *Illuminations*, ed. and introd. Hannah Arendt, trans. Harry Zohn (New York: Harcourt Brace and World, 1968); Benjamin, *One Way Street and Other Writings*, trans. E. Jephcott and K. Shorter (New York: Harcourt Brace, 1978); Harold Bloom, *Kabbalah and Criticism* (New York: Seabury Press, 1975); Bloom et al., *Deconstruction and Criticism* (New York: Continuum, 1984); and Terry Eagleton, *Walter Benjamin: Or Towards a Revolutionary Criticism* (London: Verson, 1981).

35. Cash, *Mind of the South*, 432–40; Morrison, *W. J. Cash: Southern Prophet*, 77–81.

36. Ibid., Morrison, *W. J. Cash, Southern Prophet*, 98–100.

37. Ibid., 43–44; Hannah Arendt's introduction to Benjamin, *Illuminations*, 18. This was also the self-description by Allen Tate of the New Agrarians. See Lewis P. Simpson, "The Southern Republic of Letters and *I'll Take My Stand*," in *Band of Prophets*, 67.

38. Perry Miller, "The Incorruptible Sinclair Lewis," in *Responsibility of Mind in a Civilization of Machines*, 114–15; and Kenneth S. Lynn, "Perry Miller," *American Scholar* 52 (1983): 221–27. See Walter Benjamin, "The Work of Art in the Age of Mechanical Reproduction," in *Illuminations*, 243–44, 253 n. 21, 17–18; and his "Theses on the Philosophy of History," "Incorruptible Sinclair Lewis"; 259–60.

39. Miller, "Incorruptible Sinclair Lewis"; and Miller, *Errand into the Wilderness*, 12–13.

40. Cash, *Mind of the South*, 44–45.

41. Ibid., 137.

42. Morrison, *W. J. Cash, Southern Prophet*, 12–14.

43. Ibid., 26–27. See Thomas Dixon, *Southern Horizons: The Autobiography of Thomas Dixon*, ed. and intro. Karen Crowe (Alexandria, Va.: IVW Publishing Co., 1984). Thomas Dixon wrote at least three versions of his autobiography. The oldest version was made available to Raymond A. Cook by Dixon's second wife,

Madelyn Donovan Dixon, and served as the basis for his biography, *Fire From Flynt: The Amazing Careers of Thomas Dixon* (Winston-Salem, N.C.: John F. Blair, 1968). However, the manuscript Cook used was destroyed by Mrs. Dixon after Cook returned it. The film historian Raymond Rohauer won Mrs. Dixon's confidence and was able to gain access to the two remaining versions of Dixon's autobiography which Karen Crowe edited into a single version in 1982 with Rohauer's assistance. However, this version is missing seven of the chapters that were originally part of the manuscript used by Cook.

Though there are valuable insights in this autobiographical statement, it is important to recognize that the existing version was written late in Dixon's life, between 1934 and his physical collapse in the 1940s. Once more it was likely sanitized out of consideration for the second Mrs. Dixon whom he married after suffering a cerebral hemorrhage in 1939, xxi–xxxiii.

All Dixon's writing was autobiographical in the sense that he drew on the same experiences again and again when writing his novels. Because the novels were written earlier and less guardedly than the autobiography, his fiction provides a better insight into his values and motives than does much of the autobiography. For that reason, this chapter primarily draws on the novels for explicating Dixon's views.

William Poteat was a favorite teacher of Dixon's, and Dixon included Poteat as a member of his advisory board for his last project, a great worldwide chautauqua, which was undone by the Great Depression. See Cook, 35–37, 210–11 and Dixon, *Southern Horizons*, 153: "I liked him from the moment we met." Dixon remembered. "He was the youngest member of the teaching force. If he were a sample of the teachers I was going to work under, I was in luck."

44. Cook, *Fire From Flynt*, 218–20.

45. In fact, Dixon did use Freud, but in the 1920s Freud was not yet fashionable in interpreting race relations in America. See King, *Southern Renaissance*, 170, 248; and Singal, *War Within*, 6–7. Writing of his disillusionment with political reform, Dixon wrote "a dog fight had been going on in my sub-conscious mind for a long time. I now saw the cause of the trouble. I was facing the fact deep in my soul that a tribune of the people to be successful in his hold on power must pander to the masses and be prepared always to submit to mob rule to further his career. In brief, that I must prostitute my mind to reach and hold the highest power as a leader in politics," *Southern Horizons*, 185.

46. See for example John Murray Cuddihy, *The Ordeal of Civility: Freud, Marx, Levi-Strauss, and the Jewish Struggle with Modernity* (New York: Dell, 1974), 50–58.

47. Bruffee, *Elegiac Romance*, 32–41.

48. Hofstadter, *Age of Reform*, 273–75; and Reinhold Niebuhr, *Irony of American History*. See Richard Wightman Fox, *Reinhold Niebuhr: A Biography* (New York: Pantheon, 1985), 246–47.

49. See Cash, *Mind of the South*, 51–56, 87, 140–41, 232, 321, for examples. In *Southern Horizons* Dixon claimed, as did Cash, to have been liberated from southern romanticism towards women: "I had to face the issue of woman suffrage. All my Southern instincts and education were against it . . . The brilliant mind and winning personality of Carrie Chapman Catt, the women's leader, got me. She tore my argument to shreds. I was ashamed of it . . . I saw the world needed inspired women leaders," 220. Writing of the accomplishment of his sister Delia, who became a medical doctor, Dixon eulogized her as follows: "She lived to see every sex tyrant in the State, who sought to impose his masculine will on all women, ashamed of himself and his age," 319. Nevertheless, Dixon saw women as weaker vessels who were shaped by men: "I would atone for my mistake and make a new woman leader and teacher out of my sister Delia," Dixon said was his lesson from Carrie Chapman Catt, 220.

50. See Richard Harwell, ed., *Margaret Mitchell's "Gone with the Wind" Letters, 1936–49* (New York: Macmillan, 1976), pp. 52–53.

51. Cook, *Fire From Flynt*, 73–79; and Dixon, *Southern Horizons*, 295–302. In a postscript to Dixon's autobiography, the late film historian Raymond Rohauer suggested that Dixon was very much involved with the film production of *Birth of a Nation*. Not only had Dixon copyrighted the title "Birth of a Nation" in 1905, but Dixon attempted to have *The Clansman* made into a film in 1911. Apparently Dixon and his director planned to use color and sound before the project was abandoned when other backers lost interest, 328–32.

52. Thomas Dixon, *The One Woman: A Story of Modern Utopia* (New York: Doubleday, Page and Co., 1903), 247.

53. See Willie Lee Rose, "Race and Region in American Historical Fiction: Four Episodes in Popular Culture," in *Region, Race, and Reconstruction: Essays in Honor of C. Vann Woodward*, ed. J. Morgan Kousser and James M. McPherson (New York: Oxford University Press, 1982), 134 n. 3; and Cook, *Fire From Flynt*, 131–32.

54. See John C. Inscoe, "*The Clansman* on Stage and Screen: North Carolina Reacts," *North Carolina Historical Review* 64 (April 1987): 140 n. 4. Inscoe explores the fact that *The Clansman* was wildly successful when staged as a play in North Carolina in 1905. By 1915, when *Birth of a Nation* appeared on the screen in North Carolina, reaction was quite subdued. Inscoe focuses on the easing of racial tensions in the years between 1905 and 1915 as the cause for Dixon's diminished popularity. But his eclipse by Griffith, the film's director, in the public response to the film, suggests that it was not racism but Dixon's formula for containing its contradictions which fell out of fashion in those years. Cash, who was born in 1900, illustrates this transition of a once-compelling style becoming an embarrassment. See Cash, "The Southland Turns to Books with Full Vigor," February 9, 1936, in Morrison, *W. J. Cash, Southern Prophet*, 221.

55. Dixon integrated political and religious messages of revival, yet personally

stood outside both of them. Similarly, he defended the Romantic style against Realist fiction through Realism. See Cook, *Fire From Flynt*, 201–6. For other instances of aesthetic therapy as a form of revivalism at this time, see T. J. Jackson Lears, *No Place of Grace*, 187–92. For a description of Machiavellian aesthetics as it balances its internal contradictions, see Quentin Skinner, *Machiavelli* (New York: Hill and Wang, 1981), 24–28.

56. Henry Adams, *The Degradation of the Democratic Dogma* (New York: Macmillan, 1919), and Henry Adams, *The Education of Henry Adams: An Autobiography* (Boston: Houghton, Mifflin Co., 1918), 58–59. Adams's close friend and alter ego, Secretary of State John Hay, read proofs of and endorsed the *The Clansman*, the second volume in Dixon's Reconstruction trilogy.

57. Henry Adams, *Democracy: An American Novel*, in *Democracy and Esther: Two Novels by Henry Adams* (Gloucester, Mass.: Peter Smith, 1965).

58. David W. Noble, *Progressive Mind 1890–1917*, Revised ed. (Minneapolis: Burgess, 1981), 106. See also F. Garvin Davenport, Jr., *The Myth of Southern History: Historical Consciousness in Twentieth-Century Southern Literature* (Nashville: Vanderbilt University Press, 1967), 23–43.

59. Adams, *Education of Henry Adams*, 47–50.

60. Letter to Brooks Adams, August 20, 1899, in *Henry Adams and His Friends: A Collection of His Unpublished Letters*, ed. Harold Dean Cater, (Boston: Houghton Mifflin, 1947), 473, 482–83.

61. Adams, *Education of Henry Adams*, 4–12.

62. Quoted in Jackson Lears, *No Place of Grace*, 277.

63. Adams, *Democracy*, 122. "The bitterest part of all this horrid story is that nine out of ten of our countrymen would say I have made a mistake," concludes Mrs. Lee (Democracy, 206).

64. Adams's title character's name is taken from a character in the Hawthorne story "Old Esther Dudley," who remains obsessively loyal to the old order after the Revolution has swept it away. Her father was moved to name his daughter after a fictional character because he was a member of the Puritan Dudley family. Adams, *Esther*, 220; Nathaniel Hawthorne, *The Complete Novels and Selected Tales of Nathaniel Hawthorne*, ed. Norman Holmes Pearson (New York: Random House, 1937), 982–90.

65. Adams, *Esther*, 371.

66. Ibid., 266.

67. Cook, *Fire From Flynt*, 128–29.

68. Thomas Dixon, *The Southerner: A Romance of the Real Lincoln* (New York: Grosset and Dunlap, 1913), 507–8. The novel was dedicated to "our first southern-born President since Lincoln, my friend and collegemate Woodrow Wilson."

69. Ibid., 515, 542–44.

70. See Pocock, *Machiavellian Moment*, 504.

71. Thomas Dixon, *Comrades* (New York: Grosset and Dunlap, 1909); Thomas

Dixon, *The Root of Evil: A Novel* (New York: Doubleday, Page and Co., 1911).

72. See for example, the character of old Nickaroshinski, a Jewish refugee from Poland whose "instinctive sympathies had always been with the oppressed people of the South," in Thomas Dixon, *The Traitor: A Story of the fall of the Invisible Empire* (New York: Doubleday, Page & Co., 1907), 107; and Thomas Dixon, *The Black Hood* (New York: Grosset and Dunlap, 1924), which championed the place of Jews in America. John Vassar, the hero of Dixon's *The Fall of a Nation: A Sequel to The Birth of a Nation* (New York: D. Appleton Co., 1916) is Polish-American, and he criticizes colonialist oppression against the Chinese, Indians, and South Americans (49–50, 180–81).

73. Dixon, *Leopard's Spots*, 67–68; *The Clansman*, 45–47.

74. Dixon, *The Traitor*, 330–31. See also Dixon, *Southern Horizons*, 67–71. Dixon reveals that his uncle, Lee Roy McAfee, was the model for John Graham, the protagonist of *The Traitor*, and that McAfee engaged in a struggle for control over the Klan against a dissident member named Captain Durham.

75. Dixon, *Leopard's Spots*, 385–88.

76. Ibid., 447, 467.

77. Ibid., 467–69.

78. Ibid., 313–14.

79. Ibid., 389–407, 450.

80. Dixon, *The Clansman*, 323–25.

81. See Fred Silva, *Focus on Birth of a Nation* (Englewood Cliffs, N.J.: Prentice-Hall, 1971), 94.

82. Dixon, *Leopard's Spots*, 81–83, 260–66. Allen McLeod is "adopted" into the Durham household and develops a Freudian attachment to the older Mrs. Durham as a latent love interest. The other romances are that between George Harris and Helen Lowell (394–97) and the ultimately successful pairing of Charles Gaston and Sallie Worth (465–66).

83. Ibid., 326–27.

84. Ibid., 328–29.

85. Thomas Dixon, "Booker T. Washington and the Negro: Some Dangerous Aspects of the Work at Tuskegee," *Saturday Evening Post* 178 (August 1905): 1–2. See also Dixon, *Leopard's Spots*, 265.

86. Dixon, "Booker T. Washington"; and *Leopard's Spots*, 185, 432, 395–98.

87. Dixon, *Comrades*, 101.

88. Dixon, *Root of Evil*, 3–6, 85.

89. Ibid., 35.

90. Ibid., 205–8.

91. Dixon, *Leopard's Spots*, 244, 336.

92. Machiavelli, *The Discourses*, Chapter 2, Line 21, 341–43.

93. Thomas Dixon, *The Sins of the Father: A Romance of the South* (New York: D. Appleton, 1912).

94. Ibid., 195–96; Dixon, *Leopard's Spots*, 242.

95. Dixon, *Sins of the Father*, 121–22.

96. Ibid., 131–62.

97. Ibid., 195.

98. Pocock, *Machiavellian Moment*, 63–76; Arendt, *Human Condition*, 23–37.

99. Dixon, *The Clansman*, 90–96; *Sins of the Father*, 227–30, 296–98.

100. See, for example, Thomas Dixon, *The Fall of a Nation*, 135–38. An Italian immigrant, Tommaso, unwittingly follows Weems's formula for virtuous patriotism. He writes a message to the congressman-hero, John Vassar, which concludes: "I Americano. My kid he be president—maybe—," and his son proceeds to chop down a valuable tree in emulation of George Washington. Later, the immigrant overcomes cowardice to storm battlements when moved by his need for his wife and son to be proud of him (274–78).

101. Dixon, *Sins of the Father*, 43.

102. Ibid., 153. Dixon described the transgressing of God's boundaries as a Faustian act of scientific experimentation. See, for example, *The Clansman*, 182–83. Senator Stoneman's "world alienation" is fueled by *ressentiment*. The Boston woman's arrogant sentimentality is the equivalent in *Leopard's Spots*, 49–50. Compare a similar perspective in Arendt, *Human Condition*, 9–10; and in Arendt, "Tradition in the Modern Age," in *Between Past and Future: Six Exercises in Political Thought* (New York: Viking, 1961), 39–40.

103. Dixon, *Leopard's Spots*, for example, has a chapter titled "The Thousand Legged Beast" (376–84), in which Dixon describes a mob that lynches the Negro rapist, Dick. Jim Stuart, the hero of *Root of Evil*, is almost killed by "a mob of hissing howling brutes that surged about him and all the millions like them that crawl over the earth" (180). Dixon's last film, released in 1923, was titled "Mark of the Beast." It portrayed psychological dualism as characteristic of the human condition (Cook, *Fire From Flynt*, 197–98). Dixon equated anarchists and socialists in *One Woman*, 244.

104. Dixon, *Leopard's Spots*, 284; *Fall of a Nation*, 106.

105. Dixon, *Leopard's Spots*, 199–200.

106. Thomas Dixon, *The Flaming Sword* (Atlanta: Monarch, 1939).

107. Ibid., 562, 418–22; Dixon, "Booker T. Washington," 2.

108. See, for example, *Sins of the Fathers*. Norton thinks that his son Tom has married his mulatto half-sister. The only alternative to suicide is for her to go abroad (382). Before attempting to kill his son and himself, North tells Tom that "the sin of your father is full grown and has brought forth death. We are caught to-night in the grip of the sins of centuries. I tried to give my life to the people to save the children of the future. My shame showed me the way as few men could have seen it, and I have set in motion forces that can never be stopped" (452). Though the family romance is completed between Helen, who turns out not to be mulatto, and Tom, this comes about by accident, not by destiny. Tom has no solution to offer in resolving the condition that has killed his father except never to allow a Negro to cross his threshold or enter his gates.

109. Maxwell Bloomfield, "Dixon's Leopard's Spots. A Study in Popular Racism," *American Quarterly* 16 (Fall, 1964), 387–401.

110. See Cook, *Fire From Flynt*, 112–14, 119–20.

111. Quoted in ibid., 64.

112. Ibid., 66.

113. Ibid., 209–12; and Dixon, *Southern Horizons*, 309–16.

114. Ibid., Cook, 78–80.

115. Thomas Dixon, *The Failure of Protestantism in New York and its Cause* (New York: V. O. A. Strauss, 1986), 8–20.

116. Ibid., 16.

117. Dixon, *One Woman*, 106.

118. Quoted in Cook, *Fire From Flynt*, 102.

119. Thomas Dixon, "From the Horrors of City Life," *World's Work* 4 (October 1902): 2603–11.

120. Ibid., 2603.

121. Cook, *Fire From Flynt*, 134–36.

122. See ibid., 201–2.

123. For a discussion of this theme, see Hans Robert Jauss, "Literary History as a Challenge to Literary Theory," in *New Directions in Literary History*, ed. Ralph Cohen (Baltimore: Johns Hopkins University Press, 1974), 11–41.

124. C. Vann Woodward (*Thinking Back: The Perils of Writing History* (Baton Rouge: Louisiana State University Press, 1986, 24) notes that the Dunning school was less an academic position than a white consensus setting the parameters around which "reasonable" interpretations of Reconstruction were formed. The changing conventions of the family romance were central to the transformation of that consensus from "realism" into "romanticism" by the 1960s. Cash provides another example in *Mind of the South*, 133. Speaking of Reconstruction, Cash says that politically the result of the "long training in fraud and trickery," which was part of the campaign for mastery, led to the philosophy that "if only the end be reckoned good, the most damnable means becomes justifiable and even glorious." Aesthetically, "the mounting tide of passionate defense and defiance, of glorification and brag . . . inevitably bore a people so given to oratory to even more striking extravaganzas in that direction and to greater susceptibility to it" (133).

125. Cook, *Fire From Flynt*, 203–7.

CHAPTER FIVE

1. Allan Nevins, "Tom Watson and the New South," *New York Times Book Review* 3 (April 1938): 1, 26.

2. John Herbert Roper, *C. Vann Woodward, Southerner* (Athens: University of Georgia Press, 1987), 80.

3. C. Vann Woodward, "The Historical Dimension," in *The Burden of Southern History* (Baton Rouge: University of Louisiana Press, 1960), 39.

4. Roper, *C. Vann Woodward*, 25–27.

5. See Fred C. Hobson, *Serpent in Eden*, 3–10; and Hobson, *Tell About the South*, 165–66. See Charles Scruggs, *The Sage in Harlem: H. L. Mencken and the Black Writers of the 1920s* (Baltimore: Johns Hopkins University Press, 1984), 3–17. See also H. L. Mencken, "The American Tradition," in *Prejudices: Fourth Series* (New York: Knopf, 1924), 9–42, especially 20–29.

6. H. L. Mencken, "Sahara of the Bozart," in *Prejudices: A Selection*, ed. James T. Farrell (New York: Vintage, 1955), 72–74, 77–78.

7. Mencken, "The American Novel," in *Prejudices: Fourth Series*, 282–84.

8. Quoted in Scruggs, *Sage in Harlem*, 13.

9. Ibid., 5–9. Mencken's recently published diaries suggest that Mencken fit the Ligurio image, and was not the selfless patron of deserving talent. Though his diary shows clearly that he shared in antisemitic and racist attitudes to some degree, he also held prejudices against Anglo-Saxons. See Henry L. Mencken, *The Diary of H. L. Mencken*, ed. Charles A. Fecher (New York: Knopf, 1989), 396–97, 451–52. The following excerpt from the diary seems to best characterize Mencken's own view of himself: "My life has been regulated by purely selfish motives, but I believe I have carried out my actual obligations with reasonable diligence and good humor," 147.

10. See Hobson, *Serpent in Eden*, 175–76, 185–89.

11. Ibid., 177–80.

12. Ibid., 185.

13. Charles and Mary Beard, *Rise of American Civilization*, 766.

14. Roper, *C. Vann Woodward*, 26–27.

15. See Thadious M. Davis, "Southern Standard-Bearers in the New Negro Renaissance," in *The History of Southern Literature*, ed. Louis D. Rubin, Jr. (Baton Rouge: Louisiana State University Press, 1985), 291–313.

16. Woodward, *Thinking Back*, 85–86; Roper, *C. Vann Woodward*, 52–53.

17. Woodward, *Thinking Back*, 85–86.

18. Ibid., 86.

19. See Robert Bone, *Down Home: A History of Afro-American Short Fiction from its Beginnings to the End of the Harlem Renaissance* (New York: G. P. Putnam's Sons, 1975); Robert Stepto, "Afro-American Literature," in *The Columbia Literary History of the United States*, ed. Emory Elliot (New York: Columbia University Press, 1988), 785–99; Amritjit Singh, *The Novels of the Harlem Renaissance* (University Park: Pennsylvania State Press, 1976); and Nathan Irvin Huggins, *Harlem Renaissance* (New York: Oxford University Press, 1971).

20. Bone, *Down Home*, 123–24.

21. Ibid., 120–22.

22. Ibid., xv–xxiv; Leo Marx, "Pastoralism in America," *Ideology and Classical American Literature*, 43.

23. Bone, *Down Home,* 130–36.

24. See Joseph M. Flora, "Fiction in the 1920s: Some New Voices," in Louis Rubin, ed. *The History of Southern Literature,* 279–90.

25. Andrew Nelson Lytle, "The Hind Tit," in *I'll Take My Stand,* 245.

26. Donald Davidson, "A Mirror for Artists," in *I'll Take My Stand,* 57.

27. Howard Odum, "Religious Folk-Songs of the Southern Negroes [1909]" in *Folk, Region, and Society,* ed. Katharine Jocher *et al.* (Chapel Hill: University of North Carolina Press, 1964), 7–8.

28. Robert Ezra Park, "The Negro and His Plantation Heritage," in *Race and Culture: Essays in the Sociology of Contemporary Man* (New York: Free Press, 1950), 67, 70–71.

29. See Park, "Politics and the Man Farthest Down" (1935), 167; "The Mentality of Racial Hybrids" (1929), 377; "Behind Our Masks" (1926), 247–49; all in *Race and Culture.* See also Fred H. Matthews, *Quest for An American Sociology: Robert E. Park and the Chicago School* (Montreal: McGill University Press, 1977); and Stanford Lyman, *The Black American in Sociological Thought: A Failure of Perspective* (New York: G. P. Putnam's Sons, 1972). Park's Race-Cycle theory follows the jeremiad form of promise, decline, and return through prophecy, very much as did Perry Miller's Puritans. Like Miller, Park lost faith in Faustian ideals of progress in the 1920s. See Winifred Raushenbush, *Robert E. Park: Biography of a Sociologist* (Durham: Duke University Press, 1979), 12; and Park, "Autobiographical Note," in *Race and Culture,* v.

30. See Patrick J. Gilpin, "Charles S. Johnson: Entrepreneur of the Harlem Renaissance," in *The Harlem Renaissance Remembered,* ed. Arna Bontemps (New York: Dodd Mead, 1972), 225–27.

31. Stepto, "Afro-American Literature," 798–99.

32. Howard Odum, *An American Epoch: Southern Portraiture in the National Picture* (New York: Holt, 1930), x. For an extended discussion of Odum see Michael O'Brien, *The Idea of the American South 1920–1941* (Baltimore: Johns Hopkins Univ. Press, 1979), 31–93.

33. Howard W. Odum, *Southern Regions of the United States* (Chapel Hill: University of North Carolina Press, 1936), 529–31.

34. See Hobson, *Tell About the South,* 190; and Woodward, *Thinking Back,* 20.

35. Simms, *Views and Reviews First Series,* 69–75.

36. Ibid.

37. Park, "The Negro and His Plantation Heritage, 73.

38. See Charles S. Johnson, "The Changing Attitude of the Negro" and "Can There Be a Separate Negro Culture?" in *Race Relations: Adjustment of Whites and Negroes in the United States,* ed. Willis D. Weatherford and Charles Johnson (New York: D. C. Heath, 1934), 534–54. Johnson's differences from Park on race and power are highlighted in a study of Liberia which he undertook in 1929 at Herbert Hoover's invitation. Johnson served as American representative on the International Commission of Inquiry into Slavery and Forced La-

bor in the Republic of Liberia. The study, however, was not published in Johnson's lifetime, though he worked on it over two decades. See Charles S. Johnson, *Bitter Canaan: The Story of the Negro Republic,* with an introductory essay by John Stanfield (New Brunswick, N.J.: Transaction, 1987), xliv-lvii; See also Gilpin, "Charles S. Johnson," 237–41.

39. Simms, *Views and Reviews,* 57–60, 79.

40. Ibid., 73. "It may be that the future poet who thus undertakes his delineation,—uninfluenced by that feeling of reverence which fills *our* hearts, when we approach the great hero of civilization,—will venture to delineate, as in honorable conflict for the ascendancy, the rival stars of Washington and Arnold. The one, calm, and cold, and haughty, in his secret pride of place;—the other, fiery and impetuous, hot with haste, spurring forward, sleepless always, to that glorious eminence which the jealous fate denies that he shall ever reach. It will not perhaps be difficult, a hundred years hence, to make it appear that Arnold was the victim of some great injustice,—to show that his rightful claims were denied. . . . Fate shall war against him,—his best merits shall fail their fruits."

41. Machiavelli, *The Discourses,* Chapter 1, Line 1, p. 102.

42. Pocock, *Machiavellian Moment,* 485–88.

43. Ibid., vii.

44. Rebhorn, *Foxes and Lions,* 22–25, 240–41.

45. Bone, *Down Home,* 141. See William Empson, *Some Versions of the Pastoral* (Norfolk, Conn.: New Directions, 1950), 195–209. See also Cleanth Brooks, *Modern Poetry and the Tradition* (New York: Oxford University Press, 1965), 227–29; and Kreyling, *Figures of the Hero,* 185–86.

46. Bone identifies Hughes with antipastoralism, which he sees as part of a cyclical swing alternating with pastoralism as "deep structures" within Afro-American short fiction. But in doing so, he suggests a dichotomy between Protestant religion and jazz and blues, which is as doubtful as the New Criticism's division between Classicism and Romanticism. Bone, for example, uses Hughes's self-identification with sinners to prove Hughes's detachment from Protestantism and pastoralism, when he earlier defined Protestantism and pastoralism as exultation of the lowly over the high-stationed. Bone, *Down Home,* xx–xxi. See also Arnold Rampersad, *The Life of Langston Hughes,* 2 vols. (New York: Oxford University Press, 1986), particularly 1: 13–22, and Nathan Irvin Huggins, *Harlem Renaissance,* 221–27.

47. Langston Hughes, *The Ways of White Folks* (New York: Knopf, 1969).

48. Robert Bly, "Being a Lutheran Boy-God in Minnesota," in *Growing Up in Minnesota: Ten Writers Remember Their Childhoods,* ed. Chester Anderson (Minneapolis: University of Minnesota Press, 1976), 209.

49. Rampersad, *Life of Langston Hughes,* 1: 42, 315–20.

50. Langston Hughes, *Mulatto,* in *Five Plays,* ed. Webster Smalley (Bloomington: University of Indiana, 1963), 10–11.

51. Ibid., 33. Cora says to Norwood's corpse. "You died here in this house, and you been living dead a long time. You lived dead." In choosing her son over Norwood, Cora recognizes Bert's life to be the source of the dead man's hatred, which, in turn, is indistinguishable from the mob that seeks to lynch him.

52. Rampersad, *Life of Langston Hughes*, 1: 217–18.

53. Ibid., 147–48, 213–14.

54. Ibid., 224.

55. Reprinted in Langston Hughes, *The Panther and the Lash: Poems of Our Times* (New York: Knopf, 1969), 37.

56. Rampersad, 1: 231–32.

57. Roper, *C. Vann Woodward*, 53–54.

58. Ibid., 75–76.

59. Howard Odum, *An American Epoch: Southern Portraiture in the National Picture* 97, 330.

60. Woodward, *Thinking Back*, 31.

61. Roper, *C. Vann Woodward*, 78–79.

62. Odum, *American Epoch*, 132–49.

63. Woodward, *Thinking Back*, 18.

64. Ibid., 22–23; Woodward, "Why the Southern Renaissance?" *Virginia Quarterly Review* 51 (1975): 235–36. See also Woodward, "The Historical Dimension," 31–32. Woodward discovered southern history through southern fiction, and entered "suddenly upon a new world of the imagination, a world in which the historical imagination played a supreme part."

65. Woodward, "Why the Southern Renaissance?" 237.

66. Charles A. Beard, Review of Arthur Schlesinger's *Rise of the City: 1878–98*, in *American Historical Review* 38 (July 1933), 779.

67. Charles A. Beard, "Written History as an Act of Faith" (Presidential address delivered before the American Historical Association on December 28, 1933) in *American Historical Review* 39 (January 1934): 219–29.

68. C. Vann Woodward, "America on the Way" (review of Charles and Mary Beard, *America in Midpassage;* Howard Odum, *American Social Problems;* and William T. Coach, ed., *These Are Our Lives*), in *Virginia Quarterly Review* 15 (1939): 632–36.

69. Woodward, "Why the Southern Renaissance?" 237; C. Vann Woodward, Moderator, "The Uses of History in Fiction: A Discussion with Ralph Ellison, William Styron, and Robert Penn Warren," *Southern Literary Journal* 1 (1969): 58–59, 77–78.

70. Ibid., 59.

71. See C. Vann Woodward, "Gilding the Lily," review of William Safire, *Freedom*, in *New York Review of Books* 34 (September 24, 1987): 23–26.

72. Ibid., 26; Woodward, *Thinking Back*, 144.

73. Warren and Woodward developed a friendship in the 1930s, according to

David Potter, "C. Vann Woodward and the Uses of History," in *History and American Society: Essays of David Potter*, ed. Donald F. Fehrenbacher (New York: Oxford University Press, 1972), 377. See also King, *A Southern Renaissance*, 5.

74. Woodward, "The Uses of History in Fiction," 61–62.

75. C. Vann Woodward, review of W. J. Cash, *Mind of the South*, in *Journal of Southern History* 7 (1941): 400–401.

76. Quoted in Roper, *C. Vann Woodward*, 248–49.

77. Lewis Harvie Blair, *A Southern Prophecy: The Prosperity of the South Dependent Upon the Elevation of the Negro*, ed. C. Vann Woodward (Boston: Little Brown, 1964).

78. See Roper, *C. Vann Woodward*, 226–27. Woodward's pastoral inversion of an ironically redemptive South, owing much to Niebuhr's similar inversion of an ironically redemptive America, collapsed under similar circumstances. See Fox, *Reinhold Niebuhr*, 284–85; Reinhold Niebuhr, "Vietnam: Study in Ironies," *New Republic* 156, no. 25 (June 24, 1967), 11–12.

79. C. Vann Woodward, "White Man, White South," review of Joseph L. Morrison, *W. J. Cash, Southern Prophet; A Biography and Reader*, in *New Republic*, December 9, 1967, 28–30. Woodward's earlier, more positive review of *Mind of the South* contained the same criticisms. But Woodward's frustration with Morrison's hagiography suggests that Cash's book may have become an inverted prophecy, mocking his own. See also King, *Southern Renaissance*, 266–67.

80. The Review of *The Mind of the South* was originally titled "W. J. Cash Reconsidered" when it appeared in the *New York Review of Books* on December 4, 1969, 28–34. However, Woodward retitled it to the less personal and more ambiguous "The Elusive Mind of the South" in C. Vann Woodward, *American Counterpoint: Slavery and Racism in the North-South Dialogue*, 261–84. References are taken from the latter.

81. Ibid., 264–66, 271.

82. Ibid., 267–68.

83. See Langston Hughes, *The Langston Hughes Reader* (New York: Braziller, 1958), 159–61, 492–94; Steven C. Tracy, *Langston Hughes and the Blues* (Chicago: University of Illinois Press, 1988); and Huggins, *Harlem Renaissance*, 224–27.

84. Ibid., Huggins 275.

85. Ibid., 282.

86. Woodward, *Thinking Back*, 4.

CHAPTER SIX

1. Henry Adams, *The Life of George Cabot Lodge* (Boston: Houghton Mifflin, 1911), 16–17.

2. George Cabot Lodge, *Cain: A Drama* (Boston: Houghton Mifflin, 1904).

3. Henry Adams, *Education of Henry Adams*, 406.

4. Macdonald Smith Moore, *Yankee Blues: Musical Culture and American Identity* (Bloomington: University of Indiana Press, 1985), 3–5. Moore suggests that the centennial generation was no longer able to locate its identity positively but only negatively: not immigrants, Catholics, Jews; not Southerners and not Negroes. They could, however, assimilate Midwesterners into this New England family (5). Frederick Jackson Turner was, of course, the Progressive who first described this pivotal role for the Midwest.

5. Ibid., 7.

6. Ibid., 42–43.

7. Ibid., 68–72, 88. See Robert Crunden, "Ministers of Reform: The Progressives' Achievement in American Civilization 1889–1920," 117–33; and David W. Noble, *The Progressive Mind*, 146–52 for insightful discussions of Charles Ives. On Mencken and Jazz, see "Music and Sin," in *Prejudices, Fifth Series*, (New York: Knopf, 1926), 293–96. See also Daniel Gregory Mason, "Music and the Plain Man," 28–53 in *The Dilemma of American Music: And other Essays* (New York: Macmillan, 1928). Mason compared good music to good beer—the portion between the froth and the dregs. "In other words," he explained," the 'high-brows' (Stravinsky, Busoni, Schönberg) and the 'low-brows' (jazz) divide our music between them; the plain man has no use for it . . . much to his own loss, and to that of music," 29.

8. Ibid., Moore, 145–50.

9. Ibid., 108.

10. Daniel Gregory Mason, "The Depreciation of Music," 81–100, in *The Dilemma of American Music*, 82–83.

11. Ibid., 163–68.

12. Perry Miller, *Errand into the Wilderness*, viii.

13. Will Herberg, *Protestant, Catholic, Jew* (New York: Doubleday, 1951). See also Harry J. Ausmus, *Will Herberg, From Right to Right* (Chapel Hill: University of North Carolina Press, 1987), 280 n. 12, 199; and Will Herberg, "Reinhold Niebuhr: Burkean Conservative," *National Review* 11 (December 2, 1961): 379–80; Will Herberg, "A Religious Right to Violate the Law?" *National Review* 16 (July 14, 1964): 579. See also John Rathbun, "Martin Luther King: The Theology of Social Action," *American Quarterly* 20 (Spring 1968): 4. King wrote he "nearly fell into the trap of uncritically accepting everything Niebuhr wrote." Niebuhr, despite his advocacy of civil rights agitation, in articles such as "Revolution in an Open Society" (*New Leader* 46 [May 27, 1963]: 7–8), also warned that deprived blacks might become a dangerous underclass reminiscent of Nazi Germany in "Man the Unregenerate Tribalist" (*Christian Century* 24 [July 6, 1964]: 133–34).

14. See Richard Wightman Fox, *Reinhold Niebuhr*, ix.

15. Most prominent among these is Daniel Bell. See Daniel Bell, "The 'In-

telligentsia' in American Society," in *Winding Passage: Essays and Sociological Journeys, 1960–1980* (New York: Basic Books, 1980), 124. A more recent example of a similar position to Bell's is found in John Patrick Diggins, *The Lost Soul of American Politics: Virtue, Self-Interest, and the Foundations of Liberalism* (New York: Basic Books, 1984), vii, 336.

16. C. Vann Woodward, *The Burden of Southern History* (Baton Rouge: Louisiana State University Press, 1960). Woodward discusses his debt to Niebuhr in *Thinking Back*, 106, 110.

17. Woodward, "A Southern Critique for the Gilded Age," in *Burden of Southern History*, 118–26.

18. See Richard Nelson "Carl Becker Revisited: Irony and Progress in History," in *Journal of the History of Ideas* 48 (April–June 1987): 307–24.

19. Carl Becker, *The Heavenly City of the Eighteenth Century Philosophers* (New Haven: Yale University Press, 1932). See also Charles Beard, review of *The Heavenly City of the Eighteenth Century Philosophers*, in *American Historical Review* 38 (April 1933): 590–91. Becker closes with the question of whether mankind is marching in stages towards perfection or stumbling around in a circle, says Beard. "Such is the dilemma to which the relativity of the modern historical school inevitably leads. . . . But until the knot-cutter has arrived Professor Becker's statement of the problem will remain a classic—a beautifully finished literary product."

20. See Charles Beard, introduction to J. B. Bury, *The Idea of Progress: An Inquiry into its Growth and Origin* (New York: Dover Publications, 1932), xxxi–xl. "Conceding for the sake of argument that the past has been chaos, without order or design," Beard concluded in Machiavellian terms, "we are still haunted by the shadowing thought that by immense efforts of will and intelligence, employing natural science as the supreme instrumentality of power, mankind may rise above necessity into the kingdom of freedom." See Thomas Bender, "The New History Then and Now," *Reviews in American History* 12 (1984): 612–22.

21. See Carl Becker, "The Degradation of Henry Adams," in *Detachment and the Writing of History: Essays and Letters of Carl Becker*, ed. Phil L. Snyder (Ithaca, N.Y.: Cornell University Press, 1958), 33; and David W. Noble, *Historians Against History*, 88–89.

22. Carl Becker, *How New will the Better World Be?* (New York: Knopf, 1944), 204–5, 244–45, presents a far more limiting ethic towards technology and social power than Beard's perspective. See Becker's last letters to Charles Beard, May 10, 1943; and to Mrs. Max M. Kesterton, January 25, 1945, in *"What is the Good of History?": Selected Letters of Carl Becker, 1900–1945*, ed. Michael Kammen (Ithaca, N.Y.: Cornell University Press, 1973); and Cushing Strout, *The Pragmatic Revolt in American History: Carl Becker and Charles Beard* (New Haven: Yale University Press, 1958).

23. Allen Tate, "Miss Emily and the Bibliographer," in *Collected Essays* (Denver: Alan Swallow, 1959), 58–59.

24. Lewis P. Simpson, "The Southern Republic of Letters and *I'll Take My Stand,*" in *A Band of Prophets: The Vanderbilt Agrarians After Fifty Years,* ed. William C. Havard and Walter Sullivan (Baton Rouge: Louisiana State University Press, 1982), 65–66.

25. Ibid., 68. Tate proposes the use of inversions of Enlightenment conventions so as negatively to "*create an intellectual situation interior to the South.*" Tate underscores this "because to me, it contains the heart of the matter." This Enlightenment division exists not just between science and poetry but between humanism and religion as a crisis in the frontier between time and space. See Allen Tate, "Humanism and Naturalism" (1929), in *Memoirs and Opinions, 1926–1974* (Chicago: Swallow Press, 1975), 181.

26. Allen Tate, *Memoirs and Opinions:* "Three Types of Poetry" (1934), 95–98; and "What is a Traditional Society?" (1936), 294–304.

27. Allen Tate, "Remarks on Southern Religion," in *I'll Take My Stand,* 175.

28. Ibid.

29. For an alternative interpretation of Tate's unorthodox conversion, see Robert H. Brinkmeyer, Jr., *Three Catholic Writers of the Modern South* (Jackson, Miss.: University of Mississippi Press, 1985), 63–72. See also Walter Sullivan, *Allen Tate: A Recollection* (Baton Rouge: Louisiana State University Press, 1988), 37–38, 59–61, for an unintentionally Machiavellian interpretation of Tate's religious conversion, an interpretation that should not be confused with hypocrisy. Compare to de Grazia, *Machiavelli in Hell,* especially pp. 68–70, 75–80, 379–85; and Bondanella, *Machiavelli and the Art of Renaissance History,* 144–45. In a dream doubtfully attributed to Machiavelli, he was asked if he preferred heaven or hell. Machiavelli unhesitatingly chose hell so that he could discuss politics with noble minds such as Plato and Plutarch. But he also availed himself of confession and the last rites. Political coercion and personal escape were the two poles of religion as Machiavelli understood it, and he availed himself of both, as did Tate.

30. Tate, "The Man of Letters in the Modern World," in *Collected Essays,* 382, 384–85.

31. Tate, "Remarks on the Southern Religion," 172.

32. Tate, "The New Provincialism," in *Collected Essays,* 285.

33. Ibid., 286 (my emphasis).

34. See Tate, *Collected Essays,* "The Man of Letters in the Modern World," 384; "The Symbolic Imagination," 421–22, 425–31; "The Angelic Imagination," 454; and "A Southern Mode of Imagination," 565.

35. For the origins of this term and its use by Eliot, see Craig Cairns, *Yeats, Eliot, Pound and the Politics of Poetry* (Pittsburgh: University of Pittsburgh Press, 1982), 205–7.

36. See T. S. Eliot, "Machiavelli," in *For Lancelot Andrews: Essays on Style and Order* (London, Faber, 1970), 44–46. See also Eloise Knapp Hay, *T. S. Eliot's Negative Way* (Cambridge, Mass.: Harvard University Press, 1982), 9, 11–12,

83–84, for a description of Eliot's use of negativity in shaping a positive message of redemption. On Tate and Eliot, see Karanikas, *Tillers of the Myth*, 200–202.

37. Allen Tate, "A View of the Whole South," *American Review* 2 (February 1934): 424.

38. Cairns, *Yates Eliot Pound and the Politics of Poetry*, 279–60. "As Eliot, paraphrasing Machiavelli, wrote in 1927: 'Liberty is good; but more important is order; and the maintenance of order justifies every means.'"

39. Tate, "Remarks on the Southern Religion," 173.

40. Brinkmeyer, *Three Catholic Writers*, 25.

41. Ibid., 23. See also Robert Buffington, "Young Hawk Circling," *Sewanee Review* 87 (1979): 541–56; and Robert Buffington, "Allen Tate: Society, Vocation, Communion," *Southern Review* 18 (1982): 62–72.

42. Tate appealed to the same dichotomy of a European East of civilization and an American West of frontier as did Turner and Cash. Yet both Tate and Cash viewed themselves as the "last Europeans." See Tate's manifesto for *Who Owns America?* in Simpson, *"The Southern Republic of Letters* and *I'll Take My Stand,"* in which Tate calls for "an academy of southern *reactionaries*" (Tate's emphasis) and a repudiation of Jefferson, despite his own emotional attachment to him, because "we must be the last Europeans—there being no Europeans in Europe at the present" (67–68). See also King, *Southern Renaissance,* 152.

This suggests that Bercovitch's division between the European and American jeremiads has been influenced by the New Critic's dichotomy, and that the frontier thesis actually does, contra Bercovitch, help explain "the persistence of the Puritan Jeremiad throughout the eighteenth and nineteenth centuries, in all forms of literature, including the literature of westward expansion" (Bercovitch, *American Jeremiad,* 10–11). Rather than the Puritan-Revolutionary jeremiad acting as a romantic challenge to a classical medieval European jeremiad, as Bercovitch seems to argue, the inversion of the European jeremiad into an "American Jeremiad" was part of a Machiavellian convention. The transformation of the rhetoric of the frontier to appear as a uniquely American reality does not represent a unique history or hubris. Rather the American jeremiad was, or is, a particular rhetorical mode, aimed at legitimizing the promise of an essentially antitraditional form of political redemption. It is and was a Machiavellian inversion of piety and murder. Thus, the "'conquest of a continent' was for him [Turner] also an enterprise of the spirit. It was to 'dream as our fathers dreamt and . . . [to] make their dream come true.'" (Bercovitch, *American Jeremiad,* 164 and note).

43. This is seen in Tate's self-divided "Romantic Traditionalist." See Robert S. Dupree, *Allen Tate and the Augustinian Imagination: A Study of the Poetry* (Baton Rouge: Louisiana State University, 1983), 3–11; Tate, *Collected Essays,* "Three Types of Poetry" (1934), 91–114; and "Tensions in Poetry" (1938), 75–90.

44. Allen Tate, *Collected Poems: 1919–1976* (New York: Farrar Straus Giroux, 1977), 66–69; and Tate, "What is a Traditional Society?" 295.

45. Thomas Daniel Young, *The Past in the Present: A Thematic Study of Modern Southern Fiction* (Baton Rouge: Louisiana State University Press, 1981), 48. Arthur Mizener, "The Fathers," *Sewanee Review* 67 (Autumn 1959), 604–13.

46. Tate, "Tension in Poetry," 83–86; Tate, "Preface to Reactionary Essays on Poetry and Ideas" (1936), in *Collected Essays*, xv–xvi.

47. Tate, "Three Types of Poetry," 91, 113; "The Symbolic Imagination," 420, 431.

48. Allen Tate, *The Fathers* (New York: G. P. Putnam's Sons, 1938), 5.

49. Tate, "Three Types of Poetry," 98–99.

50. Quoted in Dupree, *Allen Tate*, 128. See also Tate, "What is a Traditional Society?" 296–301.

51. Tate, "The Profession of Letters in the South" (1935), in *Collected Essays*, 281.

52. Tate, "Emily Dickinson," in *Collected Essays*, 198–99, 209.

53. Ibid., 210–13.

54. Ibid., 213; and Allen Tate, "Robert Frost as Metaphysical Poet" (1974), in *Memoirs and Opinions*, 95–109.

55. Pocock, *Machiavellian Moment*, 516 n. 15, 540–41. See also Mark Hulliung, *Citizen Machiavelli* 194–98. Hulliung argues that Machiavelli subverted stoic doctrine by saying that grandeur and nobility are impossible without fraud.

56. Robert Penn Warren, *A Place to Come to* (New York: Random House, 1977), 79–80.

57. Ibid., 83.

58. Ibid., 84–85.

59. Ibid., 104–6, 349–51.

60. Ibid., 398–401; and Robert Penn Warren's interview with Peter Stitt, March 1977, in *Robert Penn Warren Talking: Interviews, 1950–1978*, ed. Floyd C. Watkins and John T. Hiers (New York: Random House, 1980), 234.

61. Robert Penn Warren, *Flood: A Romance of Our Time* (New York: Random House, 1963).

62. See Lawrence H. Schwartz, *Creating Faulkner's Reputation*, 3–5, 27–28.

63. Lewis P. Simpson, *The Dispossessed Garden: Pastoral and History in Southern Literature* (Baton Rouge: Louisiana State University Press, 1975), 90–100.

64. Warren, *Flood*, 166.

65. Ibid., 365–66; Robert Penn Warren, *Who Speaks for the Negro* (New York: Random House, 1965), 442.

66. Warren, *Flood*, 4–5, 360–64.

67. Ibid., 439–40.

68. Biographical material and discussion of Warren's novels may be found in a number of sources, including Singal, *War Within*, 339–71; King, *Southern Renaissance*, 277–86; John Stewart, *The Burden of Time: The Fugitives and Agrarians* (Princeton: Princeton University Press, 1965), 438–55; John Burt, *Robert Penn Warren and American Idealism*; James H. Justus, *The Achievement of Robert Penn*

Warren (Baton Rouge: Louisiana State University Press, 1981); and F. Garvin Davenport, *The Myth of Southern History*, 131–70. See also Robert Penn Warren, *John Brown: The Making of a Martyr* (New York: Payson and Clarke, 1929).

69. Warren, interview with Marshall Walker in *Robert Penn Warren Talking*, 176–77.

70. Ibid., 181.

71. Stewart, *Burden of Time*, 141–42; and Thomas Dixon, Jr., *The Man in Gray: A Romance of the North and South* (New York: D. Appleton, 1921).

72. Warren, *John Brown*, 446, 141, 9–11; and Dixon, *Man in Gray*, 101–3, 106.

73. Dixon, *Man in Gray*, 303–5.

74. Ibid., 309–10. "The mob mind, once formed, is a new creation and becomes with amazing rapidity a resistless force. The reason for its uncanny power lies in the fact that when once formed it is dominated by the unconscious, not the conscious forces, of man's nature" (310, and 313–14); and Warren, *John Brown*, 317, 261, 269, 438–39.

75. Dixon, *Man in Gray*, 156, 271; Warren, *John Brown*, 317–18.

76. Dixon, *Man in Gray*, 425.

77. Warren, *John Brown*, 283, 332.

78. Robert Penn Warren, "The Briar patch," in *I'll Take My Stand*, 246–64.

79. Ibid., 248, 255–60; Dixon, *Leopard's Spots*, 280–84. Dixon devoted a whole chapter in *Southern Horizons* to rail against the mind-numbing drudgery of farm life. He titled the chapter "Hell on a Farm," and wrote that "The flight of human beings from the soul degrading toil of the farm into the town and city has not been an accident or an incident in the era in which we live. It was the resistless movement of humanity to a higher, saner and nobler life," 109.

80. Robert Penn Warren, *Night Rider* (New York: Random House, 1939). See also interview of Warren by Ralph Ellison and Eugene Walter, "Warren on the Art of Fiction" (1957), in *Robert Penn Warren Talking*, 29–30, 39.

81. Robert Penn Warren, *At Heaven's Gate* (New York: Random House, 1943). For Warren's comments on Dante's influence on the structure of *At Heaven's Gate*, see Robert Penn Warren, "Introduction to the Modern Library Edition of *All the King's Men*," in *Twentieth Century Interpretations of "All The King's Men": A Collection of Critical Essays*, ed. Robert H. Chambers (Englewood Cliffs, N.J.: Prentice Hall, 1977), 94–96; and in *Robert Penn Warren Talking*, 182. Warren ambiguously divides historical fiction from contemporary fiction to preserve his autonomy as an artist, very much as he divides the personalized violence of rebellion in *Night Rider* from the abstract violence of capitalism in *At Heaven's Gate*. This results in a powerful moral conflict between order and justice on the personal level but assumes that the abstract violence of capitalism is part of the natural fallen order in which society must exist. See *Robert Penn Warren Talking*, 251. For examples of criticisms of this strategy, see Justus, *Achieve-*

ment of Robert Penn Warren, 209–14, and 346 n. 4. See also Robert Penn Warren, *The Legacy of the Civil War* (New York: Random House, 1961), 19–20; Warren, *Night Rider,* 305–14.

82. Warren, *Night Rider,* 230–33, 403–26, 58–67.

83. Ibid., 67–76, 187–91. When hiding at Willie Proudfit's, Munn recalls the events leading to the black man's innocent death, and struggles, unsuccessfully, to remember his name (392–93).

84. *Robert Penn Warren Talking,* 179; Justus, *Achievement of Robert Penn Warren,* 119, 193.

85. See Robert Penn Warren, "Introduction to the Modern Library Edition of *All the King's Men,*" 94.

86. Robert Penn Warren, *Band of Angels* (New York: Random House, 1955); and Robert Penn Warren, *Segregation: The Inner Conflict in the South* (New York: Random House, 1956); and Robert Penn Warren, *Who Speaks for the Negro?.*

87. Warren, *Segregation,* 54–55.

88. Burt, *Robert Penn Warren and American Idealism,* 9.

89. Robert Penn Warren, "A Conversation with Cleanth Brooks," in *The Possibilities of Order: Cleanth Brooks and His Work,* ed. Lewis P. Simpson (Baton Rouge: Louisiana State University Press, 1976), 84–85.

90. John Burt has recognized that Warren uses the elegiac form both aesthetically and politically to present an ambiguously redemptive message (*Robert Penn Warren and American Idealism,* 43–49). However, he suggests the model of a pastoral elegy in his interpretation of Warren's message. *Flood,* and even more clearly, *Who Speaks for the Negro?* are clear rejections of the pastoral elegy, opening the way for a positive message in the form of a Romantic elegy in *A Place to Come to.* See *Who Speaks for the Negro?:* "The admiration for the betterness of the Negro is often little more than a simple turning upside down of the white man's old conviction of the Negro's inferiority. . . . At the same time that Negroes may recognize and resent, this upside-down condescension, some may cling, paradoxically enough, to the very superiority which they as good psychologists, have just condemned the white man for granting" (438–39). "It is sentimental to think the Negro will give us redemption in our spiritual bankruptcy. . . . For, in the end, everybody has to redeem himself" (442). "There is one more kind of sentimentality that the white man cannot afford: a sentimentality about himself. He cannot afford to feel that he is going to redeem the Negro" (443). Warren's answer to this conundrum is to posit a new realism of white self-interest, which both rejects a failed Western civilization and yet defines it as the only source of redemption. "Looking about us, we find no clear and persuasive model for imitation. We must go it alone." Not alone, exactly, Warren concludes, because there are "non-white Americans," who can only redeem America through "the standards of Western civilization developed and elaborated here" (442). Realism replaces romanticism, or "sentimentality," as a doubtful patriarchy is revitalized in the interest of balancing jus-

tice and order, innovation and piety. The black pastoral formula which, with the southern pastoral, defeated New England's redemptive culture has been put to death as a sentimentality, making it possible to formulate a new national identity constructed from Machiavellian terms.

91. Robert Penn Warren, *The Legacy of the Civil War* (New York: Random House, 1961), 84.

92. Robert Penn Warren in conversation with Cleanth Brooks, in *Possibilities of Order*, ed. Simpson, 110–11.

INDEX

Adams, Henry: and crisis of democracy, 137–41 *passim,* 197–99 *passim;* and George Washington, 138–39; mentioned 206, 207, 212. *See also* Dixon, Thomas

Agrarianism: and New Criticism, 8; and Harlem Renaissance, 169; and Charles Beard, 19; J. G. A. Pocock and, 18; Frederick Jackson Turner and, 57, 59; Puritanism and, 63; Jefferson and, 67; deconstruction of, 35; Thomas Dixon and, 274*n79;* Robert Penn Warren and, 231. *See* New Agrarian Critics; Frontier, agrarian; Populism

Anderson, Dwight, 26

Andre, Major John, 29–30. *See* Weems, Mason Locke; Simms, William Gilmore

Anti-Semitism: Henry Adams's, 138; Frederick Jackson Turner's, 249–50*n3;* H. L. Mencken's, 264*n9;* paradox of in Tom Watson, 108, 253*n67;* identified with Populism, 89; repudiated by Thomas Dixon, 261*n72*

Arendt, Hannah, 43, 44

Arnold, Benedict, 29–30, 176, 266*n4*

Bailyn, Bernard: recovers republican ideology, 10, 34, 36; American Revolution and, 10–14 *passim;* New Criticism influences, 13–15. *See also* republicanism; historiography; Pocock, J. G. A.

Basset, John, 25

Beard, Charles: and industrial republicanism, 68, 72, 187, 188; and H. L. Mencken, 166, 187; Agrarianism and, 19. *See* Turner, Frederick Jackson; New Agrarian Critics; Woodward, C. Vann; historiography

Becker, Carl L., 11, 12, 207. *See* Tate, Allen; historiography

Bell, Daniel, 89–90

Benjamin, Walter, 127–29 *passim*

Bercovitch, Sacvan, 126, 256*n16,* 272*n42*

Blake, William, 36, 37, 72. *See also* Romanticism

Bloom, Harold, 15, 247–48*n55*

Bly, Robert, 180

Bone, Robert, 169, 170, 266*n46. See* Pastoralism

Brooks, Cleanth, 75, 77

Brown, John: Langston Hughes and, 181. *See* Dixon, Thomas; Warren Robert Penn

Brown, Sterling, 168, 178

Bruffe, Kenneth, 9, 228. *See* elegy, Romantic

Buber, Martin, 75

Butler, Marilyn, 35–39 *passim*

Byron, George Gordon: *See* Byronic hero; Watson, Thomas E.

Byronic hero: defined, 95

Cash, Wilbur J.: death of, 117–18; and H. L. Mencken, 116–17, 119, 128; pastoral elegy of, 130; romantic realism and, 119, 123; on "savage ideal," 126, 129; and Joseph Conrad, 119–20; compared to Perry Miller, 118–20, 129, 204; compared to Thomas Dixon, 120, 130–31; and southern heroic narrative, 121; and Modernism, 18, 120, 123, 127, 128–29, 160, 194; and Reinhold Niebuhr, 129. *See* Dixon, Thomas; New Criticism

Cervantes (Don Quixote): and Tom Watson, 114; and Reinhold Niebuhr, 73; Robert Penn Warren and, 220